Looking into the

Seeds

of

Time

Looking into the
Seeds
of
Time

The Price of Modern Development
SECOND EDITION

Y.S. Brenner

 Transaction Publishers
NEW BRUNSWICK (U.S.A.) AND LONDON

Copyright © 1998 by Transaction Publishers, New Brunswick, New Jersey 08903. First edition published in 1979 by Van Gorcum & Comp.

This book is printed on acid-free paper that meets the American National Standard for Permanence of Paper for Printed Library Materials.

Library of Congress Catalog Number: 97-30355
ISBN: 1-56000-996-9
Printed in the United States of America

Library of Congress Cataloging-in-Publication Data

Brenner, Y. S.
    Looking into the seeds of time : the price of modern development / Y.S. Brenner. — 2nd ed.
        p. cm.
    Includes bibliographical references and index.
    ISBN 1-56000-996-9 (pbk.)
    1. Economic development. 2. Economic history. 3. Middle class. I. Title.
HD82.B692   1997
338.9—dc21   97-30355
                                                                           CIP

Foreword

This book was first published in 1979 and many things have changed since then. I have tried to discuss these changes in the introduction to this new edition. This introduction may just as well be regarded as an added chapter 12 to the old edition. Except for this, there is little difference between the old and the revised versions of the book. The changes I have made were mainly corrections of mistakes pointed out to me by colleagues, students and my wife, since the book first appeared in print.

I therefore want to take this opportunity to thank all those who convinced me to make the changes I made, and particularly to acknowledge the help given to me by my wife Mrs. Nancy Brenner-Golomb who practically rewrote a large part of chapter 5. I also want to thank Edward Elgar for not objecting to my inclusion in this book of sections of my lecture given at Utrecht University in December 1996, from the book to be published by him later this year.

Finally I wish to express my gratitude to the following: Professor Warren Samuels for suggesting to me the reissue of the book; all the

v

authors whose work I have cited and whose names and publishers are mentioned in the footnotes; to my colleagues and friends Antoon Spithoven and Maiumi Sadler-Hamada for helping me to get this new edition ready for publication.

Y.S. Brenner
Bilthoven, June 1997

Table of Contents

vii

Introduction to second edition of *Looking into the Seeds of Time* [1]

Almost a quarter of a century past since I began writing *Looking into the Seeds of Time*. In it I defined *economic progress* as the augmentation of freedom of choice, and predicted that with mankind's increasing ability to satisfy its material needs more fully and with less effort this freedom would increase. At the time I was writing the book unemployment and abject destitution appeared to have almost been banished from the *Welfare States*, and the student movement's call for a 'march through the institutions' was still reverberating through the land. I was not unaware that the decreasing material constraints gave rise to new constraints because a more

---

1. This introduction is based on my public address in Utrecht on December 13th, 1996. A shortened version of the address was printed in Vol. VII, of the *Journal of Income Distribution* (1997) and the full version will appear in J. van der Linden & A. Manders (eds), *Heterodox Economics and Income Distribution*, Edward Elgar, Cheltenham, UK & Brookfield, USA, 1998.

complex economic and social environment imposes new restrictions, but I believed that increasing productivity allows people greater freedom to choose between material goods and the satisfaction of other desires which could not be satisfied before. I believed, and continue to believe, that there is no freedom without economic security, and that economic security depends upon progress in both the natural and the social sciences because a society's institutions determine the pace and direction of technological advancement, and scientific and technological achievements determine which forms of social reorganization are possible and which illusionary. Science and technology delimit the material wants which can objectively be satisfied, and the culture of societies demarcates the nature, diversity, and extent of these wants and the techniques employed to satisfy them. As all living is action, and human action implies choices that, whether free or circumscribed, are choices to prefer one action rather than another in the hope that they lead to one rather than another kind of future, I was optimistic. I trusted in people's good sense and in democracy's provisions to make their wishes known at the ballot box and as far as practicable fulfilled by democratically elected governments.

I was too optimistic. I underrated the power of old *'habits of thought'* – the tenacity of old ideas and institutions. I forgot Keynes's admonition that the difficulty lies not in new ideas, but in escaping from old ones which ramify into every corner of our minds. I did not sufficiently realize that norms of conduct communicated to the young by elders and teachers persevere long after their original causes lost their earlier rational justification. Convinced that the relentless pursuit of gain before the coming of the *Welfare State* was the product of individuals' dire need to forestall poverty and destitution, I overlooked the possibility that in spite of the objective waning of this need the old notions would linger on.

In spite of all the signs of what was coming, and my warning the readers of the book about them, I simply could not in the climate of social engagement of the late 'sixties and early 'seventies imagine that the new affluence, which relieved the young from the fears of earlier generations and provided them with a chance to create a new more equitable social order, would give rise to trite materialism. I listened to their vocal denunciations of 'false wants' and to their calls for a new agenda for society, but turned a deaf ear to their other slogan: 'We want it all, and we want it now!'.

The object of my book was to illuminate the relationship between economic development and social mechanisms, and the role of economic planning in this process. Having witnessed the transformation of the semi-colonial economy and society in Palestine and Israel, and having worked for many years in Ghana and Turkey as a development economist, and with Jan Tinbergen on planning courses in the Hague, I believed to be qualified to write about this subject. I wanted to know whether we could interpret the signals from the past and present correctly without bias and give direction to our future. I therefore gave the book the title *Looking into the Seeds of Time*.[2] I was certain that the past and present hold clues about the future, but I wondered how we could decide which clues are relevant and which are not?

In my earlier work[3] I explained that economic growth provides nations with the opportunity, but no more than the opportunity, to choose the kind of society they wish to have. I illustrated how Capitalism driven by competition increased mankind's ascendancy over nature and gave it the power to produce the material affluence with which the citizens of the technologically-advanced countries are

---

2.   I borrowed the title from the scene in Shakespeare's *Macbeth* where Banquo asks the three witches to foretell him his destiny:

'If you can look into the seeds of time, And say which grain will grow, and which will not, Speak, then, to me, who neither beg nor fear Your favours nor your hate.'

and from the scene at the end of the play, when Macbeth comes to realize that predictions

'palter with us in a double sense. That keep the word of promise to our ear, And break it to our hope!'

3.   Y.S. Brenner, *Theories of Economic Development and Growth*, Allen & Unwin, London, 1966; *A Short History of Economic Progress*, Frank Cass, London, 1969; *Agriculture and the Development of Low Income Countries*, Mouton, The Hague & Paris, 1971; and *Introduction to Economics*, Middle East Technical University, Ankara, 1972.

endowed, or still endowed to day. But I also showed that competition, the mechanism which accounted for this wonderful achievement, was powered by constant fear: employers afraid to be driven out of business and reduced to the ranks of the proletariat, and workers fearing destitution and starvation. It was a two-pronged mechanism: competition between entrepreneurs for their respective shares of the market, and competition between employers and workers for their share in the fruits of production. Fearful of being driven out of business by more efficient competitors, entrepreneurs were inexorably driven to search for and introduce superior technological and organizational methods of production; and facing an increasingly well-organized and powerful labour force they were pressed to introduce improvements which helped them to raise output per worker sufficiently to maintain the necessary profit to finance the innovations which compensated them for the rising wages. Though not the exclusive driving force, and not always functioning smoothly, this dual mechanism was the dynamic and progressive element in old-style capitalism.

I also showed that with all its economic merit, the capitalist system even in its modified form, had a darker side. It imposed a state of mind that made *acquisition* the purpose of almost all endeavors. In fact, the spirit of acquisition seized not only upon all phenomena within the economic realm but reached over into the entire cultural sphere, including social relations, and established the supremacy of business interests over almost all other values. Enterprises took on a separate intelligence and became the locus of economic rationality quite independent of the personality of their owner and staff. It imposed on society a utilitarian valuation of people, objects and events. The motives of entrepreneurs could be many: the desire for power, the craving for acclaim, the impulsion to serve the common good and the simple urge to action, but by virtue of an inner necessity they all became subordinate to profit-making, because without economic success almost none of these desires could be attained.[4] What I underrated was the obduracy of

---

4.   This was noticed already by W. Sombart. *Vide* 'Capitalism' in *Encyclopedia of Social Sciences*, Vol. III, Macmillan, New York, 1935.

old institutions and the characteristic features and role of new ones, and I did not foresee the tremendous changes which were to transform the relationship between the ownership and the management of real capital, between old style multinational monopoly and globalization, and between advanced mechanization and automatization.

I was conscious that the pursuit of narrow materialistic self-interest continues to govern people's life in the *Welfare State* although it ceased to be a dire necessity, and that the spirit of relentless economic competition persevered. But I was convinced that given time this demon would eventually waste away. I reasoned that just as by the end of the Middle Ages faith continued for a very long time to be an area of life with boundaries extravagant to overstep even in science and business dealings, in which reason was only gradually taking the place of revelation,[5] so in the end would unbridled materialism also gradually taper off.

I knew that when social values, and the associated modes of conduct, communicated from one generation to the next become habitual, they seem to be intuitive – to be 'human nature'. But I believed that in the end reality is stronger and the old *habits of thought* eventually fade out. Alas, the process appears to be more protracted than I thought. I did not realize that in the era of pre-war capitalism the need to compete successfully in order to survive had invested egoism with almost moral quality. At home and in school, practically everywhere, competitive success met with approval and failure with contempt. Competition in all spheres of life became 'human nature', and it continued to determine people's conduct in spite of the fact that in the post-war era in many spheres of life the need to compete lost its earlier rationale. Having become 'human nature' it practically justified anything: providing African children with unsuitable milk-powder, selling arms to combatant nations, the pollution of air and water, and eventually also massive

---

5. And as I have shown in Ch. 6, thereby contained rapacity within legally conceded confines and restricted the pursuit of riches to ingenuity and business acumen.

unemployment. All became 'understandable' to most people when done in the name of competition.

What I also did not fully recognize then was capitalism's ability to socialize opposition by presenting a relative mobility of individuals within the system as an illusionary image of social progress. In fact it allows individuals to find their place in society on the basis of competitive ability, while the system as a whole remains immutable. This is a kind of running in place and leading nowhere in particular. The containment of opposition takes many forms. Blue jeans and long hair, which autocratic regimes, like the Greek colonels', forbade because they regarded them a symbol of opposition, are tolerated by liberal capitalism. They are simply turned into a fad – a fashion which often only the rich who have the least reason to challenge the existing order can afford. Similarly in the sphere of ideas, it does not disallow opposition but emasculates it by integration. When Copernicus suggested that the sun was at the center of the solar system his hypothesis was suppressed; when Galileo made his heliocentric theory plausible, he was banned by the Church, made to recant and placed under house arrest for the remainder of his life. Under capitalism, Germany's *Berufsverbote* and the British *Official Secrets Act* are exceptions. On the whole, such measures are superfluous. Studies which do not jibe with commercial interests are simply seldom funded. Substantial criticism of the system is either not published at all or printed in journals which are seldom read by anyone but the converted, and in books with too small circulation to be influential. There is no sinister conspiracy, only the logic of the market. Serious unconventional ideas are hard to sell; they seldom promise substantial profit to publishers and, naturally, offer little incentive for the establishment to subsidize their dissemination. It is the same as in industry. When a pharmaceutical firm with limited resources faces the choice to produce a medicine against River Blindness which afflicts millions of poor Africans, or a new kind of perfume that will please a few thousand rich Europeans, the decision will be in favour of the perfume. Not that the firm's managers are lacking in humanity, but because the cure for River Blindness is less financially rewarding. Shareholders neither know nor care what is produced with their investments, but they are well aware of the returns; and a management which does not make the customary rate of profit will not remain management for long.

In short, in spite of the achievements of the Welfare State the system continued to be held together by a universal pursuit of gain which permeated society to the last individual. It provided each individual with an illusion of security of life and property which led him or her to approve of arrangements, such as the legal system, that enabled him or her to enjoy what earnings or property they had but left them unmoved by the fact that it prevented them from obtaining true economic security which could be an alternative to the Marxist requirement of obtaining the full value of their work. By immediate notions of self-interest it led workers to approve of one type of insecurity in order to be protected from another. It turned all people into the system's unconscious protectors, and denied them the security they were actually striving for. It made the competitive pursuit of gain a necessity for survival, and the wish to survive a necessary rationale for accepting it – a vicious circle with an inescapable internal logic, an internal consistency that made it unassailable from within, permitting it to last long after the objective reasons which originally gave rise to it cease to be valid.

However, in the early 1980s my optimism was turning into trepidation. I realized that corruption was undermining the positive achievements of the *Welfare State,* and that democracy was loosing its socially emancipating powers and remedial control over the Free Market system.

For most people in the industrialized countries living standards in the late 1970s were higher than ever before, and the social security system seemed steadfast, but dark clouds were gathering on the horizon. Concentration and accumulation of wealth was giving rise to monopolistic or near-monopolistic business conglomerates with world-wide connections that enabled them to determine not only supply but also the structure of demand. Relatively high and rising taxes and wages, as well as political considerations,[6] led to the removal abroad of low-skill labour-intensive enterprises and

---

6.   For example, some Third World governments conditioned the sale of certain products dependent on their local production or assembly.

sometimes of entire industries. Increasing unemployment frightened workers, and the inability of governments to mitigate inflation after the oil crises scared small savers. The scramble for investment funds to finance costly technological process innovations, and the growing public debt, raised interest rates. All this is well known, but the crisis had also another reason: it was the logical conclusion of egoism, mistakenly understood as individualism, becoming a near virtue.

Classical capitalism had made a clear distinction between legitimate and illegitimate means of acquiring wealth. Thieves, swindlers, embezzlers, forgers, and the rest of that ilk, were excluded from free enterprise society. This was still so in the late 1970s, but the frontiers of social disapprobation were receding and the modus operandi changed. In their new form these practices were less easy to prosecute and socially more tolerated. Respectable businessmen increasingly regarded tax fiddles as peccadilloes and even bragged of them among their friends, and more and more working-men were also taking undue advantage of the state. In fact capitalists, workers, civil servants and self-employed ceased to regard misappropriation of company property, and public funds, as malfeasance. People collected unemployment benefit and conspired with others who needed workmen to defraud the state. The 'moonlighter' obtained an income on top of his social security benefits and the employer saved the money he had to pay the state.

The effect was disastrous. At one time or another almost everybody came face to face with these malpractices and decent people felt fooled by society, and began to resent paying taxes and national insurance contributions, and to work responsibly and honestly for normal wages, while 'smart alecs' were much better off. The old fears were still simmering in the background, but no longer as impelling as they used to be. Workers took longer sick leave, prolonged their tea-breaks, worked less diligently and responsibly, allowed more time to pass between leaving one position and finding another, and like employers they were tempted to resort to all manner of stratagems to misuse facilities provided by the state. To be sure, dishonesty was no new phenomenon, there had always been corrupt individuals, but the threshold which divided what is and what is not acceptable became lower. The old sense of decorum was waning. But without this sense of decorum – without working-men's feeling of responsibility taking the place of the old fears of unemployment and destitution, there is little left to maintain the necessary level of efficiency to sustain a highly complex industrial society and to assure the living standard it affords.

Worst of all, people lost interest in politics and confidence in political leaders. After the war democracy was meaningful and Keynesian economics placed much of income and wealth distribution in the hands of representative governments. People voted on issues which related to the welfare of the majority of citizens. Political parties were committed to programmes which clearly stated how they intended to solve the problems facing their electorates. But gradually this changed. The voice of high social, business and academic position gives access to television, radio and the press, and the voice of economic advantage being louder was regularly mistaken for the voice of the masses.[7] In the 'seventies and 'eighties democracy was practically drowned by a flood of factually true but misleading information. The failure of labour's leadership to acknowledge what was common knowledge, namely that not only capitalists but also workers were abusing the provisions of the *Welfare State* made this worse. It prevented prime of place to be given to efforts to correct this situation and afforded the oligarchy the opportunity to revive some features of the pre-war social and economic system, while ignoring others. In short, the combination of these moral and political crises, with persistent unemployment and inflation, afforded the foes of the *Welfare State* the long awaited opportunity to stage their comeback.

There was also another development since the first edition of this book was published which concerns the role of the economics profession in this process. In the introduction to the first edition I pointed out that, in their efforts to obtain the scientific status achieved by their colleagues in the natural sciences, economists tried to emulate the methodology which proved to be successful in physics and they restricted their investigations to a narrow domain. Not

---

7.   J.K. Galbraith, 'The Conservative Onslaught' in *The New York Review of Books*, New York, January 22, 1981.

prepared to abandon the neat models of Adam Smith and Léon Walras they never took on board the thought that an egalitarian society which incorporates everyone in a shared moral citizenship and high culture, without poverty, oppression or arbitrariness, and with perpetual economic and cognitive growth, is not inscribed into any historical plan. They were simply ill equipped to see that a stored surplus needs to be guarded and its distribution enforced and that no principle of distribution is either self-validating or self-enforcing.[8] Educated in the neoclassical mechanistic paradigm they excluded the long-term dynamic processes of complex economic life from their studies by labelling them 'exogenous' or lumping them together in empirically untraceable 'proxi variables' to obtain rigor by quantification.[9] They did not deny the influence of technological innovation, changes in social conduct, the emancipation of women, the increasing alertness to environmental hazards, but treated them as if they were not themselves also influenced by the economic system. Economists assumed a one-way traffic and ignored that most of the variables which they labelled exogenous do not develop in an economic vacuum. They simply disregarded the mutual influence of social and economic factors, and introduced unrealistic assumptions such as 'ceteris paribus', which may well be expedient for the prediction of short-run microeconomic processes but become a travesty where long-term macroeconomic processes are concerned. In short, they were unwilling to abandon the metaphysical foundations of the *Enlightenment's* 'Grand Design' – the all pervasive regulating mechanism of the 'invisible hand', which provided capitalism with a veneer of 'scientific' and moral justification, and with this greatly assisted the drift toward the restoration of the pre-war social and economic conditions. The point is that although good scientists' philosophical background seldom influences their answers it does determine their questions, and the final outcome can depend on

---

8.   E. Gellner, 'Introduction', in J. Baechler et al. (eds), *Europe and the Rise of Capitalism*, Blackwell, Oxford, 1988.

9.   The reference here is to terms like 'real national output per head' or 'capital-labour ratio'.

this.[10] Even the work of such brilliant economists as Hicks, Hansen and Samuelson, was tainted by 'habits of thought' which led them to ask how best Keynes's *General Theory* could be incorporated as a 'special case' in the old conception, rather than to see it as a break with it, as a step on the road to a new scientific paradigm free from the myth of the eternally valid full employment-seeking equilibrium.

What our profession overlooked was that since the eighteenth century the rising productivity in agriculture was matched by a more or less equivalent fall in the real prices of farm produce. The fall in food prices increased real incomes and allowed people to spend more on industrial goods.[11] In this way the falling demand for labour in agriculture was compensated by a rising demand for labour in industry. Later, when productivity in industry also increased, and the demand for labour in this sector began to flag, and competition reduced the price of industrial products, a growing demand for services made good the loss of jobs in industry. In other words, for as long as competition remained sufficiently powerful to pass on the benefits of technological progress to consumers, a diminished demand for labour in one sector gave rise to an increased demand in others. This sequence lasted well into the 1960s,[12] and led social scientists to believe that the rising demand for services would sustain full employment also in the future. This seemed to be a plausible prognosis because several important services can hardly be improved by labour-time-reducing innovations as they require the simultaneous attendance of consumer and provider (for example patients and doctors and pupils and teachers) and their quality depends on their duration.

---

10   This, as Heisenberg pointed out, is also true for other sciences. *Vide* W. Heisenberg, 1975, 'The Philosophical Background of Modern Physics'. Lecture notes from Dubrovnik seminar.

11.   *See* Y.S. Brenner, *A Short History of Economic Progress*, Frank Cass & Co. Ltd., London, 1969.

12.   Dettling, u.a., *Die Neue Soziale Frage und die Zukunft der Demokratie,* München, Wien, (2nd edition) 1977.

Again it appeared as if an 'invisible hand' were leading the economy toward full employment equilibrium, but it was an illusion. Old and new monopolistic practices prevented prices from falling in line with labour input, and in many services, such as banking, insurance and even marketing, the expected new employment opportunities fell prey to *automatization*. In comparison with the cost of the goods where the new technologies could be applied, the cost of services where labour-time could not be reduced greatly increased. Obviously if two cars can be produced with the labour input previously required to produce one, and the time required by a hairdresser to serve a customer remains as before, the cost of a haircut becomes expensive if compared with the cost of a car. But the real trouble with this was that this relative rising cost happened mainly in the services which have to be funded by the state.

In other words, relative to the decreasing costs of goods produced by the private sector, the public sector became dearer. This was one cause for the rising cost of the *Welfare State* – for the relatively high taxes associated with state regulation and for a good part of the growing public debt. But the main reason for the rising cost was that the general affluence of the 'sixties transformed society by placing with the state many of the obligations which traditionally rested with the family. The customary responsibility for the infirm and the aged, and for health-care and education, shifted from the household to the public sphere. This became the most visible addition to the costs imposed by the increasing complexity of the economic system itself, like the construction of new national communication networks (that at least initially were too costly to be constructed and maintained by private enterprise alone) and the cost of traditionally public goods like the protection of the public from epidemic diseases and from pollution of air and water, let alone the defence budgets. Together, they made government more costly than it had ever been before.

However, a society accustomed to assign social status to private ownership of property found it difficult to appreciate the intangible returns it was receiving from the state. Such a society tends to forget that even if all these needs were met by private enterprise the share of the national income allocated to their satisfaction would still be high and rising. The aged and infirm would still have to be housed and fed; teachers would still want to be paid; communication systems would still need to be constructed and maintained, and epidemics and pollution would still have to be prevented. In this respect the difference between a regulated and deregulated economy is inconsequential, but the distribution of the burden is significantly different. Under a system of *progressive taxation*, the rich as individuals are obliged to pay more than the poor to maintain the provisions of the *Welfare State*, while they are the least dependent on its services. This then, is the crux of the matter. The rich are allergic to subsidizing the 'undeserving poor'.

In practice, though the poor did indeed benefit from the provisions of the *Welfare State*, it was the large middle class which gained most. Tax-deductible mortgages to purchase houses; tax-deductible expense accounts; the free use of company vehicles; free or almost free health-care; redundancy pay; state pensions; free education including higher education, all these were only a few of the most direct advantages to which the middle class had better access than the poorest members of society. Yet the cultural legacy of old-style capitalism prevented the majority of the members of this class from recognizing this. Their eyes were focused on taxes and other deductions from their incomes.

Coming mainly from a rich background, or from the deluded middle class,[13] most politicians genuinely believed that the interests of individual business enterprises and those of the state must always coincide. They were easily convinced that high taxes and wages were the causes of inflation and tenacious massive unemployment, and mainstream economics, dominated by the study of the private profit-maximizing firm and its trust in the distributing powers of the 'invisible hand', provided them with 'expert' justification. Moreover, even if politicians did understand that the pursuit of the public's interest required a different attitude from that which suited the pursuit of private business, being dependent on votes they never dared say that to assure the future affluence of the industrial societies taxes must from time to time be adjusted or raised.

---

13. In *Capitalism, Competition and Economic Crisis*, p. 21, I gave several examples to illustrate this.

In reality however, the new situation requires a judicious reallocation of the fruits of the technologically generated economic growth. Such a reallocation of the added value does not imply *less* for the rich. All it means is that the poor receive a little more, and the rich a little *less more*. In other words, what was needed is state intervention to sustain effective demand in line with growing productivity, and measures to provide sufficient capital to allow innovative investment to continue. With stringent measures to reduce abuse of social security, tax evasion and the ill-use of public funds, this could probably have been achieved with little or no inflation. But instead of doing this, governments adopted *supply side economics*, and ignored that the object of private investment is profit, and that profit can be obtained from a growing consumer demand as well as from a fall in production cost. This is because there are two types of innovation: *Product innovation* and *Process innovation*. Both types usually go together, but in periods of increasing consumer demand, as was the case in the 1960s – in the era of the 'false wants', more capital is attracted to the former, while in periods of stagnating consumer demand more capital is attracted to the latter in an effort to sustain profit by reducing the cost of production. Oblivious to the fact that the preference of the latter led to a new form of competition,[14] governments feather-bedded the rich in the hope that easy money will encourage investment and revitalize demand for labour. The result was that investment continued to increase, but only in *process innovation* – in the replacement of human labour by machines, and production was scaled down in line with the resulting diminishing consumers' effective demand, thus increasing unemployment.[15]

---

14.   I discussed this in detail in Y.S. Brenner & N. Brenner-Golomb, *A Theory of Full Employment*, Kluwer Academic Publishers, Boston/Dordrecht/London, 1996, Chapters 8, 9 and 10.

15.   The explanations given by the economic 'experts' for the failure of employment to revive were various and many. It was blamed on the flight of industries with a large low-skill labour input to the Third World, on the new technologies, on competition from the Asian Tigers, etc. But as my colleague A.J.C. Manders has shown none of these explanations is substantiated by the

The often recited reason for the failure of the market system to distribute the fruits of innovation in a manner which relates consumer purchasing power to production is monopoly or oligopoly. With limited success monopoly has been subjected to a great volume of corrective legislation, but even firms acting independently are aware of their mutual interdependence. Most businesses have a good notion of their competitors sales, production, investment and even advertising plans, and make decisions on the basis of their rivals' expected behaviour. This was recognized by neoclassical economists who developed models designed to take account of co-operation and collusion. Neoclassical price theory did not ignore *monopoly* and *oligopoly*, but treated them as the exception, not the rule. Yet oligopoly is no longer an anomaly.

The power of monster conglomerates is well known and needs here no elaboration.[16] But while there is little new in the tendency toward monopoly, the stimulus it received in the 1980s from technological developments made it different because it ushered in a *new market structure*. Corporations manufacturing production technology, together with changes in the world economy, and *Computer Integrated Manufacturing* (CIM) caused a revision of large corporations' market strategy.[17] From being companies in many

---

facts. *Vide* 'Facts and Fiction: Wage Levels and the Relocation of Production' in *International Journal of Social Economics*, Vol. 22, No. V, 1995, pp. 15–27.

16. For example, in the 1970s, five Dutch conglomerates directly employed 18 per cent of the working population, and indirectly many more. These five controlled electronics, metallurgy, food processing, chemicals and oil. In Germany, some 2000 businesses employed about 50 per cent of the total labour force. In the USA some 2000 corporations controlled about 80 percent of all resources used in manufacturing. By 1994, their share in employment had fallen more steeply than the fall in overall employment, but their grip on all other resources had increased. Globalization had added an entirely new dimension to the familiar problem of economic concentration.

17. The process was triggered by three developments in the production sphere: 1) in computer-aided manufacturing (CAM), flexible manufacturing systems (FMS) and robotics; 2) in computer-aided design (CAD) and paperless

countries, important *multinationals* became *global* concerns; and their new managerial watchword became *globalization*. This new type of globalized monopoly exorcised the odium of malpractice and illegality from a great many monopolistic and oligopolistic practices.

The most obvious reasons for this change was the growing capital-intensity of manufacture; the accelerating momentum of technologies; the emergence of a growing body of universal users; and the spreading of neoprotectionist pressures. Since the late 1980s the pursuit of economies of scale was increasing the capital-intensity of manufacturing, and the increasing capital-intensity of manufacturing was, and will probably continue to be, a major source of 'globalization' in spite of the spreading of *flexible manufacturing systems* (FMS) which provide cheap short production runs. The accelerating pace at which new technologies are discovered and applied causes the costs of *research and development* (R&D) to soar, while the diffusion of new technology through the industrialized countries is so rapidly advancing that it has become difficult to sustain technological advantage. This forces companies planning to penetrate Japanese, American and European markets with new products to invade the entire zone simultaneously rather than gradually, country by country, as they used to do. Finally the emergence of an unprecedented massive body of universal users is also pushing companies in this direction.

Coalition-forming is the specific type of cooperation which accompanies globalization. It has become *the* new strategy of large enterprises. Coalitions differ from mergers and takeovers because they allow participants to retain relative independence. Their *raison d'être* is that they provide the opportunity for establishing positions in strategic markets. They have a 'synergistic' effect by recruiting partners to fill gaps in each other's operations and to increase the possibility for exploiting economies of scale. They lead to cost and

---

knowledge work; and 3) in the increased understanding of physical phenomena. The combination of all three provided the basis for computer-integrated manufacturing (CIM).

risk spreading and help to arrive at new standards.[18] This type of alliances and coalitions, especially favoured by capital-intensive industries with high R&D costs and a broad technological basis, practically dominates production in aviation, electronics and increasingly also motor vehicles. Even the largest enterprises feel that they can no longer afford the independence which previously they were jealously protecting. The choice of coalition partners depends on the companies' *core activities*. To maintain international standards large enterprises need to specialize in order to reduce the cost associated with the increasing complexity of their operations. They must avoid the risk of destroying competency by diversification, or from engaging prematurely in activities outside the technological and market paradigms with which they are familiar. This concentration on core activity, globalization and coalition-forming, is the salient feature of new strategic planning. It introduces a new *market structure* dominated by something close to what used to be known as *natural monopolies*. In conclusion, although price competition

---

18. Kenichi Ohmae in *De opkomst van mondiale konkurrentie*, 1985, listed several examples for this type of cooperation. In *aero engines:* General Electric and Rolls Royce; Pratt and Whitney-Kawasaki-Rolls-Royce. In *motor vehicles* (components and assembly): GM and Toyota; Chrysler and Mitsubishi; Volkswagen and Nissan; Volvo and Renault. In *consumer electronics:* Matsushita and Kodak; JVC and Telefunken and Thorn, Philips and Sony. In *computers,* AT&T and Olivetti; Hitachi and Hewlett and Packard; Fujitsu and Amdahl and Siemens and ICL; IBM and Matsushita.

In The Netherlands, André Manders tells us in *Sturing van produktie-technologie*, 1990, that Philips cooperates with Sony in the field of compact-disc players and with Matsushita and Yamaha in efforts to establish a standard for interactive CD and in seeking a standard for CD-video. A detailed study of the technological alliances into which Philips had entered by 1989, and of the multiplicity of relationships with other companies working with it in tandem (with five or more cooperation agreements) lists 27 agreements with Siemens, 11 with Thomson, 10 with Matsushita, 8 with Bull, Olivetti and Sony, 7 with AT&T and Bosch, 6 with DEC and Nixdorf, 5 with Alcatel (CGE), Hewlett-Packard and STC (+ICL). Of the listed inter-company agreements, 43% were finalized between 1986 and 1988. During the same period the proportion of alliances in professional products and in the systems sector (including production automation) rose from ten percent prior to 1986, to more than thirteen percent in 1989.

continues to play an important role in wholesale and retail trade, its influence on large-scale producers has been waning. The enormous and continually rising costs of breaking into markets makes prospective entrepreneurs shy away from competition with established businesses even when they are very profitable. The greater the cost of innovating the more even well established large producers tend to concentrate on what they consider to be their *core* activities. Rather than competing, they prefer to cooperate, amalgamate, buy up each other's shares, or form coalitions.

The new market structure rests on the presence of a near monopoly in certain semi-finished goods and in particular production processes. If in any of these industries a new investment leads to a greater output than an equivalent investment did before, and oligopolistic structures prevent prices from falling, then consumer demand cannot increase in line with rising productivity, and profits can no longer be made in the market place. The result is that producers turn to *process innovation* because in an sluggish or shrinking market the way to preserve or increase profitability is to reduce production costs. With this, competition shifts from markets to innovation. The most efficient process innovator makes the highest profit. As process innovation usually involves high R&D expenditure and costly new equipment, the new structure strengthens the near monopoly of successful producers. It facilitates the determination of prices in line with investment plans with little regard for market competition – variations in the volume of demand do not influence prices but determine the volume of production; it replaces familiar market competition by a scramble for investment funds, and since *process innovation* is normally associated with a reduced demand for labour it increases unemployment. The final outcome is growing unemployment together with rising rates of interest. This is the phenomenon known as *stagflation*.

With this became questionable the entire theory by which prices, wages and the rates of interest, are said to regulate the economic system toward full employment equilibrium. If prices are determined by investment plans, then the latter determine the volume of demand,

and income effects thwart price effects.[19] Effective demand remains the final arbiter of production, but instead of influencing prices it determines the volume of employment. Inflation, rates of interest and economic growth all rise together, but the volume of employment dwindles. In other words, the *new market structure*[20] allows large enterprises, or practically compels them, not to pass on to consumers the advantages of innovation by reducing prices, and with this the entire full employment equilibrium-restoring mechanism at the root of mainstream economic thought becomes a travesty. With the new market structure, competition does no longer function in the way it did before and without state intervention massive unemployment became chronic. State intervention to regulate income distribution becomes an unavoidable necessity.

There is, however, another social rather than economic reason why neither the technological achievements of the last decades nor the new markets opened by the disintegration of the communist block can break this vicious spiral by which the western economic progress is slowly grinding to a halt. This is the spreading of a new managerial culture. I called this culture *industrial feudalism*. The old *Captains of Industry* were owner-managers who operated with their own money, or with borrowed funds for which they staked their good name. Their wealth determined their position in the social hierarchy. It reflected what was taken to be evidence for their

---

19.   Whether this has always been the case because, as Post-Keynesians believe, production antecedes sales, and producers only learn ex-post from the movement of prices if their estimations of the markets were correct, or if this is a new phenomenon, is here irrelevant. The point is that the new market structure practically forces large producers to adjust their volume of output to demand and not their prices; and that it obliges them to increase expenditure on technological innovation even more when markets are stagnating or reducing than when they are expanding.

20.   In my book I noted that this new structure of capitalism was accompanied by a kind of *industrial feudalism* which threatens to demolish the achievements of the market system, and to destroy most of the capitalists themselves. I concluded that the adopted economic policies will cause society to disintegrate and result in something like South American conditions. I still hold this view.

economic sagacity. The new *'Captains'* of large enterprises are managers whose personal wealth and attainment is less directly tied to their businesses' profitability. Shareholders, the *owners* of the enterprises, are of course interested in profit, but they have no knowledge of, and only indirect control over, the businesses in which they hold their shares; and they compete in a quite different market from the managers'.

In the 1950s and 1960s top professional management was mainly recruited on the basis of the candidates' prior scientific, technological, or otherwise professional capability. This was the Galbraithian *technostructure*.[21] The more recent managerial oligarchy receives its education in schools of management which provide useful social contacts.[22] Its members' positions are determined by their social connections.[23] Once holding a managerial position, managers' true ability can hardly be assessed because the test of business perspicacity depends on a great variety of circumstances from which the role of management can seldom be disentangled. Naturally, even today there are some very competent managers, but unlike the owner-managers of the past, the least competent are less likely to be weeded out by business competition. Their economic acumen is not the most decisive factor which determines their rewards. It is the other way around, their rewards, their salaries and perks, determine their position in the social hierarchy. Business success will enhance their prestige and earning capacity, but failure need not signal their ruin. Unlike the owner-managers, they can abandon a failing enterprise and become directors in another. Such managers form a

---

21.   J.K. Galbraith, *The New Industrial State*, Houghton Mifflin Company, New York, 1967, Ch. VI.

22.   Without going into the question whether or not such schools equip their graduates with much learning that is really functional for the efficient management of enterprises, it is obvious that unlike the Galbraithian members of the technostructure the new managers can seldom show prior evidence of competence in any sphere, let alone professional capability.

23.   Above all by the prestige of the particular institution where they received this education.

new stratum of society which has more in common with a feudal estate than with a capitalist class. They exercise *power over people*, but hold this power by virtue of position, not wealth. This vests status with a new significance. Status becomes a rival to wealth in a competitive scramble for distinction.

Controlling large funds which are not their own, the members of this new élite are less careful than their forebears to avoid unnecessary costs when this can strengthen their personal prestige. Provided such expenditures can be correctly booked as business costs, or tax deductible, they will be incurred regardless of whether or not they are really necessary for the business. Wealth continues to bestow numerous advantages on those who own it, and company profits remain an indispensable necessity, but the role of salaries and profits is reversed. Not current business profits but the height of his personal remuneration reflects the manager's social status. This means that the new utility-maximizing 'Captain of Industry' is no longer Adam Smith's profit-seeking entrepreneur who is willy-nilly promoting business efficiency, but an individual who constantly weighs his own against the enterprise's best advantage. With this the concept *utility*, as it is conventionally applied in economics, no longer reflects economic reality, and if given a more realistic definition the concept undermines the premiss that the market structure is a self-sustaining economic growth-promoting mechanism.[24]

The *'Feudalisation'* of the modern economic system does not affect top management alone. It penetrates the entire structure of most large scale corporations in both the public and the private sectors. As the vertical and horizontal integration of businesses progresses and more and more firms amalgamate to achieve greater market control, their management becomes increasingly bureaucratized and hierarchical. Top managers delegate tasks and responsibilities to sub-managers, to heads of branches, departments

---

24. The fault with the concept of *utility*, which was explained earlier in this introduction, now obtains a new significance: the conventional concept of *utility* becomes too narrow to reflect conflict between personal and corporation interests, and if it is extended to include craving for status it is too broad to sustain the causal mechanisms at the root of neoclassical theory.

and sections. Each of these strata is assigned its own responsibilities and status. Beside its appropriate wage or salary, the holder of each rank is also given its specific privileges – expense accounts, official or business vehicles, housing allowances, etc. The higher the rank the greater the perks. The structural change is a natural concomitant of the growing size of corporations, but the newfangled type of competition, the scramble for position and status, introduces an economically debilitating element.

With personal status the object of attainment, each head of department or section becomes more interested in his or her own part of the organization than in the achievements of the business as a whole.[25] Within each department or section, the worth of an employee is more often measured by his or her contribution to the activities of their particular department than by their value to the organization as a whole. Sometimes it is not even the employee's actual efficacy which determines his or her employment and position but the impression that their particular section is functioning without a hitch. In this way promotion becomes less a reward for good performance and more for acquiescence, obedience, and personal relations between inferior and superior members of the organization. Criticism which does not suit the personal interests of the direct superiors upon whom an employee's advancement depends is muted. Step by step not capability but the quasi-feudal nexus, 'who one knows and who one serves', becomes the overriding factor for personal advancement. In this way a new vertical relationship is forged by which the whole hierarchy is held together. The lower ranks protect the higher since their positions depend upon their superiors' standing; the higher ranks protect the ones below, since by holding higher responsibility any mistakes made by their inferiors eventually come to rest on their own doorstep. As every individual member of the hierarchy has little personally to gain from questioning the value and efficiency of the organization but good reason to fear jeopardizing his or her chances for promotion by it,

---

25.   This comes to light, for example, in the constant squabble between the heads of sales departments and research divisions in large enterprises.

and as all members would be adversely affected by outside criticism, little is left to stimulate personal responsibility and general efficiency.

This Feudalization is however not the only debilitating social factor which disturbs the efficient functioning of the new market system. The growing size of enterprises makes 'bookkeeping supervision' almost the only means of financial control. This provides many opportunities for dubious practices, and contrary to popular belief, this is so not only in the production, purchase and sale of public goods which are shrouded in secrecy, such as military equipment or space technology. The funds involved in most transactions are not the property of those who disburse them and it is hard to ascertain whether they are well spent or not. All that can be checked is if the receipts match the claimed expenses. Consequently not only public enterprises but individuals in all firms fall prey to temptation, and corruption undermines the confidence which used to be a fundamental constituent of traditional Capitalism.[26] Confidence was an essential ingredient of transactions, and the demise of this ingredient is therefore not only a moral matter but a real threat to the proper functioning of the economic system. Not that traditional capitalists never indulged in shady practices, or that present-day managers are all corrupt, but the opportunities for engaging in dubious practices were more circumscribed under traditional capitalism. Few self-respecting capitalists would ever have admitted to have, for example, given or received a bribe. This is no

---

26. It can of course be argued, as various socialist ideologists do, that by any moral standard, except by that of the capitalist system itself, the system has always been unethical, but this is beside the point. The point is that old-style capitalists even when they were not noted for their honesty, unlike their modern peers, were at least aware of it. When they transgressed against the unwritten rules of their society they did their best to hide it. To be found out meant social disgrace and often economic ruin. The reason for this was that the entire system rested on trust and confidence. 'My word is my bond' was the slogan of the Stock Exchange; 'The Bank of England promises...' was printed on the British currency and was sufficient for making it acceptable as a medium of exchange.

longer so and herein lies another source of social and economic decline.[27]

The position of the scientific and technological research units in the large enterprises and public institutions is somewhat different. Characteristically scientists are motivated by curiosity and peer appreciation. They are therefore less keen than administrators to obtain the kind of status which comes from power and control of people. Often their successes and failures can be tested by experiments and are immediately visible. Therefore, unlike administrators whose status is determined by their level of remuneration, scientists' and technologists' remuneration only *reflects* their status which is in fact determined by their genuine achievements. It is this special position of Research and Development which permits economic growth to continue in spite of managerial inefficiency and rising unemployment. But even here the feudal culture takes its toll. When a section head in R&D is offered a new idea which deviates from well established principles he faces a dilemma. If the idea proves to be successful the acclaim is reaped by the person who suggested it or by the top managers of the organization, but if it turns out to be a failure it is he who will be blamed. It therefore becomes safer for heads of sections to avoid spending money on new or unconventional ideas.

Unfortunately this debilitating culture is rapidly spreading also to public research institutions, such as universities. Worse than this, the penetration of commercial interests into the world of science has led to a confusion between profitability and social relevance. Scientists still register tremendous achievements, particularly where science has a high degree of technological applicability, but they lost control over the direction of their work. They push back the frontiers of ignorance but leave the decision which frontiers to push back in the

---

27.   When the US agency Business International questioned the managers of 55 multinationals about their experiences with bribery it was told that bribes are taken practically everywhere. When a study group to investigate corruption was organized by the United Nations Social and Economic Council (ECOSOC) and the American delegation suggested that all payments to persons involved in the arrangement of contracts should be made public to avoid corrupt practices, this suggestion met with the strongest opposition.

hands of industrialists and bureaucrats and thus relinquish their moral obligation to society. This submission to the material interests of industry not only causes the public's currently spreading flight from science and reason, and the resort to all kinds of 'alternative medicine' and other alternative beliefs, but depreciates the role and social status of science to the point that many gifted young people prefer to become managers rather than scientists.

For several decades, well into this century, science played a major role in the promotion of welfare and economic growth. This gave scientists a special position in society. The majority of people romanticized their work and regarded scientists as selfless servants of human progress and truth. At the same time the scientists themselves developed a sub-culture of their own in the midst of an otherwise profit-dominated social environment. They found their ideal in the advancement of true knowledge and put this before the pursuit of material advantage. Not that there was a lack of people in the scientific community who were keen on money, but these did not determine either the principles of scientific practice or the public image of the scientist. Many students of medicine, engineering and the natural sciences, as well as of economics and sociology, chose their studies out of strong social commitment. Even those studying just to obtain a well-remunerated job with social status, or because their parents just wanted them to go to universities, did not escape the influence of the sub-culture's value system. In recent years this is no longer true – the scientific community is losing its soul; it is becoming part of the commercial enterprise, and apart from some exceptions forfeited its public esteem. Together with the spreading of the feudal structure, this makes scientists less and less able to produce new ideas and find financial backing for their testing and application. But just as the loss of confidence in a businessman's word is not merely a moral decline but a real threat to the proper functioning of capitalism, so this loss of the traditional scientific spirit – the search for truth – is a real hazard for the proper functioning of the new market economy, because new ideas is precisely what western society needs to sustain a humane face, and what industry requires to keep ahead its new Asian industrial competitors.

In conclusions. Since the late 1970s I discern a drift toward a society which I find neither economically expedient nor morally attractive. I see risks involved for science and society in the newfangled sophism hiding behind some of the post-modern ideas and 'political correctness', and the need for a revival of the public's political engagement and for a revision of economic theory to restore to society the humane perspective which inspired the founders of the *Welfare State*. For centuries the West, and particularly the west of the West, had turned its eyes to the morrow and eagerly embraced change, perceived as progress, and by this it marked itself off from earlier and alternative cultures. From the 1950s onwards much of this intellectual energy spent itself in practical achievements, from town planning to the Welfare State. The subsequent loss of momentum gave people the impression that the wheel is motionless – that it fails to carry them upward, as they previously believed, or downward, as they try not to fear. They immerse themselves in their daily business and immediate circle, and turn their back on the political parties who until now claimed to command the levers of change.

In the dark days of World War II, Albert Einstein declared that whatever '(science) will produce depends entirely on the nature of the goals alive in this mankind. Once these goals exist, the scientific method furnishes means to realize them. Yet it cannot furnish the very goals. The scientific method itself would not have led anywhere, it would not even have been born without a passionate striving for clear understanding. But perfection of means and confusion of goals seem to characterize the age. If we desire sincerely and passionately the safety, the welfare, and the free development of the talents of all men, we shall not be in want of the means to approach such a state.'[28]

Einstein's statement is as true today as it had been when he made it, but a society nurtured on individualism interpreted as materialistic self-interest is ill equipped to choose goals and pursue policies designed to promote *social* safety, *social* welfare and the *free* development of talent; and a scientific community which regards

---

28. A broadcast-recording for the Science Conference in London on September 28th, 1941.

expediency as its guiding principle is ill equipped to deal with truth. Nobody is against safety, welfare, and the development of talents, but events have given these desires a different meaning from those supposed by Einstein's generation to be self-evident.[29]

Unlike the depression of the 1930s, which affected the lives and hopes of millions of people from almost all classes, the depression of the 1980s had a discriminatory effect. The incomes of the employed did not diminish, as had been the case in the 1930s, but separated society into reasonably well remunerated employed people and the unemployed, poor and destitute members of the community. In the USA it led to ghettos and 'no go' areas. In most countries of western Europe this disintegration of society has been delayed by the social security system of the Welfare State, but is now rapidly moving in the same direction. Ideas like the *New Deal* lost their attraction for politicians because these can no longer secure them an electoral majority. They realize that even if all the unemployed were to cast their votes for an updated similar proposition the total number of their votes would not suffice to balance those of the employed.[30] To obtain power in a democracy one must win elections and this places politicians in a dilemma. They feel that they cannot take their electorate into their confidence, and dress up their

---

29. The director of a plant generating atomic energy may be very much concerned for his andhis family's safety but less troubled by hazards facing the rest of the community. He will move his home as far as possible from his enterprise but not shut it down because other families which do not have this option are living in its immediate vicinity. Nor will the state (barring extreme circumstances) close down the power-plant if it is deemed necessary for maintaining the country's economic competitive position. Similarly, irrespective of class and social status, many people will deplore cuts in social benefits, but they will not be prepared to reduce their own income even if they are or can be convinced that this is the only way to secure the welfare of society as a whole and in the long run possibly also their own.

30. Even an unlikely combination of environmentalists, communists, old-age pensioners, the unemployed and their dependents, and the genuinely religious-motivated supporters of a less profit-centred policy would together not muster more than 20 per cent of the votes in the Netherlands. In the USA, where most of the deprived do not even bother to register for elections, the percentage would probably be smaller.

decisions in what seem to be plausible arguments. They place their trust in rhetoric rather than in truth. The result is that people lose confidence in politics as an instrument of change. The worst is that major parties lull the large middle class into false confidence and do not alert it to its impending fate. As noted already, for a long time this middle class, which nowadays comprises the great majority of all the gainfully employed, was *the* main beneficiary of the Welfare State. Even those able to pay for it themselves enjoyed government-assisted housing, free health care and education, and many other material advantages, and if necessary even unemployment pay. Many European sociologists believed this middle class interest to be a safeguard against a return to the pre-war misery. But their confidence was misplaced. Since the late 1970s increasing unemployment has progressively, salami-like, sliced off the lower tiers of the middle class and thereby increased the number of people no longer merely enjoying but actually depending on the social arrangements of the Welfare State. At the same time, fewer and fewer working members of the class were obliged to pay more and more for sustaining those sliced off from the bottom tiers of the salami. But the politicians of the Left refused to look this process in the eye. They simply took the easy way out, and did not warn the decreasing number of employed, who make up the majority of the middle class, of the risk of approaching unemployment. Instead they used a whole array of plausible half-truths borrowed from the right wing of the political spectrum to convince the public that the malaise is only temporary, or that it is a kind of unavoidable natural disaster.

However, as long as there is no real shift of policy to address such structural issues as described, the salami-slicing process will continue. And as the number of the unemployed continues to increase and the number of those able to sustain them to diminish, a choice will eventually be forced upon industrial society. It will either have to accept South American conditions, that is its separation into a small group of affluent citizens and a large majority of poor and destitute people, or it will have to take collective political action.

Unfortunately, the virtual monopoly of the establishment over the media of public information makes the explanation of the necessary choice practically impossible.[31] It excludes the possibility to present *alternatives* to the 'received' recipe for solving the unemployment problem, as the New Deal had purported to be. Moreover, the survival of the achievements of the Western World crucially depends on education. And education, as distinct from training, is anathema to obedience and compliance. But the latter are the attributes the new oligarchy requires to ensure its hegemony. Hence, the new oligarchy has most to lose by supporting the free development of talents. The denial of the traditional role of the study of history and literature in the widening of the concept of 'humanity' ignores the traditional wish for progress associated with modernity. If the term human progress can be given any meaning at all; even if my definition of progress as the augmentation of freedom of choice is not accepted, the term human progress means the extension of equal rights to an

---

31. There is nothing sinister in this and there is no conspiracy to hide the truth, but there is the simple fact that the information given to the public is usually selected by people who do not consider themselves experts in the field of knowledge they report, and that they rely for their information on what they believe to be the best established sources. The very nature of their work allows them little time to analyze the press releases and government communiqués which they receive. Their task is to report the news, and an official press release is news. In the Gulf war reporters were in fact prevented from obtaining first-hand information, and had to rely only on press releases, and this practice is not confined to matters of defence alone. Often reporters also do not know the *true origins* of the news they are reporting, and the measure of its import on the public mind. For example, if they report information provided by an international organisations such as the OECD, they may not even be aware that it is based on the material supplied to the organization by member governments and therefore reflects no more than these governments' official policy. But by broadcasting the news the media are creating the impression that they convey independent international confirmation for the ruling point of view. The public, learning of the OECD report, finds that it conforms with what their government is saying, and concludes that what the experts have been telling them is right. The public stops thinking. If the 'experts' and everyone else agree that the world is flat, it must be true. Even the ministers and experts who originally supplied the material upon which the international report is based forget the doubts they may initially have had, and feel that their views have been confirmed.

increasing number of people.[32] Democracy promoted equal rights for all irrespective of colour, religion and sex, though unfortunately they were never fully attained. The hallmark of progress is the search for what is common to mankind, and the hallmark of reaction is the stressing of differences.[33] Striving for equality is not antithetical to individuality. Characteristically, modern science searches for the unifying principles behind events, but also emphasizes the diversity of particulars. It makes the distinction between facts and values. Equal *rights* provide the basis for the opportunity to realize individual aims and desires. But the attempt to regard pure self-interest as a unifying principle behind all behaviour, as if it was a scientifically established fact, and in the political sphere equating it to individualism, turned success itself into a kind of vindication of almost all means by which it is obtained. This attitude is more evident from day to day.[34] There is nothing new in the fact that

32.   Ancient Rome regarded slaves as 'speaking instruments'; Feudal society distinguished people with blue from red blood; early Capitalism abolished slavery and 'blood' but transformed workers into 'hands'; and late capitalism allowed workers to rise on the basis of individual competitive ability but did not provide them with equal opportunities.

33.   Nazi Germany, for example, separated mankind into superior and inferior races, as has always been done by all who do not wish to see others equal to themselves.

34.   Hardly a week goes by without the newspapers reporting some new political scandal. In the USA, Senators and even Presidents are deservedly or undeservedly reported to be or to have been involved in financial or sex scandals. In Britain, the term *sleaze* has practically become a byword for politics. In Belgium, Willy Claes is accused of accepting bribes to finance the advancement of his party. In Italy the country's seven times prime minister Andreotti is charged with links with top Mafia boss Toto Riina. In Holland, when large scale reorganisations are taking place even Trade Union leaders are suspected of making arrangements in favour of their members by circumventing the law of last in first out. The public figures whose involvement in scandals is spreading distrust in politics are too many to be mentioned here by name, but a few will suffice to illustrate the drift. In Britain the names of Jeffrey Archer, Neil Hamilton and Tim Smith spring to mind; in Italy Silvio Berlisconi, Bettino Craxi, Francesco de Lorenzo; in France Alain Carignon, Henri Emmanuel, Gerard Longuet, Michel Roussin,

politicians are corruptible; and it is a good sign that the press still finds corruption in high places newsworthy, because it indicates that decorum is not yet altogether dead. What is new is that in the public's mind high office is increasingly becoming synonymous with corruption. If the alternative to a drift to a South American situation is collective political action, then herein lies the real danger for the future: distrust in *politicians* is leading to distrust in *politics* and hence to disbelief in the possibility of obtaining desired ends by means of the ballot-box.

Collective political action must take account of the fact that economic *policy*, and not only economic *conditions*, influence the conduct of society, and the conduct of society influences the economy. This means that to be successful any attempt to revive the progressive economic policies called Keynesian must take note of its possible effect on people's conduct. The feasible success of providing economic security without deliberate, powerful and costly measures to restrict corruption is an illusion. It is certainly not enough to introduce half-heartedly some legislation to prevent corruption. But to fight the abuses of the economic security provided by the Welfare State by its abandonment, as the Thatcherites attempted to do, can only end in social and economic disaster.[35]

Having reviewed the last quarter of a century, I cannot help asking myself how the new generation can find its way out of the present wasteland of the spirit. In my latest book,[36] I do not presume to offer a route map out of it. I have been describing the charts which have been used to shepherd us into it, and the dangers of continuing to use them. All I can now do is to indicate the main

---

Bernard Tapié; in Belgium the Vice Prime Minister F. Vandenbroucke, Guy Coëme, Guy Mathot, Guy Spitaels; in Spain Alfonso Guerra, Mariano Rubio; and in Germany Jürgen Möllemann, Franz Steinkühler and Max Streibel.

35. I tried to explain how it can be done in the last chapter of *A Theory of Full Employment*.

36. Y.S. Brenner and N. Brenner-Golomb, *A Theory of Full Employment*, Kluwer Academic Publishers, Boston, 1996.

considerations which may point to a possible exit, and hope that others be persuaded to move towards it.

The fate of the humane values of western civilization is still in the balance – the battle for a more decent world is not yet lost. What is required from us – from economists, is to provide a plausible *alternative*. Discontent, and efforts to correct specific wrongs alone, cannot reverse the drift toward despondency. A realistic alternative, the vision of a future worthy to be struggled for, is indispensable. Without it discontentment breeds desperation, reaction and disaster. But given an alternative people find *hope*, and hope is the great antidote to despondency and fear.

Our social and economic system is in the process of reorganization, and the final outcome of any system's reorganization is always unpredictable. But our decisions may influence its future.

Bilthoven, June 1997

Introduction
to the 1979 Edition:
General Outline and Scope of Book

This book is concerned with *economic progress* and with the mechanisms by which such progress tends to materialize. Economic progress is the augmentation of freedom of choice. The intention is to show that the extension of such freedom is functionally related to mankind's increasing ability to satisfy its material needs more fully and with less effort, i.e. to mankind's increasing ability to overcome both the retentiveness of nature and the inertia of its social institutions.

The term *progress* is chosen deliberately because it denotes the notion of movement in a desired direction, and because it is sufficiently general to include both spontaneous and organized change. It is here suggested that there can be no freedom of choice without economic security, and that economic security depends upon man's mastery of both nature and his social modes of existence. The mastery of nature is in the domain of the natural sciences, and the mastery of man's social modes of existence in the social sciences, but in their contribution to progress they are inextricably interrelated and interdependent. I believe that society's social organization determines the direction of its technological advancement and that its scientific and technological achievements delimitate its possible forms of social organization. Science and technology determine the effort and labor-time *required* to satisfy man's material needs, and man's social forms of existence determines the nature, diversity, extent, and all but the minimum of these needs, together with the techniques adopted for their satisfaction, – that is the effort and labor-time actually expended. It follows that societies capable of producing and retaining more than the minimum produce required for their physical survival acquire a degree of freedom which is commensurate with the labor-time and effort they can devote to the satisfaction of wants which go beyond subsistence, including the want for more leisure. This 'more' is society's surplus labor-time, and the larger this surplus the greater its freedom of choice. Without such surplus choice is confined to the alternatives of existence and extinction. With the increasing efficiency of production the surplus grows and the choice widens. It becomes possible to divide the 'extra' time and effort between a greater variety of purposes. Yet, as material constraints diminish, cultural constraints proliferate. Escaping the fetters of material poverty, mankind enters the bondage of an increasingly sophisticated social environment which it both inherits and creates. In the process of this transformation a distinction must be noted between the freedom of an individual and the freedom of a society as a whole. This is because each individual is only free to choose from among the possibilities available to him is his society, and he does so with attitudes and preferences fashioned by the same society. But from the point of view of others (or even of the same individual if, for example, he happens to be a social scientist) he could have also other choices available to him if those socially determined restrictions were relaxed. It follows that progress – the augmentation of freedom of choice, can only have a social meaning, namely the proliferation of alternatives recognized by society as possible, or acceptable by it as modes of conduct. On the whole, therefore, it is the value system of society which influences and limits the individual's freedom of choice; and society's freedom –

the range of available choices, is influenced and restricted by the degree of control it holds over the natural environment. It follows that science and technology by reducing the labor-time and effort required for providing man's basic necessities for biological survival afford society the opportunity to remold its social formations – a society is given the chance, but no more than the chance, of becoming the master of its social institutions and outlook.

For centuries man's dominion over nature increased spontaneously. More or less by trial and error man learned to solve a growing number of concrete problems. Finding himself wanting in strength he employed wind and water and domesticated animals to do his work. Finding the generosity of nature inadequate he learned farming the land to supplement his means of sustenance. Chancing upon suitable ores and coal he learned to control the low but vital carbon content required to make steel by the difficult and unreliable method of stopping the blast in the furnace at the precisely correct moment. Almost unconsciously, in response to immediate stimuli, per capita output of labor and the per unit yield of land and materials increased. The improvements were the product of isolated changes in production, never the result of fundamentally new methods. The dramatic changes by which man overcame the niggardliness of nature came later when spontaneity yielded to the organized efforts of modern science. They came in the wake of the establishment of a body of systematic principles, – a theory not limited by man's practical interests and perspective but one that would transcend them. Such a theory gave man a mental image, a model of nature; a reflection of order and regularity that, until undone by contrary observations, could form the basis for the formulation of fundamental laws of wide applicability. Man formulated a law of gravity and was eventually able to construct a rocket capable to overcome the attraction of the earth and reach the moon; he formulated a kinetic theory that gave him an understanding of matter which ultimately made it possible to split the atom and gain control over sources of energy incomparably more powerful, more reliable, and less spatially restricted than wind, water and animals. Genetical, biological and biochemical theories gave rise to man's understanding of life and made it possible for him to interfere with the mechanisms of natural growth to obtain predictable results, and to reap more, better and greater varieties of crops than earlier generations could ever have imagined. The formulation of theories about the composition of substances, and of their effects upon one another – the study of chemistry – taught man to synthesize, to form compounds and recreate nature, and make materials and substances more suitable for his purposes than those nature has provided. To obtain, for example, high-quality steel it was no longer necessary to stop the blast in the furnace at exactly the right moment. Instead, one would simply burn all carbon out and then restore the correct amount at the end of the process. In short, the understanding of reality, even in the limited sense of forming a picture of mechanisms which *could* be responsible for all the observed phenomena (even though one may never be quite sure if this picture is the only one which can explain the observations) gave man the power to dominate rather than be dominated by the natural environment. Little of this kind of understanding has yet been gained by social scientists.

Except for some utilitarian notions, nothing transcending place and time and approaching a general theory capable of *explaining* social behavior; and few laws of general validity, have yet been formulated in the social sciences. In this sense it may be said that social scientists are still in a pre-scientific state of knowledge. Like the technologists in the past, who applied considerable ingenuity studying for example how iron is turned into steel without understanding the fundamental laws that could explain why these methods worked, so do social scientists. They try to answer questions like 'what will be the reaction to specific stimuli under one set of circumstances or another?' But they do not try to understand why these reactions occur, or how the sets of circumstances had come into existence. The reluctance to deal with this kind of questions is due to the wish to remain firmly within the limits of empirical science, namely within the requirement that any generalization must be tested by observation. Man's ability to learn from experience so as to alter the stimuli, and indirectly influence the 'given circumstances', and the very limited possibility to conduct controlled experiments under variable circumstances, exclude the possibility to give a scientific, i.e. an empirically tested, answer to the wider question, and this is then advanced as the reason for the social sciences failure to match the success of other sciences.

For example, economists have a fairly elegant theory of demand. This theory purports to explain consumers' behavior. It is surrounded by a good deal of learned controversy about the question whether it ought to rest upon the introspective concept *utility* or on the more positivist technique of *indifference* curves. The latter is assumed to depend upon less nebulous foundations than the former because it relies on observation – on the study of the preferences which people display when choosing between different commodities, i.e. on experience and sometimes even on experimentation. Both methods have proved to be of great practical use for specific purposes of limited empirical validity. However, they fail to explain the social character of demand in a wider sense. The laws based on either method are invariably followed by qualifications like 'all other things being equal', or 'assuming that man acts rationally to maximize utility'. These qualifications restrict them in time, place, and dimension. Very little remains 'equal' through time and conditions can hardly be called 'equal' in rich and poor countries. Moreover, having restricted economics to manageable boundaries of an empirical science, namely to social phenomena which involve exchange of goods and services which can be measured in terms of money, the assumption that man acts rationally to maximize utility obtains a correspondingly restricted meaning of utility. An attempt to escape this limitation turns the concept utility into an elusive introspective term which can no longer serve the economist's urge to quantify. In other words, the term *utility* is either too narrowly defined to cover reality or too widely defined to fit the requirements of empirical scientific analysis as practiced in the natural sciences.

All in all, economic laws suit only one form of social existence, namely that of a society technically capable of providing for its basic needs but not yet assured of its ability to do so. A good, but by no means exclusive, example for a system which fits this description of social existence is Capitalism. Seen from this point of view our economic laws do not relate to 'man's actions in the ordinary business of life...' but only to 'the attainment and the use of the material requisites of well-being' under very special circumstances. These circumstances may well be described by the words 'economic insecurity' or 'fear'. They are the fears of a society, which under the pressure of an increasingly efficient technology and *potential* capacity to produce greater economic security in the future, deprives its individual members of the *limited* security they had in the past from working the land, controlling directly their means of production, and from the social and economic safeguards that come with rural, family and tribal ties.[1] They are the fears of a society just beginning to escape the scares of imaginary ghosts and demons and entering the era of the real nightmare of unemployment and starvation. They are the fears which accompany the transformation of increasing numbers of people 'from spiritual beings who, in order to survive, devote reasonable attention to economic interests, into economic animals who also find it prudent to take some precautions to assure their spiritual well-being.'[2] Altogether therefore, it may be said that the validity of these economic laws hinges upon one or both of the following transient conditions. Firstly, that society has not reached the level of technological efficiency considered by its members adequate to ensure the desired standard of living. Secondly, that society has not adapted its social institutions sufficiently to exploit the technological capabilities to provide an adequate product and to distribute it in the necessary fashion. So, 'the love of gain', which is of course no more than a manifestation of the quest for economic security, and the 'cold fear of starvation', are the true movers defining both utility and what has been called rational behavior. Take out this fear and economic theory as we know it becomes invalid. Yet, given these motives and given the level of technology that makes possible the accumulation and concentration of a surplus product for deferred consumption, this mechanism of economic progress seems fairly obvious. It is the two-pronged mechanism of competition. Competition between the entrepreneurs themselves, and competition, if this is the correct term, between entrepreneurs and workers. Fearful of being driven out of business by more efficient competitors, entrepreneurs are inexorably forced to search for and introduce new technological and organizational improvements. Facing

---

1.   These safeguards were of course not what *we* consider adequate but the only ones that they could have.

2.   R.H. Tawney, 1922, *Religion and the Rise of Capitalism*, Holland Lecture, reprinted by Penguin Books, West Drayton, 1948.

an increasingly powerful and better organized labor force, entrepreneurs are relentlessly pressed to introduce such improvements that can help to raise output per worker sufficiently not only to compensate them for higher real wages, i.e. labor's greater share in the fruits of production, but also for maintaining a level of profit that makes innovation possible. This dual mechanism prevents the entrepreneur from satisfying labor's higher wage-claims by reducing profits, because without reasonable profit he cannot make the innovations that are necessary to survive in competition with his fellow producers. This dual mechanism can therefore be regarded as a major stimulus to science and technology – i.e. to economic progress as it was defined earlier. This description of an economic growth mechanism is no more than schematic because of the variety of devices with which entrepreneurs have tried, not without some success, to free themselves of its pressures, for example by using political power to prevent the organization of labor or by forming competition reducing cartels. In spite of all, this schematic description is still close enough to reality to illustrate the point about the relationship between individual freedom and freedom of society. Labor's choice of work is limited to the employment opportunities offered by entrepreneurs, and entrepreneurs' choice of investments, i.e. their freedom to create employment opportunities for labor, is firmly restricted by competition and the condition of the labor market. The maximization of profits, a must in the competitive struggle of all against all, becomes the final arbiter of all decisions. When individuals make their decisions in such a society their socially defined limitations are clear. What escapes their considerations is the possibility that their society may well be technologically capable of producing economic security for its members unless prevented from doing so by its social character which is inherited from a technologically insufficiently advanced era. An approach to economics which would take account of this problem could no longer be confined to the study of 'how people, either individually or in groups, attempt to accommodate scarce resources to their wants through the process of production, substitution and exchange,' – i.e. to the explanation and understanding of what already exists, but would have to be at least equally concerned with what could be, and how it can be brought about. As already pointed out, what *is* determines the degree of individual freedom, and what *could be* the degree of social freedom. But to study the could be would require the concerted effort of several social sciences and would involve both a normative and a positivist methodological approach. It would necessitate the liberation of economics from its behavioral postulates which are too narrowly observed and tested and taken from specific and not universally valid cultural environments. Buddhist monks, New York hippies, Israeli Kibbuzniks, and graveyards full of soldiers – heroes or fools – who laid down their lives for the sake of ideals other than the maximization of profit, bear witness to the fact that different cultural value systems are possible.

It is useful to define three mechanisms of economic progress and to relate them to associated levels of technological efficiency. They are growth, development and planning. *Growth* is a term borrowed from biology implying an organic process of change. In its modern economic context it may be understood as an endogenously-produced quantitative, rather than qualitative increase in physical output, or *per capita* income, of society. *Development* is conscious deliberate growth, usually but not exclusively stimulated by state authorities. It implies the introduction of exogenous directional decisions. Development may accentuate or run parallel to growth in one or more sectors of the economy, and the one may also restrain the progress of the other. *Planning* is an institutionalized, previously quantified, rationalized process of development, over a definite period of time. An economic plan is a body of economic and social policies expressed in quantified targets and defined tasks. Defined in this way, and there are other possible definitions,[3] growth is spontaneous, and development and planning are organized mechanisms of progress. By implication the earlier mentioned two-pronged competitive mechanism of economic advancement is growth. Growth becomes development when a volitional element is added to accentuate some, and restrain other, spontaneous forces in the hope of giving to

3.   For alternative definitions see A. Seldon and F.G. Penance, *Everyman's Dictionary of Economics*, London, 1965; A. Gilpin, *Dictionary of Economic Terms*, London, 1961; D.W. Pearce, *The Dictionary of Modern Economics*, 1981, and for the one used here R. Bicanic's in E. Nelson (ed.), *Economic Growth*, 1960, p. 174.

growth a desired form and direction. Development is therefore an intermediate state between spontaneity and planned social effort. It is a state in which mankind is on the one hand not sufficiently free of its socio-organizational heritage to control its powers of production and distribution at will, but, on the other hand, is sufficiently aware of its character to exert a directional influence upon them. Profit continues to be the determining force behind the selection of the goods which are produced and the technology adopted for their production, but devices are added to make the production and distribution of socially undesirable goods less, and desirable goods, more profitable. Planning differs from growth and development because it replaces the spontaneous mechanisms that hinge upon individuals' pursuit of profit by organized, pre-determined willed and conscious social effort that makes man the master instead of the servant of the process. What is socially desirable and what not is then determined by the society's political institutions, by a bureaucracy which may or may not be representative, and may or may not reflect in its decisions the wishes of the majority of people. Indeed, it may be a bureaucracy that arrogates the power to determine what is best for the people, or it may be any kind of de facto leadership representing its own or other limited sectional interests. In other words, centralized and comprehensive planning is a tool and as such may be both reactionary-retrograde or progressive-liberating depending on how, by whom, and for what purpose it is used. It becomes reactionary when it lacks inbuilt mechanisms for adjustment to change, and retrograde when it does no more than replace the old peril of starvation by new fears of administrative penalties. It is progressive and liberating when it contains adjustment mechanisms and replaces compulsion by participation. Imposed 'pragmatic' planning which does not elicit participation and has no inbuilt innovating mechanism is retrograde because innovation is relegated to the state bureaucracy whose hands are tied by rigid hierarchies of 'disciplines' and order of priorities. When economic progress can no longer result from organic growth but only from policy directives and their execution as tried in the so called socialist states; where output targets ceased to be technological predictions and became compulsory government instructions, where all unplanned forms of growth were prohibited because they diverted resources away from where the planners said that they should be employed and where the state becomes the sole agent of economic advancement. With this type of planning economics is transformed into a procedural administrative matter. Losses are hidden in the lump sums of centralized averages and justified by the claim that general social utility cannot be measured by gains or losses in individual sectors. Economic planning becomes progressive in theory and retrograde in practice, it makes man an apparent master of the system but in fact deprives the majority of people of effective means of making their subjective wishes known of having a say in the allocation of resources between alternative uses. It puts all decision making powers into the hands of a bureaucracy, with an inherent tendency to develop into an unimaginative pressure group, putting what is considered best for the people before the peoples' expressed wishes. Obviously such a system, which is by no means identifiable with the Soviet system alone, does not really lead to an augmentation of freedom of choice. It gives freedom only to a selected few who purport to have some superior knowledge about what is best for the people. One type of coercion, that of market forces, is substituted by another, that of the state authorities. In addition, such a system also tends to be reactionary, because the absence of a mechanism for assessing the profitability of any specific investment invites excessive overhead costs, empire building, nepotism, general inefficiency, and maladministration. Without some kind of adjustment mechanism and supervision from 'below' old production techniques and traditional resources are seldom replaced quickly and efficiently by new and better ones. In a bureaucracy few are keen to shoulder the responsibility for scrapping expensive investments when new materials and production methods ought to replace them – bureaucracies are not known for their high spirit of responsible initiative and risk-taking. The fact is that the transformation from the state of affairs in which economic forces determine the direction, techniques, and character of production and distribution to the state where man sets out to determine them himself, replaces also the 'invisible hand' of the price mechanism by the visible hand of the public administrator. Whereas in the former state of affairs, that was defined as growth and development, an economic mechanism plays the role of coordinator and allocator of resources, in the latter state, that was defined as planning, progress requires a political mechanism to regulate the activities of the bureaucracy. For 'without general elections, without unfettered liberty of the press and of public meetings, without untrammelled political discussion, life in all public institutions fades away, and will become a pious fiction, in which the only active element is the bureaucracy'.[4] What happens to planning, and therefore to economic progress as 'the augmentation of freedom', if this should come to pass, has already been illustrated. It follows that political democracy, on the basis of an adequate level of education and information, is the necessary mechanism for making planning progressive. In short, the character of economic planning depends upon the nature of the social and political institutions which attend it. Hence, to assure a proper equitable functioning of a planned economy in the service of society, two things are imperative. Firstly, the development or evolution of a positive *economic* methodology for the solution of administrative planning problems, i.e. for the setting and quantification of realistic production and consumption targets. Secondly, the development or evolution of a method for the solution of *socio-political* problems, i.e. for the communication of the people's priorities to the planners, and for the people's supervision over the bureaucracy. In the present transitory conditions of most welfare states this implies the development of a method for coordinating the planning of the major aggregates, such as investment and consumption, with those parts of the economy which continue to be powerfully influenced by the uncontrolled forces of the price mechanism.

As economic progress is a dynamic process, neither growth nor development or planning can ever be observed in a pure form. Growth is always adulterated by some developmental interventions, and development by a degree of planning, and planning is unlikely not to be mixed with some unplanned forces. Yet sufficient characteristics of either type of economic progress are recorded in

---

4.   Rosa Luxemburg, 1922, *The Russian Revolution*. First published in *Le Populaire* in 1922 but written several years earlier. Reprinted in 1970 by the University of Michigan Press in a volume edited by B.D. Wolfe entitled *The Russian Revolution and Leninism or Marxism*.

the economic histories of several countries to illustrate the specific problems of each of them. It has already been stated that the technical side of economic progress takes the form of an increase in the per capita output of labor and the per unit yield of land and materials. Per capita output of labor obviously depends upon the equipment with which such labor is employed, but no less upon its level of education and responsibility. Per unit yield of land and materials hinges upon the range of resources known to man and their scientific and technological possibilities for exploitation. A comparison of a day's output of two equally hardworking, or lazy, men, one working with a hoe and the other using a tractor for the same job, sufficiently demonstrates that more affluence can be produced by the latter than by the former. Similarly, comparing the petrol consumption of an ill-adjusted motor-car engine with one that is well adjusted; or the wealth produced by an orange-juice extract factory which has considerable difficulties in getting rid of orange peel, spirits and other inedible by-products, with the wealth produced by a similar enterprise that makes use of these 'unwanted' by-products for making fertilizer, perfume, fuel and candy out of them, bears out the same conclusion. The superiority of production with better technology is self-evident. However, the development of such technology requires that the allocation of resources, of labor and materials, to be diverted to the production of goods which are not wanted for their own sake, i.e. for direct consumption. It requires goods whose sole purpose is to help produce other goods more efficiently. The production of such goods necessitates the utilization of resources which can only be gained at the cost of producing less for current consumption. This means that the development and adoption of an improved wealth-producing technology requires both the ability and the wish to do so. The *ability* depends on the existence of a surplus which can be turned into equipment, i.e. into real capital, and the *wish* depends upon some powerful motive for people to abstain from consumption and hoarding and to turn savings into investment. If none of the Empires of antiquity ever produced an industrial revolution it was probably due to the absence of such a motive. If farmers in ancient Egypt provided a number of large towns with a high living standard, this was due to the excellent administrative and organizational methods of Pharaonic exploitation.

Thousands of people were made to work on land of more than average fertility, at the highest level of efficiency then known, and the combined effort was just enough to produce the necessary surplus. Each worker produced something more than he needed to survive, and all these 'little somethings', when skimmed off, amounted to a good deal; sufficient to feed the collection apparatus and the parasitic towns. Similarly in ancient Roman society, farmers received nothing in exchange for their surplus product; the rich people and the towns followed a parasitic existence and exploited the masses of farmers whose efforts to increase the yield must consequently have been very rare. Moreover, even if the wish to make such an effort had been there, the money required for turning the wish into action was not forthcoming.

A change came with the rise of the modern bourgeoisie. The advent of capitalism supplied the previously missing incentive, for capitalism provided both the ability and the wish to invest. It made possible for some people to accumulate and concentrate wealth at the expense of others, but it did not provide them with the power to do so without giving something in exchange. Unlike the rulers of antiquity, capitalists are not vested with the legal authority to take whatever and as much as they want from their fellow citizens and even from the people of their empires, but are forced to trade with them if they wish to increase their wealth. In other words, capitalism brought together the forces of both supply and demand in a growth-producing combination. Sometimes as in the early parts of the industrialization of England and Japan, the accumulation and concentration of capital was the result of the investors' ability to pay low-wage rates. Other times, as happened during the early industrialization of North America, it was the result of capital imports and rapid technological improvements. In England and Japan capital was accumulated because population accretion and competition among workers for jobs, together with a legal system that prohibited the organization of labor, prevented the workers from getting a good share of the fruits of production. In America, where the abundance of free land determined the minimum level of wages, capital accumulated because employers were forced to substitute labor wherever possible by mechanical equipment which soon proved to be sufficiently efficient to raise output per man far in excess of wage claims. Demand, in England and Japan, where wages were too low to absorb the whole volume of production, was powerfully reinforced by colonial customers. In North America high wage-rates, and the yield of good land, provided a brisk domestic demand, while exports, though considerable, played a less significant role in the encouragement of capitalists to turn their earnings into investment. Altogether, therefore, it is characteristic of capitalist growth that the national product is divided in such a way that an economic surplus is created, and appropriated by one section of the population, which under the pressure of foreign or domestic demand finds it profitable to convert this appropriated surplus into further growth-producing investments. The determination of how much and in what specific sectors investment is made, is left to be decided by a relatively small group of entrepreneurs, acting under the compulsion of the earlier described two-pronged competitive mechanism.

The social and political ascendancy of the working class brought about the transformations from growth to development. The need to maintain full employment of labor in the richer countries, and the wish to accelerate economic growth in the poorer ones, led to an increasing degree of directional interference with the autonomous growth mechanisms. The fact that the price system ignores the dual character of labor as a factor of production on the one hand, and as persons with a right to be guarantied adequately rewarded work on the other, made such intervention practically unavoidable. The inadequacy of the price system to meet the needs of societies in which the promotion of economic stability and an equitable distribution of wealth have become political objectives and necessities had led to ever more state intervention in the economic sphere. While this has not altered the basic fact that economic growth can only occur with investment taking away some of the resources which without investment would be available for consumption, it has produced a fundamental shift in the location of the power to make investment decisions. From private entrepreneurs it has moved more and more under the control of state authorities. Armed with the necessary legal instruments, the state began directing and regulating investment in three ways. It made direct use of state funds to invest, where and when it deemed such action necessary; it regulates the operation of the price mechanism through taxation, bonuses and legal impositions, making private investment in some cases more and in others less profitable than they would normally be, and by controlling the monetary system, again by way of the price mechanism, it regulated the timing of investment. Therefore economic development gives the impression of being restricted only by the availability of physical resources and the sufficiency of information, and, particularly in the poorer countries, by people's motivation, but in reality the problem is considerably more complex. This is so because without comprehensive planning it is almost impossible simultaneously to raise economic efficiency, i.e. stimulate growth, to maintain economic stability, i.e. keep stable prices, and to advance the equitable distribution of wealth. The almost incessant inflationary tendencies and the lingering income differentials in all countries bear witness to this difficulty. In a developing economy the mixture of deliberate intervention and spontaneous forces like the price mechanism, makes a steady and relatively low rate of growth imperative for the maintenance of stability. The reason for this is that the level of income depends upon the level of investment, and at least in capitalist or mixed economies, investment depends upon the rate of change of income. Therefore if stability is to be maintained attention must be paid to the maintenance of a constant increase in the level of incomes over time, i.e. to a steady rate of growth. Unfortunately however, in the presence of a great many external disturbances, and limitation on the supply of resources, this can only be achieved at low growth rates. The regulative, fiscal and monetary, instruments of economic control at the disposal of governments in capitalist and mixed economies are just not powerful enough to deal with the cumulative up or down swings in the economic indicators that would accompany high growth rates, nor would they be able to time the application of these instruments effectively when growth is more than moderate. In more technical terms, the interaction of the multiplier effect and the acceleration principle make a regulated steady but moderate growth rate a necessary part of economic policy. This necessity is the mechanism which economic development adds to the older mechanism of economic growth. The determination of a precise rate of growth which is consistent with the requirements of both equity and stability, and the finding of the administrative instruments for achieving this objective, and the timing and degree of application of these instruments, are the main problems of the economist in this type of economy.

Once again, in a capitalist society the product of labor is divided into two parts, one is returned to its producers in the form of wages and salaries, and the other is appropriated by entrepreneurs and state authorities, and passes out of the direct control of its producers. The former part becomes consumers' expenditure, the latter investment. The worker is left with no direct means of controlling the character and direction of the investments. In this sense the characteristic of both growth and development is the alienation of the worker. The freedom left to him is the ability to determine the distribution of his expenditure between the goods which investors offer in the market, and, in a political democracy, to determine once in so many years, the political leadership, which, through its bureaucracy, will try to influence investment decisions.

The interest shown before the late 1970s in *Economic Planning* on a national scale has two sources: *firstly*, in the U.S.S.R. and in the economically backward countries, the wish to accelerate the growth of per capita income and expenditure, or, as Marxists would say, the wish to perform the tasks not accomplished by capitalism in these parts of the world, namely the accumulation and concentration of capital and its transformation into efficiently productive investment; *secondly*, in several economically advanced countries, particularly in Western Europe, the wish to maintain full employment together with the achievement of sustained long-run economic growth. In both cases economic planning has emerged as a tool of policy. In the first mentioned type of economies the aim of planning is no less than the long-term transformation of economic and social structures. In the second type the aim is stability and growth within the context of private ownership and by way of reliance upon the price mechanism. Hence, plans are elaborated for the achievement of social aims and they serve as means for the systematic co-ordination of income, wages, prices and other public policies through the enlistment of private support. In Soviet-type planning almost all economic activities are under the direct control of the government. In economically backward countries public and private actions have usually been regarded as complementary rather than mutually exclusive. In both cases the purpose of formulating a plan is to identify and define the policies best calculated to achieve general economic and social objectives by translating them into physical targets for output and resource allocation and specific tasks for economic activity which are consistent with the economic and technical possibilities of the community.[5] In the more advanced Free Enterprise economies significant changes in the share of investment has normally not been a major objective of planning. The volume and distribution of investment has largely been taken as a dependent function of the increase or the alterations in the demand for consumer goods. In the first place alternative overall national growth rates are considered and the one least likely to lead to disequilibria in a dynamic balance between saving and investment, employment and the supply of labor, export and imports, together with public revenue and expenditure, is selected. On the basis of this growth rate a preliminary sketch of final demand in the last, say fifth or seventh, year of the plan is elaborated, which ought to be based of an analysis of expected consumer expenditure and assumptions about foreign trade and growth expectations in years beyond the planning period. From this a kind of input-output table is constructed, which should reflect the level and pattern of final demand and the requirements for intermediate goods and services to satisfy it.[6] After the preliminary sketch is examined and adjusted to make sure of its internal consistency, similar input-output tables are constructed for each year of the plan by working backward from the terminal to the first year. In this way quantified demand and supply estimates are predicted for each subsector of the economy; these should serve as guides to investors about the expected requirements of specific goods and services. For example, a manufacturer of motor-cars should have in the plan a reasonably good estimate for the volume of materials and services which will be available in a given year and the volume of demand for cars which will accompany it. Given this knowledge

---

5.   Vide *Report of the Secretary-General United Nations on Planning*. UNO
      document A/5533/Rev.1.

6.   This is of course not the only method of national planning but a good
      example.

the manufacturer should at least in theory comply with the expectation of the planners because this would be in his own interest. If he increases production beyond the planned output he would incur shortages in the supply of materials and services which would cause his costs to rise and consequently force up car prices. In turn this would reduce demand for cars and cause losses. Consequently, noncompliance with the plan would be punished via the operation of the price mechanism. In his own interest the manufacturer would behave in the way the planners expect him to behave. Unfortunately this is a highly idealized picture. In reality, uncontrolled foreign trade, and the character of a profit-motivated society, tend to subvert the logic of such harmony. Other socio-cultural forces are too strong for manufacturers always to act in a way that would seem most reasonable and in their self-interest. As several producers operate competitively in the same markets their attempts to gain from each other a greater share of the limited resources and demand often wholly frustrate the expectations of the medium-term planners. It follows that both command and free enterprise planning have not escaped the socially restricting characteristics that attend economic growth and development – i.e. planning does not necessarily assure the fulfillment of its objectives, namely it does not automatically promote the augmentation of freedom of choice which is economic progress. The progressive element in both is that they demonstrate the possibilities that are inherent in planning for the advancement of such freedom. It is in the study of these possibilities that the economist can no longer work in separation from the sociologist, anthropologist and political scientist and others. For there are also other forces at work which frustrate mankind's chances for a better future. These are the subjects which are addressed in this book. Each chapter deals with one set of problems which were mentioned in this introduction. In the last chapter an attempt is made to discuss the latest changes in the behavioral patterns of society. How the ideologically ill prepared welfare state undermined the dignity of labor and thereby responsibility and work discipline; and how bourgeois rapacity by shedding the last vestige of what used to be middle class morality destroyed social and economic stability. Something is said about the waning of the entire system of ethics – the things done and not done

– which provided the element of confidence that had made economic progress possible in an otherwise utilitarian society; and how the legitimization of bribery and bureaucratic wickedness by labelling it *raison d'etat* has become no less a danger for humanity than nuclear proliferation. Finally some suggestions are offered how our economic, social and educational system might perhaps be made sufficiently rational to avoid a return to a new medievalism.

1

The Beginnings of Economic Development

'If you can look into the seeds of time,
And say which grain will grow and which will not,
speak then to me,...'
Macbeth I, iii, 58

This study is concerned with the relationship between two disciplines: *History* and *Political Economy* or Economics. The historian hopes to construct logical explanations for events and developments that have taken place in the past which may or may not have a bearing on the present or the future. The economist endeavours to build up economic laws of general validity with the clear intent of using the meaning inherent in them for the attainment of wilfully selected social and economic objectives. In other words, *Political Economy* or Economics is 'the art of managing the resources of a people and its government.'[1] Both the historians' and the economists' *métier* differs from the natural scientist's because unlike the latter they are concerned with people who may react to similar stimuli in different ways, and who, by learning from

---

1.   Adam Smith.

1

experience, may try to alter the stimuli themselves. Moreover, economists cannot even conduct controlled experiments and must therefore lean heavily upon historians to supply them with the empirical information to corroborate or invalidate their laws or theories. To be sure, the very laws themselves which are in fact no more than 'statements of a general uniformity in the relationship between two or more phenomena of economic life' or statements about 'what will occur in the economic world under specific conditions'[2] could never have been conceived in the first place without the systematic organization of past and present observations – that is history.

In their efforts to build-up economic laws of general validity economists employ both inductive and deductive methods. Inductively they adduce a number of separate historical and statistical facts for the purpose of strengthening confidence in a general rule and attempt to infer general rules from the observation of such particular instances. Deductively they advance in the opposite way. They start from generals and move towards the particulars by means of theory and logical conclusions. The advantage of the inductive method is that it deals with empirical or historical facts and saves economics from becoming something like a new branch of scholastics. The advantage of the deductive method is that it allows the examination of the correctness of the economist's derived conclusions. Whether or not such logical deductions are based upon valid assumptions and hypotheses, and whether or not the actors in the 'human drama' behave in the way the economist takes to be logical is another matter. However, inductive economic evidence shares with the historical past the imperfection that, unlike physical phenomena that would exist even without the intervention of someone to describe and classify them, the historical past can only exist to the extent that there is an image of it – in other words 'to the extent that it is recreated by the mind.'[3] Not this alone; 'in order to define the role

2.   A. Seldon & P.G. Pennance, *Everyman's Dictionary of Economics*, London, 1965. A. Gilpin, *Dictionary of Economic Terms*, London, 1961.

3.   *Vide* H. Berr & L. Febvre, *op.cit.*, for statement on 'historical past'.

played by history', and for that matter by economics, 'in the achievements of knowledge it must be noted that there exists for the mind a general point of view... the point of view of change; because if everything in the realm of the real were subject to immutable laws, there would be no history;' nor would there be a possibility to write history or formulate economic laws, 'if everything in the realm of the real were universally and perpetually changing.' Yet, while no one will deny the ever changing character of human society, i.e. the 'general point of view of change,' economists developed techniques in some branches of analysis which enable them to relax several of the restrictions imposed upon their studies by this point of view for the solution of certain types of practical problems. For example, by excluding slow long-term changing variables such as population accretion and technological innovations, or stochastic shocks, and labelling them *exogenous* they obtained a conception of a system in which a number of functionally inter-related *endogenous* variables such as income, saving and investment, can be studied, and the effect of changes in one or more of them on the rest predetermined. At first sight it appears that the covering of the exogenous variables by the expression *'ceteris paribus'* renders this approach essentially static – non historical. Indeed it was likened 'to statical Mechanics', with the Laws of Exchange analogous 'to the Laws of Equilibrium of a lever.'[4] Starting from the notion of mutual interdependence of all economic quantities it is possible to determine a problem by means of a set of simultaneous equations if as many equations can be obtained as there are unknowns. A comparison of various static solutions at different times, assuming that each system of inbuilt variables has a unique steady-state solution, can then, though without telling much about the *path* of change, provide a discernible pattern of development. Moreover, by artificially partitioning time into discrete intervals and making the changes in any particular period dependent upon the events preceding it, solutions can be presented in the form of a set of relations expressing each variable as an

---

4. W.S. Jevons, 1888, *Theory of Political Economy,* 3rd edition, London, p. i and vi. Jevons compares the interdependence of economic variables to the equations in physics which are valid under certain conditions.

explicit function of time. In other words it is possible with the help of linear difference equations, by presenting the variables, or at least some crucial ones, in terms of linear functions to make this apparently static approach dynamic. The shortcomings of such dynamic models are of course that there is little empirical evidence supporting the choice of the values of the coefficients or even the type of functional relationships employed; and that the substitution of rationalized mathematical functions for the human relations of real life has remained a doubtful effort. It follows that promising as this type of quantitative semi-dynamic approach may be, particularly for the solution of short-run problems, it has not replaced other approaches especially where long-run problems are concerned. It is for the study of such problems that the economist is most dependent upon the work of the historian.

One long-run problem of this type is the achievement and sustaining of economic growth. Economic growth is the steady process of increasing productive capacity and national income per capita, i.e. the raising of the efficiency of resource utilization. Normally this takes the form of rises in the product of labour per unit of time and in the yields of produce per unit of land and materials, which may be accompanied by an expanding exploitation of previously unrecognized and technologically or economically unexploited resources.[5] The result of economic growth is that people are given the opportunity, and no more than the opportunity, to become richer and freer.[6] The reduced labour-time enables them to choose between working less hours for the satisfaction of customary wants or working as long as before for the satisfaction of increasing

---

5.   This statement was discussed in some length in Y.S. Brenner, *Introduction to Economics*, Middle East Technical University Press, Ankara, 1972, pp. 33–9 and examples from history illustrating such achievements in *A Short History of Economic Progress*, Frank Cass, London, 1969, and in *Agriculture and the Economic Development of Low Income Countries*, Mouton, The Hague & Paris, 1971.

6.   The relationship between freedom and economic growth was discussed in my inaugural lecture at Utrecht University *Economic Progress*, 1973, pp. 1–9 and in the introduction to this book.

wants. Similarly, the increasing yields from land and materials makes possible the satisfaction of the needs of growing populations or of desires for greater material affluence or both. Whether or not, and under what conditions, these potentialities are actually and equitably exploited is still another matter which may well have a decisive influence on the character, path and rate of growth at which the economic process proceeds.

Evidently economic growth depends upon the progress of science and technology and the social arrangements that accompany or give rise to it. Social forces determine the application of science and technology to the processes of production and the progress of science delineates the limits to which at any given time man's mastery of nature for the satisfaction of wants can reach. The development and application of technology itself depends upon both material and cultural pre-requisites. Materially it hinges upon the availability of the factors of production, labour, land and capital, and culturally upon the spirit of enterprise. In other words, to produce economic growth both the *ability* and the *wish* for innovation must be present; but for a structural transformation of societies – for an industrial revolution – these are only *necessary* and not *sufficient* conditions. An industrial revolution requires that they combine under specific circumstances, in precisely suitable proportions, and following a particular time sequence. Ancient Rome lacked neither in material factors of production, nor in acquisitive culture patterns, nor even in scientific and technological genius, but, it did *not* produce an industrial revolution modern capitalism did.[7]

Assuming as correct that adequate supplies of land, labour and capital[8] and acquisitive culture patterns[9] are the *necessary* conditions

---

7.   *Vide* the evidence in M. Rostovtzeff's discussion of the Roman society and economy during the Empire.

8.   The term *capital* is used here in its economic definition as *real capital*, i.e. physical assets such as machines, factories, etc.

9.   The term 'spirit of capitalism' was deliberately avoided because non-capitalist societies for example the socialist societies in Russia and China are of course acquisitive but not capitalist.

for the transformation of societies, the development economist finds himself in a position not very different from that of the chemist who, having identified the elementary substances that combined to form a given compound, needs still study the laws regulating the combination of the elements in its formation and the phenomena that accompany their exposure to diverse physical conditions before he can hope to reproduce the compound. Unlike the chemist, the development economist cannot test hypotheses under controlled conditions, – he can do no more than examine the historical evidence for verification. Unlike the historian, who is methodologically confined to the task of recording and explaining the events that actually happened, the economist may however also study 'non-events', the developments which 'ought' to have happened but did not. For example, he may legitimately not only ask how it came about that by 1848 'the bourgeoisie, during its rule of scarcely one hundred years, has created more massive and more colossal productive forces than have all the preceding generations together,'[10] but also, why in the presence of all the assumedly necessary pre-requisites for sustained economic growth in the Roman empire such growth did not persist, and why the cessation of the wars of conquest and the ensuing end to the influx of abundant slave labour did not result in the introduction of labour-substituting mechanical equipment. The more precise and detailed the historical presentation accessible to the economist the greater will be the chances that additional crucial factors and circumstances are discovered that may either strengthen confidence in his development models or invalidate them. As long as no contradictory evidence has been produced, and action taken in the light of the theory renders the anticipated results, such a theory specifies the circumstances that may be necessary and sufficient for them, and is no less valid than, say, the theory of gravitation in physics.[11] It is of course also true that no economic

---

10.   Karl Marx and Friedrich Engels, *The Communist Manifesto,* 1848, p. 5.

11.   'Physical concepts are free creations of the human mind, and are not, however it may seem, uniquely determined by the external world. In our endeavour to understand reality we are somewhat like a man trying to understand the mechanism of a closed watch. He sees the face and the moving hands, even

theory can serve as a valid guide to action outside its historical context, and that this context is eternally changing, and that different historical contexts require different theories, but in spite of all this such theories have proven to be far from worthless. In the first place, given a sufficiently explicit description of the circumstances[12] (by the historian) under which the theory was true at some point of time in the past, and an equally explicit description of present conditions (by the sociologist), and information about the path of change, the development economist is often able to amend the original theory sufficiently to allow for the changes. Secondly, most of the economically relevant socio-cultural changes in the earlier mentioned 'specific circumstances' mature only very gradually and may therefore be regarded, from the economist's point of view, as fairly stable. To mention one, the profit motive spread its domination over much of the behavior of western civilization for several centuries. Thirdly, some crucial parameters of social behavior may well be functionally related to each other and to certain economic formations and are therefore less independent and unpredictable in their totality than the cursory observer may be led to believe. On another occasion[13] I suggested that the 'love of gain' that so strongly influences the behavior of modern economically advanced societies,

---

hears its ticking, but he has no way of opening the case. If he is ingenious he may form some picture of a mechanism which could be responsible for all the things he observes, but he may never be quire sure his picture is the only one which could explain his observations. He will never be able to compare his picture with the real mechanism and he cannot even imagine the possibility or the meaning of such a comparison. But he certainly believes that, as his knowledge increases, his picture of reality will become simpler and will explain a wider range of his sensuous impressions.'

Quotation from Albert Einstein and Leopold Infeld in *The Evolution of Physics*. First published in 1938, here from 7th paperback edition, Simon and Schuster, New York, 1967, p. 31.

12. The term circumstances is employed here in the widest sense to include both socio-cultural, political and economic conditions.

13. In my inaugural lecture *op.cit.*

is in fact only consistent with a specific state of technology and human organization. I tried, then, to show that this love of gain is the product of a civilization which escaped from the technological inability to secure the necessary means for its sustenance but has not yet reached a sufficiently high level of technology to have full confidence in its ability to maintain the level of material affluence that from time to time it deems adequate. I proposed that the greed, politely referred to as the incentive for economic activity in a Free Enterprise economy is no more than a somewhat complex manifestation of fear of starvation. By implication this means that given a certain level of technology it should not be impossible in the most general terms to predict the long-run trends of the other crucial behavioral parameters that combine to influence society until the time the technological parameter has changed. At the same time it is of course also self evident that the progress of technology itself is no less dependent upon changes in the other parameters than the latter upon the technological developments. This does not propose the necessary existence of some kind of minute historical determinism, all it does propose is that in the long-run, the laws which may be adduced by isolating certain variables and leaving others as fixed parameters must from time to time be reexamined.

With this in mind, I devote the rest of this chapter to the *initiation* of economic growth, and discuss the mechanism by which it is *sustained* in the following chapter.[14] It has already been said that economic growth depends on the availability of *land, labour* and *capital* and the incentives to combine and use them. While the instinct for survival suffices to explain impulses for such activities as fruit gathering and hunting, i.e. for the utilization of *land*[15] and

---

14.   The term growth is used here to signify an endogenously produced quantitative, rather than qualitative increase in physical output, or per capita income, of a society. For my classification of growth development and planning see *Theory of Economic Development and Growth*, London, 1966.

15.   The term land in the economic sense includes natural resources such as coal, oil and water.

labour,[16] this is not necessarily so with regard to *Capital*. Land and labour are 'given' but capital must be created. *Land* is God's, or nature's, gift to mankind and has no cost of production. *Labour* arises out of the dual character of man both as a consumer and producer of goods, but *capital*, the wealth used in the more efficient production of further wealth, can only be produced at a cost. Whatever fashion it assumes, that of mechanical equipment, of inputs in land amelioration, improved education, etc., it is always obtained at the cost of something else that has a direct use. It follows that the supply of *capital*, the crucial factor for the promotion of economic growth, requires an effort directed towards the supply of something which can neither be eaten nor drunk nor satisfy any other obvious basic human want. Therefore it cannot so easily be related to the human instincts.[17] It requires foresight and an ability to produce an output that is greater than the one needed to keep the producers alive. Persons fully employed in the production of goods required to assure their survival have neither the time nor the ability to produce the very means by which they can hope to satisfy their future wants more effectively.[18] Hence, economic growth, by way of greater productive efficiency which is achieved through the production of capital, must always depend upon people's *ability* to save some of their current produce, i.e. on their ability to produce more than they need for current consumption; and upon their *wish* to use such surplus for the achievement of a better satisfaction of their wants in

---

16. Labour in the economic sense means the combination of all exertions by individuals. whether they be manual, physical or menial, directed towards the production of wealth or satisfaction of some measurable want.

17. This point was illustrated in Y.S. Brenner, *An Introduction to Economics*, p. 37.

 'If a monkey were able to enjoy himself the way humans do he would probably shake with laughter watching humans who want fruit from a high tree 'waste their time' on the ground making some kind of tool or implement which neither looks nor tastes like fruit instead of climbing up the tree to pick it'.

18. This is of course the vicious circle of poverty.

the future. If people are either too poor to save, or do not recognize the possibilities inherent in the transformation of savings into investments in their future, or see that the advantages are too remote,[19] or do not feel the need for improvements, no economic growth is likely to ensue. It will also not ensue when people do not have confidence that the savings accumulated from their restriction of consumption will remain at their disposal for investment, or that the fruits of such investments will stay in their control.[20] Consequently, *the parameters determining the limits within which an economy can grow are at any given time delineated by the difference between the volume of output produced by the society and the minimum of such output that is necessary to keep the society alive, while the actual and specific growth rate depends upon social, political and other non-purely economic circumstances which are also the product of historical developments.*

Given that even very primitive societies supported a number of people, such as priests and kings, who did not directly contribute to their material social output, it appears reasonable to say that almost all early civilizations were potentially capable of economic growth; and in fact several such civilizations gave rise to impressive trading and manufacturing communities.[21]

Taking further into consideration that even in periods of general economic reversal, for example in Medieval Europe, the spirit of acquisitiveness never completely disappeared,[22] it may well be true that growth rather than stagnation is the normal order of things – the

---

19.   For example, a person who knows that by refraining from something he can save enough money to purchase some tool which can raise his living standard may still be reluctant to save for purchasing it if he realizes that it would take him, say, twenty years until he can save enough to do so.

20.   For example, farmers in Africa may be able to save but may not be able to protect their savings from pests and fungi or may fear that their savings will be taken from them by poorer relatives, by tax-collectors and by thieves.

21.   For example: Mesopotamia, Greece, Egypt and Rome.

22.   *Vide* M. Rostovtzeff *op.cit.*; H. Pirenne, *Medieval Cities;* M. Bloch, *Feudal Society*; and F. Ganshof, *Feudalism.*

natural mode of existence.[23] If this is so, then from the development economist's point of view the study of *growth-impeding* forces may be no less fruitful than the more traditional search for *growth-promoting* factors. If indeed every society has a kind of acquisitive 'élite'[24] that in a favorable environment would try to raise its standard of living, or standards of living in general,[25] then, the elimination or reduction of growth-impeding forces would be the proper approach to stimulate development. From this point of view the sequence of events leading to the economic transformation of early modern Europe could be seen in the following manner. By the last quarter of the 11th century, if not earlier, a new era was dawning on Europe. Its manifestations were: – accretion of

---

23.   That this is true for organic forms of life needs no further explication, that it may also be true of inorganic substances is becoming increasingly probable from the study of the atomic compositions of matter.

24.   Early society stands here for historical societies because I maintain that the source of the acquisitive drive is economic insecurity, which may, of course, wane with future affluence.

25.   Growth can probably be produced by an elite pursuing its own interest and also by an elite that sees its task in the raising of a nation's or society's living standards. The former elite is the bourgeoisie who is motivated by direct self interest. the latter elite consists of the politically or socially conscious rulers of societies such as Kings, politicians, social reformers, etc., who are motivated by a kind of collective self interest. This view departs from the classical Marxist approach that sees in the era of capitalism a necessary stage in the historical dialectical development of society. According to Marx the historical task of the bourgeoisie is the concentration and accumulation of wealth (of the surplus produce required for growth) and its transformation into means of production, leaving the task of the equitable distribution of the fruits of enlarged production to the subsequent socialist era. Particularly the experience of the Soviet Union casts doubt upon such 'historical necessity' for there the task of accumulation and concentration and transformation of surpluses into means of production was carried our by order of a political elite without the intervention of the bourgeoisie, unless, of course, one cares to redefine the term class or bourgeoisie in such a way that it will include strata of the population who control rather than own the means of production. I discussed this possibility in *Theories of Economic Development and Growth*, and again in *A Short History of Economic Progress*.

population accompanied by notable improvements in agricultural practice[26] and spreading of commerce[27] which fostered the nascent trading communities in the rising towns.[28] On the one hand this accretion of population led to the settlement and conversion to tillage of 'new' land east of the Rhine and to the conquest of new *feuda* in the eastern Mediterranean;[29] on the other hand it led to an intensification of land use in the traditionally settled parts of Europe and to a gradually mounting flow of people who could no longer find adequate employment on the land into the incipient towns. Throughout the two-and-a-half centuries during which these processes continued they did not essentially differ from other growth sequels in earlier periods and other parts of the world. The historical details of these processes (as far as they could be reconstructed) have too

---

26.   *Vide* B.H. Slicher van Bath, *The Agrarian History of Western Europe AD 500-1850*, London, 1963.

27.   *Vide* M.M. Postan, 'The Trade of Medieval Europe: The North', in *Cambridge Economic History of Europe*, Vol.II, Ch. IV, pp. 119–256, Cambridge, 1952, and Henri Pirenne, 'The Low Countries', in *Cambridge Medieval History*, Vol.VIII, pp. 332–62, Cambridge, 1936.

28.   *Vide* Henri Pirenne, *Medieval Cities*, N.Y., 1925 and in *Economic and Social History of Medieval Europe*, N.Y., 1956, and in M.M. Postan, 'The Rise of the Money Economy' in *Economic History Review*, (14), 1944. Also for a Marxist view see M. Dobb, *Studies in the Development of Capitalism*, London, 1937 and K. Marx, *A Contribution to the Critique of Political Economy*, and F. Engels, *Origins of the Family, Private Property and the State*.

29.   A revealing and fairly reliable social distinction can probably be made between the land hungry peasantry which went east, and the booty seeking classes of 'crusaders' that went south-east.
      Vide S. Runciman, *A History of the Crusades*, Cambridge, 1951, 1952, 1954, and J. Prawer, 'La Noblesse et le regime feodal du royamme latin de Jerusalem' in *Moyen âge*, 1965.

often and too well been told to be repeated[30] but their relevance for the historically unique developments that followed the demographic catastrophes from the middle of the fourteenth century deserve some further exploration.

In the first place, there is no reason to believe that the sad diminution of population also eradicated the 'technological know-how', i.e. the improvements, particularly in agricultural practice, that were gained in the preceding period of growth.[31] At the same time it is however more than likely that, due to the diminution of the labour force, cultivation was restricted to the relatively more fertile holdings and many of the least productive lands were abandoned. Consequently, per capita yields of land and labour most probably increased and therefore also the material *ability* to save and invest in further improvements. Secondly, the *wish* to invest was likewise stimulated for the per capita increase in yields was accompanied by a more equitable distribution of the fruits of production which was not only reflected in free and copy-holders' higher real incomes but also in the fact that wages rose more sharply than rents and both wages and rents more sharply than the prices of manufactured goods.[32] Farmers and workers were able to maintain these economic advantages for a whole century.[33] Competition among land-lords for the relatively scarce labour force, the disarray of the central political power structure, and the destruction of the supremacy

---

30. *Vide* R.H. Tawney, *Religion and the Rise of Capitalism*, Harmondsworth, 1948. Max Weber, *The Protestant Ethic and the Spirit of Capitalism* and the Stone versus Trevor Roper controversy, as well as J. Huizinga and Marc Bloch.

31. *Vide* Charles Singer, E.J. Holmyard, A.R. Hall, and Trevor I. Williams (eds), *A History of Technology*, Vols II & III, Oxford, 1956; and Slicher van Bath, *op.cit.* and Lynn White, *Medieval Technology and Social Change*, N.Y., 1962.

32. *Vide* Y.S. Brenner, 'The Inflation of Prices in Early 16th Century England', *Economic History Review*, XIV, 1961.

33. *Vide* E.H. Phelps Brown and Sheila V. Hopkins, *Economica*, No. 92, Nov. 1956, and J. Hirshleifer, *Disaster and Recovery. The Black Death in Western Europe*, (Rand Corporation), 1966.

of the heavy cavalry and its replacement by the 'combined training bowmen'[34] peasant armies, perhaps for the first time in history, put the majority of the laboring classes in parts of Northern-Europe in a position to protect themselves against attempts of their 'betters' to deprive them of a greater share of the produce of their labour.[35] Together with this and probably because of the higher real incomes of the working population, changes in the character of some towns were also taking shape. The town-based market system that with relatively only minor reversals survived the demographic catastrophes was gradually adapting itself to the spreading of a new type of demand. Its impressive growth in the 13th century had mainly been founded on foreign trade and a domestic demand for certain high-priced goods or luxuries. The greater affluence of the working population added to this a growing market for everyday commodities. What followed was a gradual realization in the towns that fortunes which traditionally were sought in trade and money lending and to a far smaller extent in the manufacture of several expensive products could also be made in the manufacturing of less costly goods for common use. It was the emergence of this new type of demand and the response to it that really differentiates the new from the old character of some of the Northern European trading centers.[36] It was this combination of rich and profit minded urban elites with a large and relatively affluent rural population that precipitated the new type

---

34.   *Vide* Sir Charles Oman, 'War in the 15th Century' in *Cambridge Medieval History*, Vol. VIII, pp. 646–59. I discussed the relevance of peasants' ability to protect themselves against exploitation by landlords or government agents at some length in *Agriculture and the Development of Low Income Countries* (Mouton, 1971), p. 35 etc.

35.   *Vide* A.R. Bridbury, 'The Black Death' in *The Economic History Review*, XXVI (4), 1973, and my *A Short History of Economic Progress* where I try to show this in the first and third chapters.

36.   There are many similarities here with the position of towns in economically underdeveloped countries today, where also in the absence of lucrative domestic markets for local manufactures, the rich tend to engage in money-lending, export-import trade. The difference nowadays is that they can also try to whisk their money abroad.

of economic incentives. To be sure every person will make a demand but every such demand will not be answered and will consequently have no effect. The demander must have an equivalent to give, it is the equivalent, the 'effectual demand' which counts.[37] By the middle of the 14th century the demand for the goods used by the common people which could best be produced in the towns began to become 'effectual'.[38] But the growth and transformation of the towns had also other ramifications that affected rural changes and productive efficiency. The new types of productive activities in the towns required additional labour, and the more these activities proliferated the greater became the number of people who were no longer able to produce their own food and had to purchase it from others. Consequently, here and there, where the vicinity of trading towns encouraged it, cash-crops began replacing traditional subsistence cultivation. Farmers discovered that some crops, for which their land was better suited than others, could be sold in the nearby town for prices that permitted them to purchase what they no longer produced themselves and something to spare. In fact they began to specialize, and with prices instead of direct subsistence requirements, becoming the crucial determinant of production decisions, agriculture had passed the threshold of a new era of improved modes of production.[39] Within two centuries the rural maps

37.   This statement is borrowed from James Steuart, *Vide Collected Works*, first published in 1767, p. 153, in 1805 edition.

38.   It is of course possible that the above mentioned developments were the true cause of the religious movements and changes that came to a head in the late 15th and early 16th centuries. The idea behind sayings like 'ere shall the camel pass through the needle's ear than the rich man into heaven' never carried much weight with the urban élites who were *able* to become rich, and faded also with rural populations once affluence became a realistic possibility. Hence both the Protestant ethic and the adaptation of Catholicism to the new ways were perhaps both the result and the cause of the economic changes. (*Vide* also my article in the *Economic History Review* of 1961).

39.   Before this there was first the period of subsistence farming, when each household was almost entirely self-sufficient and all its produce was locally consumed. Then followed the period of the 'direct barter'; people were still

of regions thus affected were altogether changed. For example in the Netherlands, land in the vicinity of cities became almost entirely allocated to the production of vegetables, whereas the more remote areas were shared between fruits and crops required as manufacturing-materials, often at the expense of cereal production. Since the 16th century the Netherlands were actually dependent for the supply of cereals on its Baltic trade. Thomas More's tale of the sheep 'devouring' men, which is true at least for some chalk lands in early 16th century England, and of the progress of enclosure, is too well known to be repeated again in support of the contention about the reallocation of land between food and 'industrial' crops.[40] Eventually, under the influence of renewed population pressure in the 16th century, this process led to an unprecedented intensification of husbandry. More money per acre and more employment was used to increase yields. The soil was dug more deeply and manured, livestock was kept in greater numbers, and transport was developed to convey compost and ash from the towns to improve the land and bring its produce in return. By this time, however, wage rates were again falling sharply, and while part of the rural population continued in its affluence[41] and thus maintained a level of domestic demand for urban manufactures, the rest of the people became increasingly dependent on selling their labour in both town and

---

self-sufficient but produced enough to make some 'payments in kind' for services and goods which they received from persons no longer directly employed in agriculture. The rent collector, the priest, the barrel-maker, the salt merchant are examples of such persons who directly bartered goods and services for their food.

After this followed the period of the rise of an impersonal market and its concomitant, the money or cash economy. Payments in kind were almost entirely restricted to the landlord-tenant relationship and ever increasing numbers of people became dependent upon markets and middlemen and prices began playing an important role in influencing farmers' long-term decisions.

40.   *Vide Utopia* and Gonnor's *Common Land and Enclosure*, as well as R.H. Tawney's *Agrarian Problems in the 16th Century* and Slicher van Bath, *op.cit.*

41.   *Vide* the controversy about *The Rise of the Gentry*.

country at diminishing *real* wages.[42] Yet, the decline in real wages not only stimulated a rapidly spreading export trade but also gave rise to an increasing accumulation of manufacturers' wealth, i.e. to a further rise in capital – the material determinant of the limits of *possible* growth. Hence, on the one hand, the sustained growth of domestic demand over long periods, and on the other, the opportunity to satisfy foreign demand, may be regarded as the source from which the incentives for transforming wealth into growth-producing capital were flowing. So long as the pull of domestic demand or of foreign demand,[43] or their combined pull, exceeded productive capacity – the real investments required to satisfy it at the current level of technology – growth continued; for the owners of accumulated wealth found it profitable to convert their savings into productive profit-earning investments.[44] To be sure, the progress of both types of demand was far from even. Sometimes individual fortunes were lost when foreign trade underwent a reversal or when domestic demand flagged, other times such fortunes were

---

42.   Economists distinguish between money wages and real wages. The latter take into account the changing value of money in terms of its purchasing power. A wage increase may be offset by a fall in the purchasing power of money.

43.   The importance of the foreign markers in this context is apparent if one remembers the small volume of production the developed manufacturing establishments were able to produce at that time with the size of world-wide demand. which, although consisting individually of relatively poor units, was in its combined effect by sheer numbers far from insignificant.

44.   Marx gave a rather neat formulation for this transition from self-sufficiency to capitalistic modes of production and motivation. According to him prior to this period commodities were exchanged for money and money for other commodities that people wanted. Now this simple direct relationship was changed. The owner of wealth no longer sold in order to buy goods to satisfy his wants but he bought and sold in order to enrich himself The formula which presents the old situation of exchange:

Commodity ——> Money ——> Commodity

is replaced by the formula

Money ——> Commodity ——> Money

with the hope that Money after exchange, in the second formula, is more than before the exchange.

transferred and investments shifted from trade to manufacturing and to the purchase of land and back, all in accord with specific and temporary circumstances, but the overall long-term trend was growth.

In summary, since the later part of the 15th century a number of simultaneous developments combined to maintain demand on the whole ahead of productive capacity. These were: Firstly, population accretion, which raised overall demand sufficiently to compensate for the declining purchasing power of individual wage-workers which fell with diminishing wage-rates. Secondly, urbanization, which changed the ratio between people able to supply their own subsistence needs and those dependent on cash purchases, together with the ratio of people employed in food production to those unable to produce food but need to consume it, caused a sharp rise in the prices of food and other agricultural produce and in rents[45] and made investment in land and in its improvement increasingly profitable. Thirdly, expansion of world trade, which added an important source of demand in the long-run perhaps less stable but also less dependent on domestic incomes. A demand which kept investments lucrative even when, owing to domestically reduced purchasing power, investments in the production of goods for the local market were unattractive. Fourthly, falling wage-rates, which were due to the concatenation of population accretion and urbanization, and coincided with a continuing rise in the demand for goods and services, increased profits and stimulated accumulation. Thus altogether, both the *ability* and the *wish* to invest were present and before long transformed man into something like a calculating 'economic animal'[46] – into the economic-growth producer, profit accumulating and investing 'hero' of the capitalist era.

Assuming now that the essential points of this historical analysis can be generalized, namely that it cannot be shown to be relevant only to the particular European circumstances, it should be possible to base upon it a number of theoretical conclusions which *may* well

---

45.   Y.S. Brenner, 'The Inflation of Prices etc.', *Economic History Review*, XIV, 1961–2, and P. Bowden, 'Agricultural Prices, farm profits and rents', *Agrarian History of England*, E.H. Phelps Brown & Sheila V. Hopkins, *op.cit.*

46.   R.H. Tawney, *Religion and the Rise of Capitalism*, pp. 272–3.

be relevant for the formulation of modern policies for the promotion of economic growth in countries where subsistence farming still predominates. These conclusions are:

a. That the produce at the disposal of a society must exceed its current minimum requirements for survival.[47] Since, in terms of physical output, all that a society produces can either be consumed or not consumed, and as not consumed means saved, it follows that the excess of production over minimum-consumption is equal to the maximum volume of available savings. Given further that a technologically determined ratio exists between the value of real capital and the volume of output that can be produced with its assistance, it also follows that the objective parameters of growth at any given time are set by the volume of savings, i.e. by the excess of production over minimum consumption requirements, and by the technological coefficient which is the capital/output ratio.[48] For example, any rise in consumption, due either to peoples' changing consumption habits, or to the need to share the output with a greater number of claimants who do not themselves directly contribute to production, as will be the case when the number of children or old people increases more sharply than the size of the working population in a community, will *reduce* savings and hence the rate at which the economy can grow, while any net addition to savings, will *increase* the rate at which the economy can grow. Together with this, the fact that the technological coefficient, the capital-output ratio, is also dependent on the volume of available savings, for any additions to the capital stock can only be made out of savings, it may be concluded that the objective parameters of growth can only be widened by additions to the volume of savings. If the said community is already restricting its level of consumption to a bare minimum such a rise can only be brought about through outside aid; if it is not restricting consumption to a minimum, it may be attained

---

47.   If we designate the society's total produce by Y and its consumption by C and minimum required consumption for survival by C_m then the proposition can be stated $Y > C_m$.

48.   If we designate maximum savings by the letter S and the capital/output ratio by the letter α then highest rate of possible growth can be stated $Y - C_m = S$.

through reductions in the level of current consumption. It must however be remembered that the relationship of savings to the technological coefficient can only outline the limits of possible growth at any point in time. The actual rate or the actual path of growth depend upon the distribution of the savings between new investment, hoards and postponed additional consumption.

b. Under conditions of Free Enterprise the conversion of savings into productive investment will only take place if it appears to be profitable. The historical analysis has shown that profit expectations hinge upon the growth of 'effectual demand'. Such demand was at one time fed by foreign trade and at another time by rising domestic labour-incomes and occasionally by both simultaneously. Now, assuming that traders or money-lenders or any other money-elite is employing an amount of real capital[49] that with the given level of technology, is well adjusted to the volume of production necessary to satisfy the given current market demand for goods, then there will be no growth. The demand for the replacement of depreciated used-up equipment will continue, but be stable. Additional, new capital equipment, will not be necessary, and savings will not be converted into new capital-investments. Only a rise in consumers demand can change this situation by upsetting the equilibrium between the volume of existing capital-equipment, and the volume of consumers' demand it must help to satisfy. It follows that only positive *changes* in demand, i.e. additions to the level of current consumption, can induce new investment. Such *changes* in demand seem to have sprung from three sources in the historically crucial period which was discussed earlier. Firstly, from outside the system by the spreading of foreign trade. Secondly, from within the system by the rise in overall *per capita* incomes of the population occasioned by the demographic calamities. And thirdly, again from within the system, by the wider distribution of wealth which led to an increase in consumers' demand, at the expense of the accumulators', which was due to the better ability of the rural population to

---

49.   *Vide* p. 5, footnote 8 for definition of real capital.

defend and protect their temporarily enhanced level of real income.[50] Hence, a minimum of consumers' demand which would yield a maximum of savings *cannot* under conditions of Free Enterprise lead to the transformation of savings into investment, and consequently *cannot* stimulate economic growth unless the deficiency of domestic demand is made good by a growth of exports. In other words, without the advantages of a developing foreign market the *initiation* of economic growth requires a redistribution of the surplus produce away from saving and in the direction of greater consumption, away from the rich towards the poorer. However, the sustainment of such growth requires a dynamic balance between saving and consumption in such a way that increments in demand will always remain just ahead of the changes in supply that can be brought about by the savings with the current technological coefficient or with the coefficient that will be induced by the new investment itself.[51] The relevance of this is that it explains, for example, why foreign aid has been so singularly unsuccessful in initiating the economic development in almost all economically backward countries. For in the absence of expanding foreign markets for the produce of the poorer countries[52] such aid can only become productive investment when accompanied by a growing domestic market, and this requires a redistribution of wealth in favor of the working population which,

---

50. *Vide* description on pp. 13–18.

51. This problem will be discussed later in connection with the sustaining of growth. It has given rise to a great deal of learned theoretical discussion since R.F. Harrod first published in 1939 his dynamic statement of the Problem: $G_w = s_c$

52. This is apparent from the Indicative World Plan of the F.A.O.; and from the observation that qualitative changes have taken place in recent decades in the nature and structure of industrial production in the course of which labour was massively substituted by machines, unskilled labour by highly trained educated workers. and horizontal ramifications and vertical integration for the achievement of economies of scale became integral necessities for competitive industrial production. *Vide* Y.S. Brenner, *Agriculture and the Economic Development of Low Income Countries.*

in these countries means, at least initially, in favor of the peasantry.[53] What is true for foreign aid does of course equally apply to incomes such as the revenue collected by the oil-sheiks and the like of them which rest upon the export of products with a low local labour content. Hence, if not accompanied by a progressive redistribution of wealth, foreign aid though objectively raising the material capacity for growth will in effect result in hoarding, conspicuous consumption of foreign products, exportation of capital, and, in the least obnoxious case, in an augmentation of idle capacity – not in growth.[54] Paradoxically therefore, growth in a capitalist setting can only be initiated by efforts to make the distribution of income more equitable.[55] Given that technological changes require gestation periods, and may therefore be ignored in short-run analysis, and given that in underdeveloped countries such changes can normally be predicted and their impact on production preestimated,[56] it ought not be impossible to calculate in advance what the optimum division of the national product, between savings and consumption, should be to

---

53.   *Vide* ibid.

54.   No objection is implied to foreign aid, which is crucially important for the acceleration of a growth process; however objection is raised to the donation of such aid without due consideration for its proper allocation between the different sections of society with a view to matching growing effectual demand to new productive capacity. This also does not imply a new sort of colonial patronage but a politically more progressive donor policy even if it is not acceptable to the structurally reactionary, though formally progressive, governments of most if not all economically underdeveloped countries. This problem is discussed in some length in Y.S. Brenner, *Use and Abuse of Foreign Aid: some thoughts about Ghana.*

55.   Taking this proposition to its logical conclusion implies that perhaps the best way to promote *Capitalism* and growth in poor countries would be to support *revolutionary movements* which organize the peasants to protect their own direct interests against exploitation by land-lords, money-lenders, and state bureaucracies, and economic competition from richer countries.

56.   This is so because usually no entirely new inventions are necessary as is the case with most technological improvement in the rich countries but existing ones must only be adopted or adapted.

keep demand just sufficiently ahead of supply to induce investment. That such a policy must also lead to inflation, for the excess of demand over supply finds an expression in rising prices, is self evident. This is what happened *in* 16th *century* Europe.[57] Yet, carefully controlled adjustments may well reduce inflationary trends to relative mildness though not avoid them altogether.

One more point ought to be clarified: The redistribution of wealth that is essential for the initiation of growth and takes the form of the working population's rising living standards, is, from a property relations point of view, only relative not absolute. The technological improvements that accompany growth will of course reduce the labour-time and effort of producing a given quantity of produce by substituting capital, in the form of more efficient equipment and other inputs, for labour. As the input of labour will normally not be reduced, output will increase as a result of the technological improvements. The greater output will, however, seldom be shared equally between investors and workers. For reasons discussed later and which have to do with the process of *sustained* growth, additions to the investors' share in the greater output will in the long-run exceed the additions to the workers' share. As in periods of growth the investors' share will however be reinvested in the production of improved means of production, i.e. in the creation of additional real capital; and as income, and therefore effective demand, is formed by employment in the production of both consumers' and producers' goods, the further enrichment of the rich need not reduce the level of demand. Nor need it cause undue shortages in the supply of consumer goods, for increased investments tend to generate more efficient techniques of production and consequently a greater volume of output per unit of labour input. How prices bring the increased output into equilibrium with the greater demand is beyond the scope

---

57. *Vide* Y.S. Brenner, 'Inflation of Prices etc.' in Peter H. Ramsey (ed.), *The Price Revolution in Sixteenth Century England*, London, 1971 where it was shown that the prolonged rise in English prices in the late 15th and in the 16th centuries was less due to the influx of American silver and to the debasement of the coinage than to what Dr. Outhwaite in his summary *Inflation in Tudor and Early Stuart England*, (London, 1969) called 'real' economic forces. These 'real' forces were, probably, those described above.

of this discussion.[58] Here it suffices to conclude that while the initiation of growth requires the redistribution of wealth its *continuation* requires a persistent rise in consumers' income which is usually accompanied by a steeper rise in capital accumulation.[59]

    c. The historical analysis has also shown that structural changes accompany the early stages of growth. The most obvious of these were urbanization and the movement away from subsistence farming to market exchange. In a predominantly rural society this can only begin with a rise in the purchasing power of the peasantry. Ignoring

---

58.   This problem is discussed in the conventional manner in my textbook *Introduction to Economics,* Ankara, 1972, in the chapters dealing with the 'price mechanism' and the allocation of resources, and again in connection with the theory of employment and the business cycle.

59.   For example: If 10 workers produce an additional surplus worth f.20 each, and the surplus is shared between them and the employer in the proportion 75% (f.15) of each worker's surplus as addition to his wages, and 25% (f.5) of each worker's surplus as addition to employers profit, then, each workers income is increased by f.15 and employers accumulation by f.50 for 10 workers multiplied by f.5 = f.50 profit. Hence: Total additional income is f.200; increase in workers' demand for goods and services = f.150; increased accumulation and investment funds = f.50.

Technically economists tend to present the process by which changes in demand for consumer goods bring about new investment by the Acceleration Principle $\alpha(Y_t - Y_{t-1}) = I$. Where α stands for the technological coefficient (capital-output ratio); $(Y_t - Y_{t-1})$ for the difference in income between period t and t–1; and I for investment given the assumption that controllers of profits tend to adjust their real capital stock to changes in demand. Further, with the spreading of money in the economic system, economists also tend to present the effect on total income of a specific amount of real capital investment by the Multiplier ratio $Y_t = \frac{I_t}{s'}$ Where s' stands for the proportion of income saved.

The combination of both formulae (Multiplier and Accelerator) yield

$$Y_t = \frac{\alpha}{s'}(Y_t - Y_{t-1}) = \frac{\alpha}{\alpha - s'} Y_{t-1},$$ which implies a cumulative process. Hence if $Y_t - Y_{t-1}$ is positive, investment and growth should proceed exponentially to the limit of freely obtainable resources.

The reader should note that this is a simplified (only explanatory) presentation of the equations, which ignores the more realistic time factors (t–2)– (t–1) and (t+1) etc.

exports, only this class is sufficiently numerous to become an attractive market for efficient urban production. Consequently, it is initially the rising affluence of the peasants, later to be joined by the class of urban workers which comes into existence as the result of peasants growing demand for manufactures, that keeps the process going. Hence, for example, foreign food-aid to poor countries, save for in periods of natural calamities, is counterproductive, for it distorts the growth initiating processes in a Free Enterprise system. It reduces farmers' profits and thereby the main source of effectual demand and with it the incentive to turn wealth into investment.[60] Together with this, the enrichment of the peasants in the early stages of urbanization is also necessary for another reason: as urbanization changes the relationship between the number of people directly engaged in food production and the number of people who need it for consumption, a rise in agricultural productive efficiency is essential for making-up the difference.[61] Such improvements in efficiency cannot be achieved without new capital investments, i.e. without a rise in farmers' incomes. This is all the more apparent if it is further taken into account that in poor societies the rises in incomes themselves tend first of all to inflate demand for food very drastically, and only much later it leads to an abatement in this demand when it is replaced by the new demand for manufactured products. Economists use an Engels Curve to describe the variation in the intensity of demand for food in the process of development. The curve is shaped like this:

---

60. The savings which food-aid may generate can under conditions of Free Enterprise nor be turned into investment and will therefore become conspicuous consumption of foreign goods (Mercedes Benz cars) or hoards or will be re-exported.

61. Without a rise in agricultural efficiency growth will be brought to a halt either by shortages of physical inputs or by a sharp rise in prices beyond the acceptable for growth or by both.

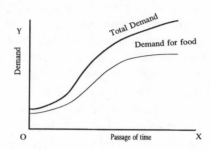

Finally the structural changes also effect the distribution of land and labour between the production of food and industrial crops, which will again result in a diminution of food production unless it is matched by greater efficiency in the utilization of land and labour – i.e. by new investment in agriculture. However, none of these requirements for economic growth can be isolated from all others. Their achievement of economic progress depends upon their dynamic combination in ever-changing necessary proportions. The more detailed and precise historical analyses of such processes become the more useful they will be for estimating the required proportions and for creating the conditions for repeating the process.

d.   Finally there arises the question whether another system instead of Free Enterprise may not achieve the initiation of economic growth more reliably or quickly. At least theoretically it may be assumed that a central authority, for example the State, with sufficient power to appropriate the whole national surplus product, could achieve a maximum rate of accumulation, i.e. the highest degree of material *ability* to produce growth. As the State need not be motivated by the profit motive for determining the rate and direction of investment, investments can be made in anticipation of demand, i.e. capacity may be created to match a predetermined growth in consumers' demand. This does not imply that the additions to production capacity and consumers' demand can at any point in time exceed the limits set by the volume of the surplus produce and the technological production coefficient (a) but within these limits growth could be maximal. If further the State would be able to control wages and prices, then, before long, the greater output produced with the new capacity should make it possible to raise also the supply of consumer goods more steeply than under a Free Enterprise competitive system. Why this is not so in practice has to do with certain human factors, the limits of political power, the character of bureaucracies and the structure of socio-cultural formations.[62] The discussion of these may be best reserved for the Sociological and Anthropological Associations.

---

62. This point was discussed with regard to economically underdeveloped countries to the best of my ability in *Use and Abuse of Foreign Aid*, The Hague, 1972. See also discussion about the Soviet Union in this book on Ch. 10.

2

Production Stimulated Growth

'In nature's infinite book of secrecy; A little I can read'
Antony and Cleopatra. Act I Sc. ii. 11

So far this discussion was concerned with the very difficult problem
of the *initiation* of economic growth, it will now turn to the
mechanism by which such growth is *sustained*. Historically, it
appears that this mechanism was *competition*. On the one hand,
competition between the entrepreneurs themselves struggling to
survive in business, and on the other hand, *competition* between
entrepreneurs and workers for their relative shares in the fruits of
production. Fearful of being driven out of business by more efficient
competitors who may capture the customers of the less efficient ones
by reducing prices, entrepreneurs become involved in a 'free for all'
struggle which inexorably forces them to improve their modes of
production by rationalizing the productive processes and introducing
more advanced technological equipment. Fearful of not being able to
accumulate the necessary resources for financing such improvements
they are, however, also forced to increase their profits, i.e. their
share in the fruits of production. Yet the improved organization and
supervision of labor and the advancing technology usually requires,
or at least required in the past, greater physical proximity of workers

29

in increasingly larger working-places, and this also gives rise to greater opportunity for workers to organize in the defence of their interests, namely for raising their share in the fruits of production. Thus, caught between the need to accumulate in order to survive in the competitive struggle among themselves, and the pressure from labor to redistribute the fruits of production between profits and higher workers' rewards in favor of the latter, entrepreneurs are again pressed hard to rationalize and mechanize production, i.e. to invest, and by implication to promote further economic growth. As with improved organization and technology less labor-time is required to produce a given quantity of output, but the time labor spends at the factory is seldom reduced and even then not very drastically,[1] there is no necessary contradiction between both labors' ability to raise its real income and entrepreneurs' ability to increase

---

1.   Examples for reductions in labor-time required to produce a given output and in the average working hours of labor:

Man-hours required for the production of one ton in USA		Net income produced per man-hour in manufacturing in UK		Average working hours per day in France (Males)	
Year	Wheat	Cotton	Year	In units of I	Year	hours
1800	137	2645	1849	185	1896	10.4
1840	86	1932	1859	266	1901	10.3
1880	56	1338	1900	387	1911	10.5
1900	40	1248	1909	121	1921	8.2
1950	10	581	1913	445	1930	8.2

Source: Colin Clark, *The conditions of Economic Progress*, 3rd edition, London, 1960. Tables XXIII, XXVIII, XI, and p. 127.

profits even more.[2] At the same time labor's rising share in

---

2. *Vide* footnote 59, Chapter 1. The total product of labor before new improvements are introduced is represented by figure A.

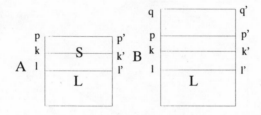

The minimum volume of the produce required to keep labor in the job is L and the surplus above it is S.

The division of the surplus can either be closer to the line 11' or to the line pp'. If it approaches too close to pp' the employer will cease producing for profits will not be attractive. Profits cannot be greater than the area pp'll' for workers will not work for less than L. Normally the surplus S will be divided according to labor's bargaining position, say at kk', when kk'll' will go to the workers and pp'kk' to profit. Now, if under the pressure of workers claims their share in S approaches closer to pp' the employer can compensate himself by introducing innovations raising the total output to the volume illustrated in figure B. Then, workers' incomes can rise to pp' but profits will increase also for qq'pp' > pp'kk'. In *time* the process will be as illustrated in figure C, where the curve Y describes the rise in total output and the axis X the passage of time from t to tn; the distance between curve P and curve Y the rise in profits, and the distance between L and P the rise in the workers' share of the produce, and the curve L the initial level of workers' real income (or subsistence level) in period t.

the fruits of production increases the demand for consumers' goods, and this *change* in demand forms the required incentive for the augmentation of the capital stock of entrepreneurs, i.e. for the creation of new investment. As the construction of new real capital is achieved through the employment of labor both the demand for new investment goods and the demand for more consumer goods tend, on the whole,[3] to keep incomes at a level that suffices, via price adjustments, to clear the market of the additional produce of consumer goods that arises out of the technological advancement.[4]

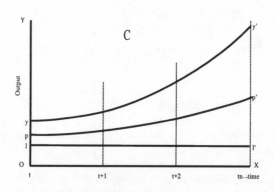

3.   The 'on the whole' refers to long-term trends for in the short-run disequilibria arise which are usually referred to as the conventional business cycles. For the discussion of business cycles *vide: The Encyclopedia of the Social Sciences,* and for example, von Haberler, *Prosperity and Depression,* J.R. Hides, *Trade Cycle,* Oxford, 1950, R.C.O. Matthews, *The Trade Cycle,* Cambridge, 1959.

4.   Figure A shows the volume of the output produced for capital goods (I) and for consumption (C). The production of both together is of course equal to all incomes received from production Y. (I + C = Y). Now with improved technology, I can produce more output of consumers' goods. Hence in figure B C' = Y of figure A., and I' is the new accumulation of profit which will lead to further output and greater incomes in the subsequent period.

How this process, which is far from smooth, is sustained with *foreign trade, competition between capitalists,* and *workers' increasing success in raising their share of the produce,* with at one time the one factor and at another time another of these there or all of them simultaneously, being the motive-force keeping it on an upward trend, is discussed in the following historical outline.

The countries in whose early economic development *foreign trade* played a most obvious role were *England and Japan.* When English wool proved to be better or cheaper than that which was produced elsewhere a kind of 'geographical' specialization began to develop which led to a new process of social and economic integration. Towns were drawn together with their rural hinterland and with other towns with similar trading interests. Before long the *nation* began to replace the town as the focal point of people's sense of 'belonging'. The disintegration of the late-feudal links gave rise to a new form of social coherence which later generations named Mercantilist-Nationalism. The object of the individual's loyalty became more abstract. The new social coherence was reflected in the construction of canals and other means of communication and by the development of a uniform customs system which quickened the pace of economic activity and specialization. By breaking down municipal and provincial autarchy mercantilism made the various regional entities into a nation, into an enlarged 'economic society'. Trade became the source of wealth and wealth a mainspring of national power. Power that could be gained by an 'increase of population, the protection of agriculture and industry, the economy of low wages, a

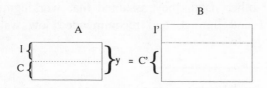

favorable balance of trade, the development of colonial systems, the accumulation of capital with the resulting low rate of interest and a reform of the revenue system.'[5] So, mercantilism was the expression and legitimization of the practice and ideology that stimulated the accumulation and concentration of wealth which preceded and accompanied Englands' early economic growth. To be sure, Man's longing for material welfare did not begin with the era of mercantilism nor did the waning of the Middle Ages totally dissipate Christian ethics, but it made the ancient vices of avarice and parsimony 'respectable' by making them subservient to what was considered the 'public good'. Usury to the mediaeval man posed a clear choice between material welfare and spiritual euphoria – 'He who takes it goes to hell, he who does not – goes to the workhouse.' The merchant of the mercantilist era is spared this choice. He could take usury without forfeiting his 'life hereafter' as long as his actions were not contrary to the mercantilist conception of the 'public good', when they would anyway be forbidden by law. From their conception that identified national power with the public good there was a logical sequence leading to the division of society into the 'people who mattered', who by the pursuit of their own interest contributed to the 'public good', namely the merchants, manufacturers and rich landowners, and the rest of the population who were incapable of saving and adding to the nation's stock of wealth. Hence, that which was desirable in the one class, the entrepreneurs' 'love of gain' – was evil in another. They believed that high profits stimulate and high wages dissuade people from economic activity. On the one hand they maintained that man's wants are unlimited and redefined the concept of achievement to make the acquisition of wealth a symbol of social distinction, – utility the end of all knowledge and vices the father of all progress;[6] while on the other hand, they assumed that workingmen's wants were constant and limited, and recommended low wages in the

---

5.   Eli Heckscher, 'Mercantilism' in the *Encyclopedia of Social Sciences*.

6.   Mandeville (edited by F.B. Kaye in 1924), *The Fable of the Bees: Or Private vices, Public Benefits*.

conviction that this would force laborers to work hard and long for their existence. Living in an era before technology was capable of dramatically raising the per capita output of labor; and in a period when, even had they been considered desirable as they were not, wage improvements would of necessity have had to remain relatively small, in any case not sufficient to induce saving and investment, mercantilists were no less than consistent in advocating starvation wages as a matter of policy. They argued that low wages help to augment the labor force by fuller employment of women and children who would be left with no choice but to seek employment in order to supplement the men's insufficient incomes. Low wages, they maintained, reduce the cost of production of manufactured goods, increase the size of the available labor force and consequently the volume of output, without significantly raising domestic consumers' demand, and hence improve the export trade and thereby the nation's wealth and power. They provided society with a body of legislation to prevent workers from combining in order to improve their wages, and to stifle entrepreneurs' appetites for gain where they considered it not in the 'public interest'. In economic terms, they devised a policy, consistent with the practices of their period, which restricted popular domestic consumption to a minimum leaving the greater share of the economic produce at the disposal of the entrepreneurial classes. Given the relatively small size of the early manufacturing and trading community in comparison with the overall foreign demand for its produce, English entrepreneurs could feel for a long time assured of the lucrativeness of reinvesting the better part of their profits in old and new business ventures. Yet some caution is necessary when assessing the contribution of foreign trade to the stimulation of the economic growth process. It was perhaps a necessary but not a sufficient factor. Had it not been for the other social and economic developments, (described earlier in this analysis);[7] had it not been for the impressive accretion of population that with varying degrees of intensity lasted from the late fifteenth to the end of the sixteenth century, and which was for a time accompanied by the enclosure movement that led here and there to

---

7.   *Vide* pp. 10–18.

the eviction of tenants and their migration to the towns in search of employment; it would have been neither possible to enforce low wages nor to evolve the socio-political conceptions that were expressed in the policies that were subsequently named mercantilist. The importance of the foreign trade for the stimulation of the economic growth process lay therefore in the fact that it added a margin of *demand* which was not matched by domestic incomes. As a rule, the volume of demand is determined by the volume of income, and investment decisions of entrepreneurs by the rate of change in the volume of demand. Consequently, given the low level of wages that persisted in England for the earlier mentioned reasons throughout much of this crucial period, the growth of domestic demand, and therefore incentives to invest accumulated wealth in business ventures, would hardly have exceeded the rate of population growth. It is for this reason, in this marginal sense, that the expansibility of the foreign trade, limited as it must have been in volume compared to the whole economic product of the country, made its truly crucial contribution. The low wages assured high profits and foreign trade filled the gap left by the low wages in the volume of effective domestic demand and kept business incentives upon an upward trend.[8] However, England's economic growth could

---

8.   If it can be taken for granted that the national income (Y) arises from the production of consumers' and producers' goods ($Y = C + I$) and that effective consumers' demand is therefore limited to the total value of production (Y) less savings (S) or investments (I) (which is the same for all that is produced can either be consumed or not consumed in which case it is saved and becomes an investment in the future, $Y = C + S$ and $Y = C + I$ hence $S = I$), and that the value of consumption is determined via an, in the short-run, fairly stable propensity to consume (c') and a fairly stable technological coefficient (α) then, by analogy with the interaction of the multiplier and acceleration principle, it can be said that the addition of foreign demand (E) to the only slowly developing growth of domestic demand $(Y_t - Y_{t-1}) + E$ must have played a very significant role in encouraging entrepreneurs to invest rather than hoard their wealth; the assumption being that entrepreneurs tend to adjust their stock of real capital to changes in demand subject to the current technical coefficient of the capital-output ratio.

Graphically this may be expressed as follows: Let time be measured along the X axis and the value of supply and demand along the Y axis. Let the curve DD represent the effective domestic demand and the curve SS capacity supply.

hardly have persisted for as long as it did in the face of the steadily growing foreign trading competition had it not been for other developments which were gradually influencing the character and growth of her domestic demand. Some of these developments such as the growth of towns and the rise of certain sections of the middle class have already been mentioned,[9] but probably most important was the abatement in the *rate* of population accretion that lasted throughout the seventeenth and first half of the eighteenth century[10]

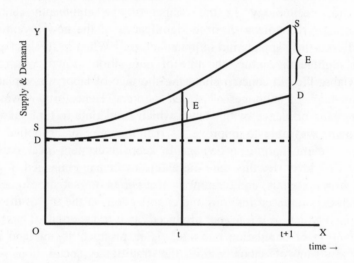

Because of the low wage rates demand is below supply at various points in time. Wealth will nor be turned into capital-investment. Foreign trade fills the gap and raises demand from D to S. This encourages investment. As long as 'free' labor is available this will create new incomes and domestic effective demand will tend to rise. As labor becomes scarcer wages rise and domestic demand increases or/and technology is improved to increase output with a constant supply of labor. As will be shown later in this discussion both processes have kept the economy growing at one time or another.

9. *Vide* pp. 10–18.

10. The abatement in population accretion is taken here in comparison with its rate of growth during most of the 16th century. *Vide* K.F. Helleiner, *Canadian Journal of Economics and Political Science*, Vol. XXIII, No. 1, 1957; Y.S.

and from time to time afforded the working class the opportunity of raising its level of real income. Indeed, the feeling that labor is scarce had become widespread in late seventeenth and early eighteenth century England and the fact that relative to the rising demand it had really become scarce made both low wages often impracticable and the old attitude to labor no longer tenable.[11] Grudgingly even mercantilists discovered that workers' wants are expansible and their attitudes towards enterprise and labor began to undergo a change. Rising demand on the one hand and wage improvements on the other also contributed to greater interest in production technology. In the course of the eighteenth century mercantilists recognized the true significance of the new inventions and advised their application in manufacture.[12] When in the later part of the eighteenth century the rate of population growth was once more rising the old concern about the shortage of labor was replaced by new fears of shortages of *skilled* workers. Henceforth it was to be the rising affluence of this class, which from time to time, as will be shown, was able to improve its real income, that supplied the necessary extra margin on demand to keep investment-incentives at a mounting level. By this time the nature of demand changed. Food, fuel, raw materials and common necessities to satisfy domestic requirements replaced luxuries and export goods at the top of the list of things which were to be produced and transported. Thus the combination of population pressure, rising productivity of land and labor, division of labor within the traditional social units and between town and country, growing numbers of wage workers in the

---

Brenner, *Economic History Review*, Vol. XV (2) 1962, & Vol. XIV, 1961, and the articles by E.H. Phelps Brown & Sheila V. Hopkins in *Economica*, 1956 and subsequent years.

11.   *Vide* D.C. Coleman in *Economic History Review*, VIII, 1956 and A.W. Coats in *Economic History Review* XI, 1958 and the contemporary literature such as Cantillon, Defoe, Steuart, Melon, Berkeley, Cary.

12.   *Vide* E.F. Heckscher, *Mercantilism*, Vol. II, p. 126; G.N. Clark, *Science and Social Welfare in the Age of Newton*, 1949; A.P. Usher, *A History of Mechanical Inventions*, 1954; H.T. Pledge, *Science Since 1500*, 1939.

cities and in road and canal construction and the resultant development of the cash economy, the spreading of foreign trade, and, particularly since the middle of the seventeenth century, the progress of technology, and, no less important, the emergence of a new social ethic, all contributed to the economic transformation of England. Yet, in the early eighteenth century only a few processes in the manufacturing industries were mechanized.[13] To be sure, technological improvements had been progressing for a long time, but neither wool nor silk had a market capable of expanding at a pace which would have put exacting strains on either the nature or the methods of production but such innovations as there were, and particularly the increasing use of the silk-throwing machine, were indicative of the future possibilities since it required only two or three people to operate many hundreds of spindles and reels, which did the work that had previously been done by many hundreds of hand-throwsters.[14] Here was a machine with the capacity to create self-sustained growth through its impact on other stages of production; a machine whose hunger for energy was too large for domestic sources of power and whose mechanical superiority was sufficient to break down the resistance of the older forms of hand production. All that was required to transform traditional manufacture into modern industry was now the application of the principle incorporated in the machine to a popular commodity with an elastic demand, i.e. a demand which swiftly reacts to changes in price. Cheap textiles fulfilled this condition. They were a popular commodity, which lent itself to mechanization, and in which the

---

13. For example in the woollen industry the water-powered fulling mill, the gig mill the knitting frame, the Dutch loom which could weave twenty-four narrow ribbons simultaneously; in the silk industry, the silk-throwing machine which had been introduced into Britain from Italy in 1716 and resulted a few years later in the construction of the first modern factory in England. For details *vide* T.K. Derry and Trevor I. Williams, *A Short History of Technology*, Oxford, 1960, and Charles Singer, E.J. Holmyard, A.R. Hall and Trevor I. Williams (Eds), *A History of Technology*, Oxford, 1958.

14. *Vide* T.K. Derry and Trevor I. Williams, *op.cit.*, p. 100. See also David S. Landes in *The Cambridge Economic History of Europe*, Cambridge, 1965, Vol. VI, p. 1 and p. 311.

mechanization of one process put a strain upon the other stages of production, so that as soon as one process was speeded up it stimulated progress in others. In addition to this, cheap textiles were the kind of product where the impact of improvements was soon felt through the economy as a whole. For these reasons it was cotton which ushered in the industrial revolution. As a raw material, cotton was more suitable for mechanization than wool because it was both more uniform and less fickle. Its supply was far more elastic than that of wool because it took less time to shift cultivation from one crop to another than it did to raise sheep. Its market as a finished product was more elastic and expansive than that for woollen goods, because each fall in its cost of production or rise in incomes brought cotton goods into the reach of a greater number of people and because its tough, yet comfortable and light fabric opened for its sales the bulk of markets in the warmer areas, in southern Europe, America, India and Africa.[15]   While Key's fly shuttle (1733) and Wyatt's and Paul's spinning frame (1738) had originally been designed for the woolen industry, they found their true importance in cotton.[16] Once they were adopted, progress was swift, and produced a chain reaction in the form of an incessant sequence of *'challenge and response'*. Under the pressure of an apparently unlimited demand for the new fabrics, the acceleration of one stage of production immediately caused bottle-necks in either the stage of production which followed or that which preceded it. Thus, for example, the fly-shuttle, which spread in the cotton industry during the third quarter of the eighteenth century, led to severe shortages in the supply of yarn, which in turn stimulated the introduction of Lewis Paul's spinning frame and a whole series of other improvements, culminating in Arkwright's water frame, and Hargreave's famous Jenny and Crompton's Mule.[17] By 1790 the Mule had been improved and adapted to take a greater variety of

---

15.   *Vide* D.S. Landes, *op.cit.*, pp. 313–4 and Y.S. Brenner, *A Short History of Economic Progress*, pp. 34–5.

16.   *Vide* Derry and Williams, *op.cit.*, p. 278 (picture) and 279.

17.   *Vide* Singer, Holmyard, Hall & Williams, *op.cit.*, pp. 278–9.

yarns and a greater number of spindles, so that it replaced no less than two hundred hand spinners. Consequently, carding was lagging behind and improvements had to be made in the preparatory processes to keep up with the demand of spinners. So, one innovation gave rise to another, and in the course of a few decades production was speeded up tremendously, while the quality of the product was also improving. The greater demand for yarn was followed by a rise in the demand for cotton, while the greater supply of yarn led to a greater demand for weavers. Consequently weavers' wages rose very sharply, and their working habits deteriorated, until in the second quarter of the nineteenth century Roberts managed to improve Cartwright's power loom to such an extent that its use became economical. When by 1822 the power loom could easily replace the work of two or three weavers, their prosperity began to diminish, but by that time the prosperity of new groups of laborers filled the gap in the demand for consumer goods left open by the weavers' and other old trades' diminished affluence. The rapid improvement of the weaving and spinning techniques could not have taken place without an equally rapid growth in the development of the preliminary and finishing stages of cloth making. Here the gains were less spectacular but not less impressive. In addition to this there were also important improvements in the quality of the machines employed at all stages which resulted in equally significant improvements in the finished textile products. Altogether the various improvements led to gradually falling production costs, and with sales competition between entrepreneurs, to reductions in the *real* prices of the finished products.[18] Consequently more people were able to afford them and demand increased.

Another, not dissimilar example of the 'challenge and response' effect on England's economic growth can be taken from the iron industry. Iron making is basically a chemical refining process, i.e. the conversion of an ore into a finer compound or pure metal through the application of heat. It follows that the iron industry was closely dependent upon developments in the nature and supply of

18.   The qualification *real* is necessary to account for rises in the nominal price
        levels.

fuels. Fuels, however, are themselves compounds containing impurities, and for this reason wood appeared to be less harmful to iron than coal. Thus while coal was employed in various other industries, it was not used in the iron industry until the eighteenth century. Even then coal could not easily be employed because the right kind of coal was seldom available near the iron ore deposits and its transportation presented great difficulties. Moreover, the utilization of coal in iron making requires a powerful forced draught, i.e. big furnaces, which for technical reasons could not have been constructed before the last quarter of the eighteenth century.[19] In addition to this it also required an alteration in the character of the blast, i.e. the application of a hot instead of a cold blast in the smelting process of iron, and this was only understood in the second quarter of the nineteenth century. Even had these improvements in the pig iron industry been realized at an earlier date they would have had little effect, as pig iron is unyielding and cannot stand up to much pressure. Only after a way to remove the remaining impurities was found did it become a really useful, malleable form of iron. Small quantities of this iron were indeed produced from the fifteenth century onwards, but the product was not always satisfactory and was very costly. The change came when Henry Court invented a technique for combining puddling and rolling in iron making. This not only produced a superior product – wrought iron – but made production far less costly and considerably faster, while the product also became more suitable for standardization. With the new process all that was necessary in order to produce identical rails or bars or other similar iron goods was to shape or groove the rollers accordingly. As a result of this iron consumption increased tremendously, and as the production of iron by this method required coal the demand and supply of coal rose similarly. Together with this, as had been the case with the textile industry, the more spectacular advances in iron were accompanied by a host of minor

---

19.   For an explanation *vide* Singer, Holmyard, Hall & Williams, *op.cit.,* pp. 103–4 and 183.

improvements which widened the basis of the industry.[20] Demand rose sharply with any new progress in the iron industry itself or in other industries that could achieve improvements by the substitution of iron for less lasting materials. Industrial machines, agricultural implements and, from the middle of the nineteenth century, also water and gas pipes and rails had an insatiable hunger for iron. This insatiable demand called forth an equally brisk demand for coal. A similar reciprocal demand and supply relationship developed in the iron and coal industry as the one described earlier in the 'seesaw effect' with weaving and spinning in the textile industry. Yet there was a significant difference. Coal is a material that cannot be replenished like cotton or wool. With each new demand mines had to be sunk more deeply and became more expensive to exploit. For centuries this problem had been growing in tin and silver mines and though from the sixteenth century onwards some very ingenious contrivances had been invented they were all dependent upon animate sources of motive power, a fact which presented a great many logistic problems. Men, horses or oxen had to be fed and this more often than not proved to be difficult to arrange and expensive. The problem was only solved with the rise to importance of the steam engine which consumed inanimate sources of power.[21]

Thus the hunger for iron generated the hunger for more coal, and the latter the development of the steam engine which added to the already existent pressure for better tools and workmanship in related industries. In time this led to an ever-increasing trend towards the substitution of inanimate energy for man and horse power whereby the power supply was increased many times and production costs were greatly reduced. While progress in agriculture increased the productivity of land, progress in industry greatly increased the productivity of labor. Together they laid the foundation for the growth of national income. The possibility of a sustained growth of

20. *Vide* Singer, Holmyard, Hall & Williams, *op.cit.*, pp. 106–7.

21. *Vide* Y.S. Brenner, *A Short History of Economic Progress* for a brief summary of the development of steam power (pp. 37–40) and for a discussion of earlier inanimate sources of power such as wind and water and their limitations (pp. 145–6).

the volume of goods and services obtainable for each unit of human effort and the accessibility of abundant other resources, became a reality, and could sustain economic growth for as long as the combination of expanding foreign markets and the rise of domestic consumers' demand persisted.

Why these developments took place in England long before they matured in France or Germany, in spite of the fact that scientific knowledge was no less and probably more advanced in these countries during much of this period, is not too difficult to see.[22] Firstly, the population of England was more concentrated in area than those of the other countries. This made possible the undertaking of tasks which are feasible only where enough people can benefit from them and sufficient manpower is available to carry them out. Secondly, being an island and well served with a good many rivers which could often be connected without too much cost into a close network of waterways Britain was in a favorable position for bringing together the different raw materials required for industrial production, and for delivering the finished products to distant markets. In contrast, on the Continent, with few exceptions, the population was scattered over vast areas, and most rivers were not suitable for heavy all-year-round navigation. Thirdly, Britain was geologically well endowed with the natural resources that were required in the early stages of industrialization and of which the continental countries were relatively poor.[23] Fourthly, Britain, again in contrast to the other countries, was politically unified, free from internal customs frontiers, free from civil wars, and free from foreign wars on her own soil since the seventeenth century. Fifthly the early

---

22.   Most of the best arguments summarized here have been borrowed from Prof. D.S. Landes earlier mentioned contribution to the *Cambridge Economic History of Europe*, Vol. VI, Pt. I, though they are used here somewhat differently.

23.   These advantages lasted until the end of the 19th century, when new methods for the treatment of mineral resources were discovered and when, as a result of further exploration, more mineral deposits were found in Continental Europe. On the whole, however, Britain's coal and iron deposits were superior in quality and more closely located to each other than Continental Europe's.

disappearance of serfdom, the uniform and more equitable legal system and its actual enforcement, gave Britain a not inconsiderable institutional advantage. On the Continent industrial progress was often prevented by deliberate policies of landlord governments, which were eager to retain the labor force on their estates, and by the survival of feudal legislation affecting the personal status of the peasants. Finally, the cultural or perhaps the socio-economic environment was far more suitable in Britain than on the Continent for economic change. For reasons which have their origin in historical developments dating back into the middle ages, poverty was never as dire in England as in France and Germany[24] and class mobility much more lively.[25] Because of the greater poverty on the Continent there was neither a market which could be stimulated by what initially could only have been marginal price reduction, nor was there enough alternative employment on the farm to place before the peasants a choice between working more on the land and purchasing, say, cloth, or making their own in their spare time. It was, indeed, not before the threshing machine made the distribution of work throughout the farming year more uniform, i.e. before the difference between the 'high' and 'low' seasons of employment in agriculture was appreciably reduced, that some of the jobs which industry could replace had any alternative cost, or *opportunity cost,* at all. In addition, there was not even the possibility of turning the relatively greater poverty into an advantage by stimulating export trade. The little that could be saved by low wages was less than was added by high transport, insurance and loan capital costs.

Moreover, in Britain, for a long time, it was quite common for 'second sons' to find their way into trade and commerce. From there the next step to industry, when the opportunity arose, was but small. On the Continent the class structure was much more rigid. Whether it was maintained by an undefined custom or merely by prejudice, as was the case in France, or by legal disabilities imposed by

---

24. Perhaps with the exception of the middle of the 19th century.

25. The difference was due, for example, to the different laws of inheritance, and the more frequent and destructive wars on the Continent.

'Estates', as in Germany or Russia, did not alter the basic fact that for a person of aristocratic descent trade or any other business activity was always associated with social degradation. A true gentleman, so it was held, did not concern himself with money matters, and least of all with commerce. Land and Office, and sometimes marriage, were the only truly noble sources of income. In sixteenth-century England someone defined a gentleman 'one who spends his money like a gentleman'. An apter definition of the continental nobility, even till the nineteenth century, might have been: 'one who gains his money like a gentleman'. The stress in the former definition on spending and in the latter on the acquisition of wealth is symptomatic of another difference with far-reaching economic consequences where industrial and cheap mass-production is concerned. This is what Professor Landes called, the 'worship of thrift that on the Continent characterized the bourgeoisie as well as the peasantry to a degree unknown in Britain.'[26] Thus, while the nobility was socially prevented from taking part in business enterprise, ambitious members of other classes were equally discouraged, because in a society where prestige was more easily attained through government service or the professions, this major incentive for showing initiative in industry was missing. 'If the aristocrat was too high to stoop to trade, the ambitious, capable, *novus homo* preferred to by-pass it and seek eminence via the professions and government service.'[27] Moreover, if some *novus homo* had after all made money in trade or industry, he was more likely to invest his profits in land than plough it back into business where it did not enhance his social standing. There were also more practical difficulties in setting up industrial enterprises as long as policy and tradition protected the old established guilds. For centuries the guilds were very useful sources of government revenue; and, no less important, they were the only method of quality control. Over the centuries their insistence upon quality had been the pride of their members. It had created a kind of class consciousness or class pride,

---

26.   *Vide* D.S. Landes, *op.cit.*, p. 361.

27.   D.S. Landes, *ibid.*

a distinction which could seldom be matched by the trade marks of industrial producers and could hardly be upheld in the face of the less personal connection between the workman and his finished product. The worker, and even the owner, in an industrial enterprise where division of labor was practiced, could no longer distinguish himself as a member of a separate class closed to all other members of society, which could be entered only by a combination of family ties (a kind of pseudo lineage), skill, and long years of experience gained through apprenticeship. Indeed, he had neither tradition nor social status to raise him above the rest of humanity even in his own esteem. To this must be added the effect of social impediments on the flow of capital to industry. Again, as Professor Landes observed, business in France and even in Germany was above all a family affair. It was so closely connected with the family that it was almost indistinguishable from it. The failure of the firm was as much a dark blot on the family name as if some serious dishonorable action had been committed by one of its members.[28] This was seldom the case with British entrepreneurs who regarded business more soberly as a means to an end and not an end by itself. These different attitudes had very important consequences regarding the conduct of enterprises. It made it difficult for continental entrepreneurs to abandon traditional methods of production, to sacrifice quality for quantity, and to engage in cut-throat competition. It gave undue preference to security and discouraged risk-taking and borrowing of funds outside the family circle. In short, it restricted expansion opportunities and held back capitalization. In addition, the social identification of the family with the business enterprise and the tendency to look on it as a source of prestige, and upon profit as a welcome coincidental advantage, also went a long way to prevent tough competition, i.e. it prevented the elimination of some of the less efficient enterprises and thereby reduced the drive for greater efficiency. To be sure, the object of business was profit everywhere, but the rules of what is permissible and what is not in the pursuit of profit were somewhat different in England and on the Continent. Unlike the English, Continental manufacturers looked for a long time

---

28.   *Vide* D.S. Landes, *op.cit.*

upon all competition as unfair and upon price competition particularly so. If wealth was made by the ruin of others it did not enhance the gainer's social prestige. It defied an important part of the whole exercise. Consequently the price level tended to settle in accordance with the least rather than the most efficient producers. Only the gradual spreading of the transport system, the greater political unity, the abolition of the legal and institutional social disabilities, and, finally, in the nineteenth century, the scientific break-through that revolutionized the technological capacity to exploit up to this time only marginally useful natural resources and materials, together with the rise of organized labor and its subsequent ability to reap a greater share of the fruits of production, all these eventually diminished the socio-cultural impediments to economic growth in France and Germany. When this happened their growth so much accelerated that in less than a century these countries caught up with, and in many respects surpassed, England's earlier industrial achievements.[29] The mechanisms that removed the impediments on the Continent were only remotely influenced by *foreign trade* and will therefore be relegated to the chapter dealing with domestic markets.[30]

The country where foreign trade did play a no less crucial role than in England, though much later, was Japan. In the 1860's economic conditions in Japan were not very different from those of England a century earlier. Japan already possessed a nucleus of skilled workers, a tradition of labor discipline, and a considerable rural manufacturing industry which was organized in a manner very similar to the pre-industrial English 'putting out' or 'cottage industry' system. In addition, also like in Britain, Japanese industrialization was accompanied by population accretion and the growth of towns. In the last quarter of the nineteenth century the total population of Japan increased by 30 per cent, the greater part of this increase was taken up by the towns. During the same period exports rose by

---

29.   The author dealt with the developments which influenced these changes in Continental Europe in *A Short History of Economic Progress*, pp. 154–71.

30.   *Vide* pp. 81–120.

approximately 600 per cent. There were, however, also significant differences between the two countries.

Firstly, in the 1860's Japan was already very densely populated by any standards; and, in absolute terms, the population engaged in agriculture did not begin to decline before the 1890's, and even then it fell only slightly. In fact there was less than one hectare of cropland per male worker in agriculture, while techniques of land exploitation were no better developed than in pre-industrial England. During the three decades from 1878 to 1908 the net output of arable land rose by approximately 76 per cent, whereas the net increase in the productivity of farm labor rose by approximately 217 per cent. This meant that the growth of the Japanese industry was accompanied during the last quarter of the nineteenth century by a rapid increase in the surplus of rural labor. In other words, industry could count on a good labor supply while at the same time the flow of labor from the country into the towns was not enough to stimulate directly a rise in the level of workers' real incomes in either sector of the economy. As a result of this the Japanese industry became increasingly obliged to look for markets overseas rather than rely upon the demand of the home market. In addition to this it directed industrialization towards those industries in which the superiority of mechanized over traditional methods of production were the highest. As a somewhat compensatory effect this saved a number of small labor-intensive workshops from going under and thereby prevented the disappearance of an industrial middle class: and it also prevented the destruction of a considerable number of rural trades which gave by-employment to families which could not make ends meet by farming alone.

Secondly, the deep-rooted cultural traditions of several centuries were carried over into the new era and influenced the organization of Japan's rising industrial labor force in a unique manner. The Japanese worker continued to feel himself a member of his family, i.e. of an organization which often retained its leadership in the countryside and in which each member had no rights as an individual except those granted to him by the head of the family. It may be said that the organization of labor continued to be vertical, quasi-feudal, rather than horizontal, following class interests.

Professor G.C. Allen,[31] describing this kind of paternalism, says that there were no recognized rates for jobs and that besides the basic wage current with each occupation, the workers' incomes were normally augmented by all kinds of extra allowances. There was an allowance for age, for education, for length of service, for family obligations, for housing, for rises in the cost of living, etc. In modern industry the worker could expect, in addition to these, bi-annual ex gratia bonuses, and even unemployment pay if he was dismissed owing to bad business. In some trades the employer was also obliged to provide accommodation for his workers. Particularly in the spinning industry, where most employees were female, he had to provide board and lodging. The girls, who were recruited by factory agents from their families in the villages, returned to their native places at the end of their contract, frequently after three or four years. The kind of accommodation and wages were usually agreed upon between the head of their families and the mill-owners. In most cases the agreement included provisions that payment was to be made in lump sums at the end of each contract, or at such intervals that would permit the girl to bring enough of it back home to her family. Obviously conditions were not favoring the development of trade unions. Nor were they suitable for promoting a higher standard of living, except by the slow, indirect process of reducing the cost of industrial goods. The absence of a more pointed and organized struggle between labor and employers may well have been another cause for the peculiar nature of Japan's development and for the great gap between the spectacular rise in output and the only very moderate rise in workers' real incomes.

Thirdly, Japan was less rich in the necessary natural resources for industrialization than Britain. Throughout the nineteenth century the country was greatly dependent upon America and Europe for machines; she did not possess adequate supplies of coke, and for this reason she was far behind in iron and steel production. Indeed, it

---

31.   *Vide* G.C. Allen, *A Short History of Modern Japan*, London, 2nd revised edition, 1962. For a detailed study of these developments see also Prof. Allen's contribution to the *Cambridge Economic History of Europe*, Vol. VI, Pt. 2, Ch. X; and W.W. Lockwood, *The Economic Development of Japan*, Princeton, 1954.

was not until the first quarter of the twentieth century that she managed, with the costly help of foreign experts, to develop a modern iron industry. Even then, Japan had to rely upon Korea and China for adequate supplies of ores. It is also significant that most of Japan's capital was recruited from internal sources and that much of her rapid development was due to the determination of her leadership, which inherited a country with certain 'political and economic institutions that could be easily adapted to serving the nation in its new role. Her social organization rooted in a special kind of family system, and the long centuries of feudal discipline helped to produce a capacity for extreme self-abnegation on the part of individuals and an aptitude to corporate effort which served the country well in a time of rapid social and economic change, and the institution of an Imperial House which by mythology invested with divine attributes provided a focus for patriotic fervor'.[32]

Thus, Japan started on the road to modern economic growth endowed with a politically suitable system and a psychological readiness. Unfortunately, however, her overpopulation resulted in an asymmetry between the more rapid rise of the country's industrial output and the only very slow improvement of the people's living standards; and her lack of the necessary natural resources led to her growing dependence upon other countries. The combination of both led Japan to look abroad not only for the supply of industrial raw materials but also for the markets in which she could sell her finished products. In fact, she had either to make sure of her markets overseas or to revolutionize her whole socio-economic structure. Until close to the middle of the present century Japan pursued the first of these two courses. The peculiar family ties caused some of the town labor's earnings to flow back to the countryside in such a fashion (lump sums, at intervals, that were relatively too large to be 'wasted') that a good part was invested in raising productivity in agriculture. The poverty of the domestic market due to the low wages forced entrepreneurs to turn abroad to the densely populated Asian mainland as the natural outlet for their produce. Like England in her early days of industrialization, Japan capitalized on the

---

32.   *Vide* note 31.

relatively enormous number of foreign consumers. This was possible because, although the individual consumer in Asia had in most cases very little to spare, the total of the many small amounts was still large enough, for a time at least, to continue the growth of Japanese production. Eventually, Japanese exports met with competition from other industrial countries and were subjected to protective tariffs. When the advantages of the shorter transport routes and low Japanese wages were no longer sufficient to keep pace with the rapid capitalization of industry in Europe and America, and when the protective tariffs imposed against Japanese goods in the European colonies in Asia, threatened the further growth of Japan's industry, Japan very rapidly adjusted the direction of her export trade. In order to control the necessary raw materials and to monopolize markets she set out to do what Britain had done before her, that is, to establish colonies. She captured and occupied part of the Asian mainland. In 1894 she invaded Korea, which was then a dependency of the Chinese Empire, and in the war that followed annexed Formosa and the Pescadores. In 1904 she attacked Russia and received Karafuto and Russia's concessions in Port Arthur and her mining rights and railroads in South Manchuria; in 1910 she finally annexed Korea; in 1915 she took Kiaochow from the Germans. In 1918 she was in full control of Shantung, Manchuria, Inner Mongolia, North Sakhalin, and parts of Eastern Siberia. By 1925, however, she was forced to retreat from the Chinese and Russian territories and to adopt the 'Open Door' policy imposed upon her in the Pacific by the Americans and British. A few years later, in 1929, the world economy collapsed and with it the Japanese economy. The old aggressive forces which had lain dormant for some time found new supporters among the worried rich and the hungry and jobless poor. To survive in a world of increasingly stringent competition, people like Premier Tanaka told the Japanese people, Japan must expand. She must first crush her great competitor the United States of America in order to be able to control China. Having China's entire resources at her disposal, Japan can then proceed to conquer India, Asia Minor, Central Asia, and even Europe. In 1931 the Imperial Army seized Manchuria and was preparing the way for an attack upon the Soviet Union. After a number of unsuccessful border skirmishes it abandoned this idea and launched a full scale assault upon China. The war with China proved 'endless and hopeless'. In 1940 Germany and Italy signed a treaty with Japan recognizing her domination of 'Greater East Asia'. The three countries also undertook to assist one another with all means at their disposal when one of them was attacked by a Power not involved in the European war or in the Chinese-Japanese conflict i.e. by the United States of America. A year later (in December 1941) Japan was at war with the United States, Britain and the Netherlands' exile government. Within a year and a half of relentless advance more than 500 million people were brought under Japanese rule. By June 1942 the tide of war began to turn and with Japan's total military, economic, and moral collapse in 1945 this first phase in her history of economic growth, the phase of growth through expansion abroad, came to an end.

Summarizing this phase, one can agree with W.W. Lockwood 'that Japan's great external opportunity arose not so much from her priority in Far Eastern industrialization, or her seizure of territory, as from the whole conjuncture of circumstances which enabled her to enter and trade peacefully in an expanding, relatively free world economy'. The conjuncture of circumstances were the tremendous growth in the world's primary production and the relatively free flow of factory technique and capital with little political interference. With Europe, Japan exchanged products which required cheap labor, little capital, and special skills, for certain raw materials; with the United States she maintained a very lucrative silk trade; and with the East she exchanged her industrial products for food and raw materials to feed her industry. She had, of course, an exceptional advantage in being linked to the world by her excellent natural suitability for water transport. Her main disadvantage, according to some historians, was the political anxiety which was enhanced by the generally nationalistic aggressive climate of the thirties, and drove the people of Japan, with those of other countries, into the arms of an economically ignorant and politically chauvinistic leadership. Whether in reality, in the face of the protectionist policies of the old established colonial powers in the East, Japan was or was not left any alternative but to pursue an aggressive line, is still open to debate.[33]

The defeat of Japan in World War II, was to alter all this and provide Japan with new sources of demand. It left Japan with no 'spheres of influence' and no investments on the continent of Asia. Moreover, her world-wide commercial network and a great part of her industry was shattered. What had remained of it was also to a great extent useless for peace-time production. Morale was low and so was the spirit of enterprise; raw materials were scarce and in most towns even food was in short supply. There was no confidence in the country's leadership and the foreign occupation forces were consciously undermining what had remained of the old social order.

---

33.   W.W. Lockwood appears to think that although 'the spread of economic nationalism in the thirties was putting brakes on further Japanese trade expansion for the moment, and clouding its outlook in the future... Japan's real economic interest could only lie in combating, not reinforcing, this inimical drift to trade restriction and bilateralism'. G.C. Allen is of the view that 'during the half-century before 1937 Japan's economic expansion was unquestionably influenced by her success in war'. The conquests led to the enlargement of territory under her control and opened up opportunities for investment and trade in areas where she enjoyed special advantages. Whatever the area of agreement and of disagreement in assessing the economic consequences of Japan's expansionist policies it remains a fact that as long as Japan continued to base her development upon foreign trade she was bound to clash with powerful competition from some of the most developed countries. From this point of view, however, the old established, say British, protectionist colonialism was no less aggressive than Japanese expansionism. Conquest had merely come earlier to India than to Manchuria, but the aims were the same monopolistic control over the country's economic potentials. The fact that Britain already had such a monopoly and exploited it, and Japan had yet to gain it, cannot be accepted as evidence for differences between the policies of the two countries. The choice with which the Japanese were confronted was not between war and peace, but between war and economic stagnation or collapse. The last would probably be followed by a social revolution. In accord with the spirit of the times the rulers of Japan chose the first alternative. In the words of Professor Schuman, writing about the year 1941, 'what choices were available to Japan's policy makers...? A policy of restoring and maintaining peace was not among them, for the Fascist combine of Big Business and Big Brass had brought into being an economy and a policy dependent for viability on armaments, war, and conquest.'

Paradoxically it was this utter defeat which extricated Japan from the cul-de-sac into which her pre-war leadership had led her. Without this crushing defeat it would have become almost impossible to break away from the unholy alliance of Big Capital and Brass and to find a way out of the vicious circle of economic growth leading to foreign military ventures and foreign military ventures stimulating economic growth. It would not have been possible to raise wage-rates – effective domestic demand, which was the only alternative to the old-style export orientation of production. The change in the socio-economic structure and the ensuing reorientation of production policies showed very soon their favorable results. Five years after the end of the war the gross domestic product per head of the total population had already regained its 1937 level, and two years later, in 1952, it has risen above it by no less than 19 per cent. Post-war Japan was again marked by a high rate of population accretion, a high rate of addition to the capital stock of the country, a high rate of growth of manufacture, and, as seldom before, by the people's rising living standards. This whole trend of growth was accompanied by increasing employment in the manufacturing and service industries, by decreasing unemployment, and by a steady reduction in working hours. Industrial production rose more sharply than employment. Only food production did not increase sufficiently, though the structure and composition of food consumption also shows definite improvements during this period.

How, then, did these surprising changes in the Japanese economy come about? The victorious powers realized that Japan could produce with the same type of technology as the United States and Europe but with lower labor costs as long as her old paternalistic ways persisted and were not replaced by workers' organized efforts to improve their wages. And so, to prevent the re-emergence of Japan as a dangerous competitor on the world markets, they employed their occupation authorities to transform the whole economic structure of the country. In this they were assisted by progressive world opinion and by the genuine climate of good will towards workers' efforts to organize in order to raise their living standards that accompanied the defeat of the world-wide Fascist alliance. Firstly, tenants were given titles to their holdings which hitherto had been the property of great landlords. Secondly, a number of labor reforms broke the traditional patriarchal relationship between employers and employees. Thirdly, anti-trust laws were imposed upon industry and the old guard of economic leaders were prevented from recapturing political and economic control. Taken together these turned out to be irreversible structural changes which helped to put the country on her new course of development. Although it may be true that these reforms made no *immediate* contribution to economic recovery it is also true that they shaped the new social relationship that prevented the revival of the pre-war pattern of economic growth even when conditions seemed to favor such a development after 1949. By that time American attitudes towards Japan changed. The Cold War and the growing strength of Communism in Asia led to the shelving of further socio-economic reform schemes in Japan and to the reconstruction of those parts of the old type of industry which could now serve the American political interests in the Far East. Inflation was checked and production, which had been stagnating during the era of social reforms from 1945 to 1949 made a big leap forward. In the following year, 1950, the war in Korea, in which Japan did not take part but served as the nearest industrial base behind the United Nations forces, boosted industrial production enormously. Once again, Japan was prospering because of war and the resultant favorable export trade. In 1952, when sovereignty was restored to the Japanese, it looked as if the old system of the pre-war era was coming back though under 'new management', but this was not entirely the case. There remained a great difference in the distribution of the gains from production. The old alliance between Big Capital and the military was not revived. This was so not only because the latter had been too much discredited by the defeat but also because the Americans, though ready to rely upon the Japanese capitalists' anti-communism, had no confidence in the military who, after all, might or might not change their political allegiances at will. This deprived capital of its 'patriotic' hegemony and of its actual control over the means of coercion. At the same time the workers themselves had gained a much greater degree of self-confidence and of actual bargaining power as a result of the early post-war period of socioeconomic reforms. Thus, while Japan's share in the production for the supply of the United Nations Force in Korea increased, her own military expenditure remained small; and after the termination of hostilities, the Americans continued to maintain bases in Japan, and they brought in a considerable additional income. The most significant facts observed during this period were the rise in workers' incomes which was higher than the rise in prices, and consequently, the rise in domestic consumers' demand, and the growth of, what as distinct from the pre-war period must be called a *normal,* foreign trade. Thus the creation of trade-unions, the new labor legislation which recognized workers' right to organize, strike, and bargain collectively, and employers' obligation to recognize the unions and to introduce certain welfare provisions, including a strict regulation of the length of working days, helped to put the Japanese economy upon a new and more stable basis than it had been in the earlier period. After 1949 some of the legally sanctioned improvements in the position of the Japanese industrial labor force were modified; and with the re-emergence of the old guard of industrialists during and after the Korean war the position of the unions became more difficult but the chance of relegating labor altogether to its pre-war status had passed. The achievements of the immediate post-war years progressive legislation in the rural sector were more lasting. Tenant farmers bought their farms from the great landlords and as they were paying for them in installments over several years their debts were almost entirely wiped out by inflation. Consequently, by 1949 Japan had already become a country of well established peasant proprietors. Unlike the industrial workers' unions, the farmers' unions were therefore gaining from the Korean war boom. It not only reduced the surplus of farm labor but greatly raised food prices, the former deficiency was rapidly made good by the introduction of modern farm equipment, while the latter advantage encouraged very considerable improvements in the exploitation of land by the wider use of fertilizers and the more selective growing of crops. Finally, when the Korean war came to its end, the Japanese economy had already gained so much impetus, and its domestic demand had already grown so far, that growth continued in the normal capitalistic pattern of competition. In this Japan was fortunate to be aided by the general economic prosperity during the 1950's in which she shared with most other capitalist countries of the world.

In summary then, in both Britain and Japan foreign demand, i.e. the export trade, played a most crucial role in the achievement of an early high rate of economic growth. Foreign trade added the margin of demand that is necessary to induce capitalists to turn their profits or accumulated resources into new productive investment. In both countries the high rate of capital accumulation, i.e. the *ability* to produce economic growth, was due to a socio-political system that made it possible to keep workers' incomes at a very low level thus letting employers reap most of the fruits of technological improvements. Had it not been for the expansibility of the foreign trade, the low level of domestic incomes would have reduced capitalists' *wish* to turn their wealth into productive investments for lack of demand, and economic growth could hardly have ensued. In the following chapter the countries where the process of development followed a different pattern is examined, where wage rates were relatively high and therefore domestic demand brisk and where notwithstanding high wages the accumulation and concentration of wealth progressed sufficiently to engender rapid economic growth.[34]

---

34.   A great part of the historical background given here is taken (sometimes verbatim) from my earlier more detailed historical discussion of these countries in *A Short History of Economic Progress*, London, 1969, Frank Cass & Co.Ltd.

3

Demand Stimulated Growth

'Tis but an hour ago since it was nine,
And after one hour more 'twill be eleven;
And so, from hour to hour, we ripe and ripe,
And then, from hour to hour, we rot and rot;
And thereby hangs a tale'.
A fool in *As you like it.* Act II Sc. IV. 26

The regions where *domestic* markets played a most obvious role in the stimulation and sustainment of economic growth were in *North America*. Here the fortunate combination of, on the supply side, a great abundance of free land, good natural resources, a population relatively free from socio-institutional economic-growth-impeding traditions; and on the demand side, an increasing number of people and, at the same time rising real incomes, produced a particularly favorable climate for investment and technological advancement.

In the first place there were few traditions which had to be broken and no old-established institutions to be swept away before economic progress could be accelerated. Secondly, the population was particularly adaptable to new forms of life; the mere fact that in order to come to America the early settlers had to leave their old environment and be ready to undertake the journey into an unknown future in a far-off land, had in itself a selective influence upon the immigrants, giving them a higher than average proportion of men with initiative, drive and ambition. Thirdly, the vast expanse of the uninhabited land, through which many of the settlers travelled and in which many of them eventually founded their isolated homes, forced upon them a much greater degree of independence and self-reliance than was common with the people whom they left behind in Europe. Finally, the great abundance of fertile land which was easily obtainable gave them the advantages of a higher living standard not only for the cultivators themselves but also for the rest of the people whose wages could hardly be diminished to the level of wage-rates paid in over-populated or quasi-feudal European countries. Thus, America was from the outset endowed with a high proportion of self-reliant, ambitious people who could avail themselves of fertile land and were free from the many restrictive institutional and social patterns of European society, and was also able to draw freely upon European technological experience in both agriculture and manufacture.

Whereas the European economic problems were mainly on the demand side of the market, the problems facing America were rather on the side of supply. Essentially the difference in this respect was that on the whole the Europeans were too poor to provide a stronger domestic stimulus for market production while the North American manufacturers, though they had a richer market, were faced with much higher labor costs and interest rates. Labor was much cheaper in Europe than in America where at least initially wages were so high that, in spite of transport costs, American manufacturers were almost unable to capture their home market for consumer goods from the British competitors. The story of the great progress of the American economy is, therefore, above all the history of vertical and horizontal industrial integration leading to an unequalled fall in production costs. As labor and capital were relatively scarce, only those industries which had a good supply of raw materials and were suitable for the introduction of very far-reaching technological and organizational improvements had a chance to succeed. Indeed, they had to be so much more efficient from an organizational point of view than their more conventional competitors across the sea that their efficiency could offset the high wage and interest rates. A good early illustration of the way this was done can be taken from the meat-packing industry. Cattle were readily available in the vast and thinly populated country and could be brought 'on the hoof' by a small number of men to the 'factory'. There they could be driven up an inclined plane to the top story of a building to be slaughtered, after which each successive group of processes was carried out at a lower level, to which the carcasses dropped under their own weight, thus saving much effort. On the level they were moved in trucks and dumbwaiters and placed with the utmost regularity before those who constantly repeated the same few operations on each carcass. In time, more of the operations on each successive level were further mechanized to save labor, and an increasing volume of the waste, for example bones, which had previously been considered useless, now found uses in a variety of quickly developing subsidiary industries. However, even with all this rationalization of the process of production, with the reduction to a minimum of the number of workers employed, and with a fuller exploitation of the materials and of their wastes, it is still doubtful whether the United States could have made such spectacular industrial progress had it not been for the high rate of population growth, the high living standards and wage rates, and the great influx of immigrants from abroad, which at the same time stimulated demand and provided the labor force to satisfy it.

The earliest industries in America, as in most colonial countries, were those which were based upon the natural resources particular to the region lumbering and shipbuilding. The shipbuilding industry enjoyed the twofold advantage of having a good supply of raw material nearby and of having easy access to a great market overseas which was ready to absorb its product. Other industries (with the exception of flour milling), which did not enjoy similar advantages on both the supply and the demand side, had very little chance to develop. In 1800 the country was too thinly populated and inland communications too poor to stimulate production. Even in the most densely populated parts the number of manufacturing industries using modern methods was small, and the total volume of their output was of little significance. The change began in 1807 as a result of the

American embargo and the subsequent curtailment of imports.[1] On the one hand the embargo caused much damage to the traditional export industries, but on the other it not only freed some capital which had previously been invested there, and made it available to other industries, but also provided for these new industries an almost monopolistic market. Thus, while in the short run the embargo caused a depression in the American economy, in the long run it helped to lay the foundation upon which America's industrial future was built. Textile prices soared, and for a time America experienced a boom in industrial investment. The boom was short-lived; with the restoration of peace in Europe even a 25 per cent protective tariff could not save the 'artificially' developed American textile industry. Only the largest and most efficient enterprises managed to survive European competition, and these became the 'pace-setters' for American industry in later decades. Revival began in the 1820's. By 1830 New England industries were already producing more than they had done before 1807. In the following decade progress was slow, but in the 'thirties it had accelerated to such a degree that even the depression which followed in 1839, could no longer reverse the upward trend. There was a considerable reduction of output between 1839 and 1844, but no large scale liquidation of business as had been the case during the depression of 1815. By 1845 the depression was over and industry progressed once more at an unprecedented pace, expanding very rapidly into new fields of production. As in England, American textile industry was the main source of early industrial development after 1820. On the one hand it helped the expansion of men's and women's clothing industries and, on the other hand, it stimulated the production of machinery for use in textile plants. In time the workshops in which textile machinery was made increasingly specialized in the production of certain machine components and left the production of others to other manufacturers. At the same time, however, they spread into new areas of machine production where similar components were required. In other words, the vertical textile-based machine industry was becoming horizontally

---

1.   This was imposed as a result of the American stand with regard to the Napoleonic wars in Europe.

inclined by specializing in the production of parts which were used in a number of different industries; this change, which was both the cause and the effect of the advantages gained from the rising degree of specialization, was soon felt by the rate at which new industries became mechanized and also by the iron industry upon which machine production was dependent. The resultant fall in the cost of machines, and consequently also the cost of machine-produced consumer goods, raised the latter's chances of holding out against foreign competition. The earliest to profit in this manner were the textile and shoe-making industries. These were followed by the woollen industry and by furniture. In this sense, then, the economic progress of the United States was largely due to the abundance of natural resources, because had it not been for the large iron and coal deposits there would have been little chance for the machine industry to develop in the way it did. Thus, while industrialization was becoming increasingly diversified in the North-East and was continually stimulated by the accretion and concentration of people, the South continued to be in a state of 'Colonial' production, i.e. producing primary materials mainly for export. (Since the end of the 18th century the South had more and more specialized in cotton, and to a smaller extent in sugar and rice.), and the West became the main source of the whole country's food supplies. All that was required now was a suitable transport system to bring the three areas closer together. The gap was filled by the spreading of the American railways in the second half of the nineteenth century. Hence, while railroads did not produce the rise of industry, they most certainly served as the catalyst which brought about the quantitative change in the rate of the United States' economic development.

In addition to its natural resources, its lack of inhibiting traditions, and a rapidly increasing demand resulting from the high rate of natural population accretion and immigration, America had also an educational advantage. Since its very early days great stress was put on education in most states, and almost everywhere the schooling of all boys under 14 years of age, for at least three months each year, was compulsory.

After the middle of the century, immigration (and with it the domestic market, and the rate of capital accumulation from both internal and external sources) increased very rapidly. The most significant change, from the point of view of industrial development in the second half of the nineteenth century, was the striking capitalization of American manufacturing industry. This was accompanied by a steep rise in productivity of labor which was due not only to the progress of technology but also to the shift of labor from the less highly into the more highly mechanized occupations. The resultant rise in *per capita* real incomes had never been equalled anywhere else in the world.

In summary, within one century the United States developed from the colonial, i.e. foreign orientated centred on primary production (until 1814); through the early industrial stage of manufacturing industry with its forward and backward links, into raw materials and machine making (1820–60); towards a highly mechanized and specialized stage of production (1860–1914). In the first stage the process was stimulated, on the demand side, by foreign markets; in the second, by the growth of the domestic market, owing to the rapid natural accretion of people and immigration; and in the third stage by the two last mentioned stimuli, which were further supported by the development of closer links with the domestic market through the expansion of the railway system and by the rising level of real incomes.

With manufacturers dependent upon their domestic markets, one government after another kept up the high protective tariff wall against foreign competition, and promoted free trade inside the country. In fact all governments made it their policy, at least until the 1930's, to interfere as little as possible in domestic economic affairs. In this way American manufacturers were freed from foreign competition and at the same time were at liberty to exploit fully their national market. A market which has been described as the largest area in the civilized world which was unrestricted by customs, excises, or national prejudice, and its population possessed, (because of its great collective wealth) a larger consuming capacity than that of any other nation. Then, between the years 1870 and 1900, competition amongst American capitalists became so brisk that there was a general feeling that profits were falling off at such a rate that all but the most efficient enterprises were threatened with destruction. Capitalist reaction to this was a growing trend towards consolidation, i.e. the creation of larger units which were able to benefit from economies of scale and monopoly. In some cases, where the consolidation of business was achieved without creating a monopoly, it served the general good, but where it resulted in monopoly it had as a rule, at least for some time, a retarding influence on the growth of the economy. Eventually, however, monopoly usually united competitors with the general public and stirred them into concerted action, leading in a good number of cases to the breaking up of the monopoly and reintroduction of competition. A good example for such a struggle is the case of the Standard Oil Company. The attempts of this company in the 1880's to free itself from competition with other oil producers took the peculiar form of a railroad war, that is of a battle for the command over the means of transport. Finding itself in a geographically more advantageous position than its competitors, and using rather unscrupulous stratagems, the Standard Oil Company was able to reduce its transport costs so far below those of its competitors that by the end of the decade it remained in almost sole control of the oil market. But then Rockefeller and his associates of the Standard Oil Company encounter a new adversary – namely the State. The creation of the South Improvement Company gave the competitors of Standard Oil the opportunity to organize public opinion to support them in their campaign. What they had been unable to achieve economically they now tried to achieve by political means with the support of the general public. The South Improvement Company had contractually agreed with the two other transport companies to divide amongst themselves the whole of the oil carrying business but were obliged to agree to an additional proviso, namely that Standard Oil shipments should be allowed rebates while all other oil companies would be made to pay the full price. The charter of The South Improvement Company was revoked under the combined pressure of the public and the competitors, but the old rebate system continued. By 1880 Standard Oil was virtually in a position to dictate its own transport rates. Ten years later, in 1890, another series of attempts was made to break up the Standard Oil monopoly by State legislation, which again resulted in nothing but the reorganization of the company to suit the new legal position. Only in 1911 was its monopoly shaken, when the Supreme Court ruled that the company had conspired by many and devious methods to build up a monopoly and was not, as the company argued, the natural product of the growth of a single business, that had never 'conspired or combined in restraint of trade.'

The success in reducing the power of monopoly at this time was undoubtedly the result of the successful co-operation between the competitors and the press, which kept informing the public about the evils of 'big business'. In 1912 competition became *the* election issue. The Democratic candidate, Woodrow Wilson, stated that American industry was no longer as free and competitive as it had been half a century before, and that something ought to be done by way of new legislation to 'prevent the strong from crushing the weak'. This the Congress tried to achieve in 1914 by passing the Clayton Antitrust Act prohibiting price discrimination and deals forbidding the parties to handle competitors' goods and the acquisition of competitors' stock in order to reduce competition and other similar monopolistic practices. The extent to which this and similar legislation was really successful in restraining monopoly is difficult to assess. It certainly had some degree of success but it did not restore the kind of 'free for all' which characterized the American economy in the late 1860's and early 1870's. For a time business consolidation abated, and the partnership between businessmen struggling for survival and the general public came to an end. In the decade that followed the end of the 1914–18 war, consolidation set in once more at an even faster rate. The leading sectors in which most of the new mergers took place, now were the metallurgical industries and public utilities. Virtually thousands of small enterprises were driven out of business within one decade. And yet although small business was going under, the general public was not really aroused. The country as a whole was experiencing a period of widespread industrial prosperity and rising living standards (1923–29) and there were no immediate grounds at the time for the workers to renew the old antitrust coalition with the middle class. In Professor Faulkner's view the causes for the relaxation of public opposition to the new wave of business consolidation were:[2] 'An appreciation of the inevitability of consolidation in a capitalist system, the futility of antitrust legislation to prevent it, the rising

---

2.   Underwood H. Faulkner, *American Economic History*, N.Y., 1964.

standard of living which has made the masses less keen to scent evils in the movement, and finally, the incessant propaganda of big business interests.'

However, while the competition between the Capitalists themselves abated, and big business was emerging victoriously from one kind of competition, *the other kind of competition between workers and employers* – was becoming increasingly powerful. Until the middle of the nineteenth century this seldom led to widespread tension. As long as labor was scarce and not concentrated in towns, and land was abundant, there was neither much need nor opportunity for the organization of labor. After the middle of the century things were changing very fast. In the 1880's already a quarter of the population of the United States was settled in towns of more than 8,000 inhabitants and in one way or another dependent on industry for their livelihood. Moreover, the total population of the United States was increasing at a rate of some 20 per cent and that of cities at a rate of close to 40 per cent per decade, while the pattern of the employment structure also showed a relatively faster growth of enterprises employing great numbers of workers than that of small workshops. Thus while, on the one hand, the traditional safeguards for the American working class' standard of living (the scarcity of labor and the abundance of free fertile land) were waning, on the other, new ones, in the form of workers' associations, were rising as a result of the growth of towns and the concentration of labor. In fact, the years in which cities grew most rapidly closely correspond with the periods of greatest activity in the labor movements. The two other factors, which were of no little importance for the rise of the American labor movement, were the development of the press and the spreading of education, which had already become a part of the American way of life. But the most important immediate cause which led to the organization of labor in the United States was probably the Civil War and its aftermath. Firstly, because the objective conditions of the working class had become worse during the war. Prices had risen and wages had not. Many of the returning soldiers could find no work because their jobs had been filled in their absence either by new immigrants or by contract labor, or had become redundant altogether because of the introduction of new laborsaving equipment. Secondly, the climate of opinion among the workers themselves had changed. They had learned a lesson in the use of violence, which deprived the employers of their hitherto almost unrivalled monopoly over it through their control of the police force; they had learned a lesson in co-operation and concerted action; and they had also learned a little about their economic reality from the Southerners' propaganda telling them, what many must have eventually recognized as the truth, that the economic position of the slaves, whom they were fighting to liberate, may not have been much worse than their own as 'free and white' men.

Thus, with the fetters of traditional attitudes falling, with little need to fear an American Peterloo, and with the dawning recognition of the economic reality in a period of falling living standards and rising unemployment, the stage was set for a new era of labor relations in the United States. Before long membership of the local unions rose and the number of unions increased and in time some of them joined together to form national associations and to publish their own newspapers. With this the struggle for better labor conditions was being carried on in both the professional and the political spheres.[3] Many unions, were however virtually destroyed in the great economic depression which took place in the 1870's. Business prospects were indeed so low at the time, and unemployment so widespread, that even where union pressure was possible, and there were few industries where this was the case, there was little hope of achieving anything but perhaps the closure of more business enterprises. Whether consciously from the examination of the situation, or merely by intuition, a number of union leaders recognized this and came to the conclusion that if something was to be done successfully it had to be done on a political level. There was indeed little to be gained from a struggle for the redistribution of the 'fruits of production' when there was no production; but there was much to be gained from making the government take active steps to restore national prosperity. Here, too, was a platform which united part of the middle class and small employers with the workers

---

3.   A very good example for the political struggle is provided in the activities of the Knights of Labor, a good example for the professional struggle in those of the American Federation of Labor.

against the growing economic and political strength of big business. The franchise, together with the shift in the distribution of population between country and town in favor of the latter, gave the leaders of the movement the necessary means for influencing the government's economic policies. These were the sources of the considerable success of the Knights of Labor.

In 1883 their membership counted about 50,000, by 1886 it had risen to almost a 1,000,000. By that time, however, the American economy was beginning very steadily to recover and the old divergence of interests between wage-workers and self-employed re-emerged. This led to considerable changes in both the aims and the organizational structure of the movements. The small businessmen and the farmers continued to be in favor of reform through political action, whereas the wage-workers, who accounted for about three-quarters of the membership, demanded direct action in the form of strikes to raise the workers' immediate incomes. The break became inevitable. The opportunity for it arose when anarchists threw some bombs after a riot. The middle-class minority was quick to use this as an excuse for its withdrawal from the union, though it was fairly obvious that the union had nothing to do with activities of this kind. After this the disintegration of the 'Knights' was very rapid, almost as fast as its rise had been only a few years earlier. By 1888 most of its middle-class membership was leaving because for them the organization had become too radical and most of its radical membership had left to join the new more militant American Federation of Labor. The middle class felt disillusioned with union politics and the workers demanded more direct industrial activity. It would, however, be a mistake to underrate the importance of the 'Knights' to the development of American industrial relations and politics. Firstly, they helped to put new life into the many smaller local unions which had almost been extinct by the end of the depression; secondly, they indicated the possibilities which are inherent in the American political system for using the working men's vote as an instrument for securing certain economic advantages; and thirdly, they showed the way which half a century later led to Franklin D. Roosevelt's 'New Deal.'

While the Knights of Labor had been primarily concerned with the political opportunity which the system offered to labor, another organization, the American Federation of Labor, was pressing the case of labor along the traditional lines of industrial action. Their policy was more purely unionistic. They did not advocate political action, though in their early days they too had demanded the abolition of contract emigration and conspiracy laws. After 1887, with the decline of the Knights, the Federation absorbed a great part of its radical membership. In 1890 it had about 100,000 members, in 1900 almost 1,000,000 and in 1910 close to 2,000,000. The years 1898 to 1904 were perhaps the most important in the history of American organized labor. It was during these years that it received widespread recognition by the employers and during which it showed its greatest drive and its members displayed a great deal of self - sacrifice and idealism. Needless to add, these were also years of prosperity and rapid economic growth.

Together with the growth of the labor movement other radical changes in the economic structure of the United States were taking place. Though it may never be possible to separate cause from effect, there can be little doubt about the close relationship between this growth of organized labor and the rate of technological progress in industry during the period 1897 to 1929. The rapid increase in the use of labor-saving equipment and its displacement of labor undoubtedly raised the membership of unions, while the resultant strengthening of the same enhanced their success in wage disputes with employers. In return, this stimulated further the tendency of employers to replace labor by machines whenever and wherever possible. In fact in the years 1899–1914 '2 per cent of industrial workers in the United States lost their jobs every five years as a result of being displaced by new machinery. But this rate of separation was counteracted by the rate of addition of jobs yielded by the rapidly expanding economy. In the same period, 15 per cent more jobs were created every five years. This expansion took care not only of the technologically displaced but of the rapid growth of population as well'.[4]

---

4.   *Vide* Daniel Hamberg, *Principles of a Growing Economy*, New York, 1961, p. 45.

In the 'twenties, American industrialists had managed to improve their technological equipment so much that the expansion of industry into new products was no longer sufficient to absorb the 'displaced' labor force. In addition to this, the persistent influx of new immigrants further increased, at least until the middle of the decade, the disproportion between the rising employment opportunities and the much more rapidly increasing labor force; and finally, the slow rise in employment opportunities and the more rapid increase of the labor force were both overtaken by an even steeper rise in the national output. Had there been less immigration during the first half of the decade, and had the organization of labor not suffered so much from the patriotic enthusiasm of the war years, it is more likely than not that the discrepancy between the rise in the rate of productivity and the rate of increase of the labor force would have resulted in a fall in prices and higher wages. As it happened, and excluding the first two years of the decade, prices did not fall but were gently rising and wages rose only very slightly from 1923 to 1928. The difference between the sharp rise in productivity and the slow rise in real incomes was taken by the employers as profit. This redistribution of income in favor of the latter led for some time to the deepening of investment which made possible the rapid rise in productivity and the displacement of labor with its resultant effects on the wage level, but at the same time it also starved the market of its effective consumers' demand. Eventually this maladjustment between the production of producers' and consumers' goods had to come to light. It did so with the Great Depression of the 1930's.

Another section of the population which did not share in the prosperity during the 'twenties were the farmers. This was because the rapid development of farming equipment during and after the first world war had led to considerable overproduction, especially when, with the coming of peace, Europe was once again in a position to provide for her needs. The position was finally made even worse for the farmers by the rising taxation of farm property.[5]

---

5.   For more on this subject *vide* Y.S. Brenner, *A Short History of Economic Progress*, pp. 212–3 and reference notes 252–6.

The most perplexing problem, regarding the twenties in the United States, is to explain the inability of the labor movement, which had been so formidable before the war, in the East and Middle-West to see to it that the American workers acquired their share in the gains from the rapid rise in industrial productivity. This was particularly surprising if one remembers that outside the United States, i.e. internationally, the position of labor was rather stronger after than before the war. One cause for this was undoubtedly the atmosphere which the American Federation of Labor had itself helped to produce during the first world war. Throughout the war the shortage of labor had given the workers a potentially very strong bargaining position, but, because of the patriotic fervor, the opportunity to exploit this was ignored. The executive of the American Federation of Labor not only neglected exploiting the situation but publicly declared that the war against Germany and her allies 'is labor's war'. In this the Federation was as good as its word and did all in its power to raise the efficiency of production. Its leadership confined its activities to ensuring that the living standards were not actually reduced. Gompers, of the American Federation of Labor, was elected chairman of the Labor Committee of the National Defence Council and called a representative conference of both workers and employers, at which both sides agreed not to take advantage of the situation. As a rule, with only a few exceptions, the workers kept the agreement. Employers had no reason not to keep it.

In line with this 'one-sided truce' a War Labor Board was set up, early in 1918, to act as a kind of tribunal between employers and employees. This too helped to prevent friction. At the end of the War labor was rewarded for its patriotic loyalty by the establishment of the League of Nations International Labor Organization, and a number of other similar achievements such as the legal recognition of unions etc. On the whole however, the effects of the war were rather detrimental for the American labor movement. It is true that it received international recognition and that the eight-hour working day became an established fact, but real wages had fallen and were lower than during the last pre-war year. However, more important than this were the lasting losses, namely the weakening of the Socialist party and the disappearance of the I.W.W. (Industrial Workers of the World) and other left wing groups from the labor movement and from the political platform. Thus labor emerged from the war with reduced vigour and received only a minor share of the economic benefits which accrued to the financiers and manufacturers as a result of the war, and employers were taught by it a lesson in violence and intolerance.

The reaction, which began after the war, was as bad as had to be expected. The unions, having lost their experience in the struggle, were unable to cope with the combination of economic depression from overexpansion; unemployment as a result of demobilization; and the return to a peace economy with the reorganization of industry that attended it. A number of ill-organized and ill-timed strikes collapsed and where the economic pressures did not suffice Federal government stepped in to break the workers' resistance. The demoralization which followed these failures was so depressing that it rendered the American labor movement impotent for almost a decade to defend the workers against the mounting inequality of the distribution of wealth. To these almost objective difficulties other less necessary ones were added. The courts which had during the war become accustomed to ignoring civil and human rights continued to do so and paid little heed to the demands of labor, and several industrialists did not shun the use of provocateurs to justify the calling up of the militia for support in labor disputes. Thus, while labor was getting weaker, capital was becoming better organized. Two other very important factors which contributed to labor's inability to capture a greater share of the national product were the increasing differentiation between skilled and unskilled workers, and the general opinion that things were getting better all around. The first of these two, i.e. the divergence of status within the working class, was due to the fall in prices of some products and the skilled workers' relative rising standard of living after the depression of 1921. Unfortunately the skilled workers used to be the hard core of the movement before the war and their lack of enthusiasm in the twenties was a severe blow to it. The second factor, namely the illusion of prosperity, had its roots partly in the fact that the conditions of one group in the working class were really improving its living standard, and partly in the subtle psychological effect of the capitalist propaganda which pretended that a redistribution of wealth in favor of the wage earners was actually taking place. The basis for this completely unfounded idea was the greatly advertised invention of the 'employee stock ownership.'

Thus, by temptation on the one hand and threats on the other, organized labor in America was rendered harmless, while employers were increasing their capital out of proportion compared with the growth of effective consumers' demand. Had labor been more successful in checking the accumulation of wealth – and had employers been less greedy in exploiting the inactivity of the labor movement – they might, perhaps, have saved the United States from the severity of the collapse which ended the decade.

The collapse, which in the course of a few years changed the 'free for all' into 'state regulated' capitalism, began with the famous stock-market crash of October 1929. Within three years unemployment rose to 25 per cent of the labor force and pay-rolls fell to less than 45 per cent of their average 1929 level. Out of the total labor force of between 45 and 48 million workers, the unemployed numbered in 1930 more than four-and-a-half millions, in 1931 approximately seven-and-three-quarter millions, in 1932 about eleven-and-a-half millions, and in 1933 over thirteen millions. For the majority of the American people, even those who were working, the depression meant wage cuts, insecurity, and frustration. Human dignity fell to a very low ebb. With the reduced demand for goods there was little to stimulate production. It decreased to about half of its pre–1929 level. Agriculture and foreign trade suffered worst of all. The former because it had already been depressed before 1929, and the latter partly for truly economic reasons, namely the depression in Europe, the lack of American loan money, and the new exchange situation, and partly because of the European retaliations in 1930 against the high American tariffs.

Thus, unless the government wished to risk a revolution, it was bound to take some initiative in economic affairs. With this the era of almost unrestrained free enterprise, the period of the American laissez faire, came to its end. Initially, President Hoover tried to stimulate the economy by tax reductions and state support to agriculture. Both the tax relief and the support of agra-prices cost the taxpayers a lot of money but were of very little avail. Equally unsuccessful were his appeals to private enterprise to keep up production. Of some use were similar appeals to State governments and municipalities, i.e. elected bodies, which were called upon to put forward some of their construction programmes in order to create employment. And yet, though all and every one of these measures did little to cure the depression they were of very great importance in creating a new state of mind. They did in fact acknowledge that government has certain responsibilities regarding the economic welfare of the people. They paved the way to the new deal of regulated capitalism. As the elections drew closer the government became increasingly aware of the need for a more progressive and active economic policy if it wished to remain in power. One factor which had a strong though mostly indirect influence in this direction during the depression was the rapid re-emergence of the socialists and communists. 'The Russian example' not only frightened the old guard of conservatives but seemed to show to those who wished to see it that where production was aimed at 'the satisfaction of social wants'[6] rather than 'the accumulation of profits,' unemployment could be totally eliminated. It was true that not all that one heard about Russia was very pleasant, the standard of living was lower than it had been in pre–1929 America, and civil liberties were at a very low ebb, but who really cares for civil liberties when he is unemployed and starving? Indeed, how much of these celebrated liberties had survived in the United States? In 1932, the socialists polled close to a million votes in the American election – a large vote indeed. Their political influence, however, went far beyond their strength in numbers. Their growth had opened the eyes of even the most stout supporters of laissez faire to what might happen to capital if no drastic steps were taken by the government to improve the economy. By scaring the opposition with the alternative to the New Deal, they helped Roosevelt to win the elections which were to begin a new phase in American socio-economic relations. What the New Deal was to be was far from clear to anyone in 1932, but it had the right ring about it to stir the imagination of the people and it implied a change – change for the better, as it was hoped. As Professor Arthur Lewis wrote: 'No single chapter can contain the

---

6.   It ought to be added here 'whether this satisfaction of real wants was as a coincidental result, or a prime objective'.

New Deal. Here combined in one administration were innumerable great measures grappling with innumerable problems.' On the economic plane alone, and there were also New Deals in the foreign and domestic political planes, there was 'a New Deal for the unemployed, for farmers, for debtors – a Relief New Deal. A New Deal for Labor, for trust-busting, for control of Wall Street, for progressive taxation – a *left* New Deal. A Recovery New Deal, designed to prime the pump and to send the economy once more vigorously upward. A social security New Deal. Each pursued in detail with vast expenditure through an ever growing network of government agencies;...'[7]

The two main problems were, of course, how to put an end to the depression and how to eliminate the 'piratical methods and practices which... not only harassed honest business but also contributed to the ills of labor'. Initially, so it appears, Roosevelt was not quite aware how indivisible the two problems – economic revival and socio-economic reform – really were. At least, in so far as revival was concerned he continued the traditional supply orientated methods of 'priming the economy by the encouragement of higher profits'. His early advisers, drawn from the camp of private enterprise, believed, or made the government believe, that support for high prices would lead to more profit and this would set the economy upon an upward trend because rising profits would be followed by increasing production and employment. When the futility of this policy had been sufficiently demonstrated Roosevelt's new advisers, the famous Brains Trust from the Universities, suggested a new, demand dominated, policy which bridged the gap between the efforts towards social reform and towards the revival of the economy. In fact, the new policy aimed at a redistribution of the national wealth in favor of the less privileged part of the population. In the monetary and financial sphere Roosevelt eased the burden of debtors by inflation – i.e. by 'increasing property values until they were greater than debts'; in the sphere of agriculture he introduced crop restrictions – i.e. payments for restricting the planted acreage and better credit facilities. In industry, the solution was not found until

---

7.   W. Arthur Lewis, *Economic Survey 1919–1939*, London, 1949, pp. 104–5.

some abortive attempts had been made to revive the World War I spirit of co-operation between government, capital and labor. As time went by, labor became more and more critical of these efforts, or rather of the evasion of the arrangements which were to be made for their representation. Eventually, by the end of 1934 the system was reorganized and by mid–1935 abolished altogether, when the Supreme Court of the United States ruled it unconstitutional. Throughout this time the actual position of labor continued to deteriorate. Yet, together with this further deterioration, the foundations were laid for a complete change in American labor relations. For the first time the government became fully concerned with the problems of labor. It provided unemployment relief, stimulated insurance and pension schemes, and, above all, viewed with favor the organization of labor in the defence of its interests. Unemployment was attacked on a wide front by the initiation of many public works and construction schemes and by making large sums of money available to the State governments to follow the federal government's example. These schemes did much to relieve unemployment in the country. Yet with all this the problem was not really solved before the next war turned unemployment into a labor shortage. In the long run, however, the most important aspect of these efforts was the principle involved; namely, that man has a right to work, and that it is part of the job of government to see that work is obtainable.[8] This point cannot be over stressed. It upheld the dignity of man and the dignity of labor. It may well rank as the greatest contribution of this century to western civilization. It abolished the degrading patronizing attitudes of charity. Whether the critics of his schemes, who accused Roosevelt of introducing them for merely vote-catching political reasons, were right or wrong makes no difference whatsoever. The net effect is clear, it introduced a new dimension into the socio-economic relations, dignity.

More directly, the economy was affected by Roosevelt's legislation aimed at increasing the social security of wage-earners, unemployment insurance, old-age pensions, etc, and the introduction

8.   This is of course the point most under attack nowadays. It was still taken as self-evident at the time the first edition of this book went to print in 1979.

of minimum wage rates and maximum working hours. Yet Roosevelt's success could not have come without the support of the workers by helping themselves. Had it not been for the revival, or perhaps re-birth, of the American labor movement, things could hardly have turned out the way they did. Had it not been for the reorganization of labor, Roosevelt could hardly have successfully pursued his labor policy. Had it not been for Roosevelt's legislation labor would have found it much more difficult to organize and assert itself. This, then, was the real importance of section 7 of the National Industrial Recovery Act, that it gave government sanction to laborers' right to organize and to bargain collectively through their freely elected representatives. The monopoly of capital over the instruments of government was broken and the free competition between employers and employees for the greater share of the fruits of production was restored. The traditional growth-producing mechanisms in the Free Enterprise economy were once again called to life.[9]

In view of the example of economic growth discussed in the previous two chapters it appears justified to summarize the following conclusions:

a. Economic growth in a profit dominated society is sustained by competition.

b. Competition can be domestic and international. Domestically it may take the form of a struggle between producers of similar types of produce for a greater share in the market, and between employers and employees for a greater share in the fruits of production. Internationally it often takes the form of a scramble for markets and scarce raw-materials between whole nations.

c. Long-term growth, in such a society, depends on rising effectual consumers' demand, i.e. on the distribution of the fruits of production in such a way that consumers incomes suffice to clear the market of the increasingly larger or better volume of output.

d. The maximally possible rate of growth depends at each point in time on the state of physical resources, (land, labor, education,

---

9.   The preceding historical discussion is taken almost verbatim from my *A Short History of Economic Progress*, pp. 171–5 & 204–17.

etc.), the level of science and technology, the volume of accumulated wealth, and the degree of addition to consumers' effective demand in the immediately preceding period.

e. The process is effected by stochastic disturbances, from outside the economic system, for example wars, which may either accelerate or hinder its progress.

f. Finally, while given the earlier stated behavioral assumptions, it is possible to determine the *general long-term trend of economic growth*, it is *not* possible to determine in this way the *short-term fluctuations* that make up the long-term path.

4

The Socio-Cultural Landscape:
Europe on the Eve of the Reformation

'The web of life is a mingled yarn good and ill together'
All's Well that Ends Well IV. Sc. iii 83

What then, are the *behavioral* assumptions upon which the economic
growth mechanisms rest? A simple answer would be the profit
motive, i.e. the love of gain or the fear of starvation. In truth,
however, the problem is more complex for man is a social being and
his actions are influenced by, and influence, his socio-cultural
environment. He desires the approbation of society and his efforts
are affected by a reigning value system. This value system is
imparted to the young by their parents and teachers, i.e. by the
preceding generations and tends therefore to be 'reactionary' for it
reflects the aspired reality and real needs and values of an earlier
period. Thus, on the one hand such a value system gives society a
necessary degree of stability and continuity, and on the other, it
hinders a more rapid adaptation to material changes occurring in the

society's environment and the creation of suitable conceptions of a changed reality.[1]

For more than a millennium people saw the universe as a system of regularity, a hierarchy in a persistent striving towards order. A regularity that could be observed, traced, described, even predicted, but not explained;[2] for its very unity and regularity was evidence of God's design which defies all explanation. This does not mean that people thought that there were no causes for the observed effects, indeed there were whole hierarchies of causes, proximate causes, efficient causes, necessary causes, etc., but they all sprang from the First Cause, the striving of the universe towards a purpose – His purpose.[3] They were not explanatory causes, answering the question *why,* but descriptive causes, answering the question *how.* They were the causes inherent in the notion that the world is uniform, rational, and arrayed in a logical hierarchical structure; – the reflection of a world in which people are born into their specific status in the social hierarchy, without knowing, or ever being able to know, *why,* but in which they are persistently admonished to know their place and behave accordingly. A world built upon authority in which 'prestige and social worth sprang less from the free disposal of property than from the free disposal of human forces;'[4] where 'superior' individuals granted protection and diverse material advantages that directly or indirectly assured a subsistence to dependents in return for their pledge to render various prestations or services and a general obligation to aid, though these relations were not always freely

---

1. These were descriptive causes. Only when the question how things happen came to mean what was the mechanism that brought them about, the answer became an explanation.

2. Ptolemy, Copernicus, Tycho Brahe and Kepler plotted the paths of the planets but never *explained* their movements. Explanation simply did not enter people's mind, it did not exist. Things happen the way they do because it is their nature to do so.

3. Aquinas was particularly explicit about the hierarchy of causes.

4. Marc Bloch, 'Feudalism' in *The Encyclopedia of Social Sciences.*

assumed or even ceased to contain a great number of constraints, violences and abuses.[5] A world into which the decline of ancient Rome had introduced so much instability and uncertainty that the gap between dire reality and better prospects became too wide to provide and make discernible rational means to bridge it so that the supernatural displaced the practical ethics which had served a guide to life in earlier times. A world in which the rational elements inherent in notions of *good* and *right*, by which social conduct is measured, were replaced by idealized ones, i.e. by mystical notions according to which right conduct, the correct manner of obtaining good, is postulated upon an imaginary world of gods and demons. One in which judgement is passed according to 'the most rightful Law of God almighty... the same always and everywhere' and of which 'any part that harmoniseth not with its whole, is offencive.'[6] A Commonwealth 'endowed with life by the benefit of divine favor, which acts at the prompting of the highest equity, and is ruled by what may be called the moderating power of reason,' in which 'those things which establish and implant the practice of religion, and transmit the worship of God... fill the place of the soul in the body.' A Commonwealth in which 'the place of the head is filled by the prince, who is subject only to God and to those who exercise His office and represent Him on earth, even as in the human body the head is quickened and governed by the soul. The place of the heart is filled by the senate, from which proceeds the initiation of good works and ill. The duties of eyes, ears, and tongue are claimed by the judges and governors of provinces. Officials and soldiers correspond to the hands. Those who always attend upon the prince are likened to the sides. Financial officers and keepers... the stomach and intestines... the husbandmen to the feet...'[7] In short, a hierarchical and all embracing world that will only be flourishing 'when the higher members shield the lower and the lower respond faithfully and fully in like measure to the just demands of their

---

5.   *Vide* Marc Bloch, *Feudal Society.*

6.   Saint Augustin *Confessions* Book. III, Cardinal Edition, N.Y. 1952, p. 38.

7.   John of Salisbury.

superiors, so that each and all are as it were members one of another by a sort of reciprocity, and each regards his own interest as best served by that which he knows to be most advantageous for the others.' A world where good government is by a Law that is the 'gift of God, the model of equity, a standard of justice, a likeness of divine will, the guardian of well-being, a bond of union and solidarity between peoples, a rule defining duties, a barrier against the vices and a destroyer thereof, a punishment of violence and all wrong doing.'[8] A Law that is not to be understood by human reason but by superior authority in a world 'that considers nothing discovered by moderns worthy of being accepted', so that it is difficult even only to discuss things arrived at by the guidance of reason, for people are so 'deceived by the picture of authority that they follow a halter... by animal credulity, and usually demand no reasonable judgement, but have faith simply in the mention of an old title.'[9] Altogether, it was a world dominated by a state of mind and a conception of the universe that reflected its social and economic real environment. An environment characterized by an economic system in which exchange although not entirely absent was comparatively rare and in which the not very abundant specie played but a restricted role;[10] where the very existence of every man depended narrowly upon the possibility of disposing of the resources of the soil placed under his control, but where an important fraction of the people also drew a revenue in the form of personal service, money or kind for the use of the land.'[11] An environment that was the product of the disintegration of effective central government, and the collapse of the money economy.

---

8.   *Ibid.*

9.   Adelard of Bath.

10.   Marc Bloch, *op.cit.*

11.   According to Marc Bloch, *op.cit.*, 'the possession of superior rights to land was for the possessor in many respects but a means for exercising an effective power of command over the men to whom he conceded or permitted the direct enjoyment of the fields.'

When by the end of the Roman Empire men lost the habit of expecting protection from a too distant and emasculated sovereign, and the market economy collapsed, people transferred their obedience to closer rulers and developed with them new ties of dependence appropriate to a self-sufficient rural mode of production; ties of dependence that proved to be singularly incompatible with rational incentives for economic improvement. Incompatible, for the usurpation of authority by locally powerful individuals increased the insecurity in all matters concerning property relations. Custom remained a powerful guardian of tenants' rights and immunities, but only as long as too little material advantages could be gained from its violation.[12] Titles to land were neither sufficiently secure nor of the required duration to induce the kind of protracted efforts necessary for the achievement of real long-term advantages. Most land was held in scattered unconsolidated strips and therefore also technically not easily improvable. Land was frequently held by some share-cropping arrangements that left tenants to bear the risk and cost involved in improvements without according them their fruits, for they would have to render a share of the increased yield to the landlord. Rarely can simple innovations, in the best of times, initially yield sufficiently greater output to allow for sharing of advantages; let alone the tenant's problem of obtaining the landlord's and community's agreement for such efforts. The various domain and corvée services, particularly the former, tended to fall into the seasons when farmers were most in need of all the labor they commanded. Hence all new incentives to raise yields that would have required more labor during these periods were hardly worthy of consideration. Further, with no institutional credit facilities innovation is prohibitively costly. People may well borrow funds at almost any price for seed or to survive times of adversity, but not in order to experiment; innovation must be expected to yield an addition to output that suffices to cover its extra cost. With too little realistic hope of doing this, it is unreasonable to attempt it. Farmers are often

---

12. In the 12th and 13th century when real advantages began to be obtainable from the eviction of tenants and alterations in the customary agreements of tenancy the power of custom gradually eroded. *Vide* R.H. Tawney, *Agrarian Problems in the Sixteenth Century*, London, 1912.

unsophisticated but seldom unreasonable. Lending in times of adversity is always prone to abuse, for the borrower is at the mercy of the lender. To protect the borrower the Church spoke out against usury. Laws against usury may not protect the needy but will always make borrowing more difficult and therefore more expensive; they close the doors to legal means of redress when borrowers fail in their obligations, and thus increase the lender's risk. Of paramount importance was also the absence of adequate crop-storage facilities. Lack of storage made almost all efforts to increase output, even where the earlier mentioned difficulties could be overcome, at best a most questionable enterprise. For without the possibility to store surpluses it is hardly reasonable to make great efforts to produce more than is immediately required. It was for lack of storage facilities that people made ostentatious feasts when harvests were particularly good; and for fear of overstocking the common that they slaughtered a great many cattle annually. Finally, even on the landlord's domain it was unreasonable to make strenuous efforts to raise output in the absence of a market or satisfactory exchange system. For unless there are people who are not employed in agriculture whose products may be accepted in exchange for the farmers' surplus; or unless the surplus can be stored for later use, what true incentive can there be to raise production beyond immediate needs?[13]

In summary then, lack of security of land tenure, absence of consolidated land holdings, share-cropping and personal and corvee services, too little personal security, lack of markets and institutional loan facilities, must all be held responsible for the absence of efforts to achieve economic improvement by honest work and technological ingenuity. Under such objective obstacles the best way to get by was not to attract attention and to accept fate as it is meted out. To be meek, – for the meek shall inherit the earth. The discrepancy between men's material aspirations and the possibilities for satisfying them was simply too wide to be bridged by rationally conceivable

13. Most of the above mentioned causes for the lack of incentives for improvement also apply to the rural stagnation in many underdeveloped countries in our time. I discussed this problem in *Agriculture and the Economic Development of Low Income Countries.*

endeavors. Resignation was therefore a state of mind well founded in the era's economic reality. It was not something that had to be implanted into people's minds by the teachings of the Church, (though such teachings may well have helped to sustain it,) but it was the true reflection of the material situation. The reflection of a world in which change through functional human effort was unthinkable, but in which life was made bearable by hope of salvation, – by hope springing from a belief in a merciful God who can be reached by prayer in humility. A world in which the distinction between the ceremonial and the functional was lost; in which only one will is capable of bringing about change, – His will.

The need to rely for both physical security and the material means of subsistence on the locally powerful people produced forms of social interdependence that were very different from the social ties common today. Modern social identification tends to gravitate towards *horizontal* links, medieval tended towards *vertical* bonds. *Horizontal* identification is related to class stratification; it is based upon real contradictions of interest: workers unite in unions or parties in order to protect their living standards and gain a greater share of the fruits of production. However, the efforts to obtain a greater share of the fruits of production separate workers from employers and make them increasingly dependent upon other workers, in other working places, even in other towns or countries. Similarly, self-employed people are drawn together in a bond of solidarity to resist pressures of big-business from 'above' and labor from 'below'. Employers too follow the same trend. When profitability dictates it they will react in union and not hesitate to shift their investments from one place or country to another with little concern for the workers left behind. This trend towards horizontal social coherence does not necessarily exclude other non-horizontal forms of adhesion; after all both workers and employers will suffer adversity from a general economic depression, and all classes of society may support the local football team. But the main characteristics of social alignment clearly distinguish pre-industrial and medieval societies from modern industrial ones. Medieval social coherence was *vertical,* based upon personal congruities of interests. A powerful master or landlord was better able to protect his tenants than a weak one, and an affluent tenant was better able to contribute to his master's power to protect him than a poor tenant When the landlord refused his master a claim, for example a contribution for a military venture, he did so for himself, but objectively he also did so for his dependents, for in the last resort it was they who had to raise the money or victuals for the campaign, and it was they who had to make available the men to accompany the master into battle.[14]

Most significant for the relative sublimation of the horizontal contradictions in medieval society, however, was the degree to which this society was subjected to uncontrollable forces of nature that

---

14.   A poor peasant in pre-industrial societies found his protection in his familial or tribal associations within the feudal hierarchy which made him a member of a collective which stretched from the head of the pyramid, the lord, down to its base, the poorest farmer. The lord of the manor though the main beneficiary of the structure had still a common interest with those socially and economically below him. This common interest united him with them against all others. The farmer relied on the aristocrat's protection and assistance and the aristocrat relied on the farmer's surplus product as his source of income. The aristocrat represented all those tied to him by the feudal hierarchy and his interests were seldom totally different from, or opposed to, those of the people under him.

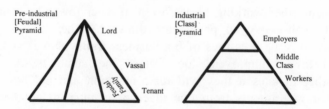

Modern society has created a new kind of alignment, horizontal as distinct from the vertical feudal nexus. Here people are linked because they belong to a similar income group or because of the nature of their employment. It is a class society and not a hierarchy in the feudal sense. The rich men, employers and money magnates, do not feel the needs and do not represent the interests of other classes because their own interests are as a rule antagonistic to all others. The upper layer of the industrialized nations' pyramid is interested in securing as much as possible of the product of the labor of the other classes for itself. This in spite of the competition among themselves makes the men at the top act in unison against all those below them. At the same time, the lower layers of the Pyramid tend to behave in a similar fashion.

affected all people alike. In modern technologically advanced societies agricultural surpluses can be stored for future use and against eventual emergencies, and many production processes are almost entirely or even wholly independent of the vagaries of weather. Adversity in such societies is therefore far less the result of forces that are obviously beyond human control than in technologically less developed societies, and far more ascribable to human mismanagement of the economy. The fate of the medieval husbandman, save for the occasional transgressions of rapacious landlords, was always in the hands of nature. God alone was seen to have the power to determine whether man should suffer dearth or enjoy abundance, and when He did so the results were felt by the high and mighty and the low and weak alike. Not so in industrial society; for when man was separated from the land, not nature, or God, but other men, those who controlled the new means of production, became the arbiters of fate. When they, the controllers of the new means of production, misjudged the market for their products and for fear of losses decided to restrict production, it was they who were the immediate cause for the misery of the unemployed. The deeds of men, not the will of God, became the *visible* sources of the new-fangled miseries. Gone was the 'harmony' that held together the feudal hierarchy by ties of mutual advantages.

In conclusion then, the medieval vision of the universe as a system of regularity, a hierarchy striving towards order, closely reflected the era's social reality. It was the reflection of a society in which each member depended on those socially above and below him for his physical and economic security and in which forces beyond human control determined all members' fate for better and for worse. It was this vision of the universe that determined people's social values; which gave meaning to such concepts as good and bad, true and false, virtuous and vicious. It was this that set the conceptions of the desirable that was influencing selective behavior, and provided criteria for selection in action, judgement, preference and choice, for more than a thousand years. It was this value system that the Middle Ages bequeathed to subsequent generations in a body of stated and implicit social theory. Its formal teaching was derived from 'the Bible, the works of the Fathers and schoolmen, the canon law and its commentators, and had been popularized in sermons and religious manuals.'[15] Its informal assumptions were those implicit in law, custom, and social institutions. Unconsciously and consciously this value system guiding the lives of medieval men was transmitted from one generation to the next well into modern times. Though gradually adapting to changing circumstances and losing in compulsion its main tenets proved very tenacious indeed. Unconsciously it was communicated by emotional and verbal contamination to successive generations of children by elders who imparted their wishes in a moralizing setting of rules variously rationalized; and, as these emotions became overladen with habitual rules the rules themselves appeared to be intuitive and inevitable. Consciously, it was transmitted by the pervasive sanction of religion, involving supernatural rewards and punishment. The mere word 'God', and the feeling and attitude of the person speaking, was sufficient to invoke a moral code invested with moral sanctions where a secular world sees only manners. God becomes part of the hidden experience of the psychic life, and a source of hope to bridge the gap between reality and a desired reality that one is impotent to bring about by instrumental efforts. The fact that the God who thus revealed himself to the medieval mind was, unlike other gods in other times, a merciful God, a God of compassion, needs here particular emphasis. For it was this aspect of the Christian God that was to play a most significant role in the formation of the post-medieval moral code of western European civilization. The God of the Jews, for example, was a God of justice; he reflected a society living by the rules of fair retribution, an 'Eye for eye, tooth for tooth,' a 'jealous God visiting the iniquity of the fathers upon the children unto the third and fourth generation'. The christian God was more merciful, he mitigated justice by compassion. He was both the image of, and the example for, the good human master ruling the lives of men on earth.

So, the combination of stated doctrine and the opinions transmitted from one generation to the next gave concrete *meaning* to such concepts as good, right and true, a meaning which was to have a

---

15. *Vide* R.H. Tawney, *Religion and the Rise of Capitalism*, Pelican edition of 1948, p. 28.

tremendous impact on social behavior long after the waning of the medieval circumstances from where they sprang, and when men's economic environment was already changing rapidly. When the realistic opportunity for material advancement arose, reverence for law and custom (though sometimes better observed by transgression than compliance) together with the unshakable christian affirmation that goodness and power are united into one, legated to western Europe a social climate that for centuries circumscribed utilitarian notions within limits consistent with rational economic behavior. It tempered the 'love of gain' with a sufficient measure of 'ancient virtues' to prevent the rise of the new-fangled egoism that accompanied the emergence of the new material opportunities from 'killing the geese that were to lay the golden eggs'.[16] It imposed legality, rationality, even a degree of humanity, upon the quest for riches, so that it confined rapacity and exploitation within legal boundaries in which ingenuity rather than brute force became a source of wealth. Self-love was circumscribed by social conventions and by the notion that one can never be sure whether or not there is retribution for injustice in a life hereafter. From a social collective point of view economic ambitions were thus kept from degenerating into self-destructive rapacity by two types of restraints: mores, the need for social approbation, and religion, the fear of heavenly retribution. The rich man glories in his riches 'because he feels that they naturally draw upon him the attention of the world'.[17] He will forfeit this approbation if he acquires the wealth by means not

---

16. It is one of the most difficult problems in many low income countries today that the bourgeoisie lacks the moral impediments discussed above and is creating by its unbridled rapacity a socio-economic climate which cannot be conducive to economic development. For example, D.R. Gadgil addressing the Convocation of Nagpur University had this to say in 1962: 'The Indian businessman happens, at present to be at a particularly unattractive stage of his development. He was never noted for any highly puritanic or moral qualities... He had also not been imbued with that high sense of social and national responsibility which characterized the Japanese...' he simply lacks the moderation and trustworthiness that inspires confidence and with no confidence business cannot promote development.

17. Adam Smith, *The Theory of Moral Sentiments*, 1759.

sanctioned by society. He needs to cloak his rapacity in a socially acceptable attire, it must appear to be in the service of some higher objective, the better salvation of his soul or the public good as contemporary society understood it. While reason was gradually taking the place of revelation and religion was ceasing to be the master-interest of mankind, Faith continued for a very long time to be a department of life with boundaries which it was extravagant to overstep.[18] Altogether therefore, the spiritual legacy of the Middle Ages left the would be rich and powerful of subsequent generations with an unspecified feeling of discomfort that, unlike in some modern communities and particularly among the emergent elites of underdeveloped countries, imposed upon them the need to justify themselves for being rich. It is in the light of this that the transformation of Christianity in early modern history has to be seen, and it is due to this that the rising bourgeoisie in much o western Europe replaced the aristocracy's violent, lawless, often irrational, and above all socially self-destructive, rapacity by its peaceful, legal and rational methods of enrichment.

If the lingering influence of religious constrictions was so important in directing the rise of the bourgeoisie, one may ask how it came about that in the eleventh century, after five centuries in which none of the western European towns made any substantial progress, city life began reviving. Perhaps it was due to the concatenation of population pressure with the restoration of contacts with the East, which had by this time become Moslem.[19] First trade revived along the Mediterranean shores, then, with the crusades, Florence, Venice, Genoa and Pisa developed as manufacturing centers trading with the coastal towns of the Near East. Similarly, in parts of northwestern Europe, along the Baltic and North Seas and along the Rhine cities began to grow, several of them forming themselves into the Hanseatic League for mutual assistance. In England too,

---

18.   R.H. Tawney, *Religion and the Rise of Capitalism*.

19.   *Vide* A.R. Lewis, *Naval Power and Trade in the Mediterranean AD 500–1100*, New Jersey, 1951; H. Pirenne, *Sozial und Wirtschaftsgeschichte Europas im Mittelalter*, Bern, 1945; M. Postan & E.E. Rich, *The Cambridge Economic History of Europe*, Vol. II, Cambridge, 1952.

various towns began to grow in the later part of the Middle Ages, and also, though more slowly, in parts of central Europe.[20] With the growth of towns traders and craftsmen became increasingly wealthy but for a very long time they did not, even in their own eyes, gain the social esteem that was traditionally accorded to people who obtained their wealth from landownership and caste privileges. In medieval society scholars and warriors were held in higher esteem than craftsmen, merchants and, needless to add, money lenders. Altogether, to be concerned with money, even work for gain, was thought socially demeaning. Though much preoccupied with what was called the 'fair price', medieval people did not recognize the *money value* of services rendered to lords and clergy. Not before Luther's time were craftsmen and traders given socially acceptable moral sanction. Only when the rising middle class began interpreting its quest for wealth as inseparably related to the traditional virtues *thrift* and *industry* and presented economic success as a sign of divine favor did the age old moral and religious disapprobation begin to wane. Only then it was no longer objectionable to think of how to increase one's wealth, except, of course, by 'the aristocrats and their dependents, the artists and scholars,' and by those who had never had any wealth.[21] This is very important for it imposed upon the rising middle class a conception of a reputable life that stimulated economic efforts and at the same time kept them within legally and morally defined boundaries; it substituted the aristocratic ideal of a life of leisure and ostentation by one of industry and parsimony. What their enemies disparaged as niggardliness, obtuseness and exploiting rapacity was thus transformed into something approaching the virtues of thrift, plain dealing and organizing genius.

There were, however, also legal arrangements which reinforced the socio-religious influences that formed the outlook of the middle class

---

20.   The rise of English towns in this period has recently most interestingly though indirectly been discussed by A. R. Bridbury in his article on sixteenth century farming in the *Economic History Review,* XXVII (4), Nov. 1974, pp. 538–56.

21.   *Vide* C. Delisle Burns on Commercialism in the *Encyclopedia of Social Sciences.*

in late-medieval and early-modern Europe. Their origins were in the rules regulating guilds and trade associations. Early in the eleventh century merchants were beginning to organize themselves for mutual assistance, and by the middle of the century some had already permanent Guild halls and funds for aiding the sick and the poor.[22] In the following century they were in many parts of Europe gaining official status with feudal lords and city authorities, and, of course, trading monopolies. At about the same time craftsmen too were organizing themselves into brotherhood or guilds of mixed religious and economic character. Increasingly city authorities subjected them to supervision in order to exact dues and protect the population against fraudulent exploitation.[23] In episcopalian towns efforts were also made to apply Catholic morality.[24] By the end of the twelfth century ordinances were more and more frequently promulgated to inspect and supervise the quality of manufactured goods offered for sale in cities.[25] In the thirteenth century artisans were organized in regulated professional associations in most western European towns. The origins of such associations must therefore be regarded as the result of a mixture of voluntary alliances and legal authority. At the same time they were already claiming self-government and participation in municipal affairs. It is however important to realize the difference in outlook which separated the guilds from post-Renaissance capitalist industrialism. What both had in common was the love of gain and hence the tendency towards protectionism. The guilds tried to protect their members' interests against

---

22.   For example the Guild of St. Omer had a fund for the sick and the poor since the eleventh century.

23.   For example, city authorities tried to prevent artisans from cheating their customers by legislating for the supervision of all weights and measures.

24.   For example, a 'fair price' was fixed for a variety of products and exceeding it was regarded as both illegal and sinful.

25.   H. Pirenne, *op.cit*, told about some butchers and bakers in Haguenan who were deprived of the right to follow their trade – the former for selling bad meat, and the latter for selling loaves of bread of less than the required weight.

competition from other cities and 'new' people who wanted to enter their trades. In this effort they did not substantially differ from the capitalists who dominated trade and industry in a later age; but, unlike capitalists the guilds also tried to prevent their members from enriching themselves at the cost of other members. To achieve this they imposed upon all uniform techniques of production, similar restrictions on the lengths and number of working days, equal wage rates and prices, even a fixed number of workers and tools that may be employed in each workshop, and, (oh blessed time!) a prohibition of all kinds of advertising. To make sure of compliance they appointed inspectors and supervisors.[26] Altogether therefore, they strengthened with legal regulations the religious and moral taboos in restraint of fraud, reinforced with self imposed rules the socio-economic pressures to maintain good standards of quality, and finally, put fetters upon any kind of personal initiative that might have stimulated technological progress. On the whole initially unconsciously, they continued the medieval collective rural way of life in a professional city setting and carried it over into early modern society. As their monopolies helped them to gain riches and with it social position in the towns their members soon gained a degree of cultural hegemony over the rest of the town-people who also began to emulate their way of life and accept their value system. This was not difficult for it did not essentially depart from the value system to which medieval men were accustomed. What medieval society had considered good, right and true, did not stop to govern peoples' sense of morality at the city gates. It remained the corner-stone of the newly emergent urban society. It continued to exert a restraining influence upon business life even when the guilds' emphasis on professional exclusiveness led, towards the end of the Middle Ages, to the emergence of new groups of business and craftsmen who, being forced outside the old trades began developing new ones, and expediency was gradually pushing aside the traditional modes of conduct.

How then did the guilds attain and maintain this cultural hegemony? In the first place because each corporation tended to

---

26.   *Vide* H. Pirenne, *op.cit.*

maintain its exclusiveness in order to protect its monopoly. Some guilds even attempted to make membership hereditary and to enforce, with no little success a strict hierarchy separating the master, the apprentices and the journeymen into different social groups. No one could become a master without satisfying certain conditions – such as the payment of dues, legitimate birth and affiliation with the local bourgeoisie, – which made the acquisition of the status rather difficult.

After the fourteenth century in many cities guild membership tended to become increasingly restricted to the families of existing masters. The length of apprenticeship increased, and the competence tests required in order to enter on mastership became increasingly difficult. To become a master an apprentice had to present a *chef d'oeuvre*, a masterpiece, i.e. a piece of work elaborate and perfect upon which it was necessary for him to work a whole year or more. And, while the 'class' of masters grew more and more exclusive,[27] the position of journeymen deteriorated to the level of wage workers. In places it even became customary for journeymen and apprentices to swear to their masters never to set up as craftsmen on their own without permission.[28] Together with the urban class differentiation a compromise also developed between the urban privileged elites and traditional feudal society. Economically this compromise took the form of land purchases by rich merchants and masters, business partnerships with the aristocracy, and the welcoming of local gentry and their sons to guild membership; socially it took the form of a desire for intermarriage, and the pursuit of titles and feudal court offices and the emulation of some aristocratic modes of conduct which did not necessarily clash with the new elite's economic

---

27.   For examples illustrating the exclusiveness of guilds *vide* Lepinasse et lonnardot, *Les Metiers et Corporations de la Ville de Paris*; H. Hauser, *Les Debuts du Capitalisme*; Levasseur, *Histoire des Classes Ouvrieres en France*; Kramer, *Craft Guilds & Government*; Pirenne, *La Fin Du Moyen Age*.

28.   The custom of making journeymen etc. swear not to engage in their trade on their own was outlawed in the 1530's. *Vide* M. Dobb, *Studies in the Development of Capitalism*, Ch. III.

needs.[29] In one respect the new class was of course unable to assimilate to the traditional elite, its members could not look upon work as a demeaning effort; but they could stress the quality of workmanship rather than the pecuniary aspect of their labor and make this the hallmark of their status, into a source of pride, a status symbol of their own separating them from all other working people. While feudalism disguised the economic characteristics of the system by ignoring the money value of the services rendered by the lower to the higher people in the hierarchy, the early bourgeoisie endeavoured to conceal its pursuit of earthly goods by stressing its excellence of skills. In this way the new city elite reconciled its way of life with both aristocratic feudal traditions and the moral senti- ments of the medieval church. Although the origins of the elite's elevated status rested upon economic achievement it was soon developing tendencies to relate it to other factors, such as social descent, modes of conduct, professional excellence and other attributes that are more difficult to attain than wealth. In this way it managed to convey the impression that its status reflected something more than what comes with wealth alone, that it holds something unattainable by others. This then became the status image that accompanied the economic ascent of the bourgeoisie and which was to leave a lasting impact on the cultural milieu in which capitalism was developing. A milieu in which, for example, money making would continue to be regarded 'vulgar' by people in privileged positions. In fact it was the search for status that provided the early bourgeoisie with its new ethics that was to bridge the gap between the ancient medieval conception of lineage, and the new middle class conception of personal endeavour and attainment as the decisive determinant of status and which found its ideological reflection in Calvinism. Lutheranism was still rural in character and theologically medieval in outlook; Luther himself, and also his English contemporaries, never really departed from the conception of the traditional stratification of rural society. Their background was of 'a natural rather than a money economy, consisting of the petty dealings of peasants and craftsmen in the small market town where

---

29.   *Vide* M. Dobb, *op.cit.*, Ch. III.

industry is carried on for the subsistence of the household and the consumption of wealth follows hard upon its production and where commerce and finance are occasional incidents, rather than the forces which keep the whole system in motion. When they criticize economic abuses, it is precisely against departures from that natural state of things – against the enterprise, the greed of gain, the restless competition, which disturb the stability of the existing order with clamorous economic appetites – that their criticism is directed.'[30]

Not so Calvinism. for Calvinism was active and radical. It was an urban movement that spread among men engaged in commerce, finance and manufacturing who were hardly disposed to idealize the 'patriarchal virtues of the peasant community'. It was a movement espoused by precisely those social groups that had already become estranged from rural society and whose occupations had long since become irreconcilable with the traditional scheme of rural ethics. It did not reject the old tenets of religion, not even its claim to moralize on economic matters. It only broke with the predominantly rural aspects of belief, especially with those that reflected the medieval objective inability of individuals to improve their material conditions. From this point of view, Calvinism in its variety of forms, did little more than make the old rural moral and ethical tenets of christianity congruent with the new needs of an urban society. It lay down rules of conduct in economic matters that were no less rigorous than those of earlier times but it no longer held on to the belief that the riches of the world are strictly limited so that the enrichment of one person always implies the deprivation of another. Nor did it look upon the accumulation of wealth as inherently sinful, – not wealth but its misuse for self-indulgence or ostentation were the things that gave cause for disapprobation. It did not reflect the social and technological impotence of medieval society to improve people's material conditions, but a society consisting of people seeking actively to improve their lot 'with the sober gravity of men who are conscious of disciplining their own characters by patient labor, and of devoting themselves to a service acceptable to

---

30.   R.H. Tawney, *Religion and the Rise of Capitalism*, p. 111.

God.'[31] This was the ideal of Calvinism – an ideal that without touching the fundamentals of religious belief, such as the popular conception of a merciful, compassionate, God watching over the deeds of men, reflected the new social and economic reality that was emerging in the cities. It was an ideal that mirrored the simple fact that people, at least some people, were indeed able to change their socio-economic position by their own efforts; that the gap between desired material improvement and its attainment was no longer unbridgeable, and that as a result of this irrational and ceremonial efforts to achieve success were beginning to give way to more rational and functional activities. It did not touch the fundamentals of morality, it only rejected some formalistic manifestations which had become dogma, – some expressions of morality that had lost their ethical content in the new material environment.

For example lending money for profit was thought morally objectionable – usury, because of its exploitative character. This did not apply to loans granted to kings and other mighty personages because the objection was not directed against the very act of lending but against the despoiling of the needy. Only the lending for profit to the poor gave rise to real moral conflict. The good christian was expected to share his worldly goods with his brother in adversity, to help the needy not turn their misfortune to his advantage; and as in the rural environment of the Middle Ages none but those in direst need, and in no position to refuse paying usurious interest rates, were borrowing, lending for interest did indeed present a moral issue. Herein lay the moral conflict, – in the collecting of interest from the poor and the defenseless. All the rest was mystification, legalism and formalism devoid of any real moral contents. Such conflict had however little to do with the borrowing of city-merchants. They were neither in dire poverty nor at the lenders' mercy. They borrowed funds to increase their fortunes not to survive when floods or drought destroyed their harvest; but then, why should the lender not have his share in the wealth to which his loan has contributed. No more could it be considered reprehensible for lenders in the city to be rewarded by traders and craft-masters

---

31. R.H. Tawney, *op.cit.*, p. 114.

for the use of their funds than for the lords of the land to be rewarded by the peasant for the use of the land. The true moral values did not change, – to take advantage of the poor remained as censurable as it had been before, – but the formalistic aspects of religion, the prohibition of all interest, were made to fit the new social reality, and by this christians were given the opportunity to seek both attainment and salvation in action.[32] Not that Calvinism had much pity for poverty; 'but it distrusted wealth, as it distrusted all influences that distract the aim or relax the fibers of the soul, and, in the first flush of its youthful austerity, it did its best to make life unbearable for the rich. Before the Paradise of earthly comfort it hung a flaming brand, waved by the implacable shades of Moses and Aaron.'[33] It continued to uphold the belief that salvation comes by grace, – not works; but it also maintained that the grace is bestowed upon those who lead an active strenuous christian life, – a life serving the glory of God. It rested on the conception of 'the holy community destined by divine mandate, but implemented by human agency, to bring a kingdom of God on earth.' From one aspect this was a collective orientation, from another, perhaps the most radical expression of christian individualism; or at least an orientation to realistic possibilities of institutionalization in secular society rather than other-worldliness or antinomian expectations.[34] It was the vision of a divinely ordained, but human implemented, flow of worldly events. A vision that stressing the virtues of industry and thrift cleared economic activities of suspicions of hedonism and raised them to the status of 'callings' serving the glory of God and the common good. 'The very rigor of its standards made Calvinism a constructive rather than a hindering force in modern economic development. The idea of 'calling' reinforced by the psychological effect of the doctrine of predestination gave a religious sanction to the most strenuous, rational, systematic labor for impersonal ends.

---

32.   Some readers may perhaps need to be reminded that the protection of the weak or poor is by no means common heritage of all civilizations.

33.   R.H. Tawney, op.cit., p. 139.

34.   Vide Talcott Parsons in International Encyclopedia of Social Sciences, Calvin.

Labor thus became a means of serving God and of proving one's own state of grace through ascetic self-discipline. Slothfulness became the deadliest of sins and fear of self-indulgence made the Calvinist a small consumer and a large saver. In Geneva this resulted in an extraordinary system of church discipline, but with the change of emphasis from church to self-discipline it later powerfully furthered the development of individual capitalistic acquisition, especially after worldly success came to be recognized as a token of grace.[35]

What was true of Calvinism was in no small measure also true of other Protestant movements. Lutherans and Anglicans wished to reform the church – not abolish it. They were never intentionally radical yet they brought ideas, patterns of behavior and social structures that were closer to human interests, reality and life. In doctrinal matters they invoked temporal power to enforce religious and moral conformity. Essentially what separated them from earlier conceptions was that unlike medieval christianity, which abhorred financial dealings and commercial activities, Protestantism was content to impose upon them its code of conduct and its own religious and moral control. Before long, Catholicism did in practice, though not theologically, undergo a similar transformation in the parts of Europe where the bourgeoisie had gained political power. It too reached a kind of compromise with the new material reality. The geographical, social and historical coincidence of the religious and economic movements is too obvious not to indicate a relationship in which both the economic and the religious factor may be regarded as the dominant and creative forces. Doubtless they were somehow causally connected and mutually stimulating.[36] However the real difference between Lutheran and Anglican Protestantism on the one hand, and Calvinism on the other, was that the former was only gradually yielding to the needs of the rising middle class, in the wake of the shift in political power, where the feudal aristocracy was

---

35.   *Vide* Talcott Parsons in *Encyclopedia of Social Sciences*, Calvin.

36.   For example compare the attitudes of Max Weber and Karl Marx to the sequence of events leading to the rise of Capitalism.

forced to share it with the rising bourgeois oligarchy, while Calvinism 'was not only interested in preserving moral and social control of the economic life but was more aggressive in promoting direct political measures for exercise of that control.'[37] Christianity was gradually lifting its inhibitions on the pursuit of wealth. Protestantism in its variety of forms stimulated economic enterprise, firstly by making the love of gain 'respectable', – the pursuit of wealth a vocation, and secondly, by making ostentation and luxury the objects of religious interdiction and social opprobrium. The former liberated the bourgeoisie from the cultural fetters inhibiting entrepreneurial incentives, and the latter stimulated saving, capital accumulation, – i.e. the material means for furthering economic growth. In its extreme forms it 'made commercial success an index of righteousness and poverty a probable badge of vice'.[38]

Altogether then; since the twelfth century a concatenation of circumstances gave rise and sustained in parts of Europe economic conditions that created opportunities also for individuals who did not belong to the traditionally privileged classes to improve their material position and consequently their social status. The social stagnation which had been characteristic of Feudal society was gradually giving way to greater social mobility. By the sixteenth century recognition of the changing reality was ferociously forced upon the Church. Religion was beginning to reformulate its moral tenets making them more congruent with the changing conception of the world that accompanied society's growing measure of socio-economic mobility. So did science; it too began revising its static conception of the universe replacing it by a new world-image pervaded by the vision of mobility. There is, and has apparently always been, a complex relationship between science and society. On the one hand science is serving as the basis for technological innovations which tend to stimulate changes in the social structures of societies, on the other it reflects in the 'scientific outlook' the very character of the societies it indirectly helped to form. Perhaps it is because people

---

37.   H. Richard Niebuhr, 'Protestantism' in the *Encyclopedia of Social Sciences*.

38.   H. Richard Niebuhr, *op.cit.*

best recognize the things they are familiar with that scientists' image of the universe tends on the whole to be similar to the social image of their environment. In any case, the socially static society of the Middle Ages was accompanied by a static image of the universe, in which Galileo's conception of a moving earth could certainly not be accommodated, just as the new era of social mobility was accompanied by the vision of an harmoniously changing universe.

It is difficult to explain the processes by which scientific perceptions of reality are arrived at, modified, or changed. According to Einstein scientific concepts are free creations of the mind which with increasing knowledge become simpler and better capable of explaining a wider range of sensuous impressions, though, of course, no one can ever be quite certain that they are the *only* ideas that can explain these impressions.[39] But then, being the 'free creations of the mind', they can hardly be far removed from the frontiers of human experience. In fact, concepts like fields, waves, particles, etc. are derived from everyday experience and only later, with the detailed expansion of their role in scientific comprehension, they obtain a more abstract meaning remote from sense experience. The scientist is a member of society, his vision is restricted by his background and limited to the range of anticipation which his background allows him. If he is ingenuous he may link certain phenomena or events in a way suggestive of a mechanism capable of explaining them. If he is very ingenuous his explanation may even be as far removed from man's sensuous experience as the conversion of time and space, matter and energy. It is possible that although the answers nature provides to scientific questions are independent, a reinterpretation of reality often means a change in the *questions* which are asked, and these, the questions, are socially or culturally determined.[40] By discovering mathematical inconsistencies which cannot be explained away in the theory representing the established vision of reality, the scientist may reach by pure logic new visions of reality ahead of those held by his society, but these may still be accepted by the

---

39.   *Vide* Ch. 1, footnote no. 11.

40.   This is perhaps the view of Karl R. Popper. *Vide Objective Knowledge.*

society which had posed the question he had sought to answer to begin with. Either way, whether or not the scientist can reach further than the limits of his place and time, his social perception, his explanations must always remain within the range of human sensuous experience for beyond this lies but obscurity and not science. This was the essence of the objection to metaphysics. Newton's science was not devoid of metaphysical assumptions, for example his perception of an orderly universe. What he objected to was the acceptance of hypotheses which could neither be tested experimentally nor mathematically proven. The scientist can be likened to a man shining the narrow light-beam of an electric torch ahead of him through the dark of night. The direction in which the beam of light is cast may well have been determined by the simple fact that the man was facing that way before the light turned on, i.e. by 'history'; or it may have been determined in anticipation or expectation of something, for example in response to some sound which attracted the man's attention in a certain direction, i.e. 'teleologically'. The objects with which he is best familiar, and which are closest in the beam of light, he can identify; those less familiar and further off may pose some problems; the unknown and least illuminated remain in the realm of more or less inspired imagination. He also knows of more things in the illuminated space; things of whose existence he has only indirect knowledge, things not sensually perceptive but evident to his senses in their effects, – in their manifestations, such as magnetic fields, radio waves, light particles, which most ingeniously he vests in familiar attire. The test of their reality, of their true existence, lies in experimentation, i.e. in acting upon the assumption that they exist, and observing whether or not the results of the actions suit the expectations. If and when they do, it will confirm the scientist's image of reality, though, other people in other times and places may find different, and perhaps equally suitable explanations for the observed events and facts. But even the most 'transcendent' cognition of reality remains limited to man's socio-cultural experience. As Einstein pointed out, there never is, nor can there be in the act of observation a fact or an event, and an observer, but it is always a joining of both.

In a medieval world where man was born into his social status, and when social mobility and economic advancement were practically unthinkable, static stability, immutability, was man's conception of the order of the world. The rising bourgeoisie brought with it the image of social mobility, of change, and the old conceptions in the natural sciences lost ground to a new principle of 'uniformitarian change'. The bourgeoisie not only viewed change as the very nature of existence but also attributed it direction. 'A world in which a man could rise from humble origins must have seemed, to him at least, a good world. Change per se was moral quality;'[41] – was progress. But if ordered change was nature, the question of its *causes* needed to be answered. The concept of cause and effect was reinterpreted to mean *mechanisms* responsible for things ordered and events following a steady sequence – a conception which did not remain confined to its social origins.[42]

The process may be illustrated by the following example. The world of the Almagest, Ptolemy's perception of a finite world contained in the sphere of the fixed stars, with the earth stationary at its center, and the sun and other heavenly bodies revolving about it in their orbs like 'jewels in their fixed mountings', was giving way to a new perception of the universe. In fact the whole Aristotelian notion that vested things with almost human wills – with an inherent striving to reach perfection in their 'natural' resting places, ('earthy' things at the center of the earth and 'airy' things up in high heaven) was crumbling. It was replaced by a world of motion. But stripped of their innate nature, events were losing their self-evidence and began requiring new types of explanations. As long as people could believe that the earth was resting stationary in the middle of the universe and all could plainly *see* that this was so, for apples were invariably falling down not up, the old conception of the universe was too obvious to call for explanations. But what about an earth in motion, an earth spinning round the sun? In such a world things are no longer obvious, no more confirmed by man's everyday experience: for with the earth rotating, stones thrown up into the air

41.   *Ibid.*

42.   Questions concerning the mechanisms responsible for change crept in. It becomes a mechanism of causes and events, of things ordered, and of events following a steady sequence of before and after.

or apples falling from high trees would hardly be expected to fall down vertically, they would rather be expected to 'be left behind', and the air would have to turn into a terrible hurricane perpetually blowing from east to west. Such a world, no longer obvious, requires explanations. Copernicus had an explanation: stones, birds, clouds, the air and even fire participate quite naturally in the motion of the earth and are carried along with it, i.e. though things falling and rising undergo a mixed motion with rectilinear and circular components, they only appear to move perpendicularly when seen from the moving earth.[43] After all a stone dropped from the mast of a moving ship drops to the bottom of the mast and not into the ship's wake.[44] The point is the change in the questions: medieval people asked why things persisted in motion when no visible force continued moving them – why a stone continued in flight after leaving the stone-thrower's hand – why does it not directly drop to earth? – But now in a world of movement, not only why the stone persists in flight, but, why it does not continue doing so infinitely becomes the problem. Thus, by having things stripped of their *innate natures*, – of their 'striving' either to the center of the earth or towards heaven, – and by turning them into inanimate matter which continues in its existing state of rest or uniform motion in straight line unless that state is changed by an *external force*, man's age old vision of the universe was deprived of its directness. Henceforth man could no longer trust the evidence of his eyes: for what seemed firmly stationary like the earth he stood on proved to be in perpetual motion, and what seemed in motion like the sun might well be stationary. Reality was placed beyond man's immediate sensory perception, it could only be observed from the 'outside' – events ceased to be self-evident, – they had to be explained by reason, and their explanations had to be proven true to reason. To reason, not to authority, for the new perceptions of reality had also cast a shadow on the time honored authorities. Try as they may to reconcile their

---

43.   A. Koyre in Rene Taton (ed.), *A General History of the Sciences*, Vol. II, (English translation) London, 1964, p. 65.

44.   Digges' *Descriptions*. Quoted here from R. Taton, *op.cit*, p. 68.

views with those of old, neither Luther nor Galileo could in the end avoid the confrontation with authority. 'Yet it does move' *'E pur si mouve'* were the words attributed to Galileo, and 'Here I stand, I cannot do otherwise,' *'Hier stehe ich, ich kann nicht anders.'* said Luther at the Diet of Worms in 1521. The world of authority and of scholastic logic was challenged by the world of facts, and in the world of facts truth could only be established by experimentation. The world was still orderly, indeed its regularity could even better be expressed in mathematical terms than that of a world at rest, – the orbit of each planet is an ellipse of which the sun's center is one of the foci, the radius vector of each planet (the line joining its center with that of the sun) moves over equal areas in equal times, and the square of the period of each planet's revolution around the sun is proportional to the cube of its mean distance from the sun,[45] but, this regularity was regularity in motion.

To be sure, change was not a new experience. For centuries man had found regularity in changing events, had known the unerring movements of the planets from which he could calculate with certainty both backward and forward the time of the last past and the next coming eclipse of the sun and the moon; had watched days follow nights and nights follow days; had seen nature's ever-recurring life-cycle; learned that the seed planted in the earth grows into a tree; the wind blowing into sails moves ships, and that stones rubbed together make fire, – and it had all confirmed his belief in God's grand orderly design of events running in a steady sequence of *before* and *after.* But while an immobile society sought for the immobile, eternally fixed, order in these motions, a society in motion with its new vision of the universe, sought explanations for this sequence of before and after, and found them in causal mechanisms.

The concept of *time* did also not escape change. In fact the concept of time is necessarily related to change: it either relates to sequence, i.e. to the order of changes, or to duration, i.e. to the period that elapses between changes. Hence it is the interconnection of *order* and *duration* that determines the process of change. But

---

45.   Johannes Kepler's (1571–1630) laws of planetary motion.

ancient and medieval farming-societies had little need for very precise measurements of time. For them a 'time' related to events, – to the cosmic cycle (the alternation of the seasons) and the human cycle (the life of men), – sufficed as the expression of duration: 'A time to be born and a time to die, a time to plant, and a time to pluck up that which is planted...'[46] The needs of urban societies are more sophisticated. For them time had to be a system of references, a measurement which could be consciously applied, – a measurement removed from the context of natural events, possessing an abstract division dissociated from immediate human experience.[47] It is not surprising that with the progress of urban life in western Europe developed also the mechanical device that could fulfill precisely this requirement, namely the mechanical clock. The first known mechanical clocks date from the thirteenth century; they were 'weight-driven' i.e. designed for controlling the force of a falling weight.[48] By the middle of the fourteenth century it became usual to divide hours into sixty minutes and minutes into sixty seconds. In the fifteenth century (and possibly earlier) a *recoil spring mechanism* was incorporated in clocks. Springs had of course been in use for a very long time. Primitive people used springs to build traps for catching animals, and less primitive people used them to make catapults and bows to kill each other, but their incorporation in mechanical equipment to aid man in the processes of production dates probably from the thirteenth century. It was then that their significance as stored energy came to light, for example in lathes where they were employed for making the shaft revolve in the restoring direction.[49] But the introduction of the spring mechanism in clocks and watches had a far greater implication for society than all

---

46.   *Ecclesiastes* III.

47.   Jack Goody discusses this aspect of time in detail in *I.E.S.S.*, XVI, pp. 30–41.

48.   H. Alan Lloyd in Ch. Singer, E.J. Holmyard, A.R. Hall & T. Williams, *A History of Technology*, Vol. III, Oxford, 1957, pp. 648 etc.

49.   *Vide* illustration of such lathes from the 13th century in Singer, Holmyard, Hall and Williams, *op.cit*, Vol. III.

its earlier applications for not only did it permit a more detailed organization of time without which an industrial society could hardly have developed, but it provided something like a mechanical model for the operation of the universe.[50] It turned the universe from what in people's conception had appeared to be a pattern into a clockwork moved by a single spring of action which before long was to be identified as gravitation.[51] In time, to become as regular as clockwork, became the bourgeois ideal and to own a watch a definite symbol of achievement.[52] So the wish *for precision* found its way into the bourgeois heritage reinforcing the earlier mentioned trends towards a culture pattern that put great store by high productive responsibility.[53]

Perhaps the most important consequence of the quest for explanations was the appeal to fact rather than authority. The need to verify the explanations led to the linking of rationality with empiricism. The traditional conception of unity and order in nature, and the success of Copernicus, Kepler and others in the sixteenth and seventeenth centuries, to embrace this unity and order in neat mathematical propositions was soon to lead people like Descartes and Newton to believe in the universal power of mathematics, and the world of hierarchies of order and of things endowed with inert 'wills' became a world of mechanisms in which the idea of sequence becomes the central concept of science. The world became a machine and the sequence – before and after – became the God within the machine.[54]

How then did all this affect the value system of society? Although it raised many questions about the formal aspects of tradition and dogmas of religion it hardly touched the basic tenets of morality; it

---

50.   Jack Goody, *op.cit*, pp. 30–41.

51.   *Vide* Dr J. Bronowski, *The Common Sense of Science*, London, 1951.

52.   Jack Goody, *op.cit.*

53.   *Vide* Ch. 4, pp. 90–6.

54.   The metaphor is borrowed from Dr. J. Bronowski's *op.cit.*

rather cleansed them of some of their formalistic distortions. Far from shattering people's belief it reinforced them with new arguments more congruent with the new socio-economic reality. Far from discrediting the belief in God's design upon earth, Newton's law of inverse squares, – his mathematical model of the world's uniform order, – confirmed it. What better proof could there be of a divine hand having designed a so perfectly systematic universe than the discovery of the universality of the law of gravitation? What the new outlook did accomplish was that it liberated the old values, good and right, from their static 'backward-looking' disposition, from their quest for legitimization in old authorities. It gave them a dynamic view that for several generations stimulated their gradual modification in the light of reason.[55]

The value of truth obtained a central position. The rise of the bourgeoisie was accompanied by the gradual realization that the understanding of nature bestows powers to control its forces. The era in which wisdom was sought in books and scholastic global arguments with little attention to detail was coming to an end, and the pursuit of truth became essential for material progress. However, several centuries were still to elapse before the gap separating the scientist explaining the natural phenomena, from the technician dealing with the practical ends of society was to be closed. Only in navigation and industrial chemistry was such a link established before the eighteenth century, in all other fields industrial progress remained in the piecemeal achievements of ingenious craftsmen. The dominance of human and animal efforts and occasionally of wind and water as sources of power, the use of hand tools, and the very limited utilization of metals remained characteristic of economic production throughout the sixteenth and seventeenth centuries. Where the power of the guilds diminished before the rise of new industries, and their insistence upon quality and general modes of conduct waned, their place was taken, especially where quality control was concerned, by the state. The state which by this time was becoming

---

55.   As we shall see in the chapter discussing the disintegration of modern society, it was much later reimposed metamorphosed in the light of expediency as the arbiter of conduct.

increasingly concerned with the safeguarding of the country's economic ascendancy for political purposes.[56]

Other changes that stimulated, and were stimulated by, the growth of towns and the rise of the bourgeoisie, which reflected the rising living standard of the emerging middle classes, were dietary improvements and the greater utilization of new clothing materials. In this context the introduction of new food crops, such as potatoes, maize, rice and oil seed, and the importation of cane-sugar and tobacco, and the new beverages tea, coffee and cocoa were of prime importance; so were the innovations in wool fabrics and the wider use of linen and silk textiles, and later, the mechanization of the metallurgical industry, the spreading use of coal and printing. All these left of course an indelible mark on the bourgeoisie's life style in centuries to come.

Finally mention must be made of the shifting emphasis in the arts that reflected man's new conception of the universe. For example paintings which throughout much of the Middle Ages had mainly reflected the *idea* of things – not their realistic visual perception - became increasingly true to nature. If one compares pictures of the crucifixion from periods before the Renaissance with those painted during or after it this becomes very evident. The early pictures show little more than a symbol, – a man on a cross his face expressionless. Not so later pictures of the crucifixion; then Christ becomes a man his face conveying an emotion either of bliss acknowledging the meaning of his sacrifice the salvation of humanity, or, alternatively, the pain – the convulsions of a tortured body. In time the old themes portrayed also change and assume a distinctly bourgeois character. The pictures show property, the property of the person who commissioned them. For example, nudes take on a facial expression and posture of submission to the spectator-owner of the painting and the background a richly decorated room, palace or park show his affluence. Perspective is added so that the eye of the viewer becomes the center of all that

---

56.   The political purposes of the state are discussed in connection with the spreading of Mercantilist ideas on Chapters 10 en 11.

is visible in the painting. 'The visible world is arranged for the spectator as the universe was once thought to be arranged for God'.[57]

By the seventeenth century scientific method and experimentation gained dominance over men's way of thinking; and reason more than revelation was gradually becoming the arbiter of social values. Religion and the old philosophies still continued to maintain their hold upon the fundamental conceptions of western European societies but their tenets were re-examined in the light of rationality and social cost. The disintegration of the unified Christian Commonwealth and its replacement by nation-states as prime sources of earthly power deprived Rome of her traditional position as interpreter of heavenly social values and substituted the latter by values based on human reason. Before very long this reason began identifying knowledge with *good*. Nature had been shown to be rational, consequently all things rational could be conceived of as nature and therefore good. Theology began to be permeated by reason, and rationalism and Deism taking the place of traditional religion.[58]

All this was also reflected in the economic philosophies of the sixteenth and seventeenth centuries. The various measures which together made up the system that later came to be known as Mercantilism were, at least to begin with, little more than efforts to augment the economic power of the emergent nation-states for political purposes. The state, not the welfare of individuals, was therefore the subject of mercantilist policies. In this sense mercantilism remained well within the medieval tradition of the essentially harmonious society, i.e. of the society in which the vertical links of allegiance and identity-of-interest prevail over the horizontal (class) identities, which were in fact just then beginning

---

57.   John Berger, *Ways of Seeing*, London, 1972.

58.   A good example for the permeation of religion by reason by way of an appeal to the rationality of nature can be seen in Dr Bentley's invitation to Newton to lecture on the laws of gravitation as the 'final example of God's design'.

to assume their modern shape.[59] What was new in the mercantilist conception was that it extended the feudal affinities to embrace the much wider social formation of the nation-state. Where in earlier periods mainly the personal nexuses had been predominant, mercantilism was concerned with aggregates, *not* individuals, and it judged the status and rights of individuals by the collective criterion of contribution to the political power of the state. Taking for granted that man's actions are ruled by some kind of universal egoism mercantilist thinkers looked upon governments as corrective agents for channelling the individuals' efforts towards the activities which they regarded most advantageous to the state. Where the pursuit of individuals' private advantages was thought to advance the political power of the state it was encouraged, where not, it was prohibited. Consequently mercantilism maintained that as a rule high profits enhance, and good wages diminish, the 'Public Good', for the former stimulate economic enterprise and production and the latter reduce employment and increase domestic consumption. The logic behind this was both simple to see and most convenient from the bourgeoisie's point of view. It gave the old vices – avarice and parsimony – 'respectability' when practiced by the rich, and retained their opprobrium for the poor. With the *public good* synonymous with strengthening the political power of the state vis-a-vis all other states, the entrepreneurs' 'love of gain' became his merit for it increased trade, and trade, so it was thought, made the difference between rich and poor nations.[60] Not so with working-men's demands for better wages, for workers' higher incomes diminished the volume of exportable goods, and reduced the compulsion to work hard and long for sustenance and deprived the nation of the labor of women and children who might then not be forced to seek employment to

---

59. *Vide* pp. 86–9.

60. Daniel Defoe wrote in 1728, 'Trade is the Wealth of the World; Trade makes the difference as to Rich and Poor, between one Nation and another; Trade nourishes Industry, Industry begets Trade; Trade dispenses the natural Wealth of the World, and Trade raises new Species of Wealth, which Nature knew nothing of; Trade has two Daughters, whose fruitful Progeny in Arts may be said to employ Mankind; namely Manufacture and Navigation.'

supplement the men's insufficient incomes. Hence, that which was desirable in one stratum of society, – the 'love of gain' was evil, nay sinful, in another. There was little new in this dichotomy; it retained the main elements of the medieval notion of hierarchy and status, i.e. the division of duties between the various layers of society, and the medieval failure to recognize the money-value of labor services. Far from seeking a confrontation with tradition the rising bourgeoisie sought and found a place fitting its newly acquired economic power within it. The nation-state that was replacing the feudal lord as the focus of social identity afforded it the opportunity to do so. By the substitution of the new collective concept, – the nation-state, for the old feudal idea of association, and the circumscription of the limits of individuals' rapacity to what was deemed to be desirable from the new collective's point of view – the public good, the acquisition of wealth was rapidly becoming a symbol of social distinction. It introduced the bourgeoisie into the old hierarchy at a level below the aristocracy but well above the laboring classes'.[61] Yet, with the social hegemony still firmly in the hands of the aristocracy, the bourgeoisie could hardly avoid being influenced by certain aspects of the aristocratic value system. Thus it felt the need to justify its actions in terms that gave them at least an appearance of traditional respectability. The rapacious exploits of the merchants venturing to distant heathen lands, and the most terrible atrocities performed upon the natives there, were therefore invariably explained and justified at home in terms of service in the public cause, or 'crusades', holy missions, to spread christianity throughout the world. In this way the search for status gave rise to what in retrospect appears to be a paradox, that precisely the rich merchants, the people who were objectively in the very forefront of the trend amending the traditional socio-economic value system, were also its most ardent followers abroad (in the colonies), and the people most anxious to imitate the aristocratic life-style at home. Perhaps the most revealing example illustrating this simultaneous

61.   The term laboring classes is used here in the contemporary sense for people who 'soil their hands by labor' as distinct from those who set them to work and 'those who fight' and 'those who pray.'

rejection and retention of traditional values, and their strange subversion without breaking them, can be observed in what happened to the christian idea of *compassion*. Far from discarding this abstract conception of brotherly love – that is *compassion,* the bourgeoisie gave it a concrete meaning, namely, *charity.* So what had once been an essentially democratic view, implying participation, – sharing the human lot in adversity, was converted into something very different implying a division of society, a distinction between classes, a separation of the christian community into those capable of giving and those only capable of receiving charitable assistance. By implication the lower classes were thus denied a *right* to the fruits of their labor, and the middle classes reinforced in their consciousness of holding an elevated status in society. Christian ethic remained intact but it became subservient, probably without people even being aware of it, to the needs of the rising bourgeoisie. What to a later age must look like sheer hypocrisy was not, and could not have been, regarded as such by a society accustomed to hierarchy and to the medieval conception of social order. The modern European reader accustomed to egalitarian ideas may find it difficult to reconcile the contradiction in the behavior of the middle class which on the one hand wished to emulate an idealized aristocratic life-style, and on the other found little reprehensible in the merciless ravaging of foreign peoples and the ruthless exploitation of their own country's working-class. Yet for contemporaries in the sixteenth and seventeenth centuries there was nothing to reconcile; they were simply unaware of any contradiction, for the contradiction arises out of a belief in the equality of man which had never really been part of the western European cultural heritage, at least where 'life on earth' was concerned. The difference between the modern European reader and a great many people in Asia and Africa has to be stressed here, because people accustomed to a Caste system do not really share the egalitarian conception.[62]

---

62. It is this aspect of society that more than anything else tends to alienate young European development assistance helpers from the people they are trying to aid in underdeveloped countries

Throughout ancient history slavery was a constant factor in the social and economic life of Europe. Greek political philosophy discussed slavery but the only question asked was whether it was a man-made institution or was based upon natural law. It was an accepted fact of life involving no moral problem. Perhaps only Hittites and Hebrews regarded slaves as human beings rather than chattel in the ancient world. In Roman times slavery was considerably brutalized by the spreading of the system of slave-gang farming. During the long periods of war, when most Italian farmers were engaged in military service, the labor shortage was made good on the growing latifundia by such slave-gangs recruited from the captives who after each war were sold into slavery. It was then that slaves became but 'speaking instruments'. In the empire and with the establishment of the *Pax Romana,* the supply of cheap slaves diminished and a gradual return to tenantry and share-cropping ensued. The increase in slave marriages and the rearing of house born slaves that accompanied the decline in the supply of slaves also exerted a humanizing influence upon the master to slaves relationship. Yet neither stoicism nor Christianity were opposed to the *institution* of slavery, for they accepted the prevalent socio-economic order. They advocated humane treatment of slaves but they did not oppose the institution.[63] However, with the exception of the two centuries of Roman wars of conquest, there was in fact on little difference between free and slave labor on the land. Both worked side by side and were subjected to the same treatment by their 'betters'. Nor was there a difference in wages or incomes. Between the tenth and the fourteenth century slavery almost disappeared from western-Europe and was replaced by serfdom which was economically better suited for the non-commercial type of agriculture of the period. Towards the end of the middle ages, probably due to the new flood of captives, and refugees, from the Eastern wars, slavery revived in Europe; but the new slaves were mainly 'heathens' and 'Foes of Christ'. Serfdom, then, that replaced

---

63.   Christianity was concerned with the spiritual destination of mankind, not with earthly matters, and in the life hereafter people were not placed by their social status on earth but by their conduct in that status.

free and slave labor, was actually a type of hereditary half free existence combined with peasant tenure. Particularly where Feudalism was imposed upon societies by conquest this tended to 'simplify' the socio-legal structure of the peasant classes at the expense of its more privileged members. In England, for example, the Normans practically eliminated the alodium and reduced most free villeins to serfdom giving the manorial lord a firm grip on local jurisdiction. Yet, altogether, the lords' exactions were usually less arbitrary than customary even when they clearly infringed upon peasants rights. What remained of class differentiation among peasants was mainly based upon the fact that those above the status of serfs were exempted from certain particular servile dues, – such as the inability to give a daughter in marriage without the lord's consent. In theory a free peasant could also in certain cases take the lord to court, which a serf could not do, but in practice he would hardly take advantage of this right. Firstly, because he rarely had the funds and opportunity to do so, and secondly, because he stood little chance of getting justice. Altogether it can therefore be said that the assimilation of slave to free labor somewhat raised the position of the former and reduced that of the latter. Consequently it created a common attitude by the upper strata of society to all engaged in manual work, reducing them to something less than people with full human capabilities. The way of life into which the economic conditions forced the working people, and which visibly distinguished them from their 'betters', further helped to reinforce this impression.[64] Having extricated themselves from a way of life imposed by poverty the bourgeoisie was ill disposed to change the order of the world. Their affluence was proof that socio-economic advancement was possible. The 'best' people took advantage of this opportunity, those who did not were not, and did not deserve to be

---

64. It is a common tendency for people in all times to judge other peoples' behavior by their own standards rather than by those of the people upon whom judgement is passed. For example, an African building worker who spends his money on hard drink rather than saving it is considered by non-Africans silly. But from his own point of view it would be more silly to save because at the level of his earnings a life time of saving cannot alter his situation – a good drink, however, can make him happy for a while.

numbered among the best people. So, society continued to be divided between the people who 'mattered' and the people who did not matter: the former were expected to live by a set of rules both inherited and self-imposed that met the needs of a trading community, the latter continued to live by the rules of religion and medieval custom. The former were encouraged to economic activity by the promise of good profits and the latter by the cold fear of starvation; the former saved and invested and thereby created the material basis for the industrial society which was to follow, and the latter paid the bill for it by their enforced low standard of living.

Much of this was reflected in Mercantilist theory. Mercantilist theory was a collection of a great number of recommendations for regulating the economy of the state and for institutions to suit this purpose which only in their totality and in retrospect may be called a theory. These recommendations included a system of taxes and penalties for the discouragement of economic activities that were considered not conducive to the 'public good', and, of course, 'liberties' and bonuses for activities that were thought to promote it. By influencing costs and prices these measures did indeed allocate resources and produced something approaching fiscal and monetary measures of economic control. On occasions Mercantilists even went as far as suggesting that the state should take a direct active part in setting-up and supporting existing enterprises which were either too costly or too risky for private entrepreneurs but were deemed crucial from what was considered by them the public good. In this way they successfully harnessed the state to improvements in the land and water transport system and to the protection of colonial ventures. Finally they also played an important role in stimulating the creation of financial institutions and Joint Stock company legislation which were essential to the process of capital concentration for investment at the scale required for the new types of industrial production. Praising the traditional virtues of austerity, for the less religious purpose of capital accumulation and investment, mercantilists further enhanced the tendencies mentioned before in connection with the spreading of a Calvinist mentality regarding economic affairs. They believed that austerity led to saving, saving to a good supply of funds, the good supply of funds to low interest-rates, low interest-rates to increased borrowing, and increased borrowing to more investment and production, and consequently to more power for the state.[65]

By the middle of the eighteenth century Mercantilist ideas concerning labor were changing appreciably. Partly this was probably directly due to the relative labor shortage in the first half of the eighteenth century that made for at least some types of work low wages impracticable, and partly it was due to the technological progress, which may well have also been stimulated by the same labor shortage and that required a somewhat better educated type of labor. In fact the first technological improvements of the early eighteenth century already divided the labor force into skilled and unskilled workers and thus left a profound mark on society's attitudes to labor. The more the number of skilled jobs and workers increased and the greater the shortage of skilled labor the more they began to 'matter', both as consumers and as members of society. On the one hand this stimulated important changes in the structure of production, i.e. it stimulated the production of cheap consumer goods for the domestic market; and on the other hand it reinforced the tendency inherited from the guilds that skill and productive excellence give social status.[66] Mercantilists did of course try to mitigate the effects of the shortage in skilled workers by attracting skilled immigrants from other countries and by training the 'poor' in the new types of employment where this was possible, i.e. in the new trades which were not controlled by the guilds, but on the whole this was of little effect. Skilled labor had at least in some periods to be well remunerated.[67]

But although this retrospectively called mercantilist theory seems to be no more than a collection of ideas derived from changing social circumstances, it reflected also the emerging new perception of a world in motion – the mechanistic world view. Perhaps the best

---

65. For a good discussion of Mercantilism *vide* Eli F. Heckscher, *Mercantilism*, 1931.

66. For growth of towns and the rise of domestic markets *vide* Y.S. Brenner, *A Short History of Economic Progress*, pp. 21–31.

67. For the rise of skilled labor *vide* Ch. 6.

example for this was the way it combined the virtue of thrift with the quest for profit in a kind of economic dynamics in which money played a central role. In 1628 Harvey described the circulation of blood in the human body. Soon after this mercantilists described the flow of business activity in similar terms. The rate of interest was given the place of the heart that pumps the money now substituting for the blood through the body. If money reached the system in adequate supply it would be pumped by low interest rates into the veins of business enterprise and stimulate all agents of production. Once these were fully employed more labor and raw materials would be attracted from outside, sales and profits increased. Profits in turn would keep interest rates low and stimulate the whole process again at a higher scale of output. So, as long as sufficient money is pumped through the veins of business by low interest rates all agents of production would be stimulated but when interest rates should rise, the flow of money diminishes and the economic system is adversely influenced and suffers.

Altogether then, by the middle of the eighteenth century, reason had taken the place of revelation, and expediency was gradually beginning to replace religious and traditional morality as the criterion by which the deeds of men were judged. Two more centuries were to pass before expediency's ominous fruit − the death of such old values as truth − was to jeopardize the future of mankind.

5

The World Begins to Move:
Reformation to the Age of Reason

'E pur si muove' – Yet it does move.
Galileo Galilei 1564–1642.

Weakened by Wiclifite, Hussite and even earlier rebellions, blemished by the Babylonian Captivity and the Great Schism, its prestige marred by corruption and worldliness, and shaken by the critical scholarship of Erasmus and others, Rome's hegemony over the minds and morals of men did not survive the onslaught of the rising nation states, capitalist economies, and growing middle classes which felt restrained by it. So the seventeenth century became the era when the champions of Reason and the champions of Religion were confronting each other fighting desperately for the possession of men's souls in a contest at which the whole of thoughtful Europe was looking on. 'What men craved to know was what they were to believe, and what they were not to believe. Was tradition still to command their allegiance, or was it to go by the board? Were they to continue plodding along the same old road, trusting to the same old guides, or were they to obey new leaders who bade them turn their backs on all those outworn things, and follow them to other

121

lands of promise?'[1] For generations the Church had held out the promise that goodwill justice and brotherly love should also reign on earth, – it never happened. Now that men, at least some men, found that by their own effort they could make life on earth less unpleasant, nay even pleasant, for themselves, old happiness-promising credos were losing their attraction and new beliefs took their places: the belief in a world in which God played the role of an architect who by a single act of creation had made the universe according to some orderly principles and then abandoned it to run its course. By this God was banished to remote heaven, and with no more God to harness the forces of nature for mankind, man had to harness them himself and this he trusted he could do with science. Even in the eighteenth century religion continued to hold the key to the life hereafter for those who chose to believe in such a life, but the key to human happiness in *this* life, 'upon this bank and shoal of time' was *science*.

'Nature and Nature's Laws lay hid in night;
God said 'Let Newton be!' and all was light.'[2]

So *truth* and *order* are raised to a newly elevated position in the scale of social values. For what is science but 'a branch of study which is concerned either with a connected body of demonstrated *truth* or with observed facts *systematically classified* and more or less colligated by being brought under general laws, and which includes trustworthy methods for the discovery of new truth within its own domain.' (1725)[3] But scientific truth is accessible to all, not only to its initiated clergy, for it is tested in the light of reason – everyman's reason; it must never be taken on trust like revelation, it needs to be examined and re-examined in order to be cleansed of

---

1.   Pierre Bayle. Quoted here from Paul Hazard, *The European Mind 1680–1715*, Paris, 1935. J. Lewis May translation. Penguin Books, Harmondsworth, 1964, p. 9.

2.   Alexander Pope (1688–1744) Epitaph intended for Isaac Newton.

3.   *Shorter Oxford Dictionary*, Science, 4, 1725.

non-truth. Its establishment requires doubt, even the expression of possibly wrong ideas, for it is only the confrontation with non-truth that can confirm its trustworthiness, and it is only doubt that can stimulate the search for new and better truth – for a superior understanding of the laws and regularity of nature. Together with truth and order the right to doubt and freedom of expression became part of the new life-style. This was the essence of the Enlightenment as a social movement. But in the seventeenth century the rise of reason was not yet divorced from theology. Rather, theology was *naturalized.* If there is a God, then the order recognizable in nature is final evidence of His existence, and it is this order – this natural law – which man must discover, and in accord with which he must form his own social laws, with which he has to live in harmony, if he wishes to attain earthly happiness. However, for making *nature* the guide to proper human conduct people had to believe that there were things that were *naturally* right, – intrinsically *good* by nature. To be sure, there was little new in this conception. Plato had asserted that there were some things which were right by nature. So did Aristotle when he spoke of the unchangeable law common to all men, though it is not clear whether he thought that this law was intrinsically founded in nature or simply admitted generally by all men. For Cicero there was a law of nature arising equally from God's providential government and from the rational and social character of man. In his own words: 'There is in fact a true law – namely, right reason – which is in accordance with nature, applies to all men, and is unchangeable and eternal.'[4] Moreover, by this eternal law all men are equal for 'out of all... the philosophers' discussions, surely there comes nothing more valuable than the full realization that we are born for justice, and that right is based not upon man's opinions, but upon Nature.'[5] The Fathers of the Church too believed in human equality and in an absolute set of values but they made God, and God alone, their source. Thomas Aquinas incorporated the Aristotelian idea about the natural law in a

---

4.   Cicero, *Republic* III, 22. Sabine and Smith translation.

5.   Cicero, *Laws I*, C.W. Keyes translation, pp. 28–9.

hierarchical system in which God's eternal law becomes *the* basis and foundation and this Natural Law is the basis for the Human Law. The last, i.e. the Human Law, is necessary for making the Natural Law more convenient for the solution of problems arising out of the specific circumstances of humans living in society. However, by the middle of the fifteenth century the idea of the equality of man assumed a new form in a new context, – that of the emerging middle class. It asserted a natural freedom for all members of society.[6] And one century later, when the *Vindiciae Contra Tyrannos* was published in 1579, the right to property had also become part of man's heritage by nature, because 'every man loves and cherishes his own', though the argument underlying this right had not yet become utilitarian. In the seventeenth century the conception of natural rights and Natural Law became, or rather commenced to become, secularized. The revived interest in Stoicism, Platonism and the new understanding of Aristotle brought with it a kind of naturalism and rationalism that was suitable for filling the gap left open by the decline in religious authority. This tendency found strong support in the conspicuous advances made in mathematics and the physical sciences which seemed to indicate that the world was not beyond human comprehension, indeed that it could be explained by logical deduction and by mathematical reasoning. Social phenomena too began to be conceived as natural occurrences open to study by observation and more especially by logical analysis in which revelation or any other supernatural element had no important place. Grotius (1583–1645) formulated these ideas as follows: 'The law of nature is a dictate of right reason, which points out that an act, according as it is or is not in conformity with rational nature, has in it a quality of moral baseness or moral necessity; and that, in consequence, such an act is either forbidden or enjoined by the author of nature, God.'[7] But God, here, as Grotius himself pointed out, implies nothing in the way of traditional

---

6.   *De Concordantia Catholica* presented to the Council of Basle in 1433.

7.   *De jure belli ac pacis* (1625) Translation F.W. Kelsey, Oxford, 1925, Bk. I, Ch. i.

sanction. For the law of nature would enjoin exactly the same if, by hypothesis, there were no God. 'Just as even God... cannot cause that two times two should not make four, so He cannot cause that which is intrinsically evil be not evil'.[8] In other words, there is nothing arbitrary in a natural law discovered by the human mind, any more than there is in a discovery in mathematics. The dictates of right reason are whatever the nature of things imply that they must be. And the human mind is capable of both discovering basic principles and deducing their implications by reason. So Grotius filled the gap left open by the demise of the religious dogmas by a number of *a priori,* apparently self-evident, propositions not unlike axioms in mathematics.

Francis Bacon, (1561–1625) a contemporary of Grotius best known for contributing to philosophy the inductive method of modern experimental science, did not find it necessary to discuss how first principles were established. For him the source of philosophic ideas was *sensuous perception,* and religious ideas *divine inspiration.* Once first principles are accepted, both in philosophy and in religion, he held it possible to draw from them logical conclusions. The difference between religious and philosophical first principles, according to him, was only this: – The former stand firm by virtue of their divine authorization, whereas the latter continue to be subjected to critical inductive examination. The world is uniform, and the inductive method, i.e. the organization of observations according to some ordering principle – around some provisional hypotheses, is valid for all sciences in spite of their separation into different branches ranging from astronomy to ethics. Man too is drawn simultaneously by the all-pervading-force of the whole, which is the general good, and the partial-force, which is the good of the individual. Ethics combines the two in harmony. Uniformity and order are still the key to Bacon's world, but so is the freedom to doubt and err – 'citus *emergit veritas ex errore quam ex confusione',* truth is easier sorted out from error than from a mixed up collection of observations. The most important thing, however, that makes the work of Bacon, in retrospect, so very interesting was its permeation

8.   *Ibid,* Bk. I, Ch. i, sect. x, 5.

by the idea that the careful analysis of the regularities in nature can give man a certain degree of mastery over it – *that man can use nature for his own purposes.* Moreover, his works implied a sense of progress – the recognition that science may provide man with a new source of worldly happiness.

Most important, however, for the new way of thinking was, of course, Galileo (1565–1642). He not only substituted an earth in motion for the earth at rest, and the idea of experimentation for scholasticism and authority, but also developed a conception of reality that was no longer reconcilable with the traditional unity between theology, science and ethics. In fact, his controversy with Aristotle's ideas, his refusal to recant the affirmation of the supremacy of *truth*, displayed a rejection of the mastery of theology over science.

Perhaps no less than the discoveries themselves it was the way by which Galileo reached them, and the way in which he presented them, and made them public, which implied the rejection of what was held right and proper until then. Claiming that the earth revolves around the sun and is not the center of the universe, is one thing, but founding such a claim upon the evidence of observations – his own observations, is something else. It implies that *seeing is* better than *believing;* that ancient usage does not necessarily bestow on statements the quality of superior truth; that nature is not concealed by mysteries comprehensible alone to the initiated few, but that it can be grasped by reason – everybody's reason, just as the observable can be observed by anybody who dares or bothers to look. As if to underline this he wrote *Italian* – not latin, and did not vest his views with some scholastic covering to reconcile them with the old authorities. Copernicus had been content to do so: he pronounced his views as 'hypotheses', but for Galileo the truth was too obvious to be disguised in such a manner. So, whether or not his works on gravitation and motion in fact anticipated Newton's first and second laws is far less relevant than his demystification of nature and reality which provided those who followed with the opportunity to combine observation with logic – experimentation with mathematical analysis. To be sure, by claiming that the Book of Nature was written in the language of mathematics, he not only broke with Aristotle's verbal-logic but substituted for it a new type of rationalism which fitted the needs of an experimental method for establishing truth, and that well suited the temper of a commercialized society.[9]

In the sixteenth century the multiplicity of medieval feudal political formations was replaced by the sovereignty of kings – by the absolutism that seemed to provide stability and order where there had been none before. In the words of Machiavelli, 'the only way to establish any kind of order there is to found a monarchical government'. In the seventeenth century this absolutism had to be based on new foundations. It had to be stripped of much of its medieval heritage – its supernatural attributes and divine rights and hierarchies, to fit the worldly needs of a rising merchant class. What the bourgeoisie required was the maintenance of a social order consonant with human intelligence; an order that imposed upon people 'the abstaining from that which is another's, the restoration to another of anything of his... together with any gain which may have been received from it, the obligation to fulfil promises, the making good of a loss incurred to one by another's fault, and the inflicting of penalties upon men according to their deserts'.[10] In short, the morality required by the rising bourgeoisie was a rational system for the protection of individuals and of their property. What the bourgeoisie needed was the supremacy of the rule of law over arbitrariness – the dominance of law to take the place of religious dogmas as the standard for correct behavior. This was the ground on which the law of nature grew – a law of nature that without mystical attributes had to be founded on reason and some basic tenets that to the rising bourgeoisie appeared to be self-evident, such as the right

---

9.   The *'Discorsi e Dimonstrazioni Matematiche in torno a due nouve scienza'* was, significantly, written in 1634 and printed by Elzevirs in Leiden in 1638. Symbolically perhaps, he died in the year Newton was born, and was born in the year Michelangelo died. (It would of course be more symbolic if it had been Leonardo who died that year). On June 21st, 1633, Galileo was sentenced to prison for having 'held and taught the Copernican doctrine' a sentence which was commuted to the house arrest which actually lasted for the remaining eight years of his life.

10.   Grotius, *Prolegomena*, sect. vi.

to self-preservation which implied the right to the preservation of one's property. However, the expansive nature of the bourgeoisie, its widening economic sphere of interest, also required the safeguarding of collective interests. It required a harmonization of individual with public needs. It required an understanding of the complex relationships, or the orderly ranking of individuals as part of a collective upon whose safety the assertion of the right to self-preservation depended. For it was the political power of the state, of the collective, that determined, for example, the individual merchant's ability to trade in foreign lands – an ability interpreted as his right to self-preservation. The state thus became not only the instrument of public order, the tool by which the law of nature was protected, but was given a dynamic function; namely the promotion of the collective interest – the public good. The validity of the laws imposed by the state could therefore be tested by reason, according to whether they did or did not fulfill their function, whether the public good did or did not conform with the first self-evident principle of nature, namely the right to self-preservation. Thus reason was transformed from a natural capacity of an individual's willed-thought, into a universal 'will' – the collective reason embodied in the mercantilist state.

Formerly people had trusted in the laws of God, now they were turning to the laws of nature. Formerly they had lived contentedly enough in a world composed of unequal social ranking, now they became absorbed in a dream of social equality. They made man's self-interest the center of their social conception, and 'disdainful of history and even of a patient study of the contemporary world, they too easily believed that they had ascertained *a priory* absolute laws, to which they ascribed a universality of application matched only by the simplicity of the underlying principles'.[11] With Luther moral values were still divine commandments suiting an image of human nature corrupted by the original sin – of an *individual* inherently corrupted by desires which are eternally subversive to the will of God. With Calvin too the moral values are divine commands defying human understanding, but they are separated from the secular rules

---

11.   G. Wenlersse, *E.S.S.*, Vol. V, pp. 348–51, 'Economics' (Physiocrats).

that regulate man's economic relations.[12] It were these secular relations which were breaking up the vertical (feudal) ties of society, and opened the way for new horizontal (class) ties which were beginning to develop; the hierarchical community of interests was being replaced by individual nexuses of mutual interest; status yielded to contractual agreement, – agreement between individuals who stand *alone* in society and alone before their creator. The desires or impulses of the individuals are still fundamentally corrupt but whether or not the individual succumbs to them is becoming a matter of choice – of the individual's choice. In the same way as men were becoming accustomed to forge their own worldly fortunes by making choices, i.e. by weighing the chances to gain profit or suffer loss, in their secular transactions so they begin visualizing that same freedom of choice in their relationship with God about the world hereafter. Henceforth morals cease to be imposed from 'above' and 'outside', and instead become subjected to individuals' decisions which are taken in the light of their likely consequences. Step by step the world of predestination becomes a world of causes and predictable effects. As Alasdair MacIntyre aptly observed:[13] 'following the age of Luther and Machiavelli' there comes the rise of 'a kind of moral-cumpolitical theory in which the individual is the ultimate social unit, power the ultimate concern, God an increasingly irrelevant but still inexpungeable being, and a prepolitical, social timeless human nature the background of changing social forms.'

Altogether then the erosion of the mystical interpretation of life in the Renaissance left man with the need to find new sources of security and stability. The dissipation of the traditional hierarchies imposed upon him the search for other types of order – for new uniformities consistent with his new-found purposeful rationality. The demise of the static hierarchical society and its replacement by a society in motion gave rise to the search for laws of dynamic

12. 'Provided that sex is restrained within the bounds of marriage and church-going is enforced, political and economic activity can proceed effectively unchecked by any sanctions whatever'. A. MacIntyre, *A Short History of Ethics*, London, 1967.

13. Alasdair MacIntyre, *A Short History of Ethics*, London, 1967.

causation – for sequences of events. While the sixteenth century had been a century of doubt and rediscovery of forgotten conceptions of man and nature, the seventeenth became the one in which these rediscoveries were systematized in a new way. It became the century in which ideas that had previously pried only vaguely in men's minds received deliberate conscious formulations; formulations upon which systems could be and were constructed that claimed to do away with scholasticism, although Descartes' idea that the application of reason alone led to knowledge of the world was in fact not less *speculative* than scholastic arguments. In fact he gave to it a new form through an unceasing search for an absolute principle of knowledge.[14]

Hobbes and Spinoza followed Decartes in an effort to construct comprehensive systems, but they were more disposed to accept the empirical aspect of the new science. With Leibniz 'the analytical tendency begins once more to assert itself – a transition to the predominant importance which the problem of knowledge and of worth were to exercise in the eighteenth century'.[15] In short, in late sixteenth and early seventeenth century people discovered a world that was not only orderly but also comprehensible. A world created by a divine architect who left it to run its course as a perfect clockwork, according to orderly principles which were comprehensible through mathematics, and consequently mathematics became the key to the understanding of God's design, the key to human understanding of nature. But the new view captured the mind of not only natural philosophers (what we would call today natural scientists), but brought with it a new conception of man by which knowledge became the key to happiness. For happiness came to mean living in harmony with the laws of nature.

Descartes (1596–1650) begins his *Discourse* (1637) with the words 'Good sense is the most evenly shared thing in the world, for each of us thinks he is so well endowed with it that even those who are

---

14.   Descartes' objection was to the scholastic use of logic for new interpretations of authoritative texts instead of using it for creating true knowledge.

15.   *Vide* H. Hoffding, *A History of Modern Philosophy*, Vol. I, London, 1900, quotations here from 1955 edition, p. 209.

the hardest to please in all other respects are not in the habit of wanting more than they have. It is unlikely that everyone is mistaken in this. It indicates rather that the capacity to judge correctly and to distinguish the true from the false, which is properly what one calls common sense or reason, is naturally equal in all men, and consequently that the diversity of our opinions does not spring from some of us being more able to reason than others, but only from our conducting our thoughts along different lines and not examining the same things. For it is not enough to have a good mind, rather the main thing is to apply it well. The greatest souls are capable of the greatest vices as well as of the greatest virtues, and those who go forward only very slowly can progress much further if they always keep to the right path, than those who run and wander off it.'[16] And, to apply one's mind well, according to Descartes, was to follow four basic rules, namely: 'never to accept anything as true that did not know to be evidently so... to divide each of the difficulties... into as many parts as might be possible and necessary in order best to solve it... to conduct... thoughts in an orderly way, beginning with the simplest objects and the easiest to know, in order to climb gradually, as by degrees, as far as the knowledge of the most complex, and even supposing some order among those objects which do not precede each other naturally... And the last, everywhere to make such complete enumerations and such general reviews that nothing is omitted.'[17] This was the chain of reasoning geometers customarily followed when teaching their most difficult demonstrations, and from here Descartes took the idea 'that everything which can be encompassed by man's knowledge is linked in the same way, and that, provided only that one abstains from accepting any for true which is not true, and that one always keeps the right order for one thing to be deduced from that which precedes it, there can be

---

16.   Descartes, *Discourse on Method.* F.E. Sutcliffe translation. Penguin, Harmondsworth, 1968.

17.   *Ibid.*, p. 41.

nothing so distant that one does not reach it eventually, or so hidden that one cannot discover it.'[18]

Here is the image of a universe that is a single whole – a unity analogous to the absolute state; a universe understandable by a single uniform science; a universe that in the minds of men can be reconstructed by the ordered logic of geometry. From sixteenth century skepticism Descartes takes the belief that nothing must be taken as truth unless it is patently self-evident to human understanding, and from the absolute structure of the contemporary mode of government and Galileo's systematic order of the movements of the heavenly bodies, he borrows the conception of the relationship between the central power and the complexity of individual drives. In this relationship he recognizes an inescapable ordering principle which led him to believe that truth is always rational and mathematical. He establishes himself, man, as an absolute *necessary* fact, – 'I think, therefore I am', as a point of departure, like an axiom in mathematics, from which he arrives at an ontological proof for the existence of God and definitions for the existence of the material world and the laws of nature that govern it. By the same necessity, imposed by his starting point, he separates mind from matter making the former abstract and the latter purely mechanistic. So, in Descartes own words, 'by the laws of nature... and the infinite perfection of God,... if God had created many worlds, there could be none in which they (the laws of nature) failed to be observed... most matter of this chaos must, in accordance with these laws, dispose and arrange itself in a certain way which would make it similar to our skies;... some particles must compose an earth, others planets and comets, and still others a sun and fixed stars.'

Yet, perhaps the most symbolic for the break with medieval conceptions was the new meaning Descartes gave to the nature of *causes*. The world of causes and effects which was beginning to replace the world of hierarchies came to mean with him, a world in which effects could be predicted from their causes and causes understood from their effects. He wrote: 'I have tried to find in general the principles or first causes of everything which is, or which

---

18.   *Ibid.*, p. 4.

may be, in the world, without considering to this end anything but
God alone, who has created it, or taking them from any other source
than from certain seeds of truths which are naturally in our minds.
After that, I examined what were the first and most ordinary effects
that could be deduced from these causes, and it seems to me that in
this way I have found heavens, stars, an earth, and even on the earth
water, air, fire, minerals and other similar things, which are the most
common and simplest of all, and consequently the easiest to know...
Following which, turning over in my mind all the objects which had
ever been presented to my senses, I dare to state that I observed
nothing that I could not easily enough explain by means of the
principles I had found. But I must also admit that the power of
nature is so ample and so vast, and that these principles are so
simple and so general, that I observe almost no individual effect
without immediately knowing that it can be deduced in many
different ways, and that my greatest difficulty is ordinarily to find
in which of these ways the effect depends upon them for to this end
I know no other expedient but then to seek certain experiments
which are such that their result will not be the same if it is in one
of these ways that the explanation lies as if it lies in another...'[19]

Altogether then, Descartes believed that he had found a system,
– that the world is everywhere alike, that it was a unity reflected in
the universal applicability of mathematics, that it could be grasped
by general rules. And of man? – All body functions, 'those which
can be in us without our thinking of them, (and therefore without
our soul,... that part distinct from the body ... that its nature is only
to think') resemble those of the animals devoid of reason.[20] Animals
are machines, man has a mind and soul – he is more than a
machine. In other words, in Descartes' opinion, matters of the soul
can remain in the province of religion and science need not touch
them. Therefore, for all his dissidence, and that of the other great
men of the seventeenth century who shared his dualist view, most
things concerning men's everyday existence – the 'thou shalts' and

---

19.   *Ibid.*, pp. 80–1.

20.   *Ibid.*, p. 65.

'thou shalt nots', remained almost unaltered. The *value system* – the notions indicating what was good and right or bad and wrong, were hardly different at all. Nevertheless, the legitimization of these notions changed. What previously had been divine commands became the dictates of good reason. The mind of man replaced the will of God. But once self-evidence is allowed prime of place over truth, the question poses itself what is the meaning of 'self-evidence' if not what society has learned to accept? In childhood people are contaminated with the moral notions of their elders and what has been bequeathed to them in this way continues to be 'self-evident', and all that is self-evident continues to be right. By giving to the value system its new foundations, by making man's mind its source of origin a door was opened through which in the fill of time a new set of values would enter, a set of values more subservient to the pressures of expediency than the medieval firm commitments ever were. But in the seventeenth century such a relativistic conception – where any value can be justified if it only serves a social purpose, was still a thing of the distant future.

Hobbes (1588–1679) independently from Descartes also reached a mechanical conception of nature and a mathematical method of reasoning. According to him, knowledge of geometry was 'the only science that it hath pleased God hitherto to bestow on mankind.' All the rest were mere opinion. To reason philosophically meant to demonstrate the effects of a phenomenon from its known causes or to demonstrate its causes from its known effects. It followed in his opinion, that the explanation of human affairs was as subject to causal laws as any other event. If society imposed upon itself rules and laws for restraining certain impulses of individuals – a demonstrable effect, then the causes of these rules and laws must of necessity be intrinsic to the conditions of humanity before society imposed them upon itself as part of the struggle to assure its self-preservation. Consequently society before it succumbed to the rules and laws *must* have been in a condition of 'continual fear and danger of violent death;' and the life of man must have been 'solitary, poor, nasty, brutish, and short.'[21] Indeed, 'a condition of

---

21.   *Leviathan*, pt. i, Ch. XIII.

war of everyone against everyone.'[22] A conclusion obtained by logic alone, not by patient study of history. A conclusion which follows from his fundamental proposition of self-preservation. It is *human nature* to seek security. It is not the tribal or feudal collective that determines the social characteristics of the individual's values but on the contrary, it is the nature of the individual – the quest for self-preservation, that determines both his own and his society's scale of values. Not God's will but the individual's pursuit of security is the source of the distinction between good and evil in society. Therefore, unlike Machiavelli whose prince is placed above the law, the absolute power of Hobbes's king follows the laws of nature, because human desires had to be subjected to rational rules in order to assure everyman's self preservation and the amenities civilized society can offer. For the world had become one of 'perpetual restless desire' not caused by man's 'hopes for a more intensive delight, than he has already attained to;... but because he cannot assure the power and means to live well, which he hath present, without the acquisition of more.'[23] This was a philosophy that accepted the world and human nature in the way the rising bourgeoisie saw it and not in the way religion suggested that it ought to be. A world in which self-centered men impose upon themselves collective arrangements to preserve themselves individually. So, whatever is done according to reason in the pursuit of this objective is right. But because not all that is reasonable and right is *naturally* binding upon men, what is reasonably right needs to be defined by positive law and it is therefore the last that in final analysis determines society's value system. Yet laws without a power to enforce them are mere words, and 'the bonds of words are too weak to bridle men's ambition, avarice, anger, and other passions, without the fear of some coercive power.'[24] Power thus becomes the sanction of positive law – power that is circumferenced by the basic

---

22. *Leviathan*, pt. i, Ch. IV.

23. *Leviathan*, Ch. XI.

24. *Leviathan*, Ch. XIV.

precepts of self-preservation; and the law itself becomes the new legitimization of the emerging constitutional state *(Rechtsstaat)*.

And again, the conceptions of good and evil were not the first to change. These remained the same but the idea that they could change and were in need of justification by reason was new. In the Middle Ages, and for that matter in economically backward regions of the earth even now, when forces beyond human control seemed or still seem to determine people's fate, experience does not give rise to the question *why.* In a world in which individuals' efforts do in fact determine and are seen to be determining the fate of individuals the questions *why* and *how* come to the foreground and *explanation* is taking the place of mere description. This then was the revolution that in the sixteenth and seventeenth centuries remodeled men's way of thinking. Men searched for explanations and in order to resolve complex problems they adapted scholasticism and the logic of geometricians to serve their purpose. The whole structure of reality was given a logical explanation based upon a single axiom-like proposition namely self-preservation. But Descartes, Hobbes and more then them Spinoza, went even further. They implied that the same structure that in nature has no moral function does hold such a function in society. They implied that the recognition of individuals' own position in society indicates to them the right mode of living. In other words, they held that *understanding* can indicate to people 'how to live' and may therefore lead to rectifications in social arrangements – cognizance holds a *moral perspective.* This, however, does not imply that these philosophers had an evolutionary or historical conception of man. On the contrary, in his view human nature was eternal, the single 'axiomatic' fact in society, only man's social arrangements were mutable and the very power to change these arrangements gave them a moral justification and made them 'right'.

Where Hobbes saw self-preservation, i.e. the negative element avoidance of death, as the point of departure for the study of man in society, Spinoza (1632–1677) saw man's positive aspirations in the attainment of the greater happiness as his point of commencement. Spinoza departed from Descartes by uniting mind and matter into one eternal and indivisible substance, which by necessity exists as it is. Descartes identified God with thought and the external world –

the world observed in space-time, with His creation. But for Spinoza, thought and extension – namely the properties of the world in space-time – were attributes of the same substance. God was both. While his contemporaries, then, conceived of the Laws of Nature as God's design – an intended, or purposeful design – the product of His thought, Spinoza conceived of them as God's own nature.[25] In an appendix to book I of his *Ethics*, Spinoza explains the superstitious character of the religious belief that the world was created for man; that storms, earthquakes and diseases result from God's anger, from his wish to punish human wickedness. The true nature of these, as of all other phenomena, he adds, 'might have lain hidden from the human race through all eternity, had not mathematics, which deals not with the final causes[26] but the essence and properties of things, offered to man another standard of truth'.[27] In reality, Spinoza concludes, there is no purpose in nature. God does not, nay, cannot have any purpose. The notions of good and evil reside in the nature of humanity, not in God.[28] But humanity is part of the same substance, and the laws of human nature are also as inevitable as all nature. 'Nothing happens in nature which can be attributed to a defect of it; for nature is always the same and one everywhere...'[29] Just as thought and matter are united in nature as a whole so is soul and body united in man. The human body can be affected in many ways so as to increase or decrease its natural ability to act. An increase in this ability causes pleasure and a decrease causes pain. All the emotions are kinds of pleasure or pain – a mental state

---

25. *Vide* Spinoza's *Ethics*, Book I. Everyman's Library, Dutton: New York, 1979 edition. In particular see proposition xvi and note to proposition xxxiii.

26. A final cause in the Aristotelian conception of causes is a purpose of an event, while the notion of a cause in the seventeenth century was called, as it is today in that system, an efficient cause.

27. *Ibid.*, p. 32.

28. *Ibid.*, p. 143.

29. *Ibid.*, p. 84.

associated with the change in the body. But each change in a mental state is conceived together with a presumed cause. This is the source of the diversity in most attitudes and opinions, because what a person believes to be the cause of an increase in his power to act according to his nature is usually not the true cause but a belief imposed on him by others. In different words, Spinoza admits the possibility that values are the product of a society: people believe what they have been taught – what elders and teachers imparted to them in a moralizing setting. Thus, if wealth is generally considered to be the cause of pleasure it is taken to be good in that society. Social systems of belief are themselves causally determined. For not only the science of nature can be conceived in terms of causes and effects, as a sequence of events, but also the knowledge of mental states. He differs from the ancients, says Spinoza, in including the occurrence of ideas in one's mind in the mechanistic explanation of all events. The only true power of the mind, he asserts, is to accept or reject such an idea.[30] However, this does not mean that values are arbitrary, or relative to a society. The true good, he explains, is that which can enable a person to attain his perfection.[31] Perfection does not imply a change in one's essential nature, which is impossible. It means the attainment of the full power of this nature.[32] The feeling of pleasure indicates passing from a state more distant from this perfect nature to one closer to it. Hence the true good is the real increase in perfection, and knowledge of the true good can only be acquired by knowledge of the real causes of the emotions which constitute human nature.

A person can attain happiness only by acquiring a deep understanding of himself as part of nature. In Spinoza's opinion man is naturally inclined to seek such knowledge but prevented from this by social pressures. A good society is the one which allows those so inclined to pursue knowledge to do so freely. However, he did not think that such a society is a guarantee to happiness for all.

---

30. *Ibid.*, Spinoza, *Treatise on the Correction of the Understanding*, p. 255.

31. *Ibid.*, p. 230.

32. Spinoza, *Ethics*, p. 143.

Blessedness consists of the love of God – of a passionate inclination for true knowledge by the application of reason, namely by accepting true and rejecting false ideas. The understanding of necessity, then, frees one from futile pursuits of unattainable goals. But if this road to happiness is so close at hand 'how could it be that it is neglected practically by all?' Because, he sadly concludes, 'all excellent things are as difficult as they are rare'.[33]

Spinoza found *order* and *unity* in the wholeness of nature, Leibniz (1646–1716) discovered it in the conception that all things are but different combinations of identical fundamental entities which he named monads. While Hobbes and Spinoza were satisfied with the discovery of 'efficient causes', Leibniz was also searching for final causes, for a moral purpose behind it all – for God's purposeful design or a ghost in the machine. The order and regularity discovered in nature became for him the final proof of divine providence. Thereby he reconciled the new materialistic tendencies in society, and the mechanistic conception of nature that accompanied them, with the still popular traditional, essentially teleological, moral outlook – the discoveries of science became manifestations of a higher moral force and ethical purpose. Man could continue to believe in divine salvation in spite of all the changes that were taking place; and society could continue to hold on to its traditional set of values with but very gradually accumulating amendments. A set of values that had been transmitted for centuries from one generation to the next by mode of conduct and verbal contamination. Leibniz proposes that *force* was an essential property of *substance*. Every monad was a primitive active force. Derived forces (those observed in nature) are modifications of primitive forces. This corresponds to his view that aggregates, namely organisms, which are themselves monads, consist of lower level monads. Hence, 'being and working' is the same. Leibniz accepts the view of his contemporary 'moderns' that everything in nature is motion, but he departs from their views when he examines the causes of motion. In his view the *force* that causes it and which remains constant even when motion itself is not perceptible, lies in

---

33.   *Ibid.*, p. 224.

matter itself. 'I am at a loss,' he wrote to Bouruet in 1714, 'to understand how they can deduce Spinozism from my doctrine. It is precisely by the monads that Spinozism is undone. For there are just as many true substances as... there are monads; while according to Spinoza there is only one single substance.'[34] In fact both Spinoza's and Leibniz's idea of substance implied the attribution of force to matter. But while Spinoza's idea seems similar to the idea of scientists in the twentieth century who attribute to energy the characteristics of both force and matter, or to Einstein's replacement of matter by matter-energy, Leibniz' saw in this the basis for a philosophy that combined a godly purpose with the individual character of the *monads* – with an individual character which could be conceived of as what with human beings is the soul. Every individual becomes a little world of its own developing according to its own laws and by its own force, as a special emanation of the divine force; the cause of the development is the common origin of all things, the harmony of the development of all other beings. God is reinstated into the contemporary scientific outlook, and the lingering christian morality and ethic reconciled with the increasingly materialistic conception of science and the individualistic behavior of the bourgeoisie in their new social reality. The mystery of God is retained and provident men will be wise to hold on to the old moral heritage 'just in case' and not too readily succumb to the logic of bare-faced expedience. Even hierarchy can be retained, though in a new form. For if the world is made of an infinite number of independent units of spiritual force or matter – the monade – the contingent (variable) world which we observe is the result of the fact that God always chooses the best among all possible worlds. Each monad acts by its own inherent urges but God directs them all to a general harmony, just as each trader follows his own interest in harmony with the general objectives of the mercantilist state or trading town.

'God alone,' in the words of Leibniz, 'brings about the union of interconnection of substances, and through Him alone do the phenomena of one man coincide and agree with those of other

---

34.   Quoted here from Hoffding, *op.cit.*, Vol. I, p. 350.

men.'[35] It is the same idea that less than a century later Adam Smith formulated claiming that 'it is the consideration of his own private profit (that) is the sole motive which determines the owner of any capital to employ it either in agriculture, manufactures or some particular branch of trade, but the study of this, his own advantage, leads him to the employment which is most beneficial to all.'[36]

What separated Leibniz's conception from that of Adam Smith was that the former accepted the harmonization of individual drives and general ends as a fact, whereas the latter concerned himself with the *mechanism,* with the laws by which the 'invisible hand' maintains this harmony.

The man who highlights the watershed that separated the interest in the description of the universe from the emerging interest in the *mechanisms* governing its laws of motion was Newton. Copernicus, Kepler and Galileo had seen that the natural state of things in the universe is motion; Descartes, Hobbes, Spinoza and Leibniz showed that the world was orderly and rationally comprehensible; and Newton (1642–1727) introduced the *mechanism* regulating motion by his two laws, namely the law of *inertia* and the law of *gravitation.* The former stating the tendency of a body to persevere in its state of rest or uniform motion in a straight line; and the latter stating that every object in the universe attracts every other object with a force which is directly proportional to the product of the masses of the objects and inversely proportional to the square of the distance between them. What his predecessors had regarded as the identity of God and nature Newton saw as the unity expressed in the likeness between the apple falling from its tree and the rotation of the moon in its orbit round the earth. God was there, but he was less directly involved with the observable events. The world of His will, becomes a world of mechanisms. 'The mechanical conception of Nature founded by Kepler, Galileo and Descartes at once received confirmation and became more comprehensive. The world was now

---

35. *Discourse*, Ch. 32. Quoted here from H. Hoffding, *op.cit*, Vol. I. p. 351.

36. Adam Smith, *An Inquiry into the True Nature and Causes of the Wealth of Nations*, 1776, Bk. IV, Ch. 11.

seen to be a huge machine. Men had, it is true, already had a suspicion that this was the case; but it was only now discovered how the machine was held together.'[37] And yet, even Newton does not abandon the idea of the existence of something *stable* – absolute and permanent, in our universe. There still is something unchanging in the eternally mobile world that surrounds him – absolute time and space. To be sure, in all practical matters man cannot go beyond his sensuous perception of space and time but *in rebus philosophicus,* in abstract, man must be aware of the absolute that he cannot sensuously grasp. For if the law of inertia represents absolute motion, there *must* be absolute time and space, just as there must be an absolute good and bad, right and wrong at the roots of any moral value system. The source of the absolute is God and Newton proves his existence from the 'purposive and harmonious arrangement of the world, and in so doing he starts a theme which received a thousand variations in the course of the eighteenth century.'[38]

---

37.   *Vide* H. Hoffding, *op.cit.,* Vol. I, p. 409. It may also be noted here that Newton introduces a combined deductive and inductive method. He first deduces the consequences of an assumption and then shows that the consequences are confirmed by experience.

38.   H. Hoffding, *op.cit.,* Vol. I, p. 412.

6

The World in Motion:
The Struggle between the Medieval and
the Bourgeois Value Systems

*'These late eclipses in the sun and moon
portent no good to us: though the wisdom of
nature can reason it thus and thus yet, nature
finds itself scourged by the sequent effects:
Love cools, friendship falls off, brothers divide:
in cities, mutinies, in countries discord, in
palaces treason: and the bond cracked twixed
son and father.'*
King Lear. Act 1. Sc.ii. I 15

So, on the one hand the old dogmas continued to exercise their
influence upon men's minds, and on the other, all that had been held
valid or true in the past was subjected to rational examination from
a new point of view, namely the point of view of its demands in
terms of inhibiting man's quest for earthly wealth and greater
comforts. Values previously taken for granted began to be judged by
their worth for man in society. Theologically revealed truth was
supplemented by an appeal to nature and reason; and reason was
taken to be dependent on the evidence of man's senses, i.e. upon

143

observation and confirmation by experience and experiment. God was relegated to the sphere of the unexplainable and man armed with his new tools of measurement became the center of his world – a world known to be orderly and reducible to a mathematical model. The natural became identified with the rational, and the discoveries which culminated in Newton's Laws seemed to set a model for every field of human inquiry. The supremacy of reason challenged the power of faith and tradition; the affirmation of the eternity of the laws of nature defied providence; and together, the supremacy of reason and the demise of providence made man himself the master of his fate. This reflected the new social reality of the rising bourgeoisie which found its affirmation in the Dutch Rebellion, the English Revolution and the Civil War in France. Man seems indeed to have become the economic animal who nevertheless found it prudent to take due precautions to assure his spiritual well-being.

For example: Defoe's (1660–1731) heroes are moved by the values of double-entry bookkeeping and human feelings are allowed to enter only into the interstices left by profitability. The little Moor without whom Crusoe could not have escaped from slavery and whom Crusoe had decided 'to love ever after' is sold into slavery by Crusoe himself for sixty pieces of eight (admittedly with a promise from the purchaser to free the slave after ten years; provided, of course, that he would be converted to Christianity). The wives of the colonists in the Farther Adventures of Robinson Crusoe are assessed wholly in economic terms. In short, as Moll Flanders puts it, 'with money in the pocket one is at home anywhere'. Defoe's conclusion: 'usefulness is the great pleasure, and justly deemed by all good men the truest and noblest end in life, in which men come nearest to the character of our B. Saviour, who went about doing good.'[1] An even better expression of the moral dilemma in which the rising middle class found itself is Jonathan *Swift's* (1667–1745) cynical 'Modest Proposal for Preventing the Children of Ireland from being a Burden to their Parents or Country and for making them beneficial to the Publick'. (1729) Employing Cartesian logic and writing in the style

---

1.   The examples from Defoe are borrowed from A. MacIntyre's *A Short History of Ethics*, London, 1968, p. 151.

of contemporary rationalism, Swift puts forward a perfectly logical preposterous scheme for dealing with poverty, the shadow-side of his increasingly affluent society. The idea that this problem can be solved in a way that, of itself, would also benefit the rich, – which is inherent in the 'Modest Proposal', and the mock-humanism – implying that it is the virtue of compassion that compels the author to make the 'Proposal', demonstrate Swift's keen awareness of both his contemporaries' unshakable trust in the orderly harmony of all things, and the discomfort they must have felt as a result of the predicament in which they found themselves holding on to the Christian heritage of moral values on the one hand, and on the other, following their quest for greater worldly affluence; a predicament which only gradually resolved itself by the transformation of compassion into charity. Beginning with the observation that 'it is a melancholly Object to those, who walk through this great Town or travel in the Country, when they see the Streets, the Roads and Cabin-doors crowded with Beggars of the Female Sex, followed by three, four, or six Children, all in Rags, and importuning every Passenger for Alms...' Swift comes to the following proposal: 'I have been assured by a very knowing American of my acquaintance in London, that a young Child well Nursed is, at a year Old, a most delicious nourishing and wholesome Food, whether Stewed, Roasted, Baked, or Boiled, and I make no doubt that it will equally serve in a Fricasie, or a Ragoust. I do therefore humbly offer it to publick consideration, that of the Hundred and twenty thousand Children, already computed, twenty thousand may be reserved for Breed, whereof only one fourth part to be males; which is more than we allow to Sheep, black Cattle, or Swine;... one Male will be sufficient to serve four Females. That the remaining Hundred thousand may, at a year Old, be offered in Sale to Persons of Quality and Fortune, through the Kingdom; always advising the Mother to let them suck plentifully in the last Month, so as to render them Plump, and Fat, for good Table... I grant this Food will be somewhat dear, and therefore very proper for Landlords; who, as they have already devoured most of the Parents seem to have best Title to the Children. I think the Advantages by the Proposal which I have made are obvious and many, as well as of the highest Importance. For First,... it would greatly lessen the Number of Papists... Secondly,

The poorer Tenants will have something valuable of their own, which by Law may be made Lyable to Distress, and help to pay their Landlord's Rent; their Corn and Cattle being already seized, and money a thing unknown. Thirdly, Whereas the Maintenance of an hundred thousand Children, from two Years old, and upwards cannot be computed at less than Ten Shillings a Piece per Annum, the Nation's Stock will be thereby increased fifty thousand Pounds per Annum; besides the Profit of a new Dish, introduced to the Tables of all Gentlemen of Fortune in the Kingdom, who have any Refinement in Taste; and the Money will circulate among our Selves, the Goods being entirely of our own Growth and Manufacture. Forthly, The constant Breeders, besides the Gain of eight Shillings Sterling per Annum, by the Sale of their Children, will be rid the Charge of maintaining them after the first Year. Fifthly, This Food would likewise bring great Custom to Taverns, where the Vintners will certainly be so prudent as to procure the best Receipts for dressing it to Perfection;... Sixthly, This would be a great Inducement to Marriage... It would increase the Care and Tenderness of Mothers towards their Children,... Men would become as fond of their Wives, during the time of their Pregnancy, as they are now of their Mares in Foal, their Cows in Calf, or Sows when they are ready to farrow; nor offer to beat or kick them (as is too frequent a Practice) for fear of a Miscarriage. Many other Advantages might be enumerated. For Instance, the addition of some thousand Carcasses in our Exportation of Barreled Beef... But this, and many others...' Swift decided to omit for the sake of brevity. He concludes: 'Supposing that one thousand Families in this City, would be constant Customers for Infant's Flesh; besides others who might have it at merry Meetings, particularly at Weddings and Christenings; I compute that Dublin would take off Annually about twenty thousand Carcasses, and the rest of the Kingdom (where probably they will be sold somewhat cheaper) the remaining eighty Thousand. I can think of no one Objection, that will possibly be raised against this proposal;... Therefore let no man talk to me of other Expedients: Of taxing our Absentees at five Shillings a Pound: Of using neither Cloaths, nor Household Furniture, except what is of our own Growth and Manufacture: Of utterly rejecting the materials and Instruments that promote Foreign Luxury: Of curing the Expensiveness of Pride,

Vanity, Idleness, and Gaming in our Women: Of introducing a Vein
of Parsimony, Prudence, and Temperance... Of teaching Landlords
to have at least one Degree of Mercy towards their Tenants. Lastly,
Of putting a Spirit of Honesty, Industry, and Skill into our
Shop-keepers; who, if a Resolution could now be taken to buy only
our Native Goods, would immediately unite to cheat and exact upon
us in the Price, the Measure, and the Goodness; nor could ever yet
be brought to make one fair Proposal of just Dealing, though often
and earnestly invited to it. Therefore, Swift repeats, 'let no Man talk
to me of these and like Expedients; till he hath at least some
Glimpse of Hope, that there will ever be some hearty and sincere
Attempt to put them in Practice... After all, I am not so violently
bent upon my own Opinion, as to reject any Offer proposed by wise
Men, which shall be found equally Innocent, Cheap, Easy, and
Effectual. But before something of that Kind shall be advanced in
Contradiction to my Scheme and offering a better;... I desire those
Politicians, who dislike my Overture, and may perhaps be so bold
to attempt an Answer, that they will first ask the Parents of these
Mortals, Whether they would not, at this Day, think it a great
Happiness to have been sold for Food at a Year Old, in the manner
I prescribe; and thereby have avoided such a perpetual Scene of
Misfortunes, as they have since gone through; by the Oppression of
Landlords; the Impossibility of Paying Rent without Money or Trade;
the Want of common Sustenance, with neither House nor Cloaths to
cover them from the Inclemencies of the Weather; and the most
inevitable Prospect of entailing the like, or greater Miseries, upon
their Breed for ever.' To make sure that no one will suspect him
that he has a personal interest in promoting his scheme, other than
the public good by advancing trade, providing for infants, relieving
the poor, and giving some pleasure to the rich, Swift adds in the
end: 'I have no Children, by which I can propose to get a single
Penny; the youngest being nine Years old, and my Wife past
Child-bearing.'[2]

---

2.   Jonathan Swift is quoted (shortened) here from the Oxford Clarendon edition,
      pp. 84–92.

Swift may not have intended his 'Proposal' to become a critique and exposition of the contradictions in western European culture in the era of the Enlightenment in the manner it is used here. His 'Proposal' was published anonymously among many others, and its purpose may have been to indicate that 'advancing trade, providing for infants, relieving the Poor and giving some pleasure to the Rich' were the only practical solutions to the Irish problem. And yet, the presentation, style, mock-logic of his argumentation, all show that he saw that both the universally assumed harmony in all things and the rigorous Cartesian logic crumble when applied to the handling of the social reality.

The author who deliberately, and most sharply, drove home the cultural dichotomy – the self-centered rationalism on the one hand and the Christian ethic on the other – was Bernard Mandeville (1670–1733). The bourgeoisie did not forgive him his indiscretion even in the twentieth century.[3] In the same vein as Newton's search for *mechanisms* that make for motion and change, Mandeville shows in his fable 'The Grumbling Hive: or Knaves Turned Honest' (1705) and again, in 'The Fable of the Bees: Or Private Vices, Publick Benefits' (1714), that it is precisely the socio-culturally unacceptable that makes a people powerful and wealthy, and precisely the socio-culturally desirable that is its undoing. The message is: civilization thrives on vices. Luxury, pride, greed, envy, self-interest, these are the *mechanisms* by which a nation becomes great, these are the motives that make men exert themselves 'to supply/ Each other's Lust and Vanity'. Here was the corollary to Newton's Law of Gravitation; all bodies attract each other but in man's immediate surroundings things are at rest for the different forces cancel each other out. Make man virtuous, take away his self-centered

---

3.   W.R. Sorley in *The Cambridge History of English Literature* (London, 1912) still cannot help 'grumbling' that Mandeville 'was clever enough to detect the luxury and vice that gather round the industrial system, and perverse enough to mistake them for its foundations'. He reverted to Hobbes's selfish theory of human nature, but was without Hobbes's grasp of the principle of order. He looked upon man as a compound of various passions, governed by each as it comes uppermost, and he held that 'the moral virtues are the political offspring which flattery begot upon pride.'

gravitation, and society will revert to poverty. Like Hobbes, Mandeville believed that by nature man is in a war of everyone against everyone, but he does not hold this to be subversive of man's material advancement. It is bad for his soul, but then, it is the very source of his own and his country's material strength.

'A Spacious Hive well stockt with Bees,
That liv'd in Luxury and Ease;...
Was counted the great Nursery
Of Science and Industry...
These Insects liv'd like Men, and all
Our Actions they perform'd in small:...

Vast Numbers throng'd the fruitful Hive;
Yet those vast Numbers made 'em thrive;
Millions endeavouring to supply
Each other's Lust and Vanity;...
Some with vast Stocks, and little Pains,
Jump'd into Business of great Gains;
And some were damn'd to Sythes and Spades,
And all those hard laborious Trades;
Where willing Wretches daily sweat,
And wear out Strength and Limbs to eat:

While others follow'd Mysteries
To which few Folks bind 'Prentices
That want no Stock, but that of Brass,
And may set up without a Cross;   (A Cross was a small coin)
As Sharpers, Parasites, Pimps, Players,
Pick-pockets, Coiners, Quacks, South-sayers,
And all those, that in Enmity,
With downright Working, cunningly
Convert to their own Use the Labour
Of their good-natur'd heedless Neighbour.
These were call'd Knaves, but bar the Name,
The grave Industrious were the same:
All Trades and Places knew some Cheat,
No Calling was without Deceit.

The Lawyers, of whose Art the Basis
Was raising Feuds and splitting Cases,
Oppos'd all Registers, that Cheats
Might make more Work with dipt Estates;   (dipt= mortgaged)
As wer't unlawful, that one's own,

Without a Law-Suit, should be known.
They kept off Hearings wilfully,
To finger the refreshing Fee;   (refreshing= retaining)
And to defend a wicked Cause,
Examin'd and survey'd the Laws,...

Physicians valu'd Fame and Wealth
Above the drooping Patient's Health,
Or their own Skill: The Greatest Part
Study'd, instead of Rules of Art,
Grave pensive Looks and dull Behaviour,
To gain th' Apothecary's Favour;...

Among the many Priests of Jove,
Hir'd to draw Blessings from Above,
Some few were Learn'd and Eloquent,
But thousands Hot and Ignorant:

Yet all pass'd Muster that could hide
Their Sloth, Lust, Avarice and Pride;
For which they were as fam'd as Tailors
For Cabbage, or for Brandy Sailors:...

The Soldiers, that were forc'd to fight,
If they surviv'd, got Honour by't;
Tho' some, that shunn'd the bloody Fray,
Had Limbs shot off, that ran away:
Some valiant Gen'rals fought the Foe;
Others took Bribes to let them go:
Some ventur'd always where 'twas warm,
Lost now a Leg, and then an Arm;
Till quite disabled, and put by,
They liv'd on half their Salary;
While others never came in Play,
And staid at Home for double Pay.

Their Kings were serv'd, but Knavishly,
Cheated by their own Ministry;
Many, that for their Welfare slaved,
Robbing the very Crown they saved:
Pensions were small, and they liv'd high,
Yet boasted of their Honesty...
Unwilling to be short or plain,
In any thing concerning Gain;
For there was not a Bee but would

Get more, I won't say, than he should;...

But who can all their Frauds repeat?
The very Stuff, which in the Street
They sold for Dirt t'enrich the Ground,
Was often by the Buyers found
Sophisticated with a quarter
Of good-for-nothing Stones and Mortar;
Tho' Flail had little Cause to mutter,
Who sold the other Salt for Butter.

Justice her self, fam'd for fair Dealing,
By Blindness had not lost her Feeling;
Her Left Hand, which the Scales should hold,
Had often dropt' 'em, brib'd with Gold;...
Tho' some, first pillory'd for Cheating,
Were hang'd in Hemp of their own beating;
Yet, it was thought, the Sword she bore
Check'd but the Desp'rate and the Poor;
That, urg'd by meer Necessity,
Were ty'd up to the wretched Tree
For Crimes, which not deserv'd that Fate,
But to secure the Rich and Great.

Thus every Part was full of Vice,
Yet the whole Mass a Paradise;
Flatter'd in Peace, and fear'd in Wars,
They were th' Esteem of Foreigners,
And lavish of their Wealth and Lives,
The Balance of all other Hives.

Such were the Blessings of the State;
Their Crimes conspir'd to make them Great:
And Virtue, who from Politicks
Had learn'd a Thousand Cunning Tricks,
Was, by their happy Influence,
Made Friends with Vice: And ever since,
The worst of all the Multitude
Did something for the Common Good.

This was the State's Craft, that maintain'd
The Whole of which each Part complain'd.
This, as in Musick Harmony,
Made Jarrings in the main agree;...

The Root of Evil, Avarice,
That damn'd ill-natur'd baneful Vice,
Was Slave to Prodigality,
That noble Sin; whilst Luxury
Employ'd a Million of the Poor,
And odious Pride a Million more:
Envy it self, and Vanity,
Were Ministers of Industry;
Their darling Folly, Fickleness,
In Diet, Furniture and Dress,
That strange ridic'lous Vice,
was made The very Wheel that turn'd the Trade.
Their Laws and Clothes were equally
Objects of Mutability;
For, what was well done for a time,
In half a Year became a Crime;
Yet while they alter'd thus their Laws,
Still finding and correcting Flaws,
They mended by Inconstancy
Faults, which no Prudence could foresee.
Thus Vice nurs'd Ingenuity,
Which join'd with Time and Industry,
Had carry'd Life's Conveniencies,
It's real Pleasures, comforts, Ease,
To such a Height, the very Poor
Liv'd better than the Rich before,
And nothing could be added more....'

But then, Mandeville went on, the 'Grumbling Brutes' were not content. Whenever something went amiss they cry'd 'Damn the Cheats,' and 'Good Gods, Had we but Honesty'. And so, '...Jove with Indignation mov'd, At last in Anger swore, He'd rid the bawling Hive of Fraud; and did.'

'The very Moment it departs,
And Honesty fills all their Hearts;...

Now mind the glorious Hive, and see
How Honesty and Trade agree.
The Shew is gone, it thins apace;
And looks with quite another Face.

For 'twas not only that They went,
By whom vast Sums were Yearly spent;

But Multitudes that liv'd on them,
Were daily forc'd to do the same.
In vain to other Trades they'd fly;
All were o'er-stok'd accordingly...

The building Trade is quite destroy'd
Artificers are not employ'd;...

Those, that remain'd, grown temp'rate, strive,
Not how to spend, but how to live,...

The slight and fickle Age is past;
And Clothes, as well as Fashions last.
Weavers, that join'd rich Silk with Plate,
And all the Trades subordinate,
Are gone...

As Pride and Luxury decrease,
So by degrees they leave the Seas.
Not Merchants now, but Companies
Remove whole Manufactories.
All Arts and Crafts neglected lie;
Content, the Bane of Industry,
Makes 'em admire their homely Store,
And neither seek nor covet more...'

So in the end:

'Hard'ned with Toils and Exercise,
They counted Ease it self a Vice;
Which so improv'd their Temperance;
That, to avoid Extravagance,
They flew into a hollow Tree,
Blest with Content and Honesty.

The Moral.

Then leave Complaints: *Fools only strive*
To make a Great and Honest Hive
T' enjoy the World's Conveniencies,
Be fam'd in War, yet live in Ease,
Without great Vices, is a vain
Eutopia seated in the Brain.
Fraud, Luxury and Pride must live,

While we the Benefits receive:
Hunger's a dreadful Plague, no doubt,
Yet who digests or thrives without?...

So Vice is beneficial found
When it's by Justice lopt and bound;
Nay, where the People would be great,
As necessary to the State,
As Hunger is to make 'em eat.'[4]

So Mandeville (who together with Swift is quoted here with deliberate inordinate length not only because it amuses me to do so, but to give the modern reader something of the tone and tenor of the times) believed that man is self-seeking and egoistic and that it is this very egoism that, provided it is kept reasonably in check by good government, provides society with the *mechanism* that makes for prosperity. Those who claim otherwise, – who say that virtue and altruism, are the springs of prosperity, are, in the eyes of Mandeville, hypocrites who try to convince the world that their efforts yield 'pleasures, comforts, and ease' and make 'the very poor live better than the rich before,' and that this, and not their own good is ever their intention.

Mandeville's attack was directed against Shaftesbury but the originator of the 'reconciliation' of traditional ethic with bourgeois reality, the one who provided the bourgeoisie with the ideology that enabled it to justify its actions in the face of the lingering morality, was John Locke. For centuries society believed that resignation to one's lot was the essence of morality and wisdom; that man's life on earth was cast in the shadow of Original Sin; that the meek shall inherit the earth; and that self-interest and the pursuit of wealth, luxury and worldly pleasures were all evil. For generations parents, teachers and priests had by verbal admonitions and moralizing demeanor inculcated these beliefs into the minds of the young until they became *self-evident truths*. And indeed, as long as the social and economic reality gave little opportunity for the successful pursuit of wealth and luxury, and a lack of 'meekness', at least by the poor,

---

4.   The 'Fable' is quoted here from F.B. Kaye, Oxford Clarendon Press edition MDCCCCXXIV.

drew painful retribution from their 'betters', no need arose to reexamine these self-evident guides to good behavior. But now, on the threshold of the eighteenth century it became cleare that it was not the meek but most evidently the self-seeking were inheriting the earth. However, people cannot cast off their beliefs and the ideas they were brought up with lightly. How long did it take scientists to abandon Ptolemy's image of the constellation, how many complicated ideas were put forward to explain-away the inconsistencies between the theory and the observations before and even after Copernicus had shown his alternative image that was so much more plausible and simple?

How then indeed did the old 'self-evident' truths erode under the impact of the new worldly reality? Renaissance Skeptics, people like Montaigne and Pico, were well aware of the contradiction between the dictates of reason and religion, but they avoided the need to choose by relegating religion to the sphere of the incomprehensible and reason to the sphere of things observable and understandable by human rationality. By taking the inadequacy of human understanding, the limitation of man's mind, as self-evident they were satisfied to make religion into the arbiter of 'final truth'. Thus they were able to regard Christian asceticism – the subjugation of worldly desires to religious rules – not contrary to *reason* but to *human nature*, to human nature that was corrupted by the Original Sin. Pierre Bayle (1647–1706), for example, maintained that religion was incompatible with both reason and human nature yet this did not lead him to reject religion, he simply precluded one from the sphere of things related to the other. Not very differently were the Deists able to maintain at one and the same time that the world was ordered by natural law, – that its workings were open to human understanding by observation and experience, and, that the origins of ethics were divine and that there was a final truth. For them the search for truth was in effect a search for the will of God. The importance of this conception, that identified the laws of nature with the will of God, was that it supplied the anti-relativistic element in what would otherwise have been a wholly utilitarian relativistic outlook. It provided the basis for the legality – for the necessary social security, which prevented the legitimization of greed to the point where it would have killed the geese that lay the golden eggs. For without all moral restraints the pursuit of wealth must lead to total instability, to highway robbery, and not to the efforts required for production and exchange. So, while on the one hand Deism held a conception leading to unbounded relativism it on the other retained the tenets of ethical and moral absolutism for economic development unavoidable. In this way did the empirical movement from Bacon to Locke prepare a reconciliation between the contradictory elements, – contingent relativism and absolute truth and virtue, which was to free the bourgeoisie from its moral dilemma. Truth and virtue were given divine origins and the laws of nature a rationality comprehensible to man by observation and experiment.

In fact John Locke (1632–1704) did much more than reconcile traditional ethics with the covetous practices of the bourgeoisie. He gave it legitimization for its new set of values. By substituting Hobbes's 'wolfish' state of nature by people's tendency to act reasonably, almost benevolently towards each other, to improve everyone's life by mutual agreement, Locke provided the middle class with a self-image that was capable of putting at ease its troubled conscience. He made the pursuit of wealth, and the life of luxury that wealth made possible, respectable, and transformed the merchant living in luxury and trading for profit from a usurious Shylock into some newfangled kind of aristocrat at least in the eyes of his peers.[5] To be sure, Locke was neither a man of great logical consistency, nor was he gifted with outstanding analytical powers of reasoning, yet he combined the new scientific conception of the universe with the social and economic reality of his contemporary society in a way that well caught the tenor of the times. That, unlike Hobbes's, his conception of human motivation rested alone upon some ill defined and unexplained 'intrinsic' characteristics of man, and was lacking a rational let alone empirical basis, bothered neither him nor his admirers. Nor was anyone disturbed by the fact that he nowhere provided any proof of his convenient assumption that the pursuit of private advantages, within the terms of the social contract,

---

5.   The new image of the bourgeoisie is of course exquisitely exposed by Locke's
      great French contemporary Jean Baptiste Moliere *L'Avare* the miser (1668),
      Le Bourgeois gertilhomme the parvenu (1670) and *Le Tartuffe* the religious
      hypocrite (1664).

must necessarily lead to the greatest public good. But, being himself a likable person he 'created' society in his own image – rational, just, liberal, and thus gave the bourgeoisie the sympathetic face that it so needed to stave off its moral uneasiness. Without being conscious of it he supplied the middle class with an image for emulation and thus with the foundations for an amended set of social values. This new image implied on the one hand a social mode of conduct partly borrowed from the aristocracy, indeed a way of life that set the bourgeoisie apart and above the poor, and on the other hand a strict adherence by the rules of utilitarian rationality and positive law. The emphasis laid upon positive law by Locke, the exponent of the doctrine of the supremacy of natural law, may seem surprising – but it is not. For Locke's conception of natural law differed from earlier conceptions in several ways: Firstly it emphasized man's *rights* where earlier conceptions stressed only *duties;* secondly it was more complex than its precursors, it upheld a kind of new 'trinity' – the right to *'life, liberty* and *property',* where earlier conceptions, for example Hobbes's, held only one namely the right to self-preservation, that is the right to life.[6] If, as Locke claimed, rights were 'inherent', part of man from birth, how then could the right to *property*, particularly property acquired by the labor of ones servants, be included? The right to property, unlike the right to life and liberty, is obviously 'external'. Things of value, i.e. property, Locke maintained, are created by labor, and by laboring a man extends his own self into the objects he produces. Hence, 'by expending his internal energy upon them he makes them part of himself', and therefore their protection part of his right to self-preservation. The fact that a man's servant expends his own 'internal energy' to create property which is then alienated and becomes the property of the master, who did not expend his 'internal energy' to create it, did not bother Locke. For him it was *self-evident* that the product of a servant was his master's, and what

---

6.   The roots of the ambivalence were therefore not in contradiction between natural and positive law, for valid positive law was considered no more than the operationalization of natural law in order to make it binding upon people in their social conduct, but in Locke's conception of the natural rights themselves.

was self-evident was of course right and did not warrant further study. The same is true of Locke's expositions on the sources of positive law. Natural law provides man with all the rights required, – positive law adds nothing but their adaptation to practical requirements. The morality implied in natural law is eternal – what is right or wrong is eternally so, but whether this eternal value system is founded upon the will of God or only upon what is rationally self-evident remains a question unanswered. At one and the same time Locke's moral values are divine, and therefore 'external' to man, and 'intrinsic', i.e. what man 'feels' or 'knows' to be right or wrong. In his *Essay on Human Understanding* he argues that things 'self-evident' cannot be taken as reliable guides to truth because any time honored custom or habit seems self-evident; and yet his whole political theory is based upon the axiom-like proposition that all individuals 'are endowed by their creator with a right to life, liberty and estate' because these rights are self-evident. He denied the right of anyone to force on people speculative opinions,[7] and maintained that 'he that examines and upon examination embraces an error for a truth has done his duty more than he who embraces the profession of the truth... without having examined whether it be true or not'.[8] Yet, he also denied the right 'to differ' to all who do not accept 'natural religion' as the common ground for their belief. Like Hobbes he grants man individual rights, but, probably unconsciously, transforms them into something different. So, Hobbes's *self-preservation* becomes with Locke *self-interest* – the psychological dimension out of which a 'calculus' of pleasure and pain was to develop. He made society, by way of the social contract, the guardian of rights that antedated it; and by emphasizing a right to *property* converts earlier conceptions of natural law, the preserver of the *common good*, into a new conception that turned it into the guardian of *individual rights*, by tacitly implying that the two are identical – an assumption for which

---

7.   *Letter on Toleration* (1667).

8.   Fox Bourne's *Life of Locke* (1876).

he has no other justification but his contemporaries' notion that the assumed harmony in nature is extended to societies.

It was precisely Locke's transformation rather than negation of older established views that appealed to the bourgeoisie and gave him his great popularity. It helped to avoid a confrontation with the old order by giving to the old values an interpretation that was no longer irreconcilable with the freedoms required by the bourgeoisie. By making property part of a man's self Locke included it in what had for long been accepted as the right or duty of self-preservation; by identifying the common good with that of some individuals he side-stepped an overt confrontation with traditional morality and made self-interest respectable, almost a virtue; by deriving the right to make laws from the inalienable rights of man, including the right to *property*, and founding *Law* on the consent of people, interpreting the absence of effective resistance as everyone's tacit endorsement of economic inequality, he provided the moral justification for the new socioeconomic order that was to influence profoundly eighteenth century society.

The idea that a benign God had created the world as an orderly pattern to serve some happy future purpose, that so delighted his contemporary scientists, evoked in Locke and his followers an almost 'sentimental' trust in social harmony – in the belief in the coincidence of individual drives with the public good. There is a striking similarity between Hobbes's universal egoism and Newton's gravitation. Both *explain* rather than describe events or changes and both provide *a simple spring of action* – a mechanism or clockwork, to account for them. Newton's was gravitation – the mutual attraction of all bodies in the universe; for Hobbes it was egoism – each individual's striving to assure his self-preservation by attracting as much wealth and power to himself. There is a wonderful symmetry here between Hobbes's and Newton's perception. Both see the universe made up of individuals, persons or objects, each of which is endowed with a kind of inherent force attracting all around it, while the system as a whole is held together by the mutual cancellation of the multitude of contrary attractions. Only, Newton's mechanism dealt with inanimate matter and Hobbes's with man in society, with man absorbed in a culture which still regarded egoism with disapprobation. The search for alternative mechanisms capable of explaining man's quest for wealth and power, by those seeking to reconcile their deeds with their contemporaries' values, that would be free from the opprobrium of sin was therefore only natural. The alternative they came up with was *altruism,* which was less logically defensible but more respectable, – it left the pursuers of wealth in the image of the benevolent creator. Thus as the eighteenth century proceeded into the nineteenth, social theory became increasingly less dependent on logic and more aligned with class interests.

In conclusion; the seventeenth century produced a calculus of measurement that made possible the formulation of natural laws capable of mathematical intelligibility and of, what was believed to be, universal applicability. Nature became rational, and arbitrary dogmas were replaced by experimentally verified certainty. However, the power of reason challenged the power of faith but did not abolish it and therefore retained for society the element of stability faith gave it. In addition, the stabilizing element was also retained in the conception of eternity, i.e. in the belief in the unchanging character of nature's laws. In the eighteenth century, men like Hume, Voltaire, Diderot, Hollbach and others, shook the old conception of proper social conduct by separating ethics from religion. But even they did not invalidate basic moral values. The *grounds* for the justification of man's desired behavior were changing – not the justifications themselves; what had been right or wrong before, though with considerable modifications, continued to be so but *it was no longer right or wrong because God so willed it but because man so conceived it to be.* The bourgeoisie had won the freedoms it required but it had not gained the power to replace the old value system by a totally new system of its own. 'Right gave way before claims of expediency', but expediency had not yet become the source of Right.[9] With Locke the knowledge of good and evil was founded in 'innate' ideas, with Shaftesbury in 'instinct'. Locke rationalized his 'innate' ideas – good is what causes pleasure and evil what causes displeasure or pain, but the rewards and retributions are directly related to the laws in which the 'innate' ideas are

---

9.   *Vide* for the developments in the conception of 'Right' also Harold Laski. 'What are the Social Sciences?' in *E.S.S.*

formalized, namely to the divine laws, the civil laws, and the social conventions. Shaftesbury's conception is less formalistic. For him the knowledge of good and evil is outside the sphere of divine instruction and human experience, it is intuitive 'natural, agreeing with nature, instinctive'.[10] Birds do not need a catechism to learn to build their nests, they do so by instinct. Man does not need instruction to distinguish right from wrong he is instinctively led to this distinction. In fact in Shaftesbury's view morality is a kind of aesthetics through which people are led to like or dislike things by an inert instinctive force. Morality is divorced from Locke's legalistic conception – from the scriptures and the social contract, but it remains what people feel themselves to be good or evil. God's harmony or even harmony with no God becomes the criterion of moral judgement, and to be in harmony with both the universe and oneself becomes the object of man's rational moral endeavors. By studying himself, his motives, man comes to know whether his actions are morally desirable; by seeing his actions rewarded by the approbation of society he *knows* them to be really desirable. Here Shaftesbury anticipated the compromise between individualism and the sense of social obligation which was to dominate economic philosophy in the later part of the 18th century. He assumes general harmony and searches for the universal mechanism, the 'gravitation', that guides men to find their proper places within the universal system. Not unlike Locke, he avoids Hobbes's opprobrious egoistic mechanism and he substitutes it by the quest for happiness, a happiness that can only be found in man himself and in common ends. The actions leading to social harmony are the same that lead to harmony in man's soul. Like Hutcheson (1694–1747) and later Adam Smith (1723–1790) Shaftesbury assumes that 'the study of man's own advantage naturally, or rather necessarily, leads him to prefer that employment which is most advantageous to society';[11] – there is 'a divinely ordained harmony of egoistic and altruistic

---

10. Anthony Ashley, the Earl of Shaftesbury, *The Moralist*, III, 2.

11. Adam Smith, *An Inquiry into the True Nature and Causes of the Wealth of Nations* (1776), Bk. IV, Ch. II.

impulses in man':[12] because self-love is always circumscribed by love for one's fellows.

According to Adam Smith, man's actions are determined by society in the sense that, to be happy, man requires the approval of his fellow men. Hence, the acquisition of wealth that sin of avarice – is not really the object of man's material egoism – it is alone a means to the veritable end, namely public esteem. It is this true end of man's egoism that puts a natural limit upon rapacity. Riches draws upon man the attention of the world, that which causes true happiness, which he would forfeit when his pursuit of self-interest oversteps the socially acceptable limits, i.e. when it becomes subversive to the general good. [How nice!] In short, greed remains greed and vice remains vice – the traditional values remain intact, only the bourgeoisie is given a free pardon, because their particular type of greed is cleansed of all sin, for it is not really motivated by the evil love of gain, but by the 'pure' quest for happiness a quest legitimized by the nature of man and its harmony with the public good – the happiness of all. What man really wishes is happiness and happiness is not always synonymous with wealth 'In what constitutes the real happiness of human life beggars may in no respect be inferior to those who would seem so much above them... for it consists in the esteem in which one is held by others and in health, freedom from debt and in a clear conscience'.[13]

It is of course the consideration of his own private profit that is the sole motive which determines the owner of any capital to employ it in whatever way he deems best but the study of his own advantage leads him to the employment which is most beneficial to all.[14] Like Newton's gravitation Smith's psychological motivation serves as the *mechanism* that maintains harmony in nature. Through profit the employer learns of the needs of society and through loss what is in surfeit supply. For producing what is in real social demand the employer of labor and capital is rewarded by profit and

---

12.   Adam Smith, *The Theory of Moral Sentiments* (1759).

13.   Adam Smith, *ibid.*

14.   Adam Smith, *ibid.*

for producing what society cannot use he is punished by loss. Here is an *'invisible hand'* – a mechanism akin to gravitation, maintaining the world in harmony. Even the selfish and rapacious cannot really disturb this natural harmony. Though the rich may select the best food they still cannot consume more than anyone else, and so, whether they intend it or not, 'they are led by an invisible hand to make nearly the same distribution of the necessities of life which would have been made had the earth been divided into equal portions among all its inhabitants.'[15] The rich landlords are obliged to exchange their surplus food with those who can provide them with their other needs, and thus their quest for wealth stimulates others and increases the wealth of the nation – ('what is good for General Motors is good for the American people'). In Adam Smith's own words: by each pursuing his own interest the general interest of society is more effectively promoted than when it is deliberately promoted (by some planner). The imperfections which men may see in their environment are merely illusions, they stem from man's limited vision. Given a wider view they would disappear, for the world as a whole is in harmony.

Calvin had made the love of gain 'respectable', though not the worldly pleasures that gain could buy. Hobbes had added the mechanism by which the love of gain was satisfied, making man the self-seeking animal in the eternal struggle of all against all. Locke endowed man with a rationality that gave him moral quality and thereby reconciled the manner in which gain was made with the traditional conceptions of morality. Shaftesbury and Hutcheson gave man an innate gravitation towards goodness, they made him the image of an 'all-loving and all-protecting' God, and by reinterpreting the love of gain as the love for prestige or happiness they lifted the opprobrium from both the pursuit of wealth and its enjoyment. By granting man with an innate power to distinguish right from wrong and making him naturally good they turned ethics into a kind of natural aesthetics – which freed them from the need of giving a

---

15.   A. Smith, *Wealth of Nations*, Bk. II, Ch. V, Bk. IV, Ch. II. See also A. Smith, *The Theory of Moral Sentiments*, pp. 465–6.

rational explanation for the way in which moral judgments are formed. *Virtue became what people felt it to be.* (In retrospect one may say that virtue became what people had become accustomed to accept – the 'things one does' as opposed to the 'things one does not do'.[16]) As affluence and luxury spread the frontiers of the socially permissible were moving further and further off, and adapted to the changing circumstances. The old biblical standards of morality continued to exert a restraining influence upon most people's minds and deeds but their force was steadily though only gradually receding.[17]

A good example for mid-eighteenth century efforts to base ethics on the observation of man's actual responses is Francis Hutcheson's (1694–1747) *System of Moral Philosophy.* A good example for the attempts to reconcile this tendency with traditional morality is Joseph Butler's (1692–1752) *Analogy of Religion, Natural and Revealed, to the Constitution of Nature.* Hutcheson, whose work is permeated with the optimism of the late seventeenth and early eighteenth century, finds in man a mixture of egoism and desire to please others; *Reason* is the indispensable instrument by which man directs his deeds to satisfy this mixture of desires. Man's moral sense, is instinctive, – neither educated nor habitual. It is the gift of God, part of the harmony with which he endowed the universe, – the 'gravitation' by which man is led by promoting his own desires to advance the good of all others. Hutcheson's system can dispense with religion. Those seeking the proximity of God and man may look upon man's moral sense as God's direct endowment, those who do not, may look upon it as part of God's design in nature – as part

---

16. This was also the opinion of David Hume, but for a different reason. He *denied* the existence of innate intuitions which he called 'habits of thought'.

17. It is perhaps symptomatic that the very people who solemnly declared (in the year Adam Smith published his celebrated *Wealth of Nations*) in the Declaration of Independence of the United States that all men are created equal (and are endowed by their creator with the right to life, liberty, and property (or the pursuit of happiness) found no fault with owning slaves and with the expropriation of the land of Red-indians even condoning their extermination when to obtain their land this deemed necessary.

of nature's harmony. To be virtuous is to harmonize ones inclinations with those of one's fellow creatures; it is unnatural to offend against this rule because it is to offend against oneself, it is to offend against one's egoistic desire for appreciation and ones innate inclination.

Butler's work is no longer permeated with the optimism that influenced the works of Leibniz, Locke, Shaftesbury and Hutcheson. He too believes in man's inherent sense of moral judgement – which he calls conscience, and which he places above all other faculties; but he does not deny man's tendency to follow also other more earthly egoistic pleasures. What places the former above the latter is only the fact that the 'pleasures' of the conscience are direct or immediate whereas the egoistic pleasures must always be preceded by desire and by self-centered efforts which can never fully satisfy the expectations. He claims that 'there is a superior principle of reflection or conscience in every man, which distinguishes between the internal principles of his heart, as well as his external actions.' In other words: Butler has no new criteria by which to distinguish between good and bad, right and wrong, all he does say is that good and right are the things one feels to be so. What he pleads for in fact is the old belief in God's good intention upon earth, and by showing that it is impossible to learn nature's good cause from observation and to predict with certainty the future effects of one's actions, and, indeed, to see 'the whole' system. The only true guide to valid judgement must be intuition, i.e. the conscience.[18] With this he destroyed the trust in the superiority of Natural over Revealed religion, for neither can be proved to have a good and righteous cause by observation.

The philosopher who most consistently theorized about the separation of moral judgement and judgement by reason was David Hume (1711–1776). Rejecting altogether the possibility of attaining certain knowledge from observation he fell back upon common sense

18.   Here begins a controversy which became part of the heritage of western civilization and is far from settled even today. In the first place it raises the question of individual responsibility, and in the second whether or not there is a scientific way for predicting the future outcome of man's actions with a satisfactory degree of confidence.

and faith. Moral judgement, so he maintained, can never be the judgement of reason, for reason cannot be an incentive to action. Yet the whole purpose of moral judgement is precisely this – to guide man's actions. Reason must always be concerned with facts or with the relations between ideas, while passions are concerned with the prospects of pleasure or pain, i.e. with the true springs of human actions. Reason can at best inform about such prospects and indicate the ways one might attain pleasure and avoid pain – it is the servant not the master of man's passions.

Hume's empiricism that stressed the uncertainty of generalizations which are based upon observation alone, and his denial of all innate ideas and a priori truth, undermined the determinist world view and the great trust in natural harmony. The first buds of a new kind of skepticism entered European thought. In his *An Enquiry Concerning Human Understanding* (1748) Hume wrote: 'All the objects of human reason or inquiry may naturally be divided into two kinds, to wit, *Relations of Ideas*, and *Matters of Fact*. Of the first kind are the sciences of Geometry, Algebra, and Arithmetic; in short, every affirmation which is either intuitively or demonstratively certain...' Propositions that are 'discoverable by the mere operation of thought, without dependence on what is anywhere existent in the universe.' Of the second kind are 'matters of fact'. These are not ascertained in the same manner; 'nor is our evidence of their truth, however great, of like nature with the foregoing. The contrary of every matter of fact is still possible; because it can never imply a contradiction, and is conceived by the mind with the same facility and distinctness, as if ever so conformable to reality. That the sun will *not* rise tomorrow is no less intelligible a proposition, and implies no more contradiction than the affirmation that *it will* rise... It may, therefore, be subject worthy of curiosity, to inquire what is the nature of that evidence which assures us of any real existence and matter of fact, beyond the present testimony of our senses, or the records of our memory... All reasonings concerning matter of fact seem to be founded on the relation of *Cause and Effect*. By means of that relation alone we can go beyond the evidence of our memory and senses... a man finding a watch or any other machine in a desert island would conclude that there had once been men on that island. All our reasonings concerning fact are of the same nature. And here it is constantly supposed that there is a connection between the present fact and that which is inferred from it.' But then, how do we arrive at the knowledge of cause and effect? It arises entirely from experience without any a priori reasonings. 'Let an object be presented to a man of ever so strong natural reason and abilities; if that object be entirely new to him, he will not be able... to discover any of its causes or effects... But the same truth may not appear at first sight, to have the same evidence with regard to events, which have become familiar to us from our first appearance in the world, which bear a close analogy to the whole course of nature, and which are supposed to depend on the simple qualities of objects, without any secret structure of parts... Such is the influence of custom, that, where it is strongest, it not only covers our natural ignorance, but even conceals itself, and seems not to take place, merely because it is found in the highest degree. But to convince us that all the laws of nature, and all the operations of bodies without exception, are known only by experience, the following reflections may, perhaps, suffice. Were any object presented to us, and were we required to pronounce concerning the effect which will result from it, without consulting past observation, after what manner... must the mind proceed in this operation? It must invent or imagine some event, which it ascribes to the object as its effect, and it is plain that this invention must be entirely arbitrary... In a word, then, every effect is a distinct event from its cause. It could not, therefore, be discovered in the cause, and the first invention or conception of it, a priori, must be entirely arbitrary. And even after it is suggested, the conjunction of it with the cause must appear equally arbitrary; since there are always many other effects, which, to reason, must seem fully as consistent and natural. In vain, therefore, should we pretend to determine any single event, or infer any cause or effect, without the assistance of observation and experience. Hence, we may discover the reason why no philosopher... has ever pretended to assign the ultimate cause of any natural operation, or to show distinctly the action of that power, which produces any single effect in the universe. It is confessed that the utmost effort of human reason is to reduce the principles, productive of natural phenomena, to a greater simplicity, and to resolve the many particular effects into a few general causes by means of reasonings from analogy, experience, and observation. *But as to the causes of these general causes, we should in vain attempt their discovery;* nor shall we ever be able to satisfy ourselves by any particular explication of them. These ultimate springs and principles are totally shut up from human curiosity and inquiry... The most perfect philosophy of the natural kind only staves off our ignorance a little longer: as perhaps the most perfect philosophy of the moral or metaphysical kind serves only to discover larger portions of it...'

Hence Hume also made a clear distinction between the possibility of explaining religion by way of reason and finding its origins in human nature. *There is no need for understanding, in Hume's view, in order to embrace a religion, for it may well arise out of the unintelligible – feelings of hope and fear, of suspense and uncertainty.* In Hume's own words, 'morality is more properly felt than judged of'.[19] 'To have the sense of virtue is nothing but to feel a satisfaction of a particular kind from the contemplation of a character. The very feeling constitutes our praise or admiration'.[20]

In fact it is impossible to ascertain by *reason* the causes of man's moral judgments. For example, the sapling destroying the parent oak is judged by other standards than the son destroying his father; the former is not subjected to man's judgement, it is neither morally approved or disapproved, it is simply taken as a fact. It follows that the fact of patricide can hardly be the reason for opprobrium and moral indignation – from the factual point of view there is little difference between one and the other the sapling and the son. Yet, man *make* a distinction, they feel that the one leaves them unconcerned and the other arouses their strongest disapprobation. Thus, at one and the same time, Hume reflects both tendencies in his contemporary society, the utilitarian-rational and the traditional-conservative. By, *on the one hand,* founding moral values in man's judgement – in *feeling* (habits of thopught) of right and wrong, he reflected the tendency towards an assimilation of morality with expediency; for with the growing material affluence and

---

19.   *Treatise of Human Nature*, II, 3. 3.

20.   *Ibid.*, III, 1. 2.

spreading luxury, and in the absence of a firmer moral commitment, these feelings were changing and gradually becoming adjusted to the needs and possibilities that accompanied the changing circumstances. *On the other hand,* by claiming that it is vain to attempt to discover the cause of all causes, for the 'ultimate springs and principles are totally shut up from human curiosity and inquiry', he confirmed the need for religion for those who from 'hope, fear, suspense and uncertainty' wished to hold on to it, even though he denied the relevance of God and the authority of religion for the formation of moral judgments for people who, like himself, were unable or unwilling to accept an unproven proposition.

Altogether then the sources of Hume's moral feelings are *utility* and *sympathy.* Yet, his view of mankind is less optimistic than that of Locke, Shaftesbury, Hutcheson, and even his friend Adam Smith. He does not believe that by very nature man will prefer that which is best for the 'public good' over his own interests. But, he believed that in order to serve his self-interest, to protect himself and particularly to protect his property, man has devised *artificial virtues* in customs and rules of law and that these constitute the mechanism by which society's long-term and collective self-interest is protected against the short-term impulses of its constituent individual members. In spite of his later somewhat less pessimistic view of human nature Hume never really abandoned this idea. Perhaps it is symptomatic of the confrontation of his contemporary's growing self-centered rationalism with the lingering traditional values that Hume combined in his life and work a moral conservatism with a strong atheistic skepticism. Missing a sense of evolution, nay, even a sense of history in spite of being a historian, Hume looks upon human nature and the rules of morality as given. He holds the rules of morality immutable because they appear to him common sense – he *feels* them to be so – in spite of being mere custom they are self-evident. In this context the possibility that things self-evident one day need no longer be self-evident in another simply did not enter his mind.

With the significant exception of Rousseau, French thought about the nature of man's moral values went little further than the English. Its tenor of presentation was sharper – more aggressive, but no more. The reason for this difference in tone is fairly obvious. The sharper tone reflected the fact that in eighteenth century France the old order was still deeply entrenched while its disintegration in England had already made considerable headway. *Montesquieu* (1689–1755) recognized the greater complexity of the relationship between individuals and society than most earlier writers admitted. He undermined the trust in the utilitarian individualism on which much of the contemporary speculation about morals and human nature was based. In contrast to Hume he believed human values to be functionally related to man's natural and social environment. Consequently he did not accept the view that there must be one single set of values valid for all times and in all places. And yet, he was too much a prisoner of his own environment to draw the ultimate conclusions from his sociological perception of society; he was still searching for stability, for some absolute standard, for some 'revealed' truth, and so, his theory becomes inconsistent. Explaining the foundations of various types of government; *fear* for despotism, *honor* for monarchy, and *civic virtue* for republic government, he in fact lists all the different and sometimes contrasting assumptions about human nature that were current in his time. *Fear* is of course the wish to avoid pain, *honor* the wish to gain the appreciation of others, and *civic virtue* a kind of altruism. In fact he reconciled the contradictory assumptions about human nature by granting each of them a greater or smaller degree of importance depending on the socio-political environment. *Helvetius's* ideas (1715–1771) are more akin to those of Hobbes, only the emphasis shifts from the avoidance of pain or fear to the pursuit of pleasure which in mid-eighteenth century seemed more proper for, with but few exceptions such as Rousseau, eighteenth century thinkers were not concerned with those who were socially and economically below their own class. Hence for Helvetius human nature was almost unmitigatedly egoistic pleasure-seeking. Yet he believed in the power of education to redirect this pleasure-seeking egoism towards ends which he regarded self-evidently desirable. He thought that man can be taught to enjoy benevolence so that his egoism is satisfied by acting altruistically. Here is not the altruism of Locke, or even more of Hutcheson, but an 'altruism' generated by a self-seeking desire for a type of pleasure inculcated into the mind of society by education, – not an innate passion but an acquired taste. An almost contrary view was held by *Diderot* (1713–1784). Diderot continued to uphold the old tradition of thought in as far as 'eternal values' were concerned, but he believed that these values, or rather the actions they prescribed to men, can be subverted by bad government. If man acts badly, commits evil deeds in spite of his better nature, there are causes for this. But by implication, looking for causes, he can no longer regard man's fall as the consequence of 'Original Sin'. In his early writings he assumes that knowledge of good and right is innate – is part of human nature, a quality of moral sense with which man is endowed by birth. Later however, he comes to the conclusion that there is no such innate moral sense and that which gives the impression of being innate is really only the result of an infinite number of in themselves insignificant experiences which men collect from their very earliest childhood throughout life. The sum of these experiences then unconsciously determines man's sense of values and his judgement on each separate occasion. 'All is experience though we may not be consciously aware of it', he wrote to Mdlle. Voland.

The true 'odd man out' among the French great thinkers of the eighteenth century was *Jean Jacques Rousseau* (1712–1778). 'Rousseau differed from his contemporaries in everything but his opinions; even when he used the same words he meant something different. His character, his outlook on life, his scale of values, his instinctive reactions, all differed essentially from what the Enlightenment regarded as admirable.'[21] Where the Enlightenment believed 'the growth of knowledge' to be 'the growth of good', he held the opinion that man, good by nature or at least neither good nor bad at birth, was corrupted by civilization; where the Enlightenment spoke of freedom and equality and meant equality before the law – the freedom of the intelligentsia to evolve and voice opinions contrary to the state and church and the freedom for the bourgeoisie to protect its business interests against claims founded upon aristocratic privileges. He spoke of total social and economic equality embracing all strata of humanity including the plebeian 'rabble' which other thinkers of his time tacitly excluded from society where the Enlightenment looked upon the pursuit of

---

21.   *Vide* George H. Sabine, *A History of Political Theory*, London, 1961, 3rd ed., p. 575.

wealth with favor, giving to wealth the status of an inalienable birth-right – part of the trinity of 'life, liberty, and property', he turned it into the 'original sin', the source of all corruption, the fountain-head of all the oppressive political and social orders that in his view served but one purpose – the preservation of inequality, the protection of those who appropriated for themselves something they had no right to, something that had been part of man's common heritage. For he transformed 'the right to property' from the individual's right to protect what is his own against all others, i.e. from a right *against* society, into a social right *within* society. His claim that 'the right which each individual has to his own estate is always subordinate to the right which the community has over all', and that 'the first man, who, having enclosed a piece of land, bethought himself of saying 'this is mine', and found people simple enough to believe him was the real founder of civil government.'

Rousseau rejected both the philosophy of the new social order, i.e. the expression of middle class opposition to the traditional beliefs that could not be made to serve its purposes, and the traditional philosophy that had given rise to this opposition. He regarded the protagonists of the new ideas as 'vain and futile declaimers' who are out 'to sap the foundations of our faith, and nullify virtue' who 'consecrate their talents and philosophy to the destruction and defamation of all that men hold sacred,' and he looked upon the upholders of the old ideas as irrational dogmatists trying to maintain their hold upon society by superstition. Rousseau's position was that intelligence is dangerous because it undermines reverence; science is destructive because it takes away faith, reason is bad because it sets prudence against moral intuition.[22] This was a note which the Enlightenment could not easily understand – unless it were a covert defence of revelation and the church as in fact it was not. In fact it reflected the growing fear that the demolition of the traditional dogmas of religion might well engender the abolition of the other moral values that were worthy of retention. What Rousseau did believe in were the redeeming powers of *good* government and education. He did not share Hobbes's individualism that turned

---

22.   *Ibid.*, p. 578.

society into the guardian of each individual's right to
self-preservation; nor did he share Locke's individualism that made
it the guardian of each member's property; nor even did he share
Hume's predilection for an enlightened self-interest. He simply did
not conceive of man outside society – he saw man as an inseparable
part of it. Society itself was for him the source of human values.
Not the satisfaction of individuals' self-interest was his testing-stone
of good government but the adherence by values of which society
as such was the final arbiter. Natural man was neither good nor evil,
his values were molded by society and therefore man's fall began
with the institution of private property. When some men first
appropriated for themselves part of the common wealth; when they
created private property; when they in order to preserve their
ill-gotten gains imposed upon society their rules and laws to confirm
them in their new position; when they created inequality; then they
distorted the true character of society and made its government its
tool of corruption. Thus Rousseau arrives at the conclusion that it
was the institution of private property that gave rise to the laws that
serve no other purpose than the preservation of inequality and the
subjugation of one strata of society by another, and that this forms
the basis of man's subverted moral values. The good society is
therefore the one that aims at controlling the corrupting influences
of property-perverted social institutions. The good society is one in
which government and education serve 'the common people who
compose the human race', and serve the great majority of men, for
'man is the same in all ranks and... the ranks which are most
numerous deserve most respect'.[23] Yet the eighteenth century
intellectual did not consider 'the common people' full partners in the
'human race'. With the poor he could commiserate in their ill plight,
pity their misfortune, deplore their ignorance, but his attitude would
invariably remain condescending. When he spoke of equality he was
challenging those who regarded themselves his 'betters', their
hereditary privileges, the prerogatives by which their superiors rank
restricted his liberties – the liberties of the middle class and those
able to maintain a similar way of life. He was not thinking of those

---

23.   Rousseau quoted here from Sabine, *op.cit.*, p. 579.

he himself regarded of inferior rank, he did not think of the working class whose way of life – whose disregard for bourgeois virtues, simply did not fit his image of equal members in the human race. To him they were in fact 'non-people'.[24] 'People' are frugal – save and invest, while 'non-people' are intemperately squandering the little money they have on drink and sordid pleasures. In short the poor were the very opposite of the aspired image of society; they were uneducated, immoderate, improvident, sinful and had more children than they could support,[25] altogether their very way of life put them outside the 'human race'. And, in an era in which *cause and effect* had risen to become *The* principle of science it was but too obvious that the poors' mode of conduct was the great cause of their poverty. The possibility that their poverty may be the cause of their mode of conduct was far too inconvenient a thought to be entertained by those whose riches and luxury rested upon the inequitable distribution of the fruits of production. So, the bourgeoisie had no reason to ask such questions and the church already knew the answer for it had always placed misfortune at the sinners' doors. No wonder then that Rousseau was misunderstood when he made all people members of society and man 'the same in all ranks', and, oh sacrilege!, society at large the source and owner of all property, i.e. the source of all evil. This claim was certainly too contrary to all that was held true and obvious by his contemporaries. Indeed, his ideas disturbed Diderot – they did not convert him.

Man, the calculating egoist, as his contemporaries saw him, was for Rousseau but man perverted by 'civil government'. The true man for Rousseau was ruled by his emotions – not by intellect. True man is sensitive to the suffering of others – more than that he has an

---

24.   It may be interesting to note, though this part of the book is dealing with things mainly written in French, that in the English language this attitude is well reflected in the distinction between such expressions as: *perspire* (for 'people') and *sweat* (for 'non-people'), or being *intoxicated* (for 'people'), and disgustingly *drunk*, (for 'non-people').

25.   The last mentioned 'fault of the poor did in fact only become vocal towards the end of the century. For example in 1798 when Malthus first published his *Essay.*

innate revulsion against the suffering of others and this revulsion cannot be explained by calculating reason – *because* it is innate. Hence the true sources of man's attitudes are *feelings*. Perverted by bad civil government man has learned to suppress his feelings – his true self, and he has allowed *reason* to govern both his thoughts and deeds. This is the explanation of the fact that the poverty of some serves the luxury of others. This is the fount of the laws and customs that give to this unnatural state of affairs the semblance of legitimacy and even of self-evidence. To be sure, Natural Man was not oblivious to self-love, but self-love was but one among several equally weighty motivations, – even animals assist one another, so why should man be inferior to them in sympathy and compassion? Natural Man, man uncorrupted by society has few desires and consequently little motivation to own property. Food, sleep and love are his true needs and they can be satisfied without the subjugation of others. It is 'artificial wants', wants created by society that give rise to civil government and all the evils it engenders. Yet even bad government cannot wholly destroy man's true self. He still retains his conscience, for his conscience is innate – inalienable. Man 'knows' the difference between right and wrong though, of course, he may not act in conformity with this knowledge.

Rousseau gave a new *progressive* content to the unity of man. In the beginning of this book I defined progress as the augmentation of the freedom of choice. I explained that I chose this concept because it includes both spontaneous and deliberate change in this direction. Rousseau's contemporaries certainly intended to augment their class' freedom, but he extended the progressive content of their ideology by introducing the idea of the unity of man. In this, his idea is what progress means in natural science, namely finding likeness in diversity. In other words, Rousseau's idea was progressive in this sense that it stressed likeness where his contemporaries saw diversity.

Man's observations and experiences are many, perhaps infinite, by dividing them into what he believes matters and what does not, and into what is alike or fitting into a pattern and what is not, he passes judgement on his observations and experiences, and this judgement then forms the basis of his beliefs. Newton saw the likeness between the 'fall of the apple and the swirling of the moon in her orbit round the earth', which no one had recognized before him, and thus produced a completely new conception of the universe. Rousseau saw the likeness in all man and thus gave a new conception of mankind, though, of course, unlike Newton's discovery, his threatened too many of the establishment's vested interests to be as readily adopted by it. The constant progressive element in science, including the social sciences, is the widening of the likenesses man selects among the facts – the creation of new visions or concepts that unify his understanding of the world. 'When we discover the wider likeness, whether between space and time, bacillus and crystal, we enlarge the order in the universe, but more than this, we enlarge its unity,'[26] as in Einstein's famous equation: energy = mass ($E = Mc^2$). And *it is this conception of the unity of nature living and dead for which our thought reaches that determines progress.* It is this unity that presents a 'far deeper conception than any assumption that nature *must be* uniform'.[27] It is the shift in the judgement of things regarded alike or unlike that determines man's values in both the natural and the social sciences. When physicists discover such a new likeness their science shifts. Events previously disregarded assume a new significance and the importance of events hitherto regarded significant is reassessed – value judgments are altered. When society discovers a new likeness a similar process of reevaluation of old value-judgments takes place. The ancient Greeks did not regard slaves to be like men, Medieval Society did not liken itself to heathens. The members of the early European bourgeoisie did not regard those unable or unwilling to adopt its style of life as men like themselves, though all did occasionally pay lip-service to the idea of the brotherhood of man. And nineteenth century Europeans never regarded themselves equal to Asians or Africans. But Rousseau did. Where others saw the dissimilarities in color, manners and beliefs, he noted the unity – the uniformity of human nature. From the *de facto* changes in his society he visualized a generalization. He observed the decline of Mercantilism in England and the growing

---

26.   J. Bronowski, *The Common Sense of Science*, Heinemann, 1951.

27.   *Ibid.* The first is a scientific, the second a theological approach to the concept and perception of unity.

social mobility in France i.e. the beginnings of the movement that demolished the old rigid rank conceptions. For in his time men of humble origins actually rose to wealth and power, and made themselves indeed equal members of Society. The Mercantilism that had divided the world into, on the one hand, merchants, manufacturers and rich landowners – *the people who 'mattered'* (who were stimulated to great deeds by the 'love of gain'), and on the other hand, *the laboring poor – the 'non-people' who did not 'matter'*, (who could only be driven to work by the cold fear of starvation), had, by Rousseau's time undergone great changes. No longer did it regard workers' wants as strictly limited, as indeed they no longer were by the middle of the eighteenth century. For under the pressure of the relative labor shortage in the first half of that century, at least sections of the labor force were able from time to time to press for and obtain higher wages. Domestic demand expanded and was becoming an increasingly important source of profit. The Mercantilist old predilection for low wages simply became impracticable in many cases. The view that low wages are a *national* necessity – because men are forced to work many hours and send their wives and children out to work and thus stimulate production and reduce domestic consumption and consequently leave more of the nation's produce for export, was crumbling, and was no longer tenable in practice. Together with this the progress of technology required a new type of better educated labor – workers who could no longer be regarded as 'non-people'.[28] So altogether, the rise of the middle class had given rise to the new class of urban workers. The economic exploitation of the latter provided the foundations of the formers' newly acquired power, wealth and life-style for their own augmentation of choice. The resistance of the urban workers to exploitation, which as yet was little more than individuals' struggles for greater shares in the fruit of their labor – for higher wages, was signalling the beginning of labor's long-drawn struggle for man's emancipation – to general progress.

---

28.   For a brief summary of Mercantilism vide Y.S. Brenner, *Theories of Economic Development and Growth*, Ch. I, Early Theories. Particularly pp. 16–17.

On the whole, however, the eighteenth century was more an era of consolidation of earlier achievements than of revolutionary innovations.[29] It was the era in which the bourgeoisie established and confirmed its position vis-à-vis the upper class and began to fortify it against pressures from below. – It was the period in which the principles established in the century that separated the publication of Gilbert's *De Magnete* (1600) from Newton's *Principia* (1684) and *Optick* (1704) were developed; and in which the approaches of Galileo and Descartes were refined into *The* methodology of systematic scientific endeavour.

The idea of the unity of nature, which claimed that the book of nature is written in mathematical language, was most impressively confirmed in mathematics and in its relation to other sciences. The most striking developments in this sphere can be ascribed to the Bernoulli's, Jacob (1654– ?) and John (1667–1748); to Daniel (1700–1782); and, of course, to Euler (1707–1783), Clairant (1713–1765), D'Alambert (1717–1783), Lagrange (1736–1813), Monge (1746–1818), Laplace (1749–1827), and Legendre (1752–1833), all of whom also contributed to other branches of science, especially the highly mathematical ones such as mechanics and astronomy.[30] On the firm foundations of Newton's *Principia* Euler developed the mechanics of particles and D'Alambert, Jacob Bernoulli, and Lagrange – analytical mechanics. Maupertius (1698–1758) provided 'final proof' for the existence of God in his introduction of the 'Law of Least Action', and also made important

---

29.   The French Revolution of 1789 was in effect the final step in this stage of the ascent of the French bourgeoisie – the brushing aside of aristocratic privileges that had since long lost their real power.

30.   For example, Euler founded the calculus of variations; Clairaut studied space curves and surfaces; Lagrange modernized analytical geometry; Monge descriptive geometry, and Laplace turned the theory of probability into an independent branch of mathematics.

contributions on impact and elasticity, of which the former formed the basis for Carnot's mechanics.[31]

31. Carnot (1753–1823) was in fact the first scientist to assert the experimental character of the principles of mechanics – in contrast to Euler and D'Alambert. Again, Clairant, D'Alambert, Euler, Lagrange and Laplace must be counted among the main students of the solar system and the developers of the more experimental parts of physics. John and Daniel Bernoulli, Euler and D'Alambert advanced the study of motion of fluids (hydrodynamics); Clairant hydrostatics; Euler, D'Alambert, Daniel Bernoulli, Mange and Lagrange made important contributions to the study of vibrations and thereby laid down the theoretical foundations for the study of sound, which like the study of heat was basically experimental. Other mathematicians who studied vibrations were Carre, Brook, Taylor and Fourier. Also G.F. Chladni (1756–1827) ought to be mentioned who demonstrated the existence of longitudinal and transversal vibrations, and measured the velocity of sound in various solids and gases; and Nallet who showed that sound travelled in water. The physician and chemist Joseph Black (1728–1799) developed thermo-dynamics by introducing the concept of fluid heat – the caloric – and latent heat, and distinguished between heat and temperature. Rumford (1753–1814), who was an army organizer, innovated methods of heating, lighting and cooking. He showed that heat is a form of energy and is subject to the general law of the conservation of energy. Next to scientist Rumford was also known as a social reformer. Daniel Bernoulli reached the conclusion (in 1728) that the pressure exerted by a gas on the walls of the container that holds it is the result of the collisions between the atoms of the gas and the walls of that container. This idea, that became the basis for the kinetic theory of gases, was however only developed further in the nineteenth century. In the new branch electricity and magnetism the best known contributors were Franklin, Gray, Du Fay and Coulomb. Benjamin Franklin (1706–1790) introduced the 'one fluid' theory and the law of the conservation of charge. In contrast to other contemporary scientists his approach was positivist. (Was it because he was an American?) Stephen Gray (1666–1736) and Charles F. Du Fay (1698–1739) were both experimental scientists. They discovered conductivity and induced charge, and, Du Fay alone, discovered that there are two types of charges. Charles Augustin Coulomb (1736–1806) developed theories of magnetism (1777) and electricity (1785). The most important innovation in chemistry was the work of Antoine Laurent Lavoisier (1743–1794) who dismissed the idea of phlogiston and may therefore no longer be regarded as a developer of earlier ideas, but as the beginner of a new era in chemistry, and indeed, his work is more properly placed in the context of nineteenth century innovation.

Perhaps the most significant aspect of this period of scientific and social consolidation was that it redirected men's interest away from the old matters of doctrine, i.e. away from questions concerned with the *purpose* of life towards the 'art of getting a living';[32] away from questions relating to the nature of the state and towards the means of increasing its opulence; away from 'what was ultimately to be wished' and towards 'what was immediately expedient'. This change gave a new look and impetus to science, for the same quest for opulence that stimulated technology did also begin to open men's eyes to the contribution science can make to technological advancement. At the same time the advancement of technology supplied the scientists with new and better instruments for the pursuit of their endeavors, so that while on the one hand, science became subservient to the demands of a technology of an increasingly materialistic society, on the other hand, the technological achievements themselves gave rise to new stimuli leading to the advancement of greater scientific insight. To be sure, in the eighteenth century science did not yet become a major force in the development of industry but it was beginning to play an increasingly important role in the transformation of manufacture into industry. Many branches of technology still remained unaffected by the new scientific ideas, but several most important ones did come under their influence. For example, the chemical industry, and through it textile manufacturing was increasingly permeated by innovations based upon the new theoretical ideas. So did Black's idea of latent heat lay the foundation for the development of steam-powered engines near the end of the eighteenth century.

Still, on the whole, the change in the foundations of technology progressed only gradually. In the middle of the seventeenth century more and more of the people concerned with economic activities were beginning to take an active interest in science. It suffices to look at the membership lists of the *Royal Society* and at the *Histories of Nature, Arts or Works,* sponsored by the Society, in the early years of its existence to discover this trend in England. On the

---

32. *Vide* T.S. Ashton, *An Economic History of England. The 18th Century,* London, 1955, p. 1.

Continent a similar tendency can be recognized from the contrast between the secrecy with which the alchemists surrounded their work and the liberality with which scientists like Descartes, Huygens and Leibniz broadcast their discoveries. Huygens experimented with the force of steam in cylinders in order to devise some mining equipment. The scientist Savery experimented with vacuum together with the craftsman Newcomen and they produced an early steam-powered water pump (1712); and the combined effort of the scientist Joseph Black, the technician James Watt, and the businessman Boulton produced the famous steam engine. Black discovered a way to measure heat-energy quantitatively, and subsequently latent heat, and Watt learned from him to apply scientific principles to the practical problems he was engaged with, and Boulton recognized the commercial chances this combination of scientific effort with technological ingenuity could offer. In fact businessmen like Boulton, craftsmen like Watt and scientists like Black, Erasmus Darwin, Samuel Galton, James Keir, Joseph Priestly and others were by this time mixing freely in the 'Lunar Society'.[33]

So the period in which science had been the sole province of an inquisitive elite trying to satisfy its curiosity about the nature of the world was nearing its end – the practical bourgeoisie was beginning to put science into the service of its material ends. Henceforth the understanding of the laws governing the universe began to be harnessed to the pursuit of the material wants of an increasingly acquisitive society. The question 'does it work?' and 'is the theorem useful?' began taking the place of the question 'is it true'. Henry Cavendish became better known in his time for his contributions to the development of new processes in bleaching, in ceramic, in coal-tar, iron making and distilling; and Antoine Laurent Lavoisier

---

33. *Vide* Singer, Holmyard, Hall and Williams (Eds), *A History of Technology*, Vol. IV, pp. 674–7 for a long list of co-operations between scientists and craftsmen.

for his contributions to the development of agriculture, gunpowder and balloons, than for their theoretical achievements.[34]

The contemporary author who reflected the new mood, and gave formal expression to its ethics, was *Immanuel Kant* (1724–1804). Kant was at one and the same time an innovator and a retainer of an older style of thought. As Schiller said of him (1795), 'there is always something about Kant... which reminds one of a monk, who has left his cloister behind him but cannot rid himself of its traces'. He was strongly influenced by Rousseau, Spinoza and Hume. From Rousseau he learned the idea of the 'dignity of man', which liberated him from his contemporaries' idealization of enlightenment, and from the despise he felt, by his own admission, for the uneducated masses. From Spinoza he learned that ideas can be independent of experience, and that moral satisfaction lies in the realization of one's own rational nature; and from Hume he learned the distinction between knowledge and feeling, and, that man is but a bundle or collection of perceptions which succeed each other with inconceivable rapidity. But it was his distinction between the *is* and the *ought,* and his conclusion that *the ought can never be derived from the is,* that more than anything else influenced the new mood of his time. It did not merely reflect the mood of a bourgeoisie that had won its first 'revolution' and was settling down intent upon maintaining its position, but anticipated the feeling of no wish for further changes – no *ought* to be desired, no *is* that *ought to be different.*

Harald Hoffding[35] describes this as follows: 'In his *Tugendlehre* (personal ethics) Kant lays chief stress on that attitude of character which corresponds to his general conception of the ethical. In his view, virtue consists in strength of soul *(fortitudo moralis),* in the power and dignity which follows from the consciousness of

---

34.   For a discussion of the permeation of technology by science and the development of applied science *vide A History of Technology, ibid.,* Ch. 23, A.R.J.P. Ubbelohde, The Beginnings of the Change from Craft Mystery to Science as a basis for Technology (Oxford, 1858).

35.   Harald Hoffding, *A History of Modern Philosophy,* Vol. II, Dover edition, p. 91.

possessing the law of our own action within ourselves and of being united by means of this law into one great whole. The ends posited in Kant's personal ethics are (1) the perfection of self, (2) the happiness of others. Not our own happiness, – for we strive after this involuntarily and with such eagerness that we hold it to be other men's duty to consider it likewise. Nor the perfection of others, – for only they themselves can effect this... for perfection consists in nothing else but in making ourselves, according to our own conception of duty, our own end...'

Kant was neither a pure empiricist nor a pure rationalist. Not unlike Helvetius and Hume he believed that knowledge begins with experience but from the rationalists he learned that it not *all* arises out of experience. Reason, he claimed, must approach nature in order to be taught by it, – but it must not approach it as 'a pupil who listens to everything that the teacher chooses to say, but as an appointed judge who compels the witness to answer questions which he himself has formulated.'[36] Experience must be attended by an ordering process of perception that gives rise to concepts with which the experience then becomes knowledge – 'Concepts without perceptions are empty; perceptions without concepts are blind'.

Like the mathematicians who so greatly influenced contemporary ways of thinking, Kant too adopted in his approach to knowledge axiom-like a priori's. Intuitively given elements, namely, *space, time* and *causation,* preceed experience, and together with quality, quantity, relation and modality they form the basis of, nay the precondition for, all human understanding. The things-in-themselves, the *noumena,* man is unable to penetrate but their spacial and temporal manifestations may be understood and are the proper objects of empirical study. Morality too is 'given' – one cannot know its foundations but one may well study the character of its concepts and percepts. God may be the benevolent creator of the world but then it is also conceivable that he is not – there is no proof either way, or, even more disturbing, both propositions can be proven logically possible. With man one is on firmer ground for man can be shown to have a tendency to socialize and at the same time

---

36.   E. Kant, *Critique of Pure Reason*, 1781.

to be egoistic. The conflict between these tendencies is nature's way of promoting human progress – of furthering the development of man's natural capacities. Superficially Kant's view here comes close to his contemporary English tradition but the similarity is really only superficial. For example, Adam Smith believed that man's study of his own advantage leads him to prefer that employment which is most advantageous to the society in general;[37] and Hutcheson believed in 'a divinely ordained harmony of egoistic and altruistic impulses in man...'[38] in which self-love always finds itself circumscribed by love for one's fellow men; both, Smith and his teacher Hutcheson, see the source of this harmony in man's egoistic impulses – in man's desire for the approval of his fellow men. As pointed out before: 'The rich man glories in his riches, because he feels that they naturally draw upon him the attention of the world.[39] It is the consideration of his own private profit which is the sole motive that determines the owner of any capital to employ it either in agriculture, in manufacturing, or in some particular branch of the... trade...[40] but the study of this, his own advantage, leads him to the employment which is most beneficial to all, because through profits he will learn of the demands of society.[41] The rich in spite of their natural selfishness and rapacity... are led by an invisible hand to make nearly the same distribution of the necessaries of life, which would have been made had the earth been divided into equal portions among all inhabitants.'[42] The rich man 'by pursuing his own

---

37.   Adam Smith, *An Inquiry into the True Nature and Causes of the Wealth of Nations*, Bk. IV, Ch. II.

38.   F. Hutcheson, *An Essay on the Nature and Conduct of the Passions and Affections*, London, 1728, 1730, pp. 193–4.

39.   Adam Smith, *The Theory of Moral Sentiments*, 1759, 1790, pp. 120–5.

40.   Adam Smith, *Wealth of Nations*, Bk. IV, Ch. II.

41.   Adam Smith, *ibid.*

42.   Adam Smith, *The Theory of Moral Sentiments*, pp. 465–6.

interest... frequently promotes that of the society more effectively than when he really intends to promote it.'[43] So egoism assumes an almost moral quality; *with Kant it does not.* For Kant too the good society is the one that allows men to develop their capacities, that allows the greatest degree of individual freedom to compete and yet prevents both anarchy (the rule of the rabble) and oppression (aristocratic privileges). In short, with him too the bourgeois state leaves little to be desired, but egoism remains the very antithesis of moral perfection. The ends of his ethics were certainly closer to the medieval christian tradition than to a justification of bourgeois expediency. His ethical conception was dominated by a quest for *self-perfection* and the *conscious advancement of the 'happiness of others'.*

Altogether Kant's conviction that faith, not knowledge, justifies belief in the freedom of the will, immortality and the existence of God, is certainly more in the tradition of medieval christianity, and closer to the ethical conceptions of the nineteenth century, than to his own generation's. And yet he abandons the Platonic and Christian search for the inner-nature of things, – man cannot know the noumena, but leaves man assured of their existence, because while man cannot know the ethical noumena themselves he can well recognize and know the ethics based upon them. He can act as if the maxim from which he acts were to become through his will a universal law of nature; he can treat humanity, whether in his own person or that of another, in every case as an end in itself never as a means. So the moral individual becomes a criterion superior to and outside the actual social order. But then, Kant never recognized that to find such a moral standpoint independent of the social order is not only impossible but may well render one a mere conformist servant of the prevailing social order. To be sure, Kant's influence on subsequent generations of moral philosophers was tremendous, for perhaps the majority of writers, including many who are self-consciously anti-Kantian, were to define ethics as a subject in

---

43.   Adam Smith, *Wealth of Nations*, Bk. IV, Ch. II.

Kantian terms,[44] but his basic premise did not much deviate from the traditional. His notions of 'right', 'good' and 'the good will' were those that had been accepted for valid before, but he gave them an 'inner', psychological, content – 'Nothing can possibly be conceived in the world, or even out of it, which can be called good without qualification, except a good will.'[45] So far the values had been external to man – they were given like space and time, now they began to lose their independent character; hesitantly they were beginning to drift – to become not yet really accommodating but adaptable to the wishes of a changing society. The subjective intentions, not objective criteria – good will, not the firm dictum of church and tradition become the arbiters of value. The old value system was breaking away from its anchorage, it was not yet drifting, but it was also no longer safely fastened in its mooring.

R.C. Lewontin[46] wrote that while it seems obvious that 'scientific discovery influences the direction of social and economic change, or at least its rate, it is even more true that social and economic world views must permeate science.' He claimed that 'no appeal to a *Zeitgeist* is implied by such a relationship, for the meaning of *Zeitgeist* is that science and other social activities respond equally to some spirit of the age whose source and power are unknown... yet there is nothing mystical about the way in which notions of *cause and effect, choice and chance, determinacy and freedom,* spread from one science to another. Equally, it is entirely within the normal picture of historical causation that *general social attitudes and economic relationships between social classes should have a profound effect upon the acceptability and apparent reasonableness of scientific hypotheses.* Science is, after all, a social activity...' Well, the bourgeois revolution reached its peak in England in the Reform Bill of 1832 based on Bentham's principle of the 'greatest Happiness for the greatest number', while on the Continent it took the more

---

44.   *Vide* Alasdair MacIntyre, *op.cit.*, for a further discussion of Kant's ethics.

45.   E. Kant, *Grundlegung*, p. 1.

46.   'Evolution' in *I.E.S.S.*, 1968, Vol. V, pp. 208–9.

violent form of the revolution of 1848, and it is in this context that the subsequent development of Kant's ideas have to be judged, and it is in this spirit that the two conceptions of progress – the one assumed in science and the one proposed by me in the beginning of this book, can be united.

7

The Ascent of the Bourgeoisie and the Rise of Utilitarianism

'Come what come may,
Time and the hour runs through the roughest day'
Macbeth Act I. Sc.iii 146

Adam Smith began his celebrated *Inquiry into the Nature and Causes of the Wealth of Nations* (1776) with the words: 'The greatest improvement in the productive powers of labor, and the greater part of the skill, dexterity, and judgment with which it is anywhere directed, or applied, seem to have been the effects of the division of labor.' To illustrate this he gave an example from the pin-making trade; 'a workman not educated to this business (which the division of labor has rendered a distinct trade), nor acquainted with the use of the machinery employed in it (to the invention of which the same division of labor has probably given occasion), could scarce, perhaps, with his utmost industry, make one pin in a day, and certainly could not make twenty. But in the way in which this business is now carried on, not only the whole work is a peculiar trade, but it is divided into a number of branches, of which the greater part are likewise peculiar trades. One man draws out the wire, another straights it, a third cuts it, a fourth points it, a fifth grinds it at the top for receiving the head... and the important business of making a pin is, in this manner, divided into about eighteen distinct operations, which, in some manufactories, are all performed by distinct hands...' In this manner even poorly equipped 'manufactory' can with only ten persons make 'upwards of forty-eight thousand pins in a day. Each person, therefore,... making four thousand eight hundred pins in a day. But if they had all wrought separately and independently, and without any of them having been educated to this peculiar business, they certainly could not each of them have made twenty, perhaps not one pin a day; that is, certainly, not the two hundred and fortieth, perhaps not the four thousand eight hundredth part of what they are at present capable of performing, in consequence of a proper division and combination of their different operations.'

In this opening paragraph of his book Smith reported man's novel way of overcoming the niggardliness of nature. He described the new mode of production which, in scarcely two centuries, was not only to provide humanity with amazing powers to increase productivity, but also transformed the whole structure and character of the societies effected by it. He outlined the innovation which, on the one hand, made man the master of unprecedented wealth, and, on the other, led to his most ominous social alienation. He mentioned the essential factor that was rapidly to separate late medieval and early modern socio-economic relations from those which were to predominate in the subsequent centuries of industrial capitalism.

A society still in the last throes of a vertically aligned social order, with guilds and crafts in which but little differentiation between capital and labor had as yet materialized, was before Smith's very eyes giving birth to a society dominated by horizontally arrayed class relations. Ushered in by men like Arkwright (roller-spinning), Hargreave (spinning Jenny), Crompton (the mule), and Watt (steam power), in the second half of the eighteenth century, the new mode of production caused more and more people engaged in manufacturing to lose control over their means of production and to miss the little protection feudal and quasi-feudal affiliations and customs had hitherto accorded them. The old society in which personal nexus and certain identities of interests between people of diverse rank had offered the poor a degree of protection and security was waning, and new safeguards, based upon the horizontal identities of class interests, were only very slow to develop. Meanwhile, at least in the fast growing urban centers,[1] the poor lost not only their habitual late-feudal sources of societal protection but also the ability to use their own tools and traditional skills for earning their necessary sustenance. The inability of a steadily growing number of craftsmen to produce competitively with the owners of the new productive-technology, and hence to sell the fruit of their labor at adequate prices to sustain themselves, rendered an ever increasing part of the working population economically and socially more vulnerable than they had ever been since Roman times. The new entrepreneurs were not slow in the nineteenth century to avail themselves of this opportunity to increase their fortunes and power.

In the historiography of the nineteenth century there is a great deal of learned controversy about the question whether the material living conditions of the working classes, in the countries affected by the new mode of production, improved or deteriorated in comparison with the preceding century. Both sides to the argument produce good factual evidence to prove their opposing views. From a variety of short periods, from different locations and from diverse trades the supporters of each point of view provide credible proof of their conflicting contentions, but, with few exceptions, they all miss the essential point – namely the qualitative change in the overall conditions of the working people.

Coming mostly from fairly settled backgrounds, the great majority of social and economic historians of the nineteenth century, are simply incapable of grasping the *real meaning* for the individual worker of missing *the sense of security and social belonging* that, in spite of the degrading obligations that had accompanied this security in earlier ages, was characteristic of the 19th century. The worker now found himself deprived of the means of providing for *himself,* (even by poaching for meat or root gathering), and without the

---

1.   The population of London was approximately 1 million in the ear 1800, 2.4 million in 1850, and 4.5 million in 1900; the population of Paris 0.5 million in 1800, 1 million in 1850 and 2.7 million in 1900.

comfort and support of a social group (such as the village community or extended family), with which he could identify and which identified itself with him. It was this 'loneliness' made worse by the cold fear of starvation that made each worker the objective enemy of everyone else in the struggle for work and survival. It is this that made life in the nineteenth century for most workers, most of the time, brutish, nasty and short. It is sufficient to glance through the works of Dickens (1812–1870) and Zola (1840–1902) to see the point. The cherished freedom for one class was solitary fear for another. Desolate fear dehumanized labor and delayed its effective resistance to exploitation, while it helped to mould the bourgeoisies attitude towards the working population.[2] An attitude that transformed traditional christian notions of compassion into charity and thus severed the last integrating link between the upper and lower strata of society. For, while compassion stresses the unity of man charity negates it – it transforms a duty into a free act of generosity, a transaction between more and less fortunate equals into an event in which a superior person gives something to an inferior who may or may not deserve it. It substitutes the old unifying conception of hierarchy that was based upon obligations and duties by a new dividing conception in which the element of duty in so far as the upper classes are concerned is lost.

While desolation and the fear of starvation characterized the social climate of the industrial working class in the nineteenth century, acquisition, competition and rationality characterized the spirit of the bourgeoisie. A new spirit imposed itself upon the long-standing human propensities 'to truck, barter and exchange one thing for another.'[3] For centuries people trucked, bartered and exchanged commodities to satisfy wants they could not satisfy themselves. When money entered such transactions it did so only as a convenient

---

2.   No one who has not himself experienced the fear and deprivation that accompanies long periods of unemployment in an industrial society without the benefits of some social security arrangements can really fathom their 'dehumanizing' effect – at best he can 'understandingly' commiserate at worst 'piously' forgive.

3.   Adam Smith, *The Wealth of Nations.*

medium of exchange, as a measure, and occasionally as a store of wealth for use at a later date. Profit too was not unknown as the reward for providing one group of people with goods produced by another at what was called the 'fair price'. The object of production was consumption. Some people produced victuals others manufactured utensils; the former sold victuals to buy the utensils they wanted and the latter sold their manufactures to buy food. The new spirit of acquisition changed all this – it transformed the mere medium of exchange, money, into a self-expanding value, into *The* novel object of endeavors. Money became capital and the owners of such capital no longer sold and bought goods to satisfy their wants but for the sole purpose of increasing their stocks of wealth. Profit became the purpose of production, the satisfaction of real wants the coincidental concomitant; and the technological superiority of the new mode of production was fast becoming the hitherto unequalled source of profit. All that was necessary in order to realize a profit was to set men to work with the new technology and reward their labor by something less than the full share of what their combined produce fetched in the market.

The luxury that was characteristic of the bourgeois way-of-life in the eighteenth century taught those able to enrich themselves the new role and power of money; the desolation and fear that was characteristic of the way-of-life of the industrial working class in the nineteenth century taught industrial discipline to those unable to find alternative sources of income and were forced to work for wages. Fear of unemployment superseded pride of craftsmanship; anxiety of falling foul with one's employer replaced the traditional obligation of obedience. Traditional obligations had imposed duties and responsibilities on both employers and employees alike, but the new relationship was one sided. Employers had little cause to respect the needs of their employees, but wage-workers could only disrespect the wishes of their employers in peril of their jobs and livelihood. So the focus of attention shifted from the *laboring person* to the *product of his labor* and hence to money. For as long as the productivity of labor had remained low – when perhaps the labor of ten men was needed to provide together a sufficiently large surplus above their own subsistence requirements to feed an extra person who was not himself directly engaged in material production, (for example a master, king, warrior or priest); and for as long as the security and prestige of the socially superior depended upon the number of inferiors each of them controlled, most social and economic objectives could not but center around people. Not so when productivity of labor rose – when people equipped with the new technology and mode of producing were able to produce, and could be forced to hand over to their employers, a volume of produce incomparably greater than had ever been possible before; Not so when the life and property of the rich was found to be better protected by the state than by private bands of retainers; Not so when the symbols of social standing the style of gracious living and the power to exercise control over men, could be bought for money When these things happened, man lost his position at the center of attention, and money – the equivalent of the produce of labor, took his place.[4] Consequently attention shifted from the old human problems of society – the 'fair price' and the hierarchies of 'social obligations', to a new set of problems related to material possessions. With acquisition becoming the object of endeavors *competition* replaced the outmoded idea of the fair price. The fair price simply became irrelevant.[5] It had been important for a society protecting itself against the almost monopolistic position of guilds and craftsmen who might overcharge the public. But the superior system of production put an end to this type of risk for producers began vying with each other for the sale of their goods, and profits were now more often realized through cost reductions that were made possible by the new technology than through price increases. Freedom thus became the freedom to compete and the old guild restrictions became symbols

---

4.   Marx wrote about this process that all older idols were pushed off their pedestals and replaced by the one and only god 'Mammon'. (Mammon is the Hebrew word for money or wealth) It is noteworthy that there is here a parallel in science; Humanity is at the center of theories until Comte; in the nineteenth century this position is lost.

5.   Though the 'fair price' was to return later in a different context, namely to protect the least efficient producers from prices below the level they were able to compete.

of oppression. Achievement became the mark of distinction and successful competition the means by which it was attained.

As competition implied falling rather than rising prices, and as the latter were attributed to the new technology and were not *seen* to be related to the miserable conditions of the workers who made the goods offered for sale, (as had been the case when prices fell in earlier ages), competition soon lost its public odium. The more competition gained in respectability the greater became the ruthlessness with which it was pursued. Thus when the object of production shifted from the satisfaction of real wants and became the accumulation of wealth labor was transformed from a necessary social activity to provide man's sustenance into a factor of production not unlike land and capital. However, the supply of labor is far less elastic than the demand for goods and consequently, as factor of production, also more vulnerable to market fluctuations. So, while employers were able to vary the volume of their output at little cost to suit diminishing demand, the number of people seeking employment remained constant, or more precisely usually increased. It is therefore hardly surprising that on the whole for a long time only the rich were able to reap the fruits of the new mode of production. It was this difference between the inelastic and growing supply of labour and the supply elasticity of goods that prevented labor from sharing, even indirectly in the new affluence by being able to purchase more goods with a constant level of income.[6] This is of course true only for the workers who were unable to organize themselves in defence of their interests, but they were by far the greater part of the working class. Altogether organization was very difficult in this period when the principle of freedom in its new guise of competition was just becoming the new idol of the social elite. It was just too easy to interpret any attempt by workers to organize as 'ring forming', i.e. as creating a monopoly to the detriment of the general public, which was in fact forbidden by law. Moreover, workers had not yet liberated themselves from the age old custom of looking for protection and guidance to those hierarchically

---

6.   Prices and wages here are always *real* not money or nominal prices or wages, i.e. in terms of their current purchasing power not their nominal values.

above them and as the latter had now become the 'captains of industry' they were more inclined to turn to them 'cap in hand' so to speak, than to their fellow workers.

However, the dehumanization of labor did not lie in the new social relations alone but had also another cause, namely the very character of the new type of technology itself. The most characteristic of the new technology was, as we have seen, the separation of each production process into a great number of very simple operations for which little skill was required. All that a worker had to do was to raise or lower a leaver or turn a screw. The advantage of this was that even a simple peasant coming directly from the land was almost immediately upon arrival in town capable of serving industry. The disadvantage was that employers found it easy to replace 'difficult' workers, especially because this was also a period in which a great many people, who either could no longer find a living on the land or were attracted by imaginary prospects, were congregating in the cities.[7] But most dehumanizing of all was the fact that the new mode of production deprived the worker of the satisfaction that comes from recognizing the results of one's labor. The absence of this satisfaction turned the worker into something like a part of the machine he worked with. His actions became mechanical and repetitive like those of the machine itself, and in time, the machines were also beginning to determine his pace of work – he became indeed a 'factor of production'. His alienation became complete; he not only lost ownership but even control over the use of the instrument he worked with. Adam Smith already observed this. In 1776 he wrote: 'The man whose whole life is spent in performing a few simple operations... has no occasion to exert his understanding... He naturally loses, the habit of such exertion, and generally becomes as stupid and ignorant as it is possible for a

---

7.   *Vide* Y.S. Brenner, *A Short History of Economic Progress*, pp. 76–7. Population growth and the growth of towns with more than 200.000 inhabitants. For example in England total population increased between 1800 and 1900 from 10 to 20 millions and of towns from 2 to 16 millions. In France total population from 28 to 38 millions and towns from 1.2 to 4.5 millions. In Germany, total 22 to 49 millions and towns from 0.2 to 7 millions.

human creature to become. The torpor of his mind renders him, not only incapable of relishing or learning a part in any rational conversation, but of conceiving any generous, noble or tender sentiment.'[8] Naturally, Smith did not want this to happen and suggested certain remedies. In spite of his general objection to deliberate interference with nature's self-regulating mechanisms he made in this case an exception and clearly advocated state sponsorship of education to counteract the negative adjuncts of the new mode of production.[9]

What for Smith was but a frightening prospect became a kind of perception of reality with Malthus. In the twenty-two years which separated the publication of Smith's *Wealth of Nations* from Malthus' *Essay on the Principle of Population* social relations, at least in England, underwent a profound transformation. Reading Malthus today one is struck with the impression that for him man is here on earth for but one purpose, namely to serve the needs of the economy. One feels as if man was created for the economic system and not the system to serve the needs of man. If there is misery and poverty it has nothing to do with the system. 'The most permanent cause of poverty has little or no direct relation to forms of government or the unequal division of property[10]' it springs from the excess of the supply of labor over its demand – from the poor's sexual immoderation. And so, 'as the rich do not in reality possess the power of finding employment and maintenance for the poor, the poor cannot, in the nature of things, possess the right to demand them.'[11] If the lower classes could be made to realize that by making scarce *'the commodity'* which they produce (children) all would be

---

8.   A. Smith, *Wealth of Nations*, Bk. V, Ch. I. One may of course argue that had the worker not become 'as stupid and ignorant as it is possible for a human creature to become' he would not have allowed the system to last for as long as it did or still does.

9.   *Vide* pp. 183–5.

10.   Malthus, *Essay on the Principle of Population*, Bk. IV, Ch. XIV.

11.   *Ibid.*

well and amen. So Malthus neatly exonerates the bourgeoisie from all traditional compunction concerning the poor by placing the responsibility for their ill plight at the poor's own doorstep. He gives a new twist to the traditional asceticism, to the association of sex with sin, turning it into a self-adjusting mechanism, not unlike Adam Smith's 'invisible hand', by which the virtuous are rewarded and the sinful damned. 'The virtue of chastity is not... a forced produce of artificial society; but it has the most real and solid foundation in nature and reason; being apparently the only virtuous means of avoiding the vice and misery which result so often from the principle of population... As it appears, therefore, it is in the power of each individual to avoid all the evil consequences to himself and society resulting from the principle of population by the practice of a virtue clearly directed to him by the light of nature, and expressly enjoined in revealed religion;... It is the apparent object of the Creator to deter us from vice by the pains which accompany it, and to lead us to virtue by the happiness that it produces.'[12] But then, contraception seems to be the answer,[13] however not for Malthus. For him the 'natural and moral evil seem to be the instruments employed by the Deity in admonishing us to avoid any mode of conduct which is not suited to our being, and will consequently injure our happiness'.[14]

So Malthus combines the old with the new – the traditional teachings of the church with those of the Church of England, the old theology of predestination with the new protestant ethics of salvation through parsimony and work, the will of God with the Law of Nature, God's design and man's freedom of choice. His God is revealed on earth through 'vice and misery' but in spite of this he remains the old merciful God for 'vice and misery' cease to be punishments – God's retribution for man's Original Sin, they become a compassionate God's instrument for human salvation. 'We cannot

---

12.   Malthus, *ibid.*, Bk. IV, Ch. II.

13.   Several means of birth control were already widely published in Malthus' time. *Vide* G.F. McCleary 'Malthus and Contraception' in *The Malthusian Population Theory*, London, 1953, Ch. VIII, pp. 83–99.

14.   Malthus, *ibid.*, Bk. I.

but conceive that it is an object of the Creator, that the earth should be replenished; and it appears to me clear, that this could not be effected without a tendency in population to increase faster than food; and as, with the present law of increase, the peopling of the earth does not proceed very rapidly, we have undoubtedly some reason to believe, that this law is not too powerful for its apparent object. The desire of the means of subsistence would be comparatively confined in its effects, and would fail of producing that general activity so necessary to the improvement of the human faculties, were it not for the strong and universal effort of population to increase with greater rapidity than its supplies. *If those two tendencies were exactly balanced, I do not see what motive there would be sufficiently strong to overcome the acknowledged indolence of man*, and make him proceed in the cultivation of the soil...'[15] The analogy of all the other laws of nature would be completely violated, if in this instance alone there were no provision for accidental failure, no resources against the vices of mankind, or the partial mischiefs resulting from other general laws. To effect the apparent object without any attendant evil, it is evident that perpetual change in the law of increase would be necessary, varying with the varying circumstances of each country. But instead of this, it is not only more consonant to the analogy of the other parts of nature, but we have reason to think that it is more conductive to the formation and improvement of the human mind, that the law should be uniform, and the evils incidental to it, under certain circumstances, left to be mitigated or removed by man himself. His duties in this case vary with his situation; he is thus kept more alive to the consequences of his actions; and his faculties have evidently greater play and

---

15.   Italics *not* in the original. Substitute he idea of *profit* for Malthus' 'Principle of Population' and you get the argument that were it not for the love of gain or fear of starvation no one would work. This idea, which may be named 'The Iron Law of Capitalism', is now usually adduced to discredit the credibility of any social system not based upon the profit motive and even against the social security arrangements of the Welfare State.

opportunity of improvement, than if the evil were removed by a perpetual change of the law according to circumstances.'[16]

So Malthus was a utilitarian moralist who believed in the improving powers of God's arrangements upon earth and in a mixture of feudal and absolutist attitudes to labor. He dressed the state in the robes of a feudal protector and master, and the workers in the loin-cloth of serfs who had a right to protection and a duty of obedience though they were denied a claim to food and employment. He attacked Pitt's Poor Law of 1796, and various other attempts based upon the traditional conception of charity to mitigate the distress that accompanied the transition from feudalism and mercantilism to industrial society, and was scornful of the utopic solutions put forward by the rationalistic utopians from Condorcet to Godwin. 'A writer may tell me that he thinks man will ultimately become an ostrich. I cannot properly contradict him. But before he can expect to bring any reasonable person over to his opinion, he ought to show, that the necks of mankind have been gradually elongating; that the lips have grown harder and more prominent; that the legs and feet are daily altering their shape; and that the hair is beginning to change into stubs of feathers. And till the probability of so wonderful a conversion be shewn, it is surely lost time and lost eloquence to expatiate on the happiness of man in such a state...'[17] What aroused Malthus' anger in the writings of Godwin was the contention that but for the irrational institutional restraints that society imposed upon itself there would be neither misery nor vice. Take away the man-made evil system and substitute for it a regime of good reason, nay, of plain common sense, a regime of equality in both property and sexual relations and all causes that have hitherto impeded the progress of mankind towards happiness would simply disappear. Not so, retorts Malthus. Not the institutions are at fault but man's 'acknowledged indolence' and weakness of character. Alone each individual's pursuit of self-interest within the framework of the established order, i.e. within the institutions of

---

16.   Malthus, *ibid.*, Bk. IV, Ch. I.

17.   Malthus, *op.cit.*, (First Edition), pp. 10–11.

property, marriage, and class division, can lead him and society as a whole towards a greater happiness. For only within the institutions can man find the restraining forces that protect him and society from the true cause of misery, namely the 'principle of population'.

The Hobbesian disharmony between individuals now receives a new aspect and becomes discongruity between classes; the war of all against all becomes the contradiction of interests between landlords, capitalists and laborers. The old conception of 'self-interest' gets a class perspective, and Smith's idea of *Natural Harmony* goes by the board and is replaced by a Ricardian specter of *class antagonisms*. Adam Smith, like Locke before him, recognized that work creates value, that the worth of a commodity is directly related to the amount of human labor bestowed upon it in its process of production. Ricardo took this observation a step further. He maintained that the value of all goods depended upon the relative quantity of labor necessary for their production and the rate of profit earned for the capital which is locked up without bringing in revenue until the goods can be sold.[18] Not the greater or less compensation which is paid for labor effects the value of goods but the quantity of labor. The quantity of labor that includes not only 'the labor applied immediately to the commodities... but (also) the labor... which is bestowed on the implements, tools, and buildings, with which such labor is assisted.'[19] But having said this, Ricardo is either unable or unwilling to recognize the full *moral* implications of his statement. Labor remains a commodity, its rewards depend upon the laws of supply and demand and not upon the value it produces. 'Labor like all other things which are purchased and sold, and which may be increased or diminished in quantity, has its natural and its market price. The natural price of labor is that price which is necessary to enable laborers, one with another, to subsist and to perpetuate their race, without either increase or diminution... The market price of labor is the price which is really paid for it... labor

---

18.   Letter of Ricardo to Mc Culloch.

19.   Ricardo, *The Principles of Political Economy and Taxation*, 1917, Ch. I, p. 5.

is dear when it is scarce and cheap when it is plentiful... When the market price of labor exceeds its natural price... (the laborer) has it in his power to command a greater proportion of the necessaries and enjoyments of life, and therefore to rear a healthy and numerous family. When, however, by the encouragement which high wages give to the increase of population, the number of laborers is increased, wages fall to their natural price, and indeed from a reaction sometimes fall below it. When the market price of labor is below its natural price, the condition of the laborer is most wretched: The poverty deprives them of those comforts which custom renders absolute necessaries. It is only after their privations have reduced their number, or the demand for labor has increased, that the market price of labor will rise to its natural price.[20] Here is a sober statement of reality and a mechanism akin to the Darwinist outlook which introduces variation as an essential factor in natural law. People have become a factor of production and poverty and deprivation are stripped of their emotional properties and become a factor in natural processes.

Yet there is a glimpse of hope for all classes thanks to the advancement of technology. 'If the improved means of production, in consequence of the use of machinery, should increase the net produce,' then, according to Ricardo,[21] 'The landlord and the capitalist will benefit, not by an increase of rent and profit, but by the advantages resulting from the expenditure of the same rent and profit on commodities very considerably reduced in value, while the situation of the laboring classes will also be considerably improved; first, from the increased demand for menial servants; secondly from the stimulus to saving from revenue which such an abundant net produce will afford; and thirdly, from the low price of all articles of consumption on which their wages will be expanded.'[22] However, these hopeful possibilities can only materialize for as long as both the 'net' and the 'gross' income of society increase simultaneously,

---

20.   Ricardo, *ibid.,* Ch. V, pp. 52–3 (in Everymans edition).

21.   Ricardo, *ibid.,* Ch. V.

22.   Ricardo, *ibid.,* Ch. XXXI, p. 268.

i.e. as long as what modern economists would call investment in the consumer goods sector and in the producer goods sector increases harmoniously. For Ricardo, unlike later apologists of capitalism, had already discovered that the twentieth century 'wisdom' that 'what is good for General Motors is good for the American people' need not necessarily be true. He was quite aware that 'the one fund from which landlords and capitalists derive their revenue, may increase while the other, that upon which the laboring class mainly depend, may diminish'; and that therefore, 'the same cause which may increase the net revenue of the country may at the same time render the population redundant, and deteriorate the condition of the laborer.'[23]   But, again, as in the case of *labor-value* so with the theory of the *wages-fund* the time was not yet ripe to recognize the moral implications. Ricardo was not yet ready to draw the ultimate conclusions from his analysis that would have finally destroyed the conception of universal harmony and the very foundations upon which the ideology of bourgeois liberalism was resting.[24] On the basis of contemporary empirical evidence he on the contrary salvages what can be saved from the sinking harmony by calling upon a kind of rachet effect by which each general increase in the demand for labor and consequent rise in real wages raises the workingman's subsistence level in a way that the following downswing can never reduce it again to a level as low as it had been before. He believed, that the oscillations in workingmen's incomes took place around a long-term upward trend. 'It is not to be understood that the natural price of labor, estimated even in food and necessaries, is absolutely fixed and constant. It varies at different times in the same country, an very materially differs in different countries. It essentially depends on the habits and customs of the people... An English laborer would

---

23.   Ricardo, *ibid.*, Ch. XXXI, pp. 263–4.

24.   It is interesting to see that the same can be said of Darwin. His principle of natural selection does *not* imply that a more complex creature – one which has evolved later, is better equipped for survival than an earlier less complex one. Nevertheless Darwin believed so firmly in progress that he included this principle in his theory without noticing the contradiction. As S.J. Gould pointed out, Darwin considered both *natural laws*.

consider his wages under their natural rate, and too scanty to support a family, if they enabled him to purchase no other food than potatoes, and to live in no better habitation than a mud cabin: Yet these moderate demands of nature are often deemed sufficient in countries where man's life is cheap... Many of the conveniences now enjoyed in an English cottage would have been thought luxuries at an earlier period of our history...'[25]

In spite of the uniting principle common to all members of the classical school of economics, that liberty and property are the keystones of every rational economic order and that political economy resembles a natural science in the universal applicability of its laws,[26] there remained between them important differences of approach and social perception. For example, Malthus never freed himself from the traces of christian medievalism. As far as the purpose of life was concerned his ethical conception of man's destiny continued to be that of the church – man's *moral improvement*. Consequently he was spared the dilemma of resolving the contradiction inherent in a system that separated mankind into classes according to their earthly wealth. This was not so with Ricardo. Coming from a completely different background,[27] Ricardo, try as he may, was never really able to ignore the injustice of the system, and thus was either consciously or unconsciously forced to fall back upon the conception of natural harmony processes, essentially progressive or leading to the advantages that accrue to all members of society from the further enrichment of the rich in order to escape the ethical predicament into which his labor-value theory would otherwise have led him. It was precisely Malthus' freedom to stress *disharmony* that made him the philosophically influential writer that he was. His conception fitted exactly the tenor of competitive individualism and the ideology which the nineteenth century bourgeoisie adopted for itself to justify its predominant position and

---

25.   Ricardo, *ibid.*, Ch. V.

26.   *Vide* Karl Diehl in *E.S.S.*, Vol. V, p. 351.

27.   His Jewish background may explain Ricardo's greater sensitivity to the principle of justice than to the christian idea of eventual salvation.

to give an ethical justification to social and economic inequality. Indeed, Darwin drew essential elements from Malthus' proposition about the 'tendency in all animated life to increase beyond the nourishment prepared for it'[28] for his theory of natural selection was the reflection of an increasingly confident propertied class which, at first only hesitantly but in the late eighteenth century with growing self-assurance, adjusted its perception of the universe in congruity with its changing economic and social position. It was the resonance of the economic and social mutation that since the days of the Renaissance was with mounting impetus transforming society from its medieval static stability (in which radical changes in status could only occur as exceptional withdrawals of extensions of divine grace) into a society in which man, no longer born into his status by divine providence, obtained and retained his status by his own conscious effort.[29] This was not an entirely new approach. Galileo and Descartes had shaken the medieval inert perception of the world by showing that the natural state of existence was motion. Hobbes carried the perception of motion a step further into the realm of social behavior by making man the servant of his *passions* and Spinoza emphasized the passive nature of these passions. Utilitarianism stirred these still essentially passive perceptions of movement into activity by making the *passions* into *wants*. It transformed observation into participation – the medieval acquiescence with fate into the new bourgeois spirit of restless activity. In the process, rationality, which had first been mainly introspective, i.e. restricted to the understanding of observed phenomena, became functional – the application of reason to the choice of means for the attainment of ends and the satisfaction of wants, and opened the way for the *question* how variation between individuals could at one and the same time be mere fluctuations about a stable, and therefore predictable, pattern of change, i.e. motion.

---

28.   Malthus, *Essay*, Bk. I, Ch. I, p. 5.

29.   *Vide* also R.C. Lewontin, *op.cit.,* in *I.E.S.S.*, Vol. V, p. 209.

The recognition of man's realistic possibilities for material advancement increasingly stimulated the separation of ceremonial from functional elements in the endeavors to achieve wealth and status. It more and more permeated the pursuit of self-interest with a new irreligious type of rationality until the old ethical values – the knowledge of good and bad right and wrong, were cut loose from their ancient moorings in the teachings of the church, i.e. *outside* man's willed experience and passions, and were set adrift upon the high seas of man's self-centered notions of morality. In fact, however, these realistic possibilities for material advancement were limited to a relatively small minority – the bourgeoisie. It was an expanding minority but even so it remained small for most of the nineteenth century. For the great majority of people the chances for improvement were as remote as they had always been; and though they were the victims of the new mentality, their own continued on the whole in the traditional mould. Their values remained anchored in the teachings of the church as transmitted to them by word of mouth and the moralizing demeanor of elders. The same was true of the aristocracy and landed gentry. Economically they had little to gain from change for the old quasi-feudal conception well suited their requirements; and socially, unlike the bourgeoisie, they had no need to find justifications for their way of life and status. The utilitarian mentality was therefore for a long time not only restricted to a relatively narrow, though very active and important, layer of society, but also permeated by other earlier ethical conceptions. It was this contamination which forced the bourgeoisie to moderate its otherwise self-destructive self-centered utilitarianism. So, for example, the conception of harmony – the oneness of christian society and the Newtonian natural order, was implicitly invoked in the identification of private gain with the public good. The stigma of the sin of avarice was thus rather evaded than denied. The utilitarian principle – the pursuit of pleasure and avoidance of pain, was not taken to its ultimate logical conclusion. It never gave legitimacy to taking the poor man's 'little ewe lamb', never approved of the bearing of false witness, theft, highway robbery and all other traditionally repugnant stealthy ways of gaining riches, (even where there was no direct fear of retribution so that it would fall within the sphere of pain avoidance) but confirmed and legitimized rapacity alone in the sphere in which traditional morality had not and could not have been well established. Thus it upheld the sanctity of property without including in it man's property in himself, i.e. man's property rights in the produce of his labor. In other words, the bourgeoisie selected from among the traditional ethical values those best suited to confirm its members' practices, and added to their compulsive force by making them the positive law of the land. Concurrently the influence of the values which remained unaffected – which did not become part of positive law, diminished for they became a matter of individual choice. *The distinction between acts punishable by law and transgressions against morality or the accepted code of manners i.e. between crime and sin, was part of the mechanism of evasion by which the old ethical values gradually adjusted to the new material circumstances.* It was like a stream making its path down to the sea first by-passing the greater obstacles in its way and then gnawing at their foundations until they wear away.[30] Rousseau had separated the 'reason of the head from the reason of the heart' and related matters of law to the one and of morality to the other. Kant distinguished between 'theoretical reason and practical reason' and made science the concern of the former and matters of conscience of the latter. Bentham, who regarded his work akin to that of the chemists and physicians, who arrange material phenomena under laws and invent expedients for increasing human control over the material world, even attempted to remove the notions of 'good' and 'right' altogether from the sphere of emotions and place them where they could be treated like mathematics. He defined the goal of social ethics as 'the greatest good for the greatest number', and *good* itself as *pleasure*. The empirical evidence that all men seek pleasure and avoid pain was taken by him as sufficient proof that pleasure must be good and pain evil, though pleasure in his conception was not confined to crude sensual satisfactions but included the gratifications of imagination and taste. Yet it would not be correct to assume that Bentham believed that the term good as used in common language

---

30. There is an analogy here with the 'evasive mechanism' by which the monopoly of the old trading and manufacturing companies was broken by the 'interlopers' (in the 17th century) who established themselves in locations or in trades not explicitly covered by the old Royal charters.

always implies that what the speaker has in mind is 'productive of the greatest happiness of the greatest number', what he did believe was that there is no other rational criterion for judgement – that there simply is no other way to make value judgments free of non-rationalistic elements.

In Bentham's own words:[31] 'Nature has placed mankind under the governance of two sovereign masters, pain and pleasure', all that mankind does, says, and thinks, is ruled by them; and as the community represents no more than the 'sum of the interests of the several members who compose it', the only remaining ethical criterion of morality could not but be the idea of 'the greatest happiness for the greatest number'.

And yet, the individualistic and hedonistic practices of the bourgeoisie in the nineteenth century did not attain full control over its conception of morality. Its ideal of *thrift, promptness, industry, honesty-as-the-best-policy, economic expediency* and *the pursuit of profit,* was rooted in a far more complex ethical conception than utilitarianism could provide. It grew out of an intellectual climate which could not easily cut itself loose from its cultural heritage. For example, education, this most vital element in the advancement of the new economic system, continued to rest in the hands of those who had been traditionally responsible for it and in the hands of those who wished to install religious dogmas and traditional beliefs in the minds of the young. Particularly the religious sects in the Protestant countries who wished to keep their children loyal to their beliefs played an essential role in this process of mixing the new with the old. They provided an education that combined the rudiments of secular learning with the dogmas they wished to impress upon the childrens' minds. Confronted with this rivalry the Catholics were soon also adopting similar practices, and it was only much later, when the state began taking over responsibility for education, that the secularization of schools really began. What was true of elementary education was almost equally true of the universities. Even in the 'cradle of utilitarianism', in England,

---

31. *Introduction to the Principles of Morals and Legislation* (1789) with a corrected edition in 1823.

classics and religion held prime place in the universities, and indeed, the development of utilitarianism took place almost entirely outside the universities.

As for the majority of people – the masses in the rural areas and the urban poor, who had no control over the vagary of nature or the shaping of their fate, they continued to keep faith with the old beliefs. The new rationalism could hardly solve their problems and the new skepticism could hardly replace the consolation they found in the trust in a compassionate God.

Another equally important factor which contributed to the intellectual climate of the first half of the nineteenth century that prevented the utilitarian tendencies of the bourgeoisie from becoming socially and economically self-destructive was the Reaction that followed the Great Revolution in France. Together with the restoration of clericalism, which neither the expulsion of the Bourbons (1830) nor the ascent of the bourgeoisie and awakening of the working class (1848) eradicated, there developed particularly on the Continent an idealized image of Feudalism that romanticized the old hierarchical relationships in a way that made them look like a real remedy for the contemporary social ills. By stressing the paternalistic aspects of the feudal system and by presenting them as a relationship in which superior members of society were obligated to accord benevolent support and protection to inferior members, the conservative reaction touched indeed upon the most painful feature of the new socioeconomic order. It presented an idealized romantic picture of the past as a yardstick by which the new masters of society – the 'captains of industry', ought to be measured. It was this confrontation of the bourgeoisie with the idealized image of the past, which on the one hand retained part of the socio-cultural hegemony in the hands of the aristocracy, and on the other hand imposed upon the bourgeoisie modes of conduct that stopped its utilitarian rationalism short of reaching its logical self-destructive consequences. Shocked by the excesses of the French Revolution the intellectual elite in Europe fell pray to a nostalgia for a harmonious past that never was. This tendency assumed a great variety of forms but stripped of individual traits it reflected a longing for a sense of social security and for stability without the curtailment of established privileges.

In Britain conservative skepticism produced authors like Thomas Carlyle (1795–1881) who presented an idealized image of the lord-serf relationship *(Past and Present* 1843) as a kind of antithesis to the new social reality, and true to his aristocratic heritage solutions based on the assumption that 'great men', like the romanticized heroes of antiquity, held the key to a better order *(On Heroes, Hero-Worship, and the Heroic in History* 1841).[32] By censuring the rich and powerful for not assuming the obligations of an idealized *Pater-Familias* or chivalric feudal lord towards their employees Carlyle reflected a kind of standard of behavior against which the bourgeoisie could not always help being measured. It was this standard which, on the one hand caused a feeling of discomfort among the members of the bourgeoisie and thereby somewhat restrained its most rapacious inclinations, and on the other hand, gave a new social content and moral justification to its elevated status. In fact it provided legitimacy for the new social inequality. It transformed the medieval conception of rank which had been founded upon *birth-rights* into a new one based on *property.* The conception was that privilege entails responsibility – *noblesse oblige,* and so should wealth if it is to be recognized as a sign of distinction. For a society accustomed to look for protection from its 'betters' this was an easily acceptable idea. Hence, if the bourgeoisie wanted to claim rank it could not permit itself, at least not overtly, to be seen flouting the obligations society associated with it. In this way a whole new code of conduct, of things 'done and not done', evolved which did not recognize the money value of labor services, just as medieval society never recognized them, and quite naturally accepted that the enrichment of some people by the appropriation of part of the fruits of the labor of other people did not become part of the things that were morally reprehensible. As yet the bourgeoisie had no need to deny its exploitative character – it could simply ignore it as natural and therefore necessary. Ricardo who did more than any other writer before him to demonstrate that all value is created by labor did not draw the ultimate moral conclusion from his

---

32.   The romantic side here is reminiscent of Heidegger etc. and the idea of 'great men' of Rorty.

analysis, he never claimed that wealth grows out of paying workers less than the full value of their work or from charging customers more than the true worth of their purchases. The thought probably never even entered his mind, it was too alien for a member of a society which was still greatly in the death-throes of feudalism. Even in the industrially more advanced countries most people were still unaffected by the new modes of production and the social relationships associated with them. For most of them the class relationship that superseded the medieval status *(Stände)* relations was merely an aberration. The 'Captains' of industry were judged by the standards applied to the traditional 'superiors'. Just as the good army captain was expected to care for his troops,[33] and the good lord for his tenants, so was the good industrialist expected to look after his workers; if he did not, he was considered unworthy of his rank and status. The true character of the newly evolving economic order simply escaped most early nineteenth century critics. They censured the new social relationships from the point of view of people belonging to an earlier society whose social arrangements suited an economic reality which was either no longer in existence or waning rapidly. But it were these critics, together with egalitarians and utopists (and not the critics which were to raise their voices in the later part of the nineteenth century) against whom the bourgeoisie was defending itself. It was against them that classical economics invoked the Law of Nature and the whole body of Newtonian science to show that it was neither the unequal division of property nor pure rapacity that were the causes of the new misery and poverty. By claiming that 'the rich do not in reality possess the power of finding employment and maintenance for the poor' and that therefore the poor can have no real right to demand it from them,[34] they did in fact accept the basic tenets of the old morality. They did not take up a utilitarian stand claiming that it was not the business of the rich to care for the poor but they remained well within the traditional conception of responsibility only exonerating the rich from

---

33.   John Ruskin used this very example.

34.   Malthus, *Essay on the Principle of Population*, Bk. IV, Ch. XIV.

blame by claiming *cannot* rather than *will not*.[35] The legacy of pre-industrial society imposed its moral values upon an otherwise utilitarian and rationalistic class of industrialists and forced them not to drive their utilitarian rationalism to its ultimate logical conclusion. It was this that provided the degree of stability without which the rapidly changing society would have fallen into anarchy and insecurity akin to that which marked the last days of Rome or the situation in many developing countries nowadays.

So, not alone conservatives, but utilitarians and radicals too, remained within the confines of traditional ethical conceptions. For example, Godwin, who believed in an altruistic human nature, and Bentham, who believed that man cannot be trusted to act for the 'general good' unless guided towards it, both clung to the same ethical principle of 'the greatest happiness of the greatest number', and for both the happiness of society meant precisely the sum total of the happiness of its individual members. Both took happiness as the fundamental criterion for *good*. Yet with Godwin the notion of *good* remained absolute, definitive, with Bentham it did not. With Bentham *good* and *evil* became introspective and measurable – all men seek happiness and avoid pain hence happiness is good and pain evil. Morality became a calculus of pleasure and pain, less unconditional than it had been – more mutable.[36] Both Godwin and Bentham were progressive in the sense that they extended humanity beyond the limits of the mercantilist conception that had divided mankind into people who 'matter' and people who do not, but unlike Godwin, Bentham opened the door for future redefinitions of social values in terms of expediency. By denying the presuppositions upon which the rights and obligations of natural and positive law had been resting he in principle (though perhaps not in practice) rejected the very basis of the whole traditional value system. It was through this door that the bourgeois conception of morality entered and within

---

35.   This was perhaps a precursor to the later Darwinian idea that fluctuations about a trend become a factor of inevitable changes in that trend. In other words, an idea that natural selection could apply also to humanity. At the time however, a trend meant a fixed nature.

36.   *Vide* Alasdair MacIntyre, *op.cit.*, Ch. 17.

half a century vacated Bentham's happiness-founded moral calculus of its progressive characteristics. By attaching weights to different kinds of pleasure the bourgeoisie quickly reinstated in its favor the old class separation by distinguishing between the pleasures of the rich, to which they gave extra weight, and the pleasures of the poor, in their contribution to society's common fund of happiness. For Bentham 'pushpin' had still rated 'as good as poetry', for J.S. Mill (1806–1873) it did not. For H. Spencer (1820–1903) 'to play billiards' was altogether 'the sign of an ill-spent youth'.[37] Happiness was no longer a criterion of morality.

The progressive element in Bentham's utilitarianism lay in the fact that it grew out of an essentially traditionalist background, that it developed in a period in which traditional non-utilitarian norms of behavior were exerting a particularly potent influence, that it emerged in an era of wide consensus about what is and what is not socially acceptable, a consensus anchored in the firm rules of inherited norms of conduct. The reactionary deterioration began with the waning of the compulsive influence of the norms, i.e. when utilitarian considerations were no longer restrained by the consensus that was based upon late eighteenth and early nineteenth century idealized interpretations of the customs and of the teachings of the church. Professor Landes[38] asks and answers a question which well illustrates this point. He asks: 'Why should a society dedicated to an economy of profit-making competitive enterprise, to the efforts of the isolated individual, to equality of rights and opportunities and freedom, rest on an institution (the bourgeois family) which so totally denied all of these?' And he answers: because 'the bourgeois family went back to an earlier, less secure age and developed patriarchal authority, privacy, and solidarity in response to the hazards and opportunities of a competitive society.' Similarly Professor Landes also explains the inconsistency in the bourgeois employer's attitude towards his employees. He writes: 'Many

---

37.   *Vide* Duncan, *Life and Letters of Spencer*, Ch. 20.

38.   David Landes. The ubiquitous bourgeoisie. A review of E.J. Hobsbawm's book *The Age of Capital 1848–1875* in *T.L.S.*, June 4, 1976, pp. 662–4.

employers saw themselves, rightly or wrongly, as good fathers and providers to their workers, who would never of their own accord bite the hand that fed them. It was the presumed virtue of the worker (through bourgeois eyes) and not his shortcomings that made the outside agitator indispensable to the master.' All this is far from denying the new cruel reality of the situation of the working class as a class, nor does it deny the exploitative character of the economic relationship between employers and employees, what, however, it does indicate is the restraining influence of the heritage from an earlier age which at least imposed a feeling of discomfort and at best a limit upon the rapacious tendencies inherent in a purer utilitarian conception of the world.

For Spencer these restraining notions seemed irrelevant, at least less relevant than they had seemed to people fifty years before. For him man was 'economic man', and the state a utilitarian instrument set-up by 'economic man' for mutual protection and the enforcement of economic contracts and agreements. For him there must be no established, or state church, no organized colonization, no poor relief, no social legislation – in short nothing in the way of collective organization to interfere with the law of natural selection.[39] Education too is superfluous, 'for the moral sense develops independently of education and ignorance has no connection with evil doing'. Education does not protect society against crime, it cannot protect its 'sacred' private property.

The change in the nature of determinism, from a unique, or universally, determined morality into the morality of individuals: not what is good for Man but for individual men, became the criterion of morality – a logical consequence of making pleasure and pain the natural causes of conduct. The old morality with its clear dicta about right and wrong was approaching its end. A new era was dawning in which the morally commendable was becoming the materially expedient. It was a period in which everything was 'pregnant with its contrary'; 'machinery, gifted with the wonderful power of shortening and fructifying human labor (was) starving and overworking it,... the new-fangled sources of wealth turned by some

---

39.   H. Spencer, *Social Statics* (1850).

strange weird spell into sources of want,... the victories of art (were) bought by loss of character, and at the same place that mankind master(ed) nature, man became enslaved to other men or to his own infamy...'[40] The bearers of progress in one sense,[41] the captains of the new industries, became its worst detractors in another; and the reactionaries who were searching the past for inspiration became the protagonists of social progress. Innovators, radicals, and revolutionaries revived old doctrines, and their conservative and reactionary opponents became the inventors of new ones.[42] The bourgeoisie, which under the banner of the Rights of Men and the slogan of 'Liberty, Equality and Brotherhood' set out to destroy the old iniquity, was setting up a new socially divisive order less humane and even harsher in its consequences for the poor than the order it replaced, while aristocrats, clerics and other admirers of the old world inspired and promoted new and progressive and humane ideas. It were men like Saint-Simon, Sismondi, Fourier and Owen who became the bearers of progressive visions. Saint-Simon believed in christian ethics and feudal economic arrangements;[43] Sismondi in romantic conservatism in a christian spirit;[44] Fourier and Owen in social utopias, in co-operatives and non-profit making stores.

This contradiction – this omnipresent pregnancy of all things with their contrary, was mirrored in Hegel's dialectics. There is perhaps something symbolic in the German word *Aufheben*. It has at least three different meanings: It can be understood to mean raising or *lifting up – in die Höhe heben,* as in *etwas vom Boden aufheben;* it

---

40. Marx & Engels, *Selected Works*, F.L.P.H. edition, Moscow, 1958, Vol. I, p. 359.

41. In one sense: Progress by providing men with the technology capable of freeing them from material want, in another sense, by extending the strata of society recognized as full and equal partners in humanity. *Vide* pp. 235–300.

42. *Vide* also Alasdair MacIntyre, *op.cit.*, Ch. 17, p. 227 etc.

43. *Vide* Comte de Saint-Simon, *The New Christianity* (1825).

44. He attacked Capitalism and required to make the new technology serve instead of subjugate humanity.

can be taken to mean to *cancel* or to *annul* – *beenden, für ungültig erklären,* as in *das Gesetz oder den Befehl aufheben,* or as in *die Tafel aufheben,* i.e. *das Essen offiziel beenden;* and it may be taken to mean to *retain* or to *keep* something – *verwahren, aufbewahren,* as in *das Buch oder die Theaterkarte bis morgen aufheben.* So, here is one word expressing the contradictions and complexities inherent in the system one word for *retaining, annulling* and *raising to a higher level,* – one word for *thesis, antithesis* and *synthesis,* a word expressing simultaneously diversity and unity capable not alone of explaining the complexity of society but also society's mechanisms of change – its 'Laws of Motion'.

Hegel was born in 1770 and died in 1831. Not unlike Fichte, he flirted in his youth with a kind of aristocratic socialism that was in vogue and fitted the Romantic currents of the time. His enthusiasm in this direction was cooled when in 1806 Napoleon's soldiers threw him into terror. When in 1812 he became head of the gymnasium at Nürnburg he was no longer prone to the currents of Romanticism, and became, like Napoleon and Goethe, 'a classic vestige in a romantic age'.[45] After the Revolution of 1830 he became altogether weary of change and was denouncing radicals as dreamers and inclined towards 'a period of peaceful satisfaction' which he found in the fold of the Prussian establishment.

Hegel's most formative years began with his reacting, like Schiller and Friedrich Schlegel, against Kant's ascetic dualism between the is and the *ought.* He was led by Schelling to seek for an absolute union of nature and mind so that the ideal could be viewed as embodied in the actual.[46] *Kant* (1724–1804), had illustrated with the help of unresolvable contradictions, (for example, by the provability that space and time are finite and infinite and that God exists and does not exist,) the failure of the intellect to deal with the 'things themselves', i.e. with the *noumena.* For him dialectics was but *'die Logik des Sheines'* – the art of reaching truths about the apparent by

---

45.   Will Durant, *The Study of Philosophy,* Pocket Books, 1952, p. 294.

46.   Morris R. Cohen, *E.S.S.,* Vol. VII, p. 311.

way of logical deductions.[47] In contrast to Kant, Schelling (1775–1854) maintained that matter and mind cannot be separated. They are differing in force by degree but not in kind and find their unity in the absolute. He saw the fundamental 'identity of opposites' and the basic secret of reality and development in the belief that every situation contains a contradiction which evolution solves by a new reconciling unity which by its very nature is more complex, more elevated, than the situation that preceded it, so that both thought and things progress incessantly from unity through diversity to diversity-in-unity. This idea, taken over and developed further by Hegel, was of course very old indeed. Heraclitus (535–475 B.C.) had already maintained that all things carry with them their opposites – being and not being are in everything – and therefore the only reality is change, i.e. the real state is one of transition and all permanence but an illusion. So did Empedecles (495435 B.C.) who taught that two opposing forces – harmony and discord – combine indestructible material particles into varying forces. And so did Aristotle (384–322 B.C.) who also regarded the universe as an ideal world, and form and matter inseparable, and who found in motion and change the realization of form in matter, and implied the dialectical process in his 'Golden Mean'.

Now, for Hegel the task of philosophy was to discover this unity behind the diversity, just as of politics to unite individuals into a state; of ethics to unify the character and behavior; and of religion to reach the absolute in which all contradictions are resolved into unity – where matter and mind subject and object, evil and good are one. For him, then, struggle, i.e. motion and growth is the natural mode of existence and *achievement* the aim of life – achievement not happiness. 'Nothing great in the world has been accomplished without passion'. 'Periods of happiness are the blank pages in the history of mankind they are the periods of harmony and stagnation unworthy of man's genius.' The history worthy of man's genius

---

47. He did not say that 'apparent truths' were not real truths, as Plato did, but that the real *(the noumena)* was simply beyond reach so that we cannot know whether the apparent is real or not. It was in this sense that Hume 'awoke him from his slumber'. All the same he did say that by rational thought we can reach some truths beyond appearances.

then, is punctuated by dialectical movement – by a sequence of revolutions in which, driven by the *Zeitgeist,* people following one upon another and one genius after another become the midwives of progress. Every situation bears the unavoidable imprint of its past and the seeds of its future, hence there is no and can never be one single permanent morality. The key to all ethics is its history, for man desires to attain socially given ends and those differ from society to society. Those wishing to reform existing institutions on the basis of reason are fools for the existing institutions are already based upon much sounder reason than theirs for they are the embodiment of historical reason. So, dialectics – the divine nature of creation, does not only explain the complexity and transient nature of situations but also indicates the mechanism of change. It is the movement from one unity through the disclosure of opposites to a new unity – the passing of a thing or phenomenon into its opposite, i.e. to its contradiction. While Newton's laws of gravitation provided the mechanism by which motion was constant, and the laws of nature eternal, Hegel's mechanism explained the fixed laws of eternal social change.

Half a century later Friedrich Engels was to illustrate the process by the following example:[48] 'Let us take a grain of barely. Billions of such grains of barley are milled, boiled and brewed and then consumed. But if such a grain of barley meets with conditions which are normal for it, if it falls on suitable soil, then under the influence of heat and moisture it undergoes a specific change, it germinates. The grain as such ceases to exist, it is negated, and in its place appears the plant which has arisen from it, the negation of the grain. But what is the normal life process of this plant? It grows, flowers, is fertilized and finally once more produces grains of barley, and as soon as they have ripened the stalk dies, is in turn negated. As a result of this negation we have once again the original grain of barley, but not as a single unit, but ten, twenty – or thirty – fold.' In Hegel's own words:[49] 'Nature must be regarded as a system of

---

48.   F. Engels, *Anti-Dühring*, p. 194.

49.   *Encyclopedia*, p. 249.

stages... not, however, in such a way that one is naturally *produced* by the other, but, in the inner idea which constitutes the ground of nature. Metamorphosis can only happen to the concept as such, since change in it alone is development...'

What philosophy, what set of ideas could better reflect the restless forward struggle of the bourgeoisie, its competitive mode of advancement, than this revolutionary notion, this vision of permanent change through the resolution of opposites? And what set of ideas could better reflect the remaining conservative influences in his era than the other notion inherent in Hegel's philosophy, that 'the real is rational' – that 'whatever is is right'. However, the analogy between the conception of nature as ever changing and of social change should be seen as *questions* asked and not in the answers. The view of nature associated with Darwin's *Origins of Species* continued to acknowledge variation as a permanent factor of evolution. But this was not so in social theories. The latter may have opened people's minds to the effects of variation and natural laws but the answers were not the same.

Since the middle of the eighteenth century industrialization was hastening the pace of social change. Mobility became characteristic of society. A new class was gaining power, new people were rising into prominence.[50] By the middle of the nineteenth century, the new class, i.e. the bourgeoisie, had established its revolutionary conception of the world in motion, but now, having attained social and economic power it was entering upon its first period of consolidation and so its conception of motion began losing its revolutionary content. The laws of motion became the laws of dynamic stability – the study of growth became the study of the laws of equilibrium. The implicit preoccupation with growth in classical economic theory yields place to the study of economics in 'close analogy to statical mechanics... treating the Laws of Exchange

---

50.   'It is surely no coincidence that Josiah Wedgwood, who began as a potter's apprentice and ended as one of he great eighteenth century magnates, was Charles Darwin's maternal grandfather. Darwin's paternal grandfather, Erasmus, belonged to the circle of new midland industrialists: James Watt, James Keir, Matthew Boulton, and of course, Wedgewood.' (R.C. Lewontin, *op.cit.*)

as the Laws of Equilibrium of the lever...'[51] Yet, while the new class was introducing its own deterministic conception of the world, placing the *Laws of Nature* where once had 'stood' the *law of God,* the Law that made providence – not man's own effort, the master of his fate, tradition was also receiving a new lease of life by the Utopians who provided it with a dynamics which it had missed before. While the consolidating bourgeoisie put stress upon the *Laws of Nature* which made man once again the helpless victim of the economic laws,[52] the Utopians based their conception upon the old christian morality and an imaginary world of the past in which the satisfaction of wants rather than the pursuit of wealth was the true and permanent, or natural, source of human activities.

In parts of Europe the ascent of the bourgeoisie was complete by the middle of the nineteenth century. It was accompanied by the growth of another social stratum – the urban working class. While the total population was increasing and the number of people engaged in agriculture remained almost as before, and in places even diminished, the share of the population engaged in manufacturing grew most of all.[53]

---

51.   W.S. Jevons, *The Theory of Political Economy* (1871).

52.   As already mentioned, 'as the rich do not in reality possess the power of finding employment and maintenance for the poor, the poor cannot in the nature of things possess the right to demand them.' R.T. Malthus, *Essay on the Principle of population,* Bk. IV, Ch. IX (1789).

53.   *Population* (in millions)

Year	U.K	Germany
1840/1	15.914	30.382
1900/1	32.528	56.367

Population engaged in Agriculture (in millions)			*Population engaged in Manufacture (in millions)*		
Year	U.K.	Germany France	U.K.	Germany	France
1841	1.458	-	-	1.816	-	-
1856	-	-	5.146	-	-	2.002
1882	-	5.702	-	-	3.721	-
1895	-	5.540	-	-	-	4.565
1901	1.390	-	5.581	4.062	-	3.083

So the rise of the bourgeoisie was inextricably connected with the advent of the new mode of industrial production, but the new mode of industrial production brought with it the concentration of labor which in turn led to a new type of social relationships between workers and employers on the one hand and among the workers themselves on the other. The former led to an increasing degree of alienation, and the latter, stimulated by the physical proximity of people working under one roof, forged new links of communication between people with similar interests. These interests were related to the workers' attempts to resist exploitation by the bourgeoisie; exploitation that the bourgeoisie was increasingly forced to intensify because of the growing impetus of business competition. So the ascent of the bourgeoisie was marked by an increasingly antagonistic contradiction with the older establishment while it also contained within itself the seeds of a new more recent antagonistic contradiction with the working class – the class upon whose growth the rise of the bourgeoisie depended. The thesis had given rise to its antithesis and the antithesis was assuming the form of labor's growing power to claim a greater share than it received of the fruits of industrial production. It was against this claim that the bourgeoisie was fortifying itself by substituting for its former revolutionary conception the new ideology of *dynamic equilibrium.*

By the time Darwin published *The Origin of Species* (1859) and Spencer *The Principles of Psychology* (1855) the ascent of the bourgeoisie was a *fait accompli* and the principle of 'progress' firmly established in all the social sciences but biology. In the second half of the nineteenth century Darwin's principle of *natural selection* transformed by Spencer into the principle of *the survival of the fittest* became the ideological justification for *laissez-faire,* but in fact it was only 'the borrowing of a metaphor to further justify a system already in full operation'.[54] Darwin and Spencer did not 'invent' the system of unbridled economic competition they merely reflected it.

Source: B.R. Mitchell, *European Historical Statistics 1750–1970*, London, 1975.

54.   *Vide* R.C. Lewontin, *I.E.S.S.,* Vol. V, p. 208 (1968).

But though they had not created it they gave to its newly aspired *status quo* an ethical justification – the moralistic underpinning it wanted; and, like Hegel, they suggested a likely *mechanism* of the way it must work – an explanation that was absolutely necessary in an era in which the discovery of mechanisms, the idea of causes, had risen to the position of being the quintessence of all scientific truth.

With *Herbert Spencer* (1820–1903), as earlier pointed out, the State became a utilitarian instrument for the bourgeoisie, the man-made contrivance for the enforcement of economic contracts and for mutual protection, and economic man reaches his goal by the free play of natural selection. Here is the difference between the revolutionary perception of the bourgeoisie during its era of ascent and the perception it adopted in the second half of the nineteenth century of dynamic equilibrium: Effort alone was no longer sufficient – the true realization was confined to the those selected by the process of natural selection. Only the fittest survive, the is incorporates the *ought,* the wealth and power of the rich is proof of their selection, the poverty of the others is proof that nature found them unfit to join their betters.

For Darwin advancement was *accidental – the survival of variations that happen to suit their environment and were therefore perpetuated.*[55] His idea of natural selection was to explain the process of organic evolution, but Spencer provided it with a selective element that gave the new class the protection it wanted against interlopers from the lower strata of society. He put the seal of legitimacy upon the position of the bourgeoisie vis-à-vis the working class by suggesting that 'the general law of organization is that difference of function entails differentiation and division of the parts performing them'.[56] He provided the bourgeoisie with the ideological justification to chase away the last remaining elements of the old deterministic morality by stating in his *First Principles* (1862) that 'the deepest truths that can be reached are simply statements of the

---

55.   *Vide* C.E.M. Joad in *E.S.S.,* Vol. XIV, p. 296.

56.   This idea is reminiscent of Adam Smith's division of labor.

widest uniformities in our experiences of the relations of matter, motion, and force.' He rejected the theory of *'special creation'*, with its 'catastrophic' or revolutionary connotations and espoused the idea of *organic evolution* defining evolution as the 'change from a state of relatively indefinite, incoherent, homogeneity to a state of relatively definite, coherent, heterogeneity.' (1862) In his *Principles of Sociology* he extended this idea from biology to the human society and thus provided the definition of evolution which implied a change from a state of 'anarchic' social mobility to a state of ordered heterogeneity within each class. In fact he says, there is nothing to be gained from *recognizing* the advantages or disadvantages of different systems for each system is the inevitable product of the conditions that gave rise to it, and these – the conditions, not people's willed intentions are its determinants.

'Like all revolutions the bourgeois revolution gave way slowly to a period of consolidation,... Once the new class had gained power, it was clearly to its advantage to prevent the revolution from going further. The static hereditary society could hardly be reconstituted, but in its place a system of dynamic stability was erected. Change and social mobility were still accepted as characteristic of society but as the running-in-place rather than an overturn of the existing order... Liberal democracy... had a vested interest in maintaining the world social order but allowed individuals, on the basis of relative competitive ability, to find their own place in the social structure.'[57] With the spreading of the Spencerian legitimization of the new class division of society, which by implication transformed compassion with its egalitarian undertone into charity with its divisive tenor set the stage for the emergence of a new type of hedonistic ethics which driven to its logical conclusion could result in total egoistic chaos. Yet this time was still far off. Even J.S. Mill, the great protagonist of anti-clerical utilitarianism was still too much immersed in the cultural heritage of Christianity to cast off its essential tenets of morality, or even to notice how they were influencing his thought. He simply did not question his fundamental values for he felt them to be self-evident. The same is true for Marx with regard to Judaism;

---

57.   R.C. Lewontin, *op.cit.*, Vol. V, p. 208.

for Marx justice and equity were too evidently *good* to require some kind of justification. Neither of them was ready to go as far as Machiavelli had done when he made *force* – the will of the ruler, moral law. Mill does not need a justification for man's right to 'life, liberty and the pursuit of happiness', it is unalienable and that is all. Marx requires no reason to support 'man's right to the fruits of his labor', – it is obvious, self-evident. Both simply accept their premises as true for they have been brought up to believe that this was so. When Marx pours scorn upon the worshipers of *Mammon* and wrath upon the exploiters of the poor (accusing them of the old fashioned sin of theft) he speaks the language of the Bible; new is only the inclusion of the money value of man's labor among the villains' loot a thought which earlier moralists had managed to ignore. When Mill (1806–1873), on the one hand, proclaims the creed that accepts utility as its moral foundation 'the greatest happiness principle that holds that actions are right in proportion as they tend to promote happiness, wrong as they tend to produce the reverse of happiness,' and, on the other hand makes the ability to live without happiness a social virtue by proclaiming that because the 'happiness is not an abstract idea but a concrete whole the ingredients of which are very various...' and the happiness of others may best be served by the absolute sacrifice of the happiness of the individual, he too is no longer far removed from old fashioned christian asceticism. But, if this is so, where then remains the utilitarian self-seeking image of man? All Mill is left with is an affirmation of 'a moral experience involving ultimate principles' for which in the end he has no other justification than *intuitive* assent.[58] Yet, what else can these ultimate principles and intuitions be than the ideas implanted in men's minds by their elders and society? Here then lies the difference between Mill and Marx: Mill rationalizes the is giving contemporary middle class behavior a kind of scientific explanation, Marx states the *ought to be* for a classless society. Whether Mill writes on economic principles, liberty, or the subjugation of women, his values remain those of the middle class. Working men who lack the necessary education and time to weigh

---

58.   A.P. Lindsay, Introduction to J.S. Mill, *Utilitarianism* (ed. Everyman).

the *pros & cons* of an argument, and working women not brought up to play the role middle class assigns to women, are simply ignored – left out of his considerations. People become part of society only once they adapt to bourgeois standards, when they infiltrate as individuals into the middle class on the middle class's own terms. In short, Mill takes the moral hegemony of the bourgeoisie as an established fact which needs no further proof whereas Marx doubts it. By converting Ricardo's *economic* labor-value theory into an ethical issue based upon another principle of property Marx claims the moral hegemony for precisely those who Mill and the bourgeoisie excluded from it. What Ricardo had shown, namely that all value was the product of labor and of labor alone, and Mill had embraced as fact even proclaiming that nothing remained 'for the present or any future writers to clear up', and bourgeois economists were very soon to abandon for the *utility* value theory, Marx made the very found of his moral indignation. If labor was the source of value whence then did profit come from? For Marx the answer was self-evident: from paying labor less than the full worth of its exertion; in moral terms from tricking workers out of part of the value they create and which by right ought to be theirs – by theft. Engels explained how it is done. 'Let us assume, that (the production of) the means of subsistence represent six hours of labor time daily. Our incipient capitalist, who buys labor-power for carrying on his business, i.e. hires a laborer, consequently pays this laborer the full value of his day's labor-power if he pays him a sum of money which also represents six hours of labor. And as soon as the laborer has worked six hours in the employment of the incipient capitalist, he has fully reimbursed the latter for his outlay, for the value of the day's labor-power which he had paid. But so far the money would not have been converted into capital, it would not have produced any surplus-value (i.e. profit). And for this reason the buyer of labor power has quite a different notion of the nature of the transaction he has carried out. The fact that only six hours' labor is necessary to keep the laborer alive for twenty-four hours, does not in any way prevent him from working twelve hours out of twenty-four. The value of the labor-power, and the value which that labor-power creates in the labor-process, are two different magnitudes... On our assumption, therefore, the laborer each day *costs* the owner of money the value of the product of six hours' labor, but he *hands over* to him each day the *value* of the product of twelve hours' labor. The difference in favor of the owner of the money is – six hours of unpaid surplus-labor, a surplus-product for which he does not pay and in which six hours' labor is embodied. The trick has been performed. Surplus-value has been produced; money has been converted into capital' – a profit has been realized.[59]

Now, as long as it was possible to exclude the lower classes from among the people who matter – as long as society simply ignored them when claiming the right to 'life, liberty and the pursuit of happiness', there was no cause for moral conflict. It is worth repeating that there was of course little new in this: the democracy of ancient Greece – the very cradle of western civilization, had been founded on slave and other 'non-people's' labor. So was the glory and riches of ancient Rome grounded on the toil of 'speaking instruments' and the sweat of the 'non-Romans'. Nor did Medieval society acknowledge the money value of the labor services rendered by serfs to their feudal masters. And Mercantilist society too divided humanity into the people who counted and those who did not – into those who are stimulated to accomplish great deeds by 'the love of gain', namely merchants, manufacturers and rich landowners, and those who must be guided by their betters to do their duty by low wages and the cold fear of starvation, namely the poor whose very life-style marks them as lesser members of society.[60] It was this convenient mechanism of self-deception that maintained the truce between liberal ethics rooted in the religious and cultural heritage of the bourgeoisie, which the bourgeoisie was not ready to abandon, and its new-fangled social and economic practices. It was this truce which Marx's interpretation of the labor value theory threatened to destroy. It is therefore hardly surprising that the new rich were quick to grasp at any other economic theory that could free them from their dilemma and help them to avoid the head on confrontation

---

59.   F. Engels, *Anti-Dühring*, pp. 282–3.

60.   For illustration of the behavior of the poor see the writings of Dickens and Zola.

between their economic and their moral needs. The *utility* theory of value was just such a theory. Dating back to Aristotle it was revived by Ferdinande Galiani (1728–1787), Etienne Bonnot de Condillac (1714–1780), Jean Baptiste Say (1767–1832), and James Maitland the Earl of Lauderdale (1759–1839). The old utility theory of value had suffered from the inability to explain why some of the most useful, indeed some of the most necessary things such as water were free or cheap while some almost useless things such as diamonds were very costly. Galiani resolved this paradox by transforming *value* into *the ratio of utility to scarcity*. Abandoning the search for an *objective* measure of value he defined the term in a way that gave it a *subjective relative* content. In this way meaningful statements about the value of a good could only be made in comparison with a given quantity of another good. So *value* came to depend upon the utility derived from a good by those who want it. Value increases or diminishes with changes in the intensity of desire – increases with scarcity and diminishes with plenty. This thought was developed further by Condillac who stated that value was altogether a function of want, so that 'a more keenly felt want gives to things a greater value', i.e. that 'a thing does not have value because of its cost... but it costs because it has value'.[61]

Here finally was a theory capable of delivering the merchants from the old sin of 'unjust' profit making – buying cheap and selling dear, and in a way also from the physiocratic suspicions of contributing but little to the nation's stock of wealth – merely exchanging goods unlike the farmers who physically increase their volume.[62] For if value depended on utility and scarcity then trade

---

61. De Condillac, *Le Commerce et le gouvernement consideres relativement l'un a l'autre*, Paris, 1776.

62. According to the Physiocrats inputs of labor and capital were self-reproducing and therefore not wasted in the process of production, and brought forth a net surplus – the farmer puts a seed into the ground and has it returned manifold, but manufacture and certainly trade added nothing to the total quantity of tangible goods – at best it only transformed one kind into another. Manufacture consumes raw materials in the course of a metamorphosis, raises their price but not their quantity and value.

itself was value producing for in the process of exchange one partner offers the good he has in abundance – which has little value for him, to another who is in need of it and therefore finds it of greater value.

Naturally, as long as the essence of science had been the search for the *absolute* unifying truth, when the idea of *order* and Newtonian simplicity was ruling the minds of men, there was little to recommend itself in this kind of *relative subjectivism.* Yet in the nineteenth century – in the era in which Bentham's *psychologism* was gaining converts rapidly, there was little to restrain its popularity.[63] To be sure, this solution to the value-paradox has been suggested in the 16th century and a similar solution was advanced many times even before the eighteenth century, but it had never been given the importance that was attributed to it in the nineteenth; never had it been regarded as anything else than it really was, namely a *price theory*, never had it been interpreted as a *theory of value.* Galiani himself, unlike his followers in the nineteenth century, was well aware of this for he himself hinted at the difference between price and value. He went indeed so far as to elaborate it, anteceding Ricardo's labor value theory, by stating that the quantity of labor, *fatica* to use his own term, was the only factor of production and true source of value. Condillac already 'lost' this distinction when he identified value with usefulness, but it was Say who really gave it the form the middle class required, who made the entrepreneur the 'hero' of society the servant of humanity. For if value is determined by utility then the one who anticipates demand, who combines land, labor, and capital in order to satisfy a need, deserves well of his profit because the height of his profit indicates the value people put upon the goods he produces, i.e. their scarcity in relation to the intensity of desire for them. Obviously, the other factors of production ought also be rewarded for their *efforts,* but *not* because they are the cause of value: land by rent, labor by wages, and capital

---

63.   According to Bentham 'The greater the quantity of the matter of property a man is already in possession of, the less the quantity of happiness he receives by the addition of another quantity of the matter of property to a given amount.' *Works*, IX, 18, Edinburgh, Edition of 1843.

by interest. The idea was developed further in the first half of the nineteenth century by people like Samuel Mountifort Longfield (1802–1884), who showed that wages are in fact determined by the productivity of labor and the rate of interest by a combination of the willingness of savers to sacrifice the present for the future and by the productivity of capital; and Johann Heinrich von Thünen (1783–1850), who in effect began the use of marginal analysis in the relation between capital and labor and interest and wages. It all suited well the state of mind that put the *is* before the *ought,* it suited the mood of dynamic stability, and above all it allowed the bourgeoisie to do what it was doing without abandoning the values ingrained in western society from childhood. Where utility was a function of scarcity and scarcity – not labor, the source of value, Marx's moralizing attitude had no leg to stand on; where capital was the reward of abstinence[64] – not an accumulation of 'stolen' labor time, the pursuit of wealth was nowhere in conflict with the Eighth Commandment 'Thou shalt not steal', and with Man's laws regarding the sanctity of private property.

The avoidance of a confrontation between objective and subjective reality was of course not confined to the sphere of labor-value but entered all spheres of life. Taking for example the concept of *freedom* one can easily see how the destruction of Feudal bondage and the unleashing of man's ingenuity in the mastery of his natural environment was interpreted as the attainment of individual freedom. But, in fact, as Hegel and Marx already observed, the impression was of illusionary. From a less superficial point of view the only freedom really attained was the freedom to enter the market system which upon entering imposed on the newly 'liberated' individual a set of other no less compulsive forces limiting his freedom. Instead of being forced by legal obligations he is immediately obliged by economic and social necessity to abide by equally and even more powerfully compulsive rules. This was no less true for the rich than for the poor. The latters' freedom of choice was limited to sell their labor on the conditions offered to them or starve – which is of

---

64.   *Vide* Nassau William Senior (1790–1864) and Eugen von Böhm-Bawerk (1851–1914).

course no choice at all; and the former were caught-up in relentless competition that left them with the alternatives of either complying with the rules of capital accumulation or go under – which again is little of a choice. It is therefore possible that the confusion of price and value was also no more than society's inability to understand itself except in a form distorted, perhaps unconsciously, by those who were relatively better off and therefore the beneficiaries of the system. On the one hand these men found themselves in the grip of impersonal powers, which were their objective forms of social existence, but on the other hand interpreted these impersonal powers as 'the fruits of their own actions falsely objectified and endowed with independent existence.' Men saw themselves as free agents in areas of their life where the economic and social forms were in fact dictating the roles they lived out. These inescapable illusions constituted the loss of their grasp of their own nature, the 'alienation of Man'.[65]

Even Marx himself cannot escape the values he inherited for he has no other set of morals to judge by and so he condemns the bourgeoisie upon its own premises.[66] Alasdair MacIntyre in his *Short History of Ethics* explains Marx's attitude to morality as follows: 'The use of moral vocabulary always presupposes a shared form of social order. Appeal to moral principles against some existing state of affairs is always an appeal within the limits of that form of society; to appeal against that form of society we must find a vocabulary which does not presuppose its existence. Such a vocabulary one finds in the form of expression of wants and needs which are unsatisfiable within the existing society, wants and needs which demand a new social order. So Marx appeals to the wants and needs of the working class against the social order of bourgeois society. But he never raises two questions which are crucial for his own doctrine. The first concerns the role of morality within the working-class movement... we remain uncertain as to how Marx conceives it possible that a society prey to the errors of moral

---

65.   Alasdair MacIntyre, *Hegel and Marx, op.cit.,* p. 212.

66.   *Vide* the *Communist Manifesto.*

individualism may come to recognize and transcend them. Marx's second great omission concerns the morality of socialist and communist society. He does indeed speak in at least one passage as though communism will be an embodiment of the Kantian kingdom of ends. But he is at best allusive on this topic...'[67]

Returning to the ethical problem the labor-value theory posed for the bourgeoisie, and its solution by transforming value into price, it may be observed that this particular expedient was only part of a more general tendency to shift the emphasis from *essence* – from the essential properties of the things described, to the emphasis on *processes* – on how things happen. A bourgeoisie locked in the grip of competition, in an inexorable economic struggle of all against all, was in fact left with no real alternative but of finding immediate solutions to its practical problems. It had neither the leisure nor the strong need to question the essence, the truth or the '*noumena*', of things. What it needed to know was whether or not the actions taken upon a given proposition yield the expected results – whether '*it works*' or not. Not the *noumenon* but the *phenomenon* was what mattered, and so the phenomena became the only true object of knowledge, indeed, the only reality. The rise of the middle class put man in the center of the universe and his senses became the final judge of reality. Only what the senses or the mind could directly perceive became worthy of attention. Value is not directly perceptible but price is. Hence, price must be the true object of analysis not value. In the late eighteenth century Lavoisier introduced quantification into chemistry and turned 'the scales into the most important physical instrument of all' and forced scientists to give to the old word atom a new meaning. At the same time electric energy was also converted into a measurable quantity the ampere and with it spread such units of measurement as the Volta, Gauss, Ampere and Faraday, which were named after their inventors. 'Meanwhile, from Priestly to Dalton, more and more elementary bodies came to be defined by their characteristic atomic weights... (and) because all the new units seemed to fit into a coherent framework, some scientists gained the impression that physics had discovered the very

---

67.   Alasdair MacIntyre, *op.cit.*, p. 214.

mainspring of the Universe – *that man had at last discovered God.* However, most scientists preferred to restrict their observations to the taking of readings, leaving metaphysical speculation to the philosophers. In Kant's day it had still been possible for men with open minds to take an over-all view of human knowledge but in the nineteenth century... no scientist worth his salt could continue to prize speculation above experiment... The age of positivism had dawned.'[68] Henceforth, and until Einstein once again was able to show the inadequacy of our senses for grasping the full meaning of reality, true knowledge was thought to be founded exclusively on sense experience and all inquiry into ultimate origins was abandoned.[69] To be sure, Henri Poincare (1854–1912) had run up against some of the problems that nineteenth century positivism imposed upon science, but not before Einstein was the system really shaken. What Einstein was to show, just at the time when the bourgeoisie began losing its uncontested hegemony, was that 'the unity of the beholder must give pride of place to the unity of the external reality he beholds.' The Universe ceased to be a reflection in the human mind; but, on the contrary the human mind had limits which are in need of urgent definition. 'Time and space are interrelated in ways which transcend common experience.'[70] Not that phenomenalism and nineteenth century positivism were not extremely successful in solving the practical problems which provided the progressive element of the bourgeois era – the conquest of man's natural environment, but by its very character, being governed by extreme empiricism which brought about this success, it avoided the questions that could have thrown doubt on the prevailing social arrangements – on the true nature of man and society. The nineteenth century defined the *questions* worthy of an answer. These were the questions the middle class needed answered in order to

---

68.   From *A General History of the Sciences*, ed. Rene Taton, Vol. III, Science in the Nineteenth Century, p. 2.

69.   *Vide* Auguste Comte's *La Philosophie Positive* (1854).

70.   The above quoted passages are summarized from Taton's (ed.) work, *op.cit.*

compete in manufacture and industry, i.e. in order to maintain its mode of existence.[71]

So by the middle of the nineteenth century 'a system of production, involving social relationships, in which the primary object is the gain of profit through exchange',[72] was well established in western civilization, but its bearers had not yet really succeeded in liberating themselves from the moral values of earlier ages; indeed they stressed some of those values that could serve their purposes and avoided others which hindered them in worshiping their new found God of gain. They made rationality the determining factor in economic and technological decision-making, but did not succeed in barring religion and mysticism from all other spheres of their existence; they continued praying for riches and living in the fear of God's retribution, but they no longer expected prayer to have the same results as their own determined efforts, but they were still worried about the negative effects of supernatural forces that might defeat their rational endeavors. The decline of the landed aristocracy did not put an end to bourgeois aspirations to land and titles; and the rise of utilitarianism did not wrench the universities out of church control, nor had the rational skepticism of the new 'masters of society' much impact on the thoughts of the majority of people who remained members of their churches and evangelical sects. Utilitarian individualism, or egoistic rational hedonism was spreading but as yet its spread was mainly confined to one class – the bourgeoisie.

---

71. With all that, the importance of science – of applied science, was tremendous in the nineteenth century perhaps because it was governed by extreme empirical elements until close to its last quarter. The technological achievements of the period were above all the product of the accumulated experience of craftsmen, the enterprise of management, and the skill of individual designers. Few scientists were employed in connexion with such manufactures, and in investigating the design of product and plant they were rarely consulted; that is, until towards the end of the century when international competition no longer permitted the bourgeoisie to ignore the more profound scientific discoveries, unstabilizing as they were for the dynamic equilibrium upon which its hegemony was resting. (See definition of P. Rostock of Capitalism)

72. This is P. Rostock's definition of Capitalism.

Workers, either from inertia – continuing the tradition of men taking pride in their crafts, or and more likely, from fear of being given 'the sack' kept up the necessary labor-discipline to keep the system going.

8

Dynamic Equilibrium:
The Era of Bourgeois Consolidation

The sorcerer Bu Fu is giving a painting lesson to Chi Po.
'No, no!' says Bu Fu. 'You have merely painted what is.
Anybody can paint what is! The real secret is to paint what isn't!'
Chi Po, puzzled, replied: 'But what is there that isn't?'
Chi Po and the Sorcerer.
(A chinese tale for children and philosophers.
Quoted from Oscar Mandel)

In the second half of the nineteenth century the bourgeoisie attained the position of power it had coveted. In the hundred years that separated the middle of the nineteenth from the middle of the twentieth century it consolidated this position and strove to fortify it against the rising claims of the working class to share in it. Perhaps not surprisingly bourgeois society was therefore marked 'by a concern for equilibrium conditions, dynamic stability, and a playing down of progressivist and perfectionist elements.'[1] It appeared to live by the principle of *plus ca change, plus c'est la meme chose*. It's economic philosophy was dominated by three principles: *acquisition,*

---

1. *Vide* R.C. Lewontin, *op.cit.*, p. 208.

competition and *rationality.* The purpose of all endeavors was
acquisition, the means to this end competition, and the methods
employed were strictly rational. The new spirit of acquisition was
different from that of earlier ages because it eclipsed the restriction
inherent in the mere need of earning a livelihood and replaced it by
desires which have no quantitative upper limits.[2] The means differed
from those of earlier times by their claim to freedom from traditional
and conventional restrictions, by the assertion of free use of
individuals' natural capabilities provided they do not violate the
penal code. The method differed by its predilection for long range
planning and the development and adoption of indirect, roundabout,
methods of production; by a strict adaptation of means to ends and
banning of metaphysical elements; and, above all, the utilization of
precise cost benefit calculations, which in time tended to penetrate
almost all spheres of life. Together, the aims, means and method
gave rise to an almost purely utilitarian valuation of people, objects
and events. For the spirit of acquisition seized not only upon all
phenomena within the economic realm but reached over into the
entire cultural sphere, including social relations, and tended to
establish the supremacy of business interests over all other values.[3]
Indeed all seemed to mirror the fact that change and social mobility
were still characteristic of society but only within the confines of the
existing order, i.e. that individuals could still rise on the basis of
relative competitive ability, and find a new place for themselves
within the bourgeois structure, provided of course they did so on the
bourgeoisie's own terms. *Progress* became the accumulation of
capital, the advances in cost reducing technology, and the spreading
of trade and enterprise, just as human beings became 'labor power'
and nature a 'factor of production'. When acquisition took prime
place among all other human drives systematic rational behavior
became a social value – a virtue in itself. Consequently compassion

---

2.   Man's wants became boundless, for there is no end to the accumulation of
      wealth, and Economics became 'the science which studies human behavior as
      a relation between ends and *scarce means* which have alternative uses.' –
      Lord Robbins.

3.   *Vide* W. Sombart's discussion of capitalism in *E.S.S.*, Bk. III, pp. 195–208.

turned derisive sentimentality and individuality, except in the pursuit of economic aims, mere eccentricity. Quantification, so ably introduced into chemistry in the second half of the eighteenth century by Lavoisier, became in the nineteenth the essential tool of social stratification; the spreading of exact methods of business accounting reflected the pre-eminence of pecuniary values.

The result was that while almost all individual activities were guided by the principle of highest rationality the system as a whole remained conspicuously irrational. It placed its overall co-ordination with a self-regulating mechanism that was founded upon a belief in a particular metaphysical kind of natural order which could be trusted to regulate the overall allocation of resources by an 'invisible hand' to everybody's best advantage – to a mechanism that was supposed to lead man 'through the study of his own advantage willy-nilly to employ his resources in the way which is most beneficial to all'. It not only assumed the universality of the acquisitive drive but regarded it as part of nature's harmony – as a natural law. It continued to assumed, as Adam Smith already did, that because every individual is continually exerting himself to find out the most advantageous employment for whatever capital he can command; that because each individual is seeking his own advantage, his search for his own advantage necessarily leads him to prefer that employment which is most advantageous to society. Here is the image of a world in which private gain or loss, rising or falling prices, indicate constantly whether resources are well or ill employed; where correct employment is rewarded by profit and maximum consumers' satisfaction, and bad employment is punished by loss and consumers' disappointment; when the prices of certain goods or services rise it indicates a shortage of the same, which will, thanks to every individual's pursuit of his own advantage, sooner or later be corrected. For the high prices will attract resources to where they are most needed. Similarly is redundancy communicated and punished by low rewards, which in turn will tend to ward-off resources from where they are ill employed and redirect them towards more rewarding and hence assumably more socially necessary employment.

The nineteenth century was an era that regarded the discovery of mechanisms as the quintessence of science and in economics it found such a mechanism in the regulative effect of price and profit fluctuations. It was this 'coexistence of well nigh perfect rationality and of great irrationality' from which, as Sombart pointedly remarked, 'originated the numerous strains and stresses which are peculiarly characteristic of the economic system of Capitalism'. Here lay both the merits and the abominations of capitalist society. Rationality and freedom – the assertion of natural rights in the pursuit of profit, restricted only most marginally by usage and laws to forestall criminal dealings, enabled the bourgeois society to study dispassionately all the material aspects of nature, to which the era's magnificent victories of man's genius over the niggardliness of his environment must be credited. At the same time, it was the very same assertion of individuals' natural rights – the same freedom that had proved to be so successful in the application of rationality to the study of man's physical environment, that prevented the application of rationality to the analysis of man's social arrangements. There simply was no equivalent motive force to the quest for profit to stimulate individuals suitably placed in society to study rationally and dispassionately the structure of society as a whole, and to question the theory that rested upon so firm a scientific basis as the trust in universal order and in the regulative mechanism of price variations. The poor were ill equipped to do so and preferred to seek their salvation as individuals within the framework of the bourgeois system, and those capable of doing it had little to gain from it in a world dominated by the spirit of acquisition. The exceptions to this rule, men like Marx, were therefore singularly unsuccessful in transforming their theoretical insight into practice in their time. They simply could not make those most in need of change conscious of the irrationality of their social existence, while those not in need of change had little reason to discard their old conceptions.

Since long man had known how, for example, to make steel. By chancing upon suitable ores and coal and by controlling the low but necessary carbon content of iron with the help of the difficult method of stopping the blast in the furnace at the correct moment he could do it. But only the systematic and rational approach to nature – the formulation of theories about the composition of substances, and of their effects upon one another, also taught him to synthesize, to form compounds and recreate nature, and make, among other things, high quality steel not by the earlier mentioned chancy process but with certainty and confidence. No longer was it necessary to stop the blast in the furnace at exactly the right moment. It was now sufficient to burn all carbon out and then merely add the required amount to obtain the expected quality. Here, in the making of high grade steel, there was a direct motive, an obvious gain for those engaged in it to study reality and turn their knowledge to profitable use. But no similar mechanism was there to stimulate social analysis, and no way of drawing the practical consequences. For this to happen, not one person but millions would have first to be made conscious, and then prefer to organize themselves, and take upon themselves the personal deprivation that accompany the struggle for so general a conversion. To the few who might have recognized the irrationality of the system it must have seemed simpler to seek their own personal salvation in the existing system than attempt to overthrow it. Only when on the one hand the practical possibilities of changing the system became apparent and on the other the possibilities of improving one's life within it became so remote that they seemed hopeless; only then began thoughts about more rational social alternatives gain admittance to people's consciousness. But this development lay still in man's distant future. In the nineteenth century, the organization of labor was little more than attempts to resist local exploitation; to mitigate the specific evils that attended the system, not yet an effort to replace it by another. It lacked a practicable positive perception of an alternative society.

Throughout the second half of the nineteenth and early decades of the twentieth century the number of people employed as wage workers in manufacture, construction and other non-agricultural services was increasing very rapidly in the industrial countries. For example in the United Kingdom they increased by approximately 150.000 on average annually and in Belgium by 47.000 and although they were acquiring most characteristics of a separate social class they remained slow in developing a social class conception capable of contesting that of the bourgeoisie.[4] Partly this sluggishness in gaining a class consciousness must be ascribed to the fact that bourgeois society was less closed to entrants from the lower classes than the aristocracy had been and to the general difficulty with new insights penetrating established value systems, but there were also other reasons. For class consciousness to develop people must regard themselves as belonging to one group – they must either have a common descent or a recognizable similarity of occupation, wealth, education, life style and stock of ideas that enable them to meet one another on equal terms.[5] Marx's emphasis on economic factors in the definition of class, and Weber's separation of class from status, whereby he reserved the former term for the economic and the latter for the quality of perceived social interaction – i.e. for the positive or negative estimation of persons or positions, only describe objective class reality but not the subjective self-classification that serves as foundation for constructive class consciousness. Constructive in the sense that it creates a claim to power by similarly placed members of society which is something else than the consciousness that merely takes notice of the similarity and relates it to the vicissitudes of fate. It is simply this: the existence of a large group of people in a common economic position need not automatically lead them towards *conscious* common action. People in the same situation may exhibit similar behavior and attitudes without having a sense of class consciousness. Consciousness is heavily weighted by cultural environment and by the ideas common to a society or part of it, it is not solely determined by purely economic relations. Antagonism towards higher placed strata of society may develop spontaneously but class consciousness among the lower placed will only arise when the collective opportunity to eliminate their inferiority is demonstrated, when this inferiority is recognized as a product of the existing class structure of society and not as a natural situation. The

---

4.   For details about the growth of the working class and its share in the general increase of population see B.R. Mitchell, *European Historical Statistics 1750–1970*, London, 1975.

5.   For a wider description of the term class consciousness see Morris Ginsberg in *E.S.S.*, Vol. III, pp. 536–8.

slaves led by Spartacus who revolted in 71 B.C. and for a time dominated much of southern Italy were of course a group of people in a common economic position who exhibited similar behavior and attitudes, but they did not develop a class consciousness. They did not strive to abolish the institution of slavery, they did not confront Roman society with the image of an alternative social structure; but they accepted the existing system except for their own place as individuals within it, which became the main cause of their undoing or at least saved the Roman establishment from the menace of a much wider uprising in many provinces of the empire.

The conflict of interests between employers and workers in the nineteenth century was interpreted within the framework of a normally functioning market system. There were buyers and sellers; some bought and others sold labor and everyone, indeed each individual who participated in this transaction tried to make for himself the best bargain he could. When workers found it useful to combine in a certain trade or working place to improve their bargaining position they tried to do so, just as the London coal merchants did before the 'anti-ring' law forbade it. But this did not require great imaginative perception – class consciousness does. Class consciousness requires an abstract vision and class action requires a practicable alternative perception of society. Throughout most of the nineteenth century the working class lacked the intellectual leadership capable of producing such a perception. It developed in the wake, not in advance, of the labor unions, just as it had happened with the bourgeoisie in earlier times. To oppose exploitation and serve their own immediate interests workers got organized. The contradicting interests that split the bourgeoisie and weakened their power to resist the organization of labor, of which the struggle between landlords and industrialists that was reflected in the clash between Tories and Liberals about the Corn Laws is but one example. Time after time one or the other conflicting interest groups within the bourgeoisie found it necessary to extend greater political rights to the working class in order to serve their immediate needs which were threatened by another group. Sometimes this took the form of rearranging the electoral constituencies, other times of reducing the minimum qualifications for voting in elections, and other times again it was done by abolishing the laws prohibiting the establishment of labor unions.[6] The organization of labor in itself already quasi stressed the distinction between 'us' and 'them' and evolved a kind of class coherence and consciousness. The problem only was that in the early stages of this development the 'them' was mainly identified as the directors and managers with whom the workers' contact was direct and immediate, and not as those profit-hungry 'them', namely the class of shareholders and financial magnates. The 'them' was identified with a life-style rather than with the economic character of the relationship. In fact by confusing life-style with economic relationship, the working class divorced itself from the people capable of providing it with the necessary ideological leadership by regarding all those who did not share their own style as 'them' the working class not only alienated its own better educated members and the greater part of the middle class intelligentsia but it practically drove them into the fold of the bourgeoisie. By making a life-style and by implication the level of income that made this life-style possible the holemark of a persons class, the working class not only missed the other aspect of class relationship, namely the difference between exploiters and exploited, but divorced itself from all those in the middle class who were its objective allies. For there could be little attraction for the middle class in the acceptance of a life-style whose only *raison d'etre* was poverty. So without being aware of it the proletariat left the social hegemony in the hands of the bourgeoisie by simply presenting the image of poverty as their sole alternative. For almost a century this identification of poverty with membership of the working class remained so strong that even the belated attempts to stress the true societal importance of labor – for example with the slogans about the dignity of labor, could not disperse the fears of the middle class of being reduced to proletarians. But there were also other reasons why Labor found it so difficult to dislodge the bourgeoisie from its position of power.

In the early days of bourgeois dominance, in the era of merchant capitalism, industry was thriving on expanding foreign markets. The

6.   *Vide* 'Industry' in Y.S. Brenner, *A Short History of Economic Progress.*

backbone of unionism in this period were the journeymen[7]. But journeymen had it within their reasonable perspective to become employers themselves and were therefore on the whole less strongly motivated to engage in class struggle. They were much more than less well qualified workers inclined to find a solution to many of their problems in co-operation, i.e. in setting up co-operatives in order to eliminate middle-men, and, in desperation in a kind of Proudhonian anarchism. Later, when merchant capitalism became technological capitalism the labor movement began to separate into two camps: one that wished to do away with capitalism altogether, and another which did not necessarily reject capitalism but was ready to bargain with it. This is the period beginning about 1880 when the labor movement splits up into communists, syndicalists, guild socialists and industrial unionists. Part of the labor movement begins to look for solutions politically and another in craft unions. All Unions reflect workers' desire to protect or improve their living standards. The *revolutionary* unionist tradition is rooted in Marx's theory of dialectical and historical materialism. The *neoclassical* unionist tradition regards unions as logical constructs organized like business firms to maximize their members' gains. *Revolutionary* unionism which predominated in western Europe upheld a class perception of society in which the exploitation of workers by a profit grasping bourgeoisie occupied a central position. It had therefore both a material and a moral dimension. *Neoclassical* unionism which was more common in North-America than in Europe was less 'ideological' – had no alternative perception of society, and made no claim to moral ascendancy. The basis of the revolutionary unions' perception was Marx's dialectical and historical materialism which also provided them with a guide for action. For with the acceptance of dialectics as the general law of development it became possible to predict the future by analyzing the past and understanding the present. The idea was that the development of human society is ruled by necessity and necessity is independent of people's consciousness, but the recognition of the necessity and the formulation of policies

---

7.   A Journeyman was atrained workan who was working for a master-owner of a workshop.

that conform to it is the essence of progressive labor leadership. The laws of necessity do not operate automatically but are formed as a result of men's actions. The laws merely determine the general trend, which is the outcome of an objective situation. The development itself, however, the actual course of events, must depend on the pull of contradictory forces. For example, socialism is bound to replace capitalism – a historical necessity – but the actual date of the downfall and the manner in which it will occur depends on a variety of circumstances. The forces which provide these circumstances are the product of ideas, or ideas themselves. Scientific socialism is itself the reflection of the objective conflict between the old capitalist productive relations and the new productive forces, and the superstructures which arise out of each of these productive relations. The recognition of each new reality is the factor which eventually causes the transition from one stage to the next. The idea, i.e. the recognition of the new economic and social reality, becomes itself an integral part of the cause of change because it can unite people to conscious practical action. In this sense, according to Marx, an idea when taken up by the masses becomes a real material force.[8] So, according to this view, the correctness of union policy in any given situation depends upon its leaders' correct appreciation of the situation within the wider historical context. But facts seldom speak with a single voice; how can one ever be *sure* of having the correct appreciation of the future consequences of one's actions? Some orthodox converts to socio-economic determinism claimed, and perhaps continue to claim, that scientific Marxism – the method of historical and dialectical materialism, can do just that. Yet, there were at least three streams in the revolutionary union movement[9] with three different interpretations of historical situations and

---

8.   *Vide* Marx & Engels, *Selected Works*, Moscow (Foreign Languages Publishing House) edition of 1958, Vol. I, pp. 362–3.

9.   'Revolutionary' refers here to *objectives* rather than *methods* – it includes reformist movements working for the overthrow of Capitalism by gradualist non-violent measures as well as those preparing for it a sudden and violent doom.

necessity and consequently with different prescriptions to guide their policies and actions.

All trade unions are organizations for the purpose of protecting and improving workers' economic status. All revolutionary unions aspired the overthrow of the socio-economic order but their methods varied. The non-revolutionary, or 'neoclassical' unions as they were also called, were content to struggle within the prevailing social and economic system to obtain the best possible living conditions for their members; the aims of the revolutionary unions went beyond this, they wished to abolish altogether the social and economic system that made this struggle necessary. At the one end of the revolutionary unions' spectrum one finds the *reformists* who were revolutionary in their aims (the abolition of Capitalism) but evolutionist or gradualist in their methods. At the other end one finds the *Leninist-Stalinist,* and also, but very distinct from them, the *anarcho-syndicalist* union ideologies whose bearers did not share the reformists' optimism regarding the possible peaceful transformation of the system.[10] The reformists believed that persistently exerted pressure on employers to increase workers' share in the fruits of production and in influence on the running of enterprises would, in the fill of time, result in the peaceful socialization of industry. Some even proposed the utilization of union funds to create a union owned industrial sector to compete with the capitalistic sector with the object of abolishing capitalism by its own methods, i.e. by competition. The champions of this idea maintained that the establishment of union enterprises would in the short-run raise workers' incomes in the private sector, because wages in the union sector would influence the level of remuneration everywhere, and in the long-run exert unbearable pressure on private enterprise leading to its waning out of existence. Union enterprises presumably being less than private business in constant need to maximize profits would be free to pursue political ends. Instead of investing in the sectors and regions where profits were highest, unions could establish their enterprises where they would serve the cause of labor. It goes

---

10. For the ideological divisions in unions see also Mark Perlman in 'Labor Unions', *I.E.S.S.*

without saying that unlike their capitalist competitors union enterprises were expected to be able to rely on their workers to support them for example by moderating their wage demands in periods of recessions.[11] A well known representative of this line of thought was Eduard Bernstein (1850–1932).[12]

At the opposite end of the revolutionary union spectrum one finds the *Leninist-Stalinist* Communist conception. This conception denied the correctness of the gradualist or reformist approach. In the light of Scientific Socialism it regarded the intensification of class contradictions as a historical necessity which made unavoidable the violent confrontation that would bring about the overthrow of Capitalism. Taking less from Marx than from Lenin and Stalin the followers of this line argued that the increasing rate of capitalistic exploitation, and the accumulation of capital that attends it, must inevitably result in a decline in the profitability of capital investments and in the sagging of workers' living standards. Ignorant of, or just ignoring, the observable fact that workers' living conditions in the industrial countries on the whole improved rather than deteriorated in spite of the accumulation and concentration of capital, 'traditional' communists continued to maintain the Stalinist scenario. This scenario in which the progressing impoverishment of the working class took a central position predicted the violent doom of capitalism as follows: Unable to go on suffering the deprivations that accompany and are part of the recurrent and with each recurrence intensifying economic crisis (which are inherent in the capitalistic mode of production) the laboring masses were to be left with no choice but revolt. However, aware of this threat the bourgeoisie would take its counter measures and surround itself with

---

11.   It may be mentioned here that though not strictly comparable something of this kind actually took place in Palestine during the last decades of the British Mandate preceding the establishment of the state of Israel. There major economic enterprises were established by the General Federation of Labor (the *Chevrath Ovdim* of the *Histadruth*) with a clear political purpose to give to Zionism its territorial dimension and economic basis with a socialist imprint. See also Y.S. Brenner, *A Short History of Economic Progress*. pp. 238–45.

12.   *Vide* E. Bernstein, *Evolutionary Socialism*, 1898.

persons who in one way or another could be bribed or bought to protect the system – and so violence would become unavoidable.[13] When the 'bribing' of some intellectuals and the professionally-qualified labor-elite, and the 'buying' of the monopoly of the means of violence, i.e. the army and police, would no longer suffice to protect the regime, even then, would the bourgeoisie not give up without a final struggle. In its desperation it would take control of the whole state machinery, as indeed it did earlier in this century, though with a different ideology, in Italy, Germany and Spain, and plunge the whole world into a war. Given this scenario the duties of the unions became self-evidently political rather than economic. Their true place in society was determined by their political contribution to labor's cause and not by the material achievements they obtained for workers in their day to day haggling with employers about wages and working conditions. However, once socialism has replaced capitalism, the role of unions is revised. For with the passing of the means of production into the hands of the people – or rather into the hands of the government acting on behalf of the people, the struggle for higher living standards would cease to be a matter of class contradictions and become the struggle of man against nature – the struggle for efficiency. For without private ownership the means of production, exploitation of men by men would become a thing of the past. The new detractors of the welfare of society become, according to this view, those who because of a legacy of capitalist-mentality continue to exploit their fellow workers though of course they can no longer do so in the same manner as before. These are the workers who do not do their best – who do not contribute to the people's wealth to the best of their ability, and the managers of enterprises who misuse the powers delegated to them by society by discriminating against individuals or in any other

13. *Vide* Lenin, *State and Revolution* for the origins of this conception. It is perhaps noteworthy that in Marx's writings there is little evidence (with the exception of a statement to this effect in the *Manifesto* – which was after all a propaganda paper produced on the stir of the events of 1848) to suggest that the overthrow of the bourgeois' regime must be ushered in by sagging living standards. Also the place of violence in the demise of capitalism is less explicit in Marx than in Lenin.

way. And so, under socialism the unions become on the one hand the guardians of society against individuals who try to exploit their fellow men, and on the other hand, the guardians of individuals against managerial or bureaucratic high-handed arrogance. Wish it was true!

Between the extremes – the Gradualists and the Stalinists – one finds of course all the other colours of the revolutionary union spectrum. On the moderate right one finds such socialist-pragmatists as Hayes and Berger and later Sam Gompers of the pre–1924 American Federation of Labor;[14] while on the left one finds Rosa Luxemburg who was for revolution but against armed rebellion – for the destruction of capitalism but not without the democratic support of a conscious working class.[15]

Also on the extreme left of the union movement and deserving special mentioning here are the anarcho-syndicalists. Unlike the Communists they did not believe in a teleologically deterministic 'historical necessity'. In fact they believed that capitalism could last for a very long time indeed, and this because of its inherent consistency. Being held together by the universal pursuit of gain that permeates all layers of society to the last individual, the system provided an internal logic which assured its durability. It provided each individual with the illusion of security for life and property and an incentive to behave precisely in a manner best suited for the perpetuation of the system. It leads him to approve of, say, a legal system and its guardians that help him to enjoy what earnings or property he has, and leaves him unmoved by the fact that it is the very same legal system and its guardians that prevent him if, for

---

14.   The A.F.L. became less ideological under William Green, and something altogether strange under George Meany and after the merger in 1955 with the C.I.O. it became a Neoclassical union adopting questionable methods to maximize members(?) profits.

15.   In spite of her part in the Spartacus affair, into which she was forced against her better judgement by the party leadership majority, Rosa Luxemburg, unlike Karl Radek later on, never supported the idea of a revolution without the prior 'complete spiritual transformation of the masses.' *Vide* Rosa Luxemburg, *Leninism or Marxism*, p. 71.

example, he is a worker from receiving the full value of his labor from his employer. He is therefore led by his immediate notion of self-interest to approve of one type of 'theft' in order to be protected from another. Thus everyone intent on satisfying his immediate wants is unconsciously turned by the system into a defender of the system at large and with this destroys his chances of attaining the security of person and property he is striving for. Engulfed in competition the pursuit of gain or profit becomes a necessity for survival, and the wish to survive gives rise to the pursuit of gain – a vicious circle which provides its own inescapable logic and makes the system rationally unassailable from within. It had to be destroyed from outside – by acts unexplainable in terms of bourgeois rationality. Only 'a spanner in the works' can dislocate the system, and this – to throw the spanner in the works was precisely what anarcho-syndicalism set out to do.

There was a parallel development in nineteenth century conventionalist science which can help explain the anarchist conception of society. Conventionalist science held that as science advances the power of empirical evidence recedes. For example, if Newton's mechanics can be 'saved' from experimental refutations by the introduction of auxiliary hypotheses capable of reconciling the anomalies with the general theories – by reconciling theory and facts, this is what is done (Poincare). But altogether no experiment can ever be crucial and force the scientist to reject an accepted theory for every experiment is itself at least partially dependent upon the acceptance of the theory as a whole. For example, to assert thermic expansion one uses a thermometer but the assumption of uniform thermic expansion is already built into the thermometer itself. This then makes science a complex system theory – a system of interrelated hypotheses, experimental equipment, and methodological procedures. It follows that when a hypothesis is tested and refuted there is no way of deciding whether it is the hypothesis that is false or any one of the many other factors that are involved, – including the observation when it implies the reading of an instrument. The system is a closed system and as Duhem (1861–1916) said, no physical theory ever crumbles under the weight of refutations alone but it may crumble under the weight of continual repairs.

Yet anarchism reached further back in time into the classical and romantic heritage of inherent truths. It started from the proposition that man is essentially good but corruptible by the institutions of authority; that he tends spontaneously towards voluntary co-operation, i.e. towards natural society in which he finds fulfillment but is forced instead into the unnatural structures of the state; that he is individualistic and creative but his creative individualism is impaired by the institution of private property, which, together with the other artificial institution the state, is the prime evil – the instrument of exploitation. Take out private property and the state becomes superfluous for it serves but one purpose namely to protect such property. Take out private property and direct, mass based, spontaneous, social change will follow, and mankind will be free from Hobbes' war of everybody against everyone else and find its natural forms of social co-operation. Man just does not wake in the morning saying to himself 'what evil deed and what harm can I do unto my neighbor this fine day?' On the contrary, he is well disposed towards one and all for he is 'a social animal'. However, the institution of private property and the authority that accompanies it, leave him with little choice. If he wishes to survive he must live according to the rules (the conventions); he must compete and exploit and protect the gains of exploitation by more exploitation, for if he ceases treading the treadmill he will fall and be destroyed.

Here then was a philosophy that bestowed upon man the qualities Christianity had attributed to a Deity which man was encouraged to emulate; and here then was man's fall – a paradise lost, because of the institutions of private property and the state. It were these essentially traditional values that stirred the hearts and minds of men coming from so varied a background as Proudhon and Count Kropotkin, Czolgosz and the Andalusian peasants who fought Franco. What they had in common was an exaltation of individualism and an abomination of private property; confidence in man's inherent goodness and hate and disgust for the institutions of authority that corrupt him and subvert the natural harmony of society. From the bourgeoisie they took the conception of individual rights and carrying it into the economic sphere they stripped it of its class content thus making it into a new progressive factor.[16] Yet there was little in all that united anarchists to indicate the method best suited to overthrow the bourgeois system. William Godwin (1756–1836), the author of the *Enquiry concerning the Principles of Political Justice* who may well be counted among the forefathers of the anarchist ideology, was apparently convinced of the powers of education to bring about a voluntary piecemeal transformation of society. Pierre Joseph Proudhon (1809–1865), the author of *What is Property?* (to which he gave the unequivocal answer 'property is theft') also abhorred violence but still implied that it may perhaps become necessary. Peter Kropotkin (1842–1921) the author of *Mutual Aid,* who rejected the Darwinist idea of the survival of the fittest and the idea of the party as an instrument of revolutionary change, suggested violence as the best, perhaps the only means for the abolition of that-sentinel-of-the-all-corrupting-private-property – the state. Mikhail Bakunin (1814–1876) the prophet of *'anarchism, collectivism and atheism'* saw violence as The means for gaining freedom. He opposed Marx and was expelled by him from the First International. Georges Sorel (1847–1922) the author of the *Reflections on Violence,* who fathered the anarcho-syndicalist idea and myth of the General Strike, had altogether little concern for the ideological tenets of anarchism. For him democracy was but 'the triumph of mediocrity'. Being more concerned with action than ideology, with techniques of revolution than revolutionary theory, he recommended *organized* (union) action led by revolutionary *elites* – a recommendation hardly consistent with the original conception of anarchism. It is hardly surprising that his writings found a considerable echo later also in the Fascist movements. Finally there were men like Leon Czolgosz (1873–1901), the assassin of President McKinley, who not only advocated violence as an instrument of policy but actually practiced it themselves, and Big Bill Haywood, a labor leader who helped to found the Industrial Workers of the World (I.W.W.), and was thrown out of the socialist party for preaching violence. Yet with all its differing tendencies anarcho-syndicalism must still be regarded as the purest form of union opposition against the growing omnipotence of

---

16.   For the definition of progress *vide* p. xli.

the capitalist state. While Socialists were tempted to fight capitalism politically, by obtaining the socio-political transformation by reformistic measures, and while the non-revolutionary unions were ready to come to terms with the capitalistic state for a greater share in it, anarcho-syndicalism wanted no dealings with it nor with any of its institutions. French anarcho-syndicalism in particular, which became quite formidable in the last decade of the nineteenth century, was strongly opposed to all parliamentary or otherwise political action. It combined Proudhonist emancipationalism and distaste for state authority with the Marxian idea of antagonistic class contradictions, and Sorel's belief in the role of the militant elite, with Bakunin's predilection for violence. For them, direct action and above all the General Strike was the only true road to salvation.[17] But, again, anarcho-syndicalism was never fully representative of anarchism as such. This was not only due to the tactical deviations such as Sorel's elitarian tendencies but above all to the inherently unindividualistic elements in the syndicalist conception. This departure from the individualistic tradition gave anarcho-syndicalism, as distinct from pure anarchism, a degree of familiarity with both Fascism and Leninism. The increasing tendency of the means to take precedence over the aims, and of negation over construction, deprived anarcho-syndicalism of its most progressive element namely its liberating individualism. Tactical considerations which made it necessary to work with organizational frameworks, and the frustration with capitalism that was real and more concrete than the intellectual speculations of the pure anarchists, divested anarcho-syndicalism of its essential tenets of belief. This came to its logical, or rather illogical, conclusion, with Edouard Berth's syndicalist anti-intellectualism – the ideology of deeds rather than thought, – the ideology of medieval metaphysical racism, anti-semitism, and eventually, monarchism. On the whole, however, as Val. R. Lorwin summarizes in the *Encyclopedia*, 'The unionists did not share Sorel's

---

17.   The belief in the General Strike did however not exclude other activities such as local strikes, demonstrations and where necessary acts of sabotage because these must be regarded as exercises in the art of making revolutions, as schooling in revolutionary consciousness towards the great day of the General Strike.

pessimistic view of the world; they were optimistic in that expectation of an imminent social revolution which was part of the radical mood of the generation before 1914. The unionists denounced socialist intellectuals for their party politics, but they did not make a cult of anti-intellectualism and anti-rationalism, as did Sorel and Berth. The unionists often seemed to urge direct action for its own sake, but they did not urge violence for its own sake, as did the intellectuals. The general strike was for the intellectuals a great social myth. But the union people saw it as a real tactic for pragmatic purposes.'

With all this there remained an essential difference between anarchists and socialists. Socialists regarded the state at least in the early post-revolutionary period as a necessary evil. Anarchists did not. For them it was just evil and had to be abolished forthwith. In the socialist scenario 'The proletariat seizes the state power, and transforms the means of production in the first instance into state property (and with this) it puts an end to the state as the state' in the old sense. 'The first act in which the state really comes forward as the representative of society as a whole – the taking possession of the means of production in the name of society – is at the same time its last independent act as a state. The interference of the state power in social relations becomes superfluous in one sphere after another, and then ceases of itself. The government of persons is replaced by the administration of things and the direction of the processes of production. *The state is not 'abolished', it withers away.* It is from this standpoint that we (i.e. the socialists) must appraise the phrase 'free people's state' (of the anarchists)... and also the demand of the so-called anarchists that the state should be abolished overnight.'[18] This was certainly not the way the anarchists saw

---

18.   F. Engels, *Herr Eugen Dühring's Revolution in Science (Anti-Dühring)*, Edition of 23 May 1899. English Translation 1939, reprinted in 1970, pp. 306–7. Italics not in the original. The statement continues: 'Former society moving in class antagonisms, had need of the state that is, an organization of the exploiting class at each period for the maintenance of its external conditions of production; that is therefore for the forcible holding down of the exploited class in the conditions of oppression (slavery, villeinage or serfdom, wage-labor) determined by the existing mode of production...'

things. Leaning upon a philosophical tradition ranging from Zeno of Citium to the Levelers they were convinced that not unlike private property the state too 'has a life of itself' which is intrinsically evil.[19]

Real influence on the political and labor scene anarcho-syndicalism gained for a time in France, Italy and Spain. In France it became powerful in the last decade of the nineteenth century and maintained its influence to World War I. But Syndicalist support for the war effort and cooperation with the Socialists and even the Government after the war eroded its anarchism which turned mere revolutionary verbalism. Italian Syndicalism which was greatly influenced by Sorel's ideas, also cooperated with the Socialists and for a time even shared in the government of the country, under the slogan of realism – the acknowledgement of the need to adjust the *strategy* to the political reality. Spanish Syndicalism was the most impressive and long lasting of the three. It upheld its belief in spontaneity, its hostility to the state and to its bureaucratic institutions, and its opposition to the church. Yet its most heroic period came, paradoxically, when it joined forces with the other movements on the left and even entered the government in the civil war.[20]

Of the other countries where anarcho-syndicalism gained some degree of influence the Netherlands and the United States of America ought perhaps to be mentioned. Dutch anarcho-syndicalism was distinguished by Christian Cornelissen's theoretical contribution, while, in contrast, American anarcho-syndicalism was mainly influenced by men of action. It's power was in the I.W.W. (Industrial Workers of the World) and in its leaders', aggressive rhetoric. Its lack of discipline and opposition to the war provided the American bourgeoisie with the opportunity to suppress the

---

19. The fact that the nationalization of the means of production has not led the state to *'wither away'* in the Soviet Union, and that in the eyes of many it had rather worsened its hold on the lives of people – one may think of Stalin's reign of terror, seems to lend some support to the anarchists' distinction between economic and political powers of oppression.

20. The Anarchist participation in government lasted from November 1936 to May 1937.

movement. 'A hopelessly impractical organizational structure, internal dissension, and the competing new appeal of communism to revolutionaries completed the down fall in the 1920's of an organization which had carried antiauthoritarianism and worker exclusivism to fatal extremes'.[21]

Not alone practical considerations separated anarcho-syndicalist from socialist and from neoclassical trade unions, but also the social value systems from which their resistance to exploitation emanated differed. The neoclassicists' value system was plainly that of the bourgeoisie itself. What the neoclassicists wanted was a greater share in the fruits of production and they employed for the attainment of their purpose the bourgeoisie's own devices. They accepted as a fact that man is *homo economicus* and the competitive character of human relations – *homini homo lupus*. The socialists also recognized this reality in the existing social relationships but did not accept it as permanent – hence their revolutionary character. In their view this social reality was but the product of specific production relations. But with this they did not altogether abandon the utilitarian conception of humanity – consciousness of being exploited is the revolutionary motor, self-interest was with them too the main factor in human behavior; only that they saw the pursuit of self-interest in a wider, even social, and more sophisticated form; and they retained the belief in a number of absolutes such as the objective existence of matter (materialism) and the traditional values of good and bad, right and wrong, truth and untruth etc. which in their view did not depend upon expediency. Anarchism, in contrast, adopted a much earlier tradition, namely the tradition of natural harmony and the inherent characteristics of man. With this they came much closer to pre-capitalist ideas than to the utilitarian assumptions. Only, that they endowed them with an individualistic atheism – with the exaltation of man as an individual. It contained therefore not only the negation of capitalism but also the prospect of an alternative society based upon the spontaneous voluntary co-operation of non utilitarian individuals who by their very nature are well inclined one towards

---

21.   This is the verdict of Val. R. Lorwin, *op.cit.*, p. 450. *Vide* also Oscar Jaszi, 'Anarchism' in *E.S.S.*

each other. It may therefore be said that none of the three movements did really abandon the cultural heritage of contemporary society though all of them, even the neoclassical unions, have gnawed at its foundation.

The non-revolutionary, i.e. the neoclassical unions which work with and within the capitalist system are primarily concerned with the immediate wants of their members – with wages and working conditions. They do not relate to any particular vision of a future society but like any kind of business try to maximize advantages. Hence their leadership is far less concerned with ideological considerations than with the effects of wages on the economic system as it exists and on the level of employment. Yet even these relatively limited concerns have increasingly and perhaps unintentionally forced them to adopt ideologically and politically loaded positions. They often cannot avoid exerting their power as pressure groups to prevent or abolish some elements of state legislation that limit their freedom of action; and, perhaps more significantly, they find it increasingly necessary to get representation on management boards or other employers' decision-making bodies to gain both the information they require for the realistic assessment of the chances for wage claims, and to protect their members' jobs where the management is unable or unwilling to do it. Recurrent periods of mass unemployment and periods of sharp rising prices have led even some of the least revolutionary unions whose leaderships maintain a positive approving attitude towards the capitalist system to adopt political positions which whether they want it or not are in fact revolutionary. They are revolutionary in content but of course not in design and they do not arise out of the moral value system by which the revolutionary movements judge and reject capitalism. Their attitude is pragmatic and this pragmatism leads them step by step towards the modification of the capitalist system in most practical matters by which the system had in the past elicited and evoked the opposition of the working class. As their opponents from the left would say, they give workers better living conditions but no justice. The theoreticians of the nonrevolutionary unions are concerned with organizational problems, with the selection of suitable instruments for the attainment of their objectives (different types of strikes and harassment of employers) and with the general relationship between wages, prices and employment. Particularly the more powerful unions are also forced to study the relationship between wages, technological improvements or innovations, and various price elasticities in order to protect their members. In spite of all that certain sections of the bourgeois press claim to the contrary, the union leaders are well aware that they cannot drive the enterprises in which their members are employed out of business and must not by unreasonable wage claims subject the economy to unacceptable rates of inflation. This is so not because of an ideological desire to keep the system going but because of the simple pragmatic need to maintain their members' working-places and not have wage increases cancelled by even sharper price rises. In addition to this, union theoreticians are increasingly concerned with the whole problem of social legislation on a national scale. They occupy themselves with working conditions, social security and pensions, which are now no less important than the direct wage claims. Finally they cannot help, even if they did not want to, being concerned with government policy regarding things like taxation and subsidies because these matters have a direct bearing on union members' living standards. It is not alone the problem whether capital or labor have to pay the greater share for the country's social and political programmes, but also how the burden of reviving the economy after a recession or depression should be shared between the social partners, which is of vital concern for unions. As a result of these needs that reality imposes upon them the unions, whether neoclassical or revolutionary, have taken an ever increasing share in the running of the bourgeois states. In doing so they have greatly reduced the excesses of the system, i.e. the poverty that had been the original cause of labor's antagonism towards it, but they have not touched the core of the system itself – the profit hunger that permeates all aspects of capitalist society. Marx had in fact recognized this possibility in the chapter on the *Berauschende Mehrung von Reichtum und Macht, Relative Verarmung der Arbeiterklasse* in *Das Kapital*. Commenting there on Gladstone's speeches of 13th February 1843 and 17th April 1863 he wrote: *Wenn die Arbeiterklasse 'arm' geblieben ist, nur 'weniger arm' im Verhältnis, worin sie eine 'berauschende Vermehrung von Reichtum und Macht für die besitzende Klasse produzierte, so ist sie relativ gleich arm geblieben. Wenn die äussersten Grade der Armut sich nicht vermindert haben, haben sie sich vermehrt mit den äussersten Graden des Reichtums...* [22] But for Marx the issue with capitalism was as much a moral as a practical issue and for this reason he would hardly have been appeased by the truly impressive achievements of the working class in the rich countries during the century that followed his above quoted statement. But the diminished poverty (in the economically advanced countries), and the greater security, also blunted the opposition of the working class to the bourgeois state and system, and with it the difference between socialist and pragmatic unions. It diminished the moral resentment against the system's inequity, and left the revolutionary opposition to the students, young clergy and the idealistic sections of the middle class. This tendency, which was well demonstrated during the student riots in 1968 and in the anti-Viet-Nam war campaign in the United States,[23] is one of the subjects to which we will return in more detail in another chapter of this book. Here it may suffice to point out that until the mid-nineteen-seventies, when the security of employment was once again shaken in the industrialized countries of the west, the working class has with few exceptions come to terms with capitalism and adopted its crude utilitarian philosophy and value system. The decline of religion on the one hand, and the decline of revolutionary engagement on the other, show how well bourgeois materialism has conquered the hearts and minds of labor. With the declining poverty also went the working-class's opposition to the bourgeoisie's social and cultural hegemony. With the exception of some traditional labor sub-cultures – for example the British miners', the proletarian alternative never even budded.

---

22. 'The enthralling increase of riches and power, and the relative impoverishment of the working class.'
'If the working class remained 'poor', only relatively '*less poor*' while it was producing an enthralling increase in riches and power for the propertied class, it *remained relatively equally poor*. If the outer limits of poverty did not diminish then they increased with the outer measures of riches...'

23. Which Herbert Marcuse already discovered and discussed in his *One Dimensional Man.*

In spite of the diminishing importance of ideological divisions, practical problems continued to divide the labour movement. One such important issue was whether or not unions should be politically engaged or should confine themselves to 'industrial action'. In the concluding paragraph of his short summary of *British Trade Unions 1875–1933*[24] John Lovell writes: 'There is indeed much to be said for viewing trade unions in terms of their relationships with employers and the state. A union's capacity to influence working conditions and therefore to attract and retain members, is intimately bound up with these relationships. It is the great strength of Clegg *et al.* that their *History* focuses not on unions in isolation but on the process of interaction among unions, employers and government. Above all, it focuses on the evolution of collective bargaining: the principal means by which unions have been able to influence working conditions. It has sometimes been objected that such an approach neglects the political and ideological dimensions of union activity... however,... trade unions are constrained by their needs as institutions to subordinate political to industrial activity. A union that is to survive and grow must give priority to the short-term economic interests of its members, for this is the common bond that holds organization together'. This is indeed one of the main reasons for the British unions' inability or even unwillingness to take upon themselves direct political responsibility. As a result of this British working-men's representation in Parliament was first left in the hands of the Liberals[25] and later in the hands of the Labor Party 'bods' (recruited mainly from Eton and Harrow) who with few exceptions had little in common with the British working-people.

---

24. *Studies in Economic and Social History*, London, 1977.

25. H. Pelling for example writes about the Union leaders who joined the L.R.C. that 'They had no policy which was in advance of Liberalism... It was in deference to their views that the Labor Party remained, in the years before the First World War, uncommitted, not merely to Socialism, but to any programme whatsoever'. After the Second World War the Labor Party was led by men like Harold Wilson who made a great show of never having read Marx as if ignorance was a qualification for a Labor politician.

In England the beginnings of organized labor were punctuated by sporadic outbursts of violence such as the Luddite Riots of 1811 and 1816. These were explosions of rage by workers against the introduction of machines which they held responsible for reducing employment opportunities. They were not attempts to do away with the system – to abolish the bourgeois hegemony. The first attempt to challenge this hegemony in England came only in the wake of the *Reform Bill* (1832) and the *People' Charter* (1838) and was abruptly terminated in 1848 with the suppression of the Chartist riots. During the prolonged period of prosperity following the middle of the century skilled workers' unions reorganized and achieved a great many economic advantages for their members. Employers were in need of skilled workers and so their bargaining position was strong. The new model unionism was therefore less militant than its predecessors and was restricted to industrial action. The depression that began in the late 1880's soon lay bare the weakness of this type of unionism which proved to be powerful in times of labor shortage but weak in times of unemployment. Within less than a decade its importance was overshadowed by unskilled workers' unions in docks, mines and gas-works. Unlike the skilled workers' unions of the 'sixties and 'seventies who had tacitly accepted the bourgeois system the unskilled workers' unions were led by socialists. Yet until close to the end of the century the leaders did not succeed to enlist their union membership's support for political objectives. Nor did they manage to dissociate the British working class from the Liberal Party or from the Lib-Lab alliance. When early in the twentieth century they finally established a political representation for labor – the parliamentary Labor Party, it was dominated by the unions and did not until 1918 adopt socialism as part of its official program.[26]

So, to the end of World War I. the labor movement in Britain was reformist, Fabian, – not revolutionary. It steered a middle course

---

26.   For the general background of the Luddite riots see Y.S. Brenner, *A Short History of Economic Progress*, p. 18. For the history of Trade Unions in Britain in the early period, see Sidney and Beatrice Webb, *The History of Trade Unionism*, (New Edition) 1920; and G.D. Cole, *A Short History of the British Working Class Movement*, (London 1925–27); and R.H. Tawney, *The British Labor Movement*.

between French style syndicalism, i.e. the policy of abandoning party politics and economic bargaining in favor of efforts to abolish capitalism by means of the 'General Strike', and the German style domination of union activities by the Social-Democratic Party. It adopted a policy of promoting workers' control over industry at shop floor level. In the period of economic stagnation after the war – in the 'twenties, the fortunes of the labor movement were reversed. It's membership declined, the general strike called by the T.U.C. (1926) failed, and the passing of the Trades Disputes and Trade Union Act, which made all strikes in sympathy etc. illegal, marked the end of this phase in British unionism. The center of gravity was passing from the unions to the Labor Party. In 1923–24 the party even formed a short-lived minority government. In the ill fated year 1929 Labor once more formed a government but unable, or perhaps unwilling, to pursue socialist policies was defeated in 1931 and replaced by the National Government.[27]

In Germany, except for the short spurt, following the events of 1848, there was little union activity until the eighteen-sixties. In 1863 Ferdinand Lassalle organized the first German workers' political party with the aim of achieving universal suffrage in order to gain workers control over the state. Emphasizing the role of the state – its powers to extend credit and levy taxes and give subsidies, he believed in the possibility of using the state for the promotion of workers' *producers' co-operatives*, i.e. he hoped for a state system of workers co-operatives. Lassalle did not believe in unionism; he did not regard it adequate for solving labor's problems because of what he called 'the Iron Law of Wages'. The Iron Law of Wages was the old idea that when wages rise above subsistence level an increase in population will inevitably follow and force wages down again. This was an assertion which Marx was unable to accept. It led to a split in the German labor movement. Lassalle thought it necessary to abolish the wage system but not the institution of ownership as a whole. In the *Critique of the Gotha Programme*

---

27. The outstanding events in the period 1929–31 were the extension of franchise to women over 21 years of age, the cotton lock-out with two millions unemployed, and the financial crisis of 1931 .

Marx stated his objection to Lassalle as follows: 'If I abolish wage-labor, then naturally I abolish its laws also, whether they are of iron or sponge. But Lassalle's attack on wage-labor turns almost solely on this so-called law. In order therefore, to prove that Lassalle's sect has conquered, the wage system must be abolished together with the iron law of wages and not without it. It is well known that nothing of the iron law of wages belongs to Lassalle except the word iron borrowed from Goethe's great eternal iron laws. The word iron is a label by which the true believers recognize one another. But if I take the law with Lassalle's stamp on it and consequently in his sense then I must also take it with his basis for it. And what is that?... it is the Malthusian theory of population... But if this theory is correct, then again I cannot abolish the law even if I abolish wage labor a hundred times over, because the law then governs not only the system of wage labor but every social system. Basing themselves directly on this, the economists have proved for fifty years and more that socialism cannot abolish poverty, which has its basis in nature, but can only generalize it, distribute it simultaneously over the whole surface of society,' which was not what Marx believed to be the case.[28]

So, Marx and his followers abandoned and Lassalle and his followers retained the main tenets of German idealistic philosophy. Marx materialized dialectics into class struggle and Lassalle did not. Lassalle set his hope upon politics – upon the attainment of State Socialism, he wanted the state to help workers to organize themselves into co-operatives of producers. In 1863 he established the Universal German Workingmen's Association to promote this aim. In the following year (after the First International) Marx sent Liebknecht to Germany to organize the Marxist labor movement later to be led by Bebel. In 1875 both movements united and formed the *German Social Democratic Party* which in the short period until it was forbidden in October 1876 was dominated by Lassalle's wing of the labor movement.

In October 1876 the *Reichstag* passed the Anti-Socialist legislation that prohibited meetings, publications and collections of money for

---

28.   *Critique of Gotha Programme*. Revised translation edited by C.P. Dutt.

socialist or similar parties aiming, in the words of the law, 'to overthrow the existing order of state or society'. The labor movement was driven underground. When it reemerged into legality in 1890 it had become Marxist. It was during this time that Germany following hard upon Britain and the U.S.A. rose to take third place among the industrial powers. The number of people dependent upon industry in Germany had risen to more than sixteen millions and the number of people living in towns with more than 20.000 inhabitants had increased to over eight millions. To take the wind out of the sails of the socialists, whose underground influence was growing in pace with the industrial labor force, Bismarck introduced several measures in favor of the working class; namely Sickness Insurance (1883), Accident Insurance, (1884) Old-Age and Invalidity Insurance (1889). In 1890, after two readings of the bill extending the anti-socialist legislation for a further period it was suddenly forgotten. The new emperor (William II who succeeded to the German throne in 1888) favored a milder policy. He hoped to win the workers from socialism through social legislation. In July 1890 industrial courts were established to solve labor disputes, employment of women and children was restricted, and Sunday was declared an obligatory day of rest. In June 1891 factory inspection was improved, and workers were given the right to form committees to negotiate employment conditions. In March 1892 a Department of Labor was established to deal with labor problems in general. But in spite of these efforts 'from above' socialist ideas spread very rapidly. With the repeal of the anti-socialist legislation the socialists returned in 1890 35 deputies to the *Reichstag,* and in the following year at their congress (Erfurt) adopted a Marxian program. Between 1890 and 1906 the Social Democratic Party shared power equally with the Unions. But its failure in the elections of 1906 greatly strengthened the (Revisionist) non-Marxist wing of the labor movement. Under the pressure of the combined force of socialist and liberal agitation, Hohenlohe passed in 1899 a law permitting the federation of societies. Under Bülow in 1900 the social insurance legislation was extended, and in 1903 also sickness insurance. The conservative government, formed in 1907 to combat Center and Socialist policies, restricted factory work for women and children in 1908.[29] In 1910 an insurance code was passed that consolidated all previously made arrangements and extended their provisions. In the 1912 elections the Socialists polled more than four million votes and became the strongest party in the *Reichstag*. But by this time the party had become moderate and in favor of gradual progress through parliamentary reforms. Though it continued to be influenced by radicals, especially by Kautsky and Rosa Luxemburg, it mainly followed the moderate course of the rapidly growing trade-unions. This tendency towards moderation had been further extenuated after the Socialists' election setback in 1907. The party became reformist to the point of co-operation with the Progressives in the *Reichstag*. Though not in theory it had in fact accepted the bourgeois hegemony. In 1914 both the trade unions and the Social Democratic Party supported the government when it asked the *Reichstag* to approve war credits to defend the *Fatherland* against 'autocratic Russia'. Once again nationalism had gained the upper hand and had routed the forces of class struggle.[30]

In the war the unions gained power and prestige, – they were represented on many government boards, and after the war they obtained official status in the republican constitution. It was the Socialist leader, Scheidemann, who in November 1918 proclaimed the German Republic. The Republican Constitution not only confirmed the trade unions' official status and made 'Yellow Unions', i.e. company unions, illegal, and forbade discrimination against union members, but also reduced the working day to 8 hours

---

29.   The new rules were that children under the age of 14 would work no more than 6 hours per day, and between the age of 14 and 16 years no more than 10 hours per day. Children up to the age of 13 years were henceforth no longer allowed to work in factories.

30.   This ill fated turn of events had far reaching consequences for it left an odium of suspicion about the Social Democrats that eventually resulted in a lasting breach between the revolutionary and the reformist wings of the international labor scene. Worst of all, it deprived Russian Communism of the chance of inheriting the great humanist tradition of western revolutionary socialism.

and set up a number of joint boards for conciliation in labor disputes.

So German social democracy obtained considerable economic advantages for the working class without actually challenging the system, – but challenging the system was precisely what the revolutionary, i.e. the political wing of the labor movement wanted. The *Spartacus* revolt in 1919 against a social democratic government was the reflection of this long-standing conflict. It was the confrontation between on the one hand those who, perhaps not in theory but in practice, accepted the bourgeois system and within it tried to reinforce collective action to obtain greater economic advantages to working people, and on the other hand those who believed that the system as such was neither just nor rational nor even capable in the long run to assure the economic achievements which reformist government and union power were able to obtain. Whether or not abstract logic was on the side of *Spartacus* in 1919, concrete achievements and that which goes as common sense (until it is overcome), was on the side of the government. In any case, the crushing of the Spartacists finalized the split that had been with the German labor movement since its division over Germany's participation in the War. And though until 1932 the German Social Democratic Party remained the largest party in the country, and the German Communist Party the most powerful Communist Party outside the Soviet Union, German labor could no longer find sufficient common ground to co-operate even in the face of the Fascist threat. Since 1929 the *National Socialists* under Hitler were becoming a powerful threat to all union and social democratic achievements. In the presidential elections of March 1932, Hindenburg secured 18,651,497 votes and Hitler, supported mainly by the middle class, disappointed workers, industrialists and landlords, 11,300,000 votes. The Communist Thälmann obtained 4,983,341 votes.

In 1920 the trade unions had been sufficiently strong to defeat a reactionary monarchist putsch by a general strike alone. Twelve years later, in 1932, a large part of the German working class had become so politically disorientated that it was no more able to recognize

Hitler and his policies for what they really were.[31] The defeat of the *Spartacists* had rid German Social Democracy of its revolutionary wing and left the party in the hands of moderates who were hoping and working for the gradual non-violent abandonment of Capitalism. But in the meantime, until that happy day, they continued to accept the bourgeois world, and, with this, though of course without wanting to, the inevitable economic instability that is inherent in the capitalist economic system – the alternating periods of prosperity and depression.[32] So the Social Democratic leadership was in fact 'programmed' to disappoint its followers: it had no alternative perception of society capable of replacing that of the bourgeoisie, and in practice the achievements gained in prosperity were bound to be partly, if not altogether, lost in the next inevitable depression. Thus by not attacking the roots of economic instability but only its manifestations, Social Democracy was in the depression bound to lose face with the working class as indeed it did. By not challenging the socio-cultural hegemony of the bourgeoisie it prevented the workers from directing their rage towards the true causes of their miseries, the Capitalist system, and thus left this door open for its adversaries from both the left and the demagogic right to enter by.

Altogether then, the split in the labor movement deprived Germany of a constructive alternative perception of society capable of appealing to both the working class and the progressive sections of the middle class. In the absence of such an alternative the depression raised in the working class the old fear of destitution and starvation and revived in the middle class the scare of being reduced in social status. Worst of all, the absence of attainable solutions within the bourgeois system – the simple truth that in a capitalist

---

31.   At the election to the *Reichstag* in July, Hitler's National Socialists returned 230; the Socialists 133; the Center 97; and the Communists 89 candidates.

32.   Why the alternations between prosperity and depression are unavoidable in a Free Enterprise system has often been explained for example, by R.C.O. Matthews, *The Trade Cycle*, Ch. I–IV; and Y.S. Brenner, *Introduction to Economics – The Theory of Income and Employment*. Since Keynes one has learned to reduce some of the ill effects of the fluctuations but only by mitigating the Capitalism system by planning.

industrial society the unemployed worker really cannot find work and income by his own efforts – also produced the 'medieval' reaction of escapism, of the flight into the irrational that tends to take place when the gap between the desired and the attainable is too wide to be bridged. In an era on the one hand heavily burdened with nationalism, and on the other with expectations for social advancement, the two words *national socialism* had just the right ring to convey the illusion of an answer. The lack of a rational solution for the pressing problems of German society within the bourgeois conception, and the inability of the extreme left to advance its own alternative with any degree of credibility,[33] left the doors wide open for the entry of the irrational led by the 'saviour' who thinks and decides for all – the mythical leader and father figure, that will deliver the individual from the impossible task of finding his own solutions.

So the stage was set for the rise to power of a party led by a man supposedly gifted with some supernatural charismatic powers, demanding unquestioning obedience, whose party, unlike the Social Democrats, did put an alternative conception of society in front of the bewildered German people. Instead of the unattainable objectives, National Socialism offered to the Germans new objectives, not founded upon difficult to achieve hopes of economic welfare but upon the myth of 'Teutonic honor' and old rooted prejudices against intellectuals,Jews, pacifists, liberals, socialists and communists, and upon a value system with which the bourgeoisie was not unfamiliar and which the aristocracy had often preached but never practiced. The conception of society in which the individual was meaningless except as part of the nation, and a conception which was insensitive to individual deprivation – a conception concerned with 'shame', not poverty. Cows think of food, men aspire to higher things; Cows and Socialists are concerned with stomachs, Men and Germans seek spiritual fulfillment. Here was a movement capable of delivering the middle class from its fear of being reduced in status, the working class from confronting its reality, and the rich from the risk of social

---

33. The developments in Russian were not particularly suitable to make a Communist alternative very attractive except for the dogmatic devotees.

revolutions. And more practically it offered the middle class, hard hit by inflation and depression, to rid itself of its Jewish competitors in business and in the professions, the unemployed bread and uniforms in the ranks of the Storm Troops, and the industrialists, some of which actually despised Hitler and his pseudo-philosophies, but were still ready to support him, to fend off Communism.

What National Socialism had in common with the left was that it could not conquer without first destroying the bourgeoisie's social and cultural hegemony. But whereas the genuine socialist movements attacked the bourgeois values from a materialistic and rationalistic point of departure, giving prime place to welfare – the satisfaction of peoples' needs and wants, – the National Socialist onslaught came from quite a different direction. Without a genuine philosophy, and fed only by the people's disillusionment with their particular situation in a time of extreme crisism, the Nazi leadership managed to pass for ideology a formula that could mean anything to anybody. By claiming for this 'ideology' an affinity to the German irrationalist philosophical tradition of the nineteenth century – to Schopenhauer and Nietzsche, it not alone gave to it's hotchpotch of ideas a semblance of respectability in the eyes of its 'respectable' petit-bourgeois following, but also managed to catch precisely the somber pessimistic mood of the people – the mood of the Great Crash of 1929 and of the Depression that followed.

Nineteenth century irrationalism assumed that *life controls reason,* not reason life, a note which must undoubtedly have struck a cord with thousands of people who had planned their future in the 1920's and found their dreams and hopes all shattered in the 1930's. More than just that: Nineteenth century irrationalism maintained that a natural (herd) instinct, inherent in race or blood, guides nations to their destinies; that the pursuit of individual happiness runs contrary to man's true urges, namely to heroism which is satisfied by sacrifice and devotion to duty; and that 'instinct', not reason, is the great mover of society – instinct not reason because life is in any case too deep and complex to be grasped by the common human mind, though it may be grasped by intuition, – not by *divine* intuition, but by the instinct of the Genius. Neither the bourgeoisie's weighing of costs and benefits, nor the scientists' patient weighing of facts, nor even divine insight, but the instinctive *will* to act was taken as the true source of genius. Here indeed was a philosophy that could reduce the burden of responsibility for their fate that weighed so heavily upon the minds of the people shaken by the Great Depression; here was a philosophy that dangled the thought of action – 'the deed' before the eyes of the unemployed; here was a philosophy that promised status to all those who had none – to be a man and a member of a nation with a destiny; and here was a philosophy that rejected the most essential characteristics of the bourgeoisie that had failed the German people *utilitarian individualism and rationalism,* and offered instead, a sham revival of a romanticized feudal past, presented as an alternative to a life of endless hopeless struggle against forces that cannot be understood. Here also was the alternative to the proletarian way, which neither Brecht, Becher and Tucholsky, nor 'the dignity of labor' could deliver from the unattractive image that too much poverty for too long had imposed upon it in the West, and Stalin and the Russian heritage imposed upon it in the East. (Not to mention that before long all those who were willing to try this alternative were 'persuaded' by the Gestapo not to do so).

To be sure, Schopenhauer (1788–1860) had considered life the struggle of a blind force *will,* 'endlessly striving to no purpose'; and an 'incessant mutual confrontation of conflicting wills never to be satisfied and therefore condemning mankind to eternal suffering'. Schopenhauer despised the bourgeois efforts for improvements, and its scientists' vain hope to comprehend reality – to press the world into their 'Natural Laws' of human logic. But, Schopenhauer also felt compassion for this eternally suffering mankind, and recognized that in the face of this destiny-of-sorrow all men were equal, all men were the same. Nazism had use for Schopenhauer's pessimism, for it reflected the mood of the times, and for his irrational struggle of blind forces, but it had no use for his compassionate egalitarianism, for this could not serve its purpose. Nietzsche (1844–1900), however, who *really* despised the vaunted culture of the bourgeoisie *(Unzeitgemässe Betrachtungen)* and who put forward a counter-culture founded upon the predominance of a Superman (the Genius as opposed to common man), and who rejected almost all accepted moral values, including compassion, in his universe that moves in a succession of identical cycles *(Also sprach Zarathustra),* was better suited to serve the Nazi cause. His last great work on Will and Power *(Der Wille zur Macht)* remained unfinished, (perhaps symbolically for what the Nazi's later made of it because he had a mental breakdown from which he never recovered.) Nietzsche's 'natural aristocrat' – the man 'made' by the will to power, i.e. the superman, was, like Machiavelli's *Prince,* beyond *good* and *evil,* and destined to destroy decadent democracy. Again, the fact that Nietzsche was neither a nationalist, nor even showed excessive admiration for Germany, was conveniently ignored. The description of his 'new vast international aristocracy' would rather fit the Jews than the Germans, and though he was in favor of restricting further immigration of Jews into Germany his writings were not anti-semitic, – he admired the Old Testament while he disliked the New.[34] Bertrand Russell summarized Nietzsche's image of the 'noble' man as follows:[35] 'The 'noble' man will be capable of cruelty, and, on occasion, of what is vulgarly regarded as crime; he will recognize duties only to equals. He will protect artists and poets and all who happen to be masters of some skill, but he will do so as himself a member of a higher order than those who only know how to do something. From the example of warriors he will learn to associate death with the interests for which he is fighting; to sacrifice numbers, and take his cause sufficiently seriously not to spare men, to practice inexorable discipline; and to allow himself violence and cunning in war. He will recognize the part played by cruelty in aristocratic excellence: 'almost everything that we call higher culture is based upon the spiritualizing and intensifying of *cruelty.* The 'noble' man is essentially the incarnate will to power'. Here was a new value system indeed – a truly 'revolutionary' ideology, but what real prospects did it hold for the solution of the German people's problems? All it could do was to transform the people's fear into a lust for power, a lust for power which itself is but a manifestation of fear. For what else does it imply but the eternal need to subjugate

---

34.   Perhaps Women's Lib can find consolation in the fact that Nietzsche's contempt for Christianity even exceeded his contempt for women.

35.   *Vide History of Western Philosophy*, London, 1940, p. 794.

others in order to avoid being subjugated by them. The victors by this very fact show that they are superior to the vanquished and for this reason the vanquished ought to be ruled by the victors. What Hitler was thinking about was again something different. He was thinking, or rather talking, of a new *'Weltanschauung'* which was to transform the State from 'a product of economic necessity or, at best, of the political urge for power' into the means for the racial division of mankind into more and less valuable societies and individuals.[36] The belief in the equality of nations, according to Hitler, engenders the belief in the equality of persons which goes against the 'aristocratic' foundation of nature which grades every race and creature according to its worth.[37] At the top of the pyramid of individuals stands, of course, the Führer; at the top of the racial pyramid the Germans; together history will call upon them to solve the great problems of the world, – *'Wir alle ahnen, dass in ferner Zukunft Probleme an den Menschen herantreten können, zu deren Bewältigung nur eine höchste Rasse als Herrenvolk, gestützt auf die Mittel und Möglichkeiten eines ganzen Erdballs, berufen sein wird'.*[38]

---

36. Adolf Hitler, *Mein Kampf*, München, 1938 edition, pp. 409 & 420 'in die faule und feige bürgerliche Welt sowohl wie in den Siegeszug der marxistischen Eroberungswelle sollte eine neue Machterscheinung treten... nicht eine neue Wahlparole oktrohiert, sondern eine neue Weltanschauung von principieller Bedeutung...'

37. 'unsere heutige landläufige politische Weltauffassung beruht im allgemeinen auf der Vorstellung, das dem Staate zwar an sich schöpferische, kulturbildende Kraft zuzusprechen sei, dass er aber mit rassischen Voraussetzungen nichts zu tun habe, sondern eher noch ein Produkt wirtschaftlicher Notwendigkeiten, bestenfalls aber das natürliche Ergebnis politischen Machtdranges sei. Diese Grundanschauung führt in ihrer logisch-konsequenten Weiterbildung nicht nur zu einer Verkennung rassischer Urkräfte, sondern auch zu einer Minderbewertung der Person...' Hitler, *op.cit.*, pp. 419–20.

38. '... die völkische Weltanschauung... glaubt somit keineswegs an eine Gleichheit der Rassen, sondern erkennt mit ihrer Verschiedenheit auch ihren höheren oder minderen Wert und fühlt sich durch diese Erkenntnis verpflichtet, gemäss dem ewigen Wollen, das dieses Universum beherrscht, den Sieg des Besseren, Stärkeren zu fördern, die Unterordnung des Schlechteren und Schwächeren zu verlangen.' Hitler, *op.cit.*, p. 421.

('We all have a foreboding that in the distant future poeple could be confronted which only the highest race as a master race, supported by the resources and possibilities of an entire globe, can be called upon to solve.') The first such great problem that really faced the world, and required a global effort to be solved, was Hitler himself and his dazzled 'Herrenvolk'. Whether Hitler's *'Völkische Weltanschauung'* really contained realistic alternatives to bourgeois utilitarian materialism is doubtful, but it certainly *seemed* to promise something to most strata of German society. To the aristocrat it conveyed the illusion of the old respect for blue blood and rank; to the industrialist it promised discipline and devotion to duty – not his own but his workers'; to the man from the middle class, fearful of social decline, it seemed to restore the sense of order, and provide a coveted military uniform that would give him status – make him feel almost as good as his betters who never soil their hands by work but follow their calling to defend the 'higher values' of society, and to the worker the feeling of belonging – of sharing in the nation's great mission, and an end to the *shame* of being poor. (With their petit-bourgeois mentality the Nazi ideologists were never able to understand that it was hunger – the real thing, that worried the workers and not some bourgeois airs of 'shame'.) In fact, with the exception of the immature, who could be influenced in school and in the youth movement, and the adults who mentally never grew up, it all conveyed something quite different. The aristocracy on the whole despised Hitler's 'virtues', and never took his new *Weltanschauung* seriously; nor did the industrialists who supported him because they found the movement useful in their efforts to resist labor's wage claims and influence, and so did the middle class which saw in the new regime the last chance to protect itself against the relentless competition which threatened to reduce many to the ranks of labor; and the working class was never really impressed with the new-fangled *Weltanschauung* but it recognized that shortly after Hitler's rise to power he succeeded where his parliamentary predecessors had failed, namely to create employment. The bill for this success was presented only a decade later.[39]

So but for the aristocracy which did not require a *new* idealistic *Weltanschauung* in order to reject the values of the bourgeoisie, all those who embraced the new creed did so only because they wished to hold on to their bourgeois values – precisely because Hitler confirmed them in their world which seemed threatened from all sides.

'Die das Fleisch wegnehmen vom Tisch, Lehren Zufriedenheit.
Die, für die die Gabe bestimmt ist Verlangen Opfermut.

Die Sattgefressenen sprechen zu den Hungernden
Von den grossen Zeiten, die kommen werden.

Die das Reich in den Abgrund führen
Nennen das Regieren zu schwer für den einfachen Mann.'[40]

Even the desire for legitimacy – the appeal to the philosophical tradition of Schopenhauer and Nietzsche, shows the Nazi's lack of spiritual independence and shows how little these people who spoke of providing the world with a new order were able or indeed willing to free themselves from the bourgeois climate. What they wanted was recognition. They did not wish to destroy bourgeois values they just wanted a way to be acceptable to the bourgeoisie, and if this required to abandon some traditions, say liberalism and christian humanism, and stress others, say, romantic irrationalism, then they abandoned the former and stressed the latter and pretended that they had something new to offer. That farce, Hitler getting formally married like any other little bourgeois shortly before his and Eva

---

39. 'Die Arbeiter schreien nach Brot.
     Die Kaufleute schreien nach Märkten
     Die Hände, die im Schosse lagen, rühren sich wieder:
     Sie drehen Granaten.'

     Bertolt Brecht, *Deusche Marginalien*, 1938

40. Bertolt Brecht, *Hundert Gedichte 1918–1950*, Berlin, 1953, p. 181.

Braun's end, in the besieged Berlin bunker, is perhaps the ultimate metaphor of what by way of abolishing bourgeois values Nazism really was.

To be sure, the millionfold murder and the atrocities committed by the Nazi regime were real enough, but can hardly serve as evidence for new values. Nor was there anything new in racialism and religious persecution or in the idea of 'a chosen people' which Hitler claimed for the aryans. It was all part of the western cultural legacy, alone that it was proclaimed and practiced just at the time when really new values – progressive liberal humanism seemed to be in ascend. That banal little bureaucrat Eichmann who was responsible for the technical execution of the greatest crime in modern history, was, (and the record of his trial in Jerusalem leaves no doubt about it) more concerned with the fact that another bureaucrat of no higher rank than himself had been made his superior on the assignment than with the monstrosity of the assignment itself. This was the true reality of the 'New Order' and not the 'great aryan mission'. With all its efforts to 'dehumanize' the Jews and the other 'inferior' peoples, Nazi propaganda never dared tell the German people what was really happening to them. Even after years of massive indoctrination the Nazi's knew all too well that most people would abhor rather than approve of their loathsome deeds. What Nazi propaganda did achieve was a temporary disorientation of society. But this had happened in tyrannies before. Thucydides already described this state of affairs in ancient Sparta:[41] 'Reckless daring was held to be loyal courage; prudent delay was the excuse of a coward; moderation was the disguise of unmanly weakness; to know everything was to do nothing. Frantic energy was the true quality of a man... The lover of violence was always trusted... The tie of party was stronger than the tie of blood... The seal of good faith was not divine law, but fellowship in crime.' No wonder Nazi education had a predilection for this part of Greek history. That in spite of the perseverance of traditional reactions with most people sufficient psychopaths could be found to commit the crimes is understandable for in any country of the earth one finds a

---

41.   *Thucydides*, Bk. III.

number of misfits and mentally deranged people capable of any type of crime, only that in normal circumstances they are not given official tasks. They are committed to prisons or lunatic asylums because they have to pursue their urges privately without the excuse of acting for the state. The legitimization of this type of crime, though in fact the actual deeds were kept secret, tells more about the state of mind of those who authorized the crimes than about the values of the German people. It does not indicate, what Kuhn may call, a shift in the paradigm, but it does show the potential of people with great political power to create an atmosphere in which normal people, even without fear of retribution, (though in this specific case fear played an important role) will condone and ignore things that are alien to the values they have learned to respect since their childhood. Fortunately the Third Reich did not last long enough to produce a generation that was both in early youth and in adulthood subjected to its influences. The irrationalism, which to begin with was no more than the reaction to the loss of hope to achieve the material advancement and security people had expected from capitalism and from its magnificent scientific and technological successes, might having been given more time led society back to barren mysticism and the most inhuman Roman days.

Altogether therefore, the rise of National Socialism must be regarded as the result of the successful exploitation by a group of political opportunists of the failure of the bourgeoisie to satisfy the material expectations of the German people – the material expectations to the fulfillment of which the bourgeoisie had itself attributed moral and social status. Having no real solution for the problems the bourgeoisie was unable to solve, National Socialism offered instead a return to old values that by-passed and evaded the issue. In spite of the short spurt of nationalistic enthusiasm that accompanied the movement in its victorious years.[42] German society, at least in the West, reverted to utilitarian materialism (if ever it really abandoned it) as soon as it recovered from the Great

---

42. To fall back to irrationality is of course a common phenomenon in all countries in times of war, for war itself is irrational from the individual's point of view.

Depression and its immediate aftermath.[43] Perhaps no other country, including the United States of America, has in the post-war period been more dedicated to the pursuit of wealth, and its citizens more devoted to 'money-making' and more respectful towards their rich, than West Germany. Dr. Adenauer's *Wirtschaftswunder* is the unequivocal evidence for the perseverance of the bourgeoisies acquisitive spirit, and his efforts to do restitution to the Jews for the survival of old-fashion morality.

Earlier in this book the term progress was related to the unifying elements in man's perception of the universe, and *economic progress* to man's ability to overcome the reticence of nature and then to control it for his material advantage. From this point of view National Socialism was certainly reactionary. It stressed the dividing characteristics of men color, race and status; and it regarded nature uncontrollable by human rationality.[44] In comparison the bourgeoisie was progressive. It recognized class and race differences but did not give them the rigidity and metaphysical attributes Nazism did; and it maintained a firm trust in man's rational ability to understand nature and wield it to his purposes. The Socialists believed not only in the equality of all men but also in mankind's propensity to control nature and provide plenty for everyone. What separated the bourgeoisie in this respect from the socialists was that its conception of equality, unlike that of the socialists, was conditional was the belief in the *potential*, not the actual, equality of all. Provided people act in a certain way, i.e. are diligent, parsimonious and play altogether according to the rules, they have, irrespective of background, race and color, an equal chance to share in what society can offer. For the socialists equality was unconditional. They

---

43.   Materialism here means only the simple wish for *more* and *better* goods for private use.

44.   In fact Nazi Germany was trying hard to split the Atom and produce synthetic materials in spite of its disbelief in man's dominion over the forces of nature. This continued preoccupation with technology was the cause of Heidegger's disillusion with the Nazi party though he held on to his national socialism *per se*. He was disilutioned with the party in power not with national socialism as an ideology.

regarded the *ought* as the *is*, and claimed what was *visibly* not so,[45] that all men *are* equal. Moreover, they could not prove that the abolition of the ruling social system would lead to the satisfaction of the people's wants. They were unable to show convincingly that the system that would replace capitalism can really release new forces capable of providing economically relevant, organizationally and technologically more advanced methods of production, that have it in their power to satisfy the needs of all. Unable to produce such evidence the socialists left the impression that what they had to offer was but the *redistribution* of the available – a little more for the poor, much less for the rich. It appealed to the destitute and to the moralists among the intellectuals, but left unmoved the great mass of people with something, even those with only a little to lose.

In fact, this inability of socialists to present a convincing alternative to capitalism was not confined to Germany. As if to prove right Marx's assertion that the state of productive technology – the economic structure of society – determines its cultural, social and legal relationships, social-democracy and communism were really unable to give to the working class the insight – the class consciousness, that would have been required to effect the 'Leap' from capitalism to socialism. In his own words *'Eine Gesellschaftsordnung geht nie unter, bevor alle Produktivkräfte entwickelt sind für die sie weit genug ist, und neue höhere Produktionsverhältnisse treten nie an die Stelle, bevor die materiellen Existenzbedingungen derselben im Schoss der alten Gesellschaft ausgebrütet worden sind'.* (A social system never disappears before all the productive forces which suit it have developed, and new higher conditions of production never take their place, before their conditions have matured in the womb of the previous society). Marx regarded it the historical task of capitalism to *create* the 'cake' that socialism would equitably divide. But in fact capitalism, in spite of appearances, had *not* completed its 'historical task' in pre-World War II Germany or anywhere else. It was not before the late 1960's that science and technology reached the level of efficiency at which

---

45. That the children of the poor were less well educated than the children of most rich could hardly be ignored.

mankind is able to satisfy the material needs of all people in the economically most advanced countries, at a standard of consumption which even the better remunerated would consider adequate, without reducing for this purpose the standards of living of a great many people who have more.[46] For this reason the majority of the votes gathered by communist and social democratic parties in the period between the end of the nineteenth century and the Fascists' rise to power were above all votes of protest – votes that reflected labor's and part of the liberal bourgeoisie's exasperation with poverty and exploitation. They were votes of protest which could, and indeed did, switch to the established order including National Socialism.

What attracted a not inconsiderable part of the bourgeoisie to the left and forged the firm bond between the class-conscious working class and many intellectuals was the ideal of social and economic egalitarianism and the quest for equity which has deep roots in Jewish-Christian culture. The whole basis of modern liberal civilization is based upon these tenets. The love for one's fellow human beings (elevated to compassion with some and debased to utilitarian charity – a ticket to heaven 'in the life to come', with others). The example of Christ, sufferings for the sake of all, as well as the Old Testament's Jewish claim to justice, were part of a heritage that even a utilitarian profit-seeking bourgeoisie could not, and mostly would not, easily repudiate. It was this legacy, made strong by generations of educators, that upheld the values of humanism against the rising floods of vulgar utilitarian materialism and even Nazi barbarism. Time after time Hitler derided compassion as cheap sentimentality, and time after time Nazi propaganda stressed that the 'noble' is, and must be 'capable of cruelty,... and of what is vulgarly regarded as crime...', but to no avail. The great majority of the people continued to believe in what they did before, though few were strong enough to follow their convictions under the threats of the New Order in Germany. But prior to the rise of Nazism, it was this Jewish-Christian and humanist tradition that was the bond between the socialist proletariat, the German intellectuals and the

---

46.   We shall return to the tremendous rise in productivity after World War II, in more detail in Chapter 10.

liberal middle class. On the Left it created the formula of 'the dignity of labor' (Arbeit Adelt), and the vast *Proletarian Literature* (which workers rarely read), produced by men and women like Stefan Heym, Heinrich Mann, Bertolt Brecht, Fritz von Unruh, Anna Seghers, Johannes R. Becher and all the many other excellent progressive Germans. In the moderate center it produced authors like Thomas Mann, Hermann Hesse, Feuchtwanger, Zweig, Werfel, Holthusen and later Borchert, the work of men who were often disgusted with the self-satisfied bourgeois mentality but who were not prepared to abandon the rest of the liberal bourgeoisie's heritage.

French Trade Unionism was restricted by law until 1884. From 1884 to 1895 was its development held back by an intricate relationship with no less than five rival socialist parties. From 1895 to 1902 it was greatly influenced by Syndicalism. The Confederation Generale du Travail which was organized at the beginning of this period reflected the French workers' frustration with both the political and the trade union activities of the labor movement.[47] The amalgamation of the Confederation General du Travail with the Federation des Bourses du Travail in 1902 led to the complete separation of trade union engagement from political engagement. The amalgamated movement restricted itself to direct union work, but after a decade of fairly successful progress the approaching war put an end to the era of political withdrawal. Not unlike labor in Germany, French labor too supported its country's war efforts and some union leaders even found their way into the Cabinet. The failure of the General Strike in 1920 and the court order to dissolve the C.G.T. in 1921 finally led the union to abandon its syndicalist tendencies which had in any case been waning since the war. Again, not unlike in the rest of the industrialized countries, the time was not ripe for labor to take over the economic enterprises and replace the profit-minded managements by workers' co-operatives intent upon the satisfaction of men's real needs the old dream of the syndicalists. In

---

47. Political labor activity because it had little to show by way of transforming the system of 'production for profit' into 'production for use'; and the trade unions disappointed the revolutionary section of the C.G.T. by the very fact that their demands for collective bargaining 'unmasked' them as people inclined to 'trade' with capitalism.

the period that followed, the C.G.T. became a union like most others, resorting to political militancy and to industrial action as the occasion demanded. Next to the C.G.T. there were also other unions pressing for improvements in the conditions of labor, the Confederation Generale du Travail Unitaire, the Communist trade union and a number of Catholic unions. However, the lack of most French unions' political engagement does not imply an absence of political engagement of the working-class. The contrary is true. There was perhaps no other country that had an equally militant-socialist working-class.[48] French working-class consciousness, unlike that of other countries, was not only the product of economic grievances but had deep roots in the political history of nineteenth century France. Particularly in the events of 1871. Radical Paris that had fruitlessly endured the long siege felt plainly betrayed by the National Assembly's peace terms with the Germans, and by the very composition of the Assembly which was obviously unfriendly to the Republicans. The bloody events of May 1871 which terminated the Paris Commune uprising left a legacy which the French working class was never able to forget.[49] It was thanks to this legacy that French labor was spared some of the difficulties that caused a great deal of confusion in other countries between the labor unions and parties especially when long-term policies could not be harmonized with immediate needs, and when the general policies of the workers' parties could not be harmonized with the specific union needs in particular enterprises or parts of industry. This does not imply that as a rule the unions were not massively supported by the labor parties or that the union members' votes did not on the whole go to the left, but what it does imply is that both the unions and the parties maintained a great measure of freedom of action in their separate spheres. The parties could concentrate on the political promotion of their aims and the unions on industrial action. The earlier start and then slower progress of industrialization in France,

---

48. It is difficult to say in how far the working-class in the Soviet Union was class-conscious in this time in the western sense of the term.

49. *Vide* also Y.S. Brenner, *A Short History of Economic Progress*, Ch. 10.

in comparison with Germany, also influenced the character of the French labor movement somewhat differently. It stimulated the development of a co-operative business sector which created in addition to the wage earning class a class of partly self-employed working-men. This division in the working-class, in spite of periods of co-operation, – (for example, the Communist support for the Popular Front government of Radical Socialists and Socialists in 1936,)[50] contributed to the growing rift between French Communists and Socialists. The latter's moderation towards the bourgeois-state, and the formers' identification with the Soviet Union's foreign policy objectives, including the Russian-German non-aggression pact in the summer of 1939,[51] lost for the one its revolutionary elan and for the

---

50. The First Popular Front government, under the Socialist Party leader Leon Blum, established the 40–hour working week in France; nationalized the Bank of France, and the munitions industry; suppressed the fascist organizations; and introduced holidays with pay etc. All these measures created an atmosphere that led the French working-class to believe that they stand 'at the Dawn of a new era'. The inflation that followed somehow reduced the initial enthusiasm. In March 1937 Blum is forced to halt his reform plans. In June he is forced to yield the leadership of the government to the Radical Socialist Camille Chautemps. In January 1938 the Socialists desert the Radical cabinet. In March the Chautemps cabinet falls. In October the Radical Socialist government of Daladier finally breaks with the socialists and communists. Soon the communists voted against it and the socialists abstained. The Popular Front is finished and the Radicals move to the right.

51. Here was one of the problems which complicated matters between socialists and liberals on the one side. and communists on the other, since the rise of Fascism in the 1930's. In essence the problem was to decide whether or not the Soviet Union is the most important source of labor's power to resist capitalism. Those who answered this question in the affirmative, i.e. who believed that the Soviet Union is the last 'bulwark' of the working men against exploitation, found it necessary to desist from criticizing the Russian communists come what may. They defended deeds they never could really approve of because in the face of the fascist threat any criticism would weaken the Soviets. By implication whoever did criticize the Soviet Union became in their eyes 'objectively' an enemy of the working class. Those who answered the question negatively were alienated from the communists because they could not help identifying communists everywhere with that which went by the name of socialism in the USSR and because of the communists'

other its ability to attract many of the socialists who did not approve of their movement's timidity.[52] Indeed it may well be that while the socialist *revolution* in Russia scared the western bourgeoisie into making economic, social and political concessions to their working class, the specifically Russian character of the *First Socialist Revolution* removed it so far from the western cultural heritage and from the western value system that it scared no less a great section of the western working class not to mention the progressive middle class.[53] Soviet centralism rested on Lenin's demand for 'the blind subordination, in the smallest detail, of all party organs, to the party center, which alone thinks, guides and decides for all,' and on 'the rigorous separation of the organized nucleus of revolutionaries from its social-revolutionary surroundings', – i.e. upon the traditional organization of pre-revolutionary Russia.[54] In the west centralism rested on another tradition, namely upon 'the existence of a large contingent of workers educated in the political struggle' and on 'the possibility for the workers to develop their own political activity through direct influence on public life, in a party press, and public congresses etc.'[55] 'It is a mistake' said Rosa Luxemburg representing as it were the western tradition against Lenin's 'Russian' outlook, 'to believe that it is possible to substitute 'provisionally' the absolute power of a Central Committee (acting somehow by 'tacit delegation') for the yet unrealizable rule of the majority of conscious workers in the party, and in this way replace the open control of the working masses over the party organs with the reverse control by the Central

---

estrangement from the western liberal socialist tradition.

52.   The relationships after Wold War II, will be discussed in another chapter.

53.   Andre Gide may serve as a good example for the disillusioned left in France, though of course Luis Aragon and Paul Eluard remained loyal to the First Socialist Revolution.

54.   Rosa Luxemburg, *Leninism or Marxism*, Neue Zeit, 1904, p. 88 (All quotations here from D. Wolfe's re-edition).

55.   *Ibid.*, p. 89.

Committee over the revolutionary proletariat'.[56] 'The only way to a rebirth is the school of public life, the most unlimited, the broadest democracy and public opinion...' For when all this is eliminated what really remains? – A crippled political life. For 'without general elections, without unrestricted freedom of press and assembly, without a free struggle of opinion, life dies out in every public institution, becomes a mere semblance of life, in which only the bureaucracy remains as the active element. Public life gradually falls asleep, a few dozen party leaders of inexhaustible energy and boundless experience direct and rule. Among them, in reality only a dozen outstanding heads do the leading and an elite of the working class is invited from time to time to meetings where they are to applaud the speeches of the leaders, and to approve resolutions unanimously – at bottom then, a clique affair – a dictatorship, to be sure, not the dictatorship of the proletariat, however, but only the dictatorship of a handful of politicians, that is a dictatorship in the bourgeois sense...'[57]

The French Communist Party was perhaps the one which more than all others in western Europe adhered by the Leninist principles. In spite of his many gifts Thorez with all the credit he deserves for his party's struggle against the Nazi's, (after the invasion of the Soviet Union) never became much more than a bureaucrat interpreting Soviet policy to make it palatable to his following. How then can the survival of the French Communist party as a powerful political factor be explained? Partly the explanation can be found in the earlier mentioned historical events that made the French left much more suspicious of the bourgeoisie and of its institutions than the working class in other western countries; but more important was the 'family' spirit that surrounded the French Communist party. One of the most felt features of industrialization everywhere was the breakdown of the old sense of security that the rural family, the guild, and even the Feudal relationship provided. Until late in the

---

56. Rosa Luxemburg, *ibid.*, p. 91.

57. Rosa Luxemburg, *The Russian Revolution*, The Problem of Dictatorship, pp. 71–2.

nineteenth century capitalism offered little to make good this loss. The French Communist party did. Organized unlike most other communist parties by working places (not regions) it not only stimulated a high degree of solidarity among workers but it also provided a whole range of social services from Kindergartens to medical care which held its members together. For this reason to disagree with the party meant more than just changing one's views. To dissent meant to risk expulsion from 'the great family' and miss both the solidarity at work and the material services it offered. But even without the risk of expulsion the absence of positive stimuli to develop members concern with national and international politics beyond what the party leadership wanted them to be concerned with – the absence of critical political discussion, reduced class consciousness to little more than enmity towards the bourgeoisie and opposition to exploitation. In fact it led to a *'depolitization'* of the party cadres substituting party discipline for wider consciousness and party loyalty for the development of thought. Tacitly policy decisions were left the sole province of the party leadership in spite of its Moscow inspired somersaults. Not before February 1976 did the French Communist Party drop the formula of the 'dictatorship of the proletariat' from its constitution and not before 1977 the concept of the 'democratic centralism' – the two pillars upon which the undemocratic, Russian, tradition of the French communist party rested.[58]

As for the non-communist left – the socialists and the radical socialists, they were more like electoral associations than disciplined

---

58.   Marx himself was not quite sure about the dictatorship of the proletariat. In a letter to Joseph Weydemeyer he wrote (March 5th, 1852) that the class struggle must inevitably lead to it. However, in later years he also regarded a parliamentary road to socialism possible.

For Lenin's 'democratic centralism' there is no support in Marx's writings. Yet, it was with the help of this principle that the French Communist Party managed to purge itself of its original founders of whom none was left in the party by 1932.

The *Great Soviet Encyclopedia* in the 1957 edition claims that 'The principle of the dictatorship of the proletariat is the most important of the teachings of Marx'. (This would probably have been great news for Karl had he lived long enough to read it).

party organizations. The socialists remained a class party as it had been before 1921 when the communists broke away from it and its aims continued to be the socialization of the means of production and exchange and the abolition of the bourgeois state by democratic means. Not unlike labor's parliamentary representation in Britain, French socialist representatives in the Chamber were much more ready to compromise with the bourgeoisie than their party organs not to mention even their party rank and file. The Radical Socialists were non-Marxist and collected their support from a wide social basis. It was in fact a party of the more or less progressive or liberal middle class − not of the proletariat.

The development of labor's claim to a greater share of the fruits of production in the United States of America was rather along *neoclassical* than political socialist lines. American unions were on the whole not only non-political since the middle of the nineteenth century but often among the foremost assailants of socialist ideas. Perhaps because capitalism had become best established in the United States it was there that the union movement first established itself in the form of a typically capitalist business enterprise: they were not committed to the abolition of capitalism but on the contrary, they were, and continue to be, ideologically tied to it for they accepted the principle of the *maximization of profits,* i.e. the maximization of their members' immediate economic advantages, as the prime cause of their existence. That this cause may sometimes best be served by the use of political pressure, and that such pressure is exercised from time to time, does not alter the fundamental fact that they are 'a-political' in the sense 'political commitment' is understood by west European trade unionists. Their members do not expect their leaders to solve long-term national or world-wide social and political problems. They expect them to make the best possible deal with the employers regarding wages and working conditions here and now. That in the long-run these *ad hoc* 'here and now' achievements may add up to a general transformation of the capitalist system is not taken into account. In fact they may not even be conscious of the effect their consistent economic and political pressure has on the state. That the state is more and more incumbent with responsibilities which lie well outside its province in a strictly capitalist system is rarely related to them. The directional interference in the country's economy, and the provision of social services by the state, on the scale introduced by F.D. Roosevelt and the growth of the state owned and state controlled industrial sector since World War II, is also seldom attributed to the unions, but in fact they indirectly played an important role in all this. In the absence of a strong socialist movement American labor learned its lessons in workers' solidarity in the unions.

The workers on the S.P. Line to strike sent out a call
But Casey Jones, the engineer, he wouldn't strike at all:
His boilers they were leaking and his drivers on the bum,
And his engine and its bearings they were all out of plumb.

Casey Jones kept his junk pile running
Casey Jones was working double time.
Casey Jones got a wooden medal
For being good and faithful on the S.P. Line.

The workers said to Casey, 'Won't you help us win this strike?'
But Casey said, 'Let me alone; you'd better take a hike.'
Then someone put a bunch of rail-road ties across the track,
And Casey hit the river with an awful crack.

Casey Jones hit the river bottom;
Casey Jones broke his blooming spine.
Casey Jones was an Angelino
He took a trip to heaven on the S.P. Line.

When Casey Jones got up to heaven to the Pearly Gate,
He said: 'I'm Casey Jones, the guy that pulled the S.P. freight.'
'You're just the man', said Peter, 'Our musicians are on strike,
You can get a job a-scabbing any time you like.'

Casey Jones got a job in heaven,
Casey Jones was going mighty fine,
Casey Jones went scabbing on the angels
Just like he did to workers on the S.P. Line.

The angels got together and they said it wasn't fair
For Casey Jones to go around a-scabbing everywhere.
The Angels Union No. 23, they sure were there,
And they promptly fired Casey down the Golden Stair.

Casey Jones went to hell a-flying
Casey Jones, the devil said, Oh fine.
Casey Jones, get busy shovelling sulphur,
That's what you get for scabbing on the S.P. Line.[59]

The fact that the unions did not oppose the bourgeoisie on ideological grounds and actually embraced the bourgeois values did of course not stop their opponents from calling them 'red' whenever this served their purpose.

I am a union woman, Just as brave as I can be,
I do not like the bosses And the bosses don't like me...

I was raised in old Kentucky, In Kentucky borned and bred,
And when I joined the union, They called me Rooshian Red...

This is the worst time on earth That I have ever saw,
To get killed out by gun-thugs, And framed up by the law.

When my husband asked the boss for a job, This is the words he said
'Bill Jackson, I can't work you, sir, Your wife's a Rooshian Red.'

If you want to join a union, As strong as one can be,
Join the dear old CIO, And come along with me...[60]

It need hardly be said that the American Federation of Labor Congress of Industrial Organizations (AFL-CIO), with leaders like Samuel Gompers who rejected socialist or radical programmes and maintained that the just aims of labor were simply shorter hours, more wages, and greater freedom, was not communist. But the very thought that accusing union members of being communist discredited them in the eyes of the masses shows how well entrenched capitalist principles really were in American public opinion.

And yet, in spite of their deliberate avoidance of anti-capitalist ideological commitment, the unions did undermine the capitalist system in two ways. In the first place they nibbled at the basis of

---

59.   Words by Joe Hill.

60.   Words by Aunt Molly Jackson.

capitalism by enforcing the principle of collective bargaining and raising labor's working conditions, i.e. they shook the universal applicability of the price or market mechanism. Secondly, using their mass membership during election times they wrought from the state a great number of social and economic concessions – for example the New Deal which in effect transformed the old style capitalism into something like a regulated capitalism which acknowledged the state's responsibility to provide work and a degree of social security for the citizens.

> My name is William Edwards, I live down Cove Creek way.
> I'm working on the project They call the T.V.A.
>
> The Government begun it When I was but a child,
> But now they are in earnest And Tennessee's gone wild.
>
> Just see them boys a-comin' Their tool kits on their arm;
> They come from Clinch and Holston And many a valley farm...
>
> All up and down the valley They heard the glad alarm,
> 'The Government means business'. It's working like a charm.
>
> Oh, see them boys a-comin' Their Government they trust;
> Just hear their hammers ringing They'll build that dam or bust.
>
> I meant to marry Sally But work I could not find;
> The T.V.A. was started And surely eased my mind.
>
> I'm writing her a letter These words I'll surely say:
> 'The Government has surely saved us, Just name our wedding day.'[61]

Naturally, the new style capitalism, and the growing share of the state in the ownership and control of the means of production, does not mean that the United States have abandoned the Free Enterprise system. American capitalism continues as before to hold on to the most essential element in bourgeois reality, namely the principle of profit. Production in the United States continues to be dominated by the urge to maximize profits – not to satisfy needs, but even

---

61.   Words by Jilson Setters. T.V.A. stands for (Tennessee Valley Authority).

American capitalism has lost a little of the worst ill attending this urge – the cold fear of starvation of those who have nothing else to sell but their labor.

There were two powerful factors that accounted for the difference between American and European labor opposition to exploitation and poverty. One was the availability of free land in America until late in the nineteenth century, and the other the successive waves of immigrants from the 'old country'. The first factor made for a long time the struggle for higher minimum wages less pressing, and the second made the organization of labor and the exertion of pressure by threat of strikes very difficult. The availability of land meant that wages could seldom for long fall much below what a man could earn by working his own land, and the ethnic and national antagonisms and the language difficulties meant that organized labor-opposition was greatly impeded by simple communication and educational problems. Each new wave of immigrants gave employers the opportunity to replace the workers who were getting organized by new workers who had not yet adjusted to their new surroundings. As because of the availability of land American minimum wages were in any case well above those earned by the new immigrants in their countries of origin, and as the immigrants did not really feel the need to organize in their early days of settling down to the American life style, American unionism never really got off the ground before World War I. Between the wars its membership and influence declined but political pressures for progressive labor legislation, and in times of prosperity *the need* for labor, filled the gap left open by the unions.[62] The Gross National Product of the United States increased approximately fourfold between the beginning and the middle of the 20th century; the average weekly hours of work declined from about 58 to 39, and disposable personal income increased more than fourfold.[63] So in fact the technological progress

---

62. For a more detailed analysis see Y.S. Brenner, *A Short History of Economic Progress*, and Harold Underwood Faulkner, *American Economic History*, 1963, Part V.

63. *Vide* U.S. Department of Commerce, *National Income Statistics. U.S. Income and Output. Survey of Current Business.*

that accompanied the competitive mechanism of capitalistic advancement in America benefited American labor, in spite of the absence of a socialist opposition and a powerful union movement, no less than it did the working-class in western Europe. The roads by which American and European labor reached a higher living standard and greater social security differed but the results were similar. John Maynard Keynes, in spite of his outspoken anti-socialism, and President F.D. Roosevelt, who was certainly no 'communist', were greatly responsible for giving to these achievements a degree of permanence by modifying capitalism and eliminating from it some of its worst abuses. Classical capitalism, which by this time shed much of the old values it had inherited from the distant past, looked upon labor as a factor of production. One bought labor when it was required and dismissed it when no longer needed. The consequences of unemployment of labor were regarded as sad but unavoidable. If the state wanted to do something about it, the investors held the key to the solution and it was through them that the state had to work. It had to make investment attractive for them. It had in addition to the low wages, the normal concomitant of mass unemployment, supply investors with low interest loans. Low wages and cheap capital were then expected to make investment profitable again even when because of too little demand prices were beneath their normal level. Now, what Keynes discovered did not really disturb the fundamental tenet of capitalism – the profit motive. It merely suggested that profits may just as well be made from high revenues as from low costs. What he offered as a solution to the depression was to put money in the pockets of the workers to stimulate the economy from the demand side. More purchasing power would revive profits, profits would stimulate production, and more production would raise the demand for labor which in turn would raise demand even further. And yet Keynes' ideas were really revolutionary. They not only upset conventional economics but deprived the bourgeoisie of two of its most cherished holy cows: The low-wage-rates and low-interest-rates ideology, and the 'Victorian morality' with regard to what is right and proper.

Keynes proposed to put money into workers' pockets by allowing governments to initiate public works, i.e. to provide employment with tax-payers' money from the treasury during a time of depression when state revenues were low. He expected the exchequer to pay out money for this purpose not only from current surpluses and reserves but also on account of future incomes. In other words he wanted to increase spending with 'borrowed' money, a sheer aberration of all that was held prime virtue in bourgeois society such as thrift, good husbandry, thou shall not spend more than you can afford, and the unrestricted freedom of the market mechanism, going by the board. In fact he converted bourgeois economics from 'the study of wealth' (Adam Smith) and 'the practical science of production and distribution of wealth' (John Stuart Mill), in which man was compelled to adapt to the economy rather than that the economy was created in the service of man, in spite of the fact that latter better agrees with individualism. Keynes converted economic theory, from a perception in which it almost seemed as if mankind was created to serve the economy rather than the economy to serve man, into a discipline in which man took up the central position. No wonder then, that Keynes's ideas appeared to many of his contemporaries both sinful and foolish. Sinful, for they undermined the very foundations of morality, for they could be construed as implicitly approving of the spendthrifts and debunking the reasonable, parsimonious, and provident. Foolish, for instead of reducing the forces which distort the 'natural order of things', i.e. the price mechanism, he proposed increasing them. Rather than recommending the elimination of labor's resistance to wage reductions, he wished to impose upon governments the duty of sustaining full employment and maintaining a minimum level of incomes sufficiently high to keep consumers' expenditure on a steadily increasing standard. Rather than restricting the role of the State in economic affairs to that of the guardian of the price mechanism against distortions, (such as the 'monopolization' of the factor of production labor by the unions) he proposed the extension of continuous and massive government interference in the economy; and he proposed all this not for compassionate reasons, providing incomes for the poor, but for what he claimed to be sound economic reasons, also in accord with the needs of the rich! Contrary to established economic theory he insisted that investment decisions do not depend on costs alone, but upon investors' expectations of profit. Unlike Ricardo, a century earlier, he did not believe that entrepreneurs will invest all they can at all times, but that they invest when they feel the time is ripe, when they can reasonably expect good profits. However, as expectations need concrete foundations, some evidence of a rising trend in demand must be present to convince investors. This evidence Keynes wanted the governments to provide by initiating state-employment.

This, to be sure, was only one of several aspects of the 'Keynesian Revolution', but in a way it may have been the most important for it restored a moral content to the study of economics. It destroyed the divisive bourgeois conception of society – its division of mankind into the 'two nations' of the rich who are best fitted by nature to enjoy wealth and are encouraged to perform great deeds by the love of gain, and the poor who are incapable of enjoying the better things in life and may only be stirred to activity by the fear of starvation.[64] By acknowledging the dependence of profit-seeking-investors upon consumers' demand Keynes in effect deprived the bourgeoisie of its self-appointed patronizing role in society as the benefactor of the people for providing them with work and income. In other words Keynes restored economics to the social sciences turning it from a field of study concerned with developing techniques for the achievement of optimum allocation of resources, from the point of view of those who control them, into a science concerned with the welfare of the people, from the point of view of all people. Thus the Keynesian approach presented an intermediate position between the traditional acceptance of the hegemony of the bourgeoisie on the one hand, and the Marxian total rejection of the system inducing efforts towards its replacement by the socialist system on the other. It presented an alternative sufficiently wide and realistic to permit both the survival of the most important part of the capitalist economic system and the upholding of the dignity of labor. Essentially it reflected the precise position of the technological level of attainment of the time and the material production relations that suit it i.e. it conformed to the level of development to which

---

64.   For this view see Y.S. Brenner, *Theories of Economic Development and Growth*, 'Classical and Neoclassical Theories'. Also Pigou, *Economics of Welfare*, Note 32, p. 17.

capitalism had exhausted its economic potentialities. Keynes's views therefore mirrored the economic and political reality of his time, a reality which many other economists and politicians had not yet recognized.

In practice the 'Keynesian approach' gained ground in the United States long before it was even partially adopted in Keynes' home country in the United Kingdom. Moreover, it was adopted in the United States on what in British eyes must have looked like very emotional grounds. In America, where society was more pragmatic and less weighted down by traditional class myths than in Europe, the political institutions held considerable possibilities for a piecemeal erosion of the oligarchical approach to the solution of socio-economic problems. Unlike in England there was no need in the United States to convince the government of the theoretical folly of the traditional solutions, (a hopeless task as anyone who has had dealings with bureaucracies will know) because it was for all to see that the old approach simply did not work and was no longer maintainable in the face of an irate electorate. With the elections approaching (1936) both major parties contesting for the presidency of the United States were pressed to provide programmes which could at least give the impression of answering some of the most immediate problems of the majority of the voters. Even if only for the purpose of vote-catching it was therefore necessary in the 1930's to approach the problem of unemployment not from a detached theoretical long-term point of view but practically, committed, and with the prospect of immediate solutions. Obviously, it would hardly have been good electioneering to say to the majority of the American people, so many of whom were at that time experiencing all the evils attending unemployment, wage-cuts, and falling living standards, that they should vote for a President who intends to let wages fall even further and unemployment increase until sometime, who knows when, the economic regulative price mechanism would restore prosperity. In other words, neither socialist agitation nor the organized union force, nor even theoretically convincing arguments, played a direct role in the American 'leap' from 'old style' to 'regulated capitalism.' It was the political system of capitalism's own creation. The democratic political system in the United States shifted the center of gravity in the search for economic solutions to the nation's problems from the study of micro-economic theorems (optimal resource allocation of firms) to macro-economics (the human sphere of employment).

The American leader who became identified with the new trend, and who became President in 1933, was Franklin Delano Roosevelt. However, even before this time, President Hoover already attempted new ways for reviving the economy which were unconventional. He tried tax reductions and state support for agriculture but to little avail. He tried to appeal to private enterprise to keep up production with equally little success. Finally he also appealed to State Governments and municipalities to advance some construction programmes for the explicit purpose of reducing unemployment. All these efforts show the gradual change of mind which anticipated the approaching new view of the role of government, and the novel responsibilities it was increasingly charged with. It foreshadowed the coming of a capitalism of *consensus* in place of *confrontation*, a system in which workers' co-operation is bought by full employment and a rising share in the fruits of production rather than exacted by fear of unemployment and destitution.

And yet, it would be an exaggeration to say that European style opposition to the capitalist system was altogether absent in America but it never really gained and maintained the kind of influence it enjoyed in western Europe.

I hate the capitalist system, I'll tell you the reason why,
They caused me so much suffering And my dearest friend to die...

Oh, what can you do about it, To these men of power and might?
I tell you Mr. Capitalist, I'm going to fight, fight, fight.[65]

We'll chase the capitalists around the stump
And give them a kick at every jump.
We'll make them pay for the blood they've shed,
And for the way our babies have been fed.
The workers are a-movin', movin', movin',
The workers are a-movin', and I'm so glad.
The workers are a-movin', movin', movin',

---

65.   Words by Sara Ogan Gunning.

The workers are a-movin' and I'm so glad.[66]

Perhaps the fact that the socialists polled close to a million votes in the 1932 elections and that their influence went far beyond their numbers also helped to accelerate the change of heart in the American establishment. In 1933 the *Economy Act;* the *National Industrial Recovery Act;* and the *Agricultural Adjustment Act,* were passed. The era of the *New Deal* had begun. In the years that followed there were many more social relief acts, and many court decisions declaring them unconstitutional, but step by step resistance to the new approach faded. All this time the unions did also continue to press for improvements. Noteworthy were above all the widespread troubles in 1937 that resulted from the employers efforts to prevent the C.I.O. to organize the workers in the automobile and steel industries on the basis of industrial unionism. The sit-down strike that spread from General Motors to the Chrysler Corporation and from there to the Republic Steel Corporation, Youngstown Sheet Steel and Tube Company, Inland Steel, Bethlehem Steel and others, even caused some bloodshed. It divided public opinion but led in the end to the unionization of the industries that had until that time stubbornly resisted their workers' demands for the right to collective bargaining.

The position of the intellectuals in the United States, in the early part of the century, was on the one hand dominated by the search for 'eternal values' – the problem of 'Time and Eternity', and on the other, by the growing self-consciousness of the American 'here and now'. The precursors of the second of these tendencies in literature were men like Walt Whitman, Mark Twain, Henry James, O. Henry, and Jack London. With Theodor Dreiser and Upton Sinclair the description of the 'here and now' becomes in effect social critique. Dreiser's *Sister Currie,* the story of a working girl who forms two liaisons as steps to success, was still withheld from circulation (1900) on the grounds of 'immorality'; but Upton Sinclair's *The Jungle,* which he wrote under the impression of an investigation of the Chicago stockyards (1901), became a best-seller and even led to

---

66.   *Ibid.*

some reforms in the Chicago meat-packing industry. Later, in the period between the two world wars, his stories took on a strong Marxist undertone. The foremost critical writers, who also repudiated the Time and Eternity tradition but did not join the revolutionary stream, were Carl Sandburg, Ezra Pound, who later became a Fascist, and of course, the Nobel prize winners Sinclair Lewis and Ernest Hemingway. Sinclair Lewis depicted the emptiness and conformism of middle-class life in the United States and its shallow meaningless idealism. Ernest Hemingway portrayed the pleasure-seeking disillusioned generation of post World War I. Americans, and reflected the violence of American life. Perhaps significantly, his best known work *For Whom the Bell Tolls* (1940), which is also his first presenting a positive note, was set in Spain among the people fighting Fascism.

The 1920s were altogether years in which American literature was gaining in self-consciousness. In spite of what now seems to have been a decade of economic prosperity it was really one of disillusionment, at least for intellectuals. The works of O'Neill (another Nobel prize winner) were again in the Time and Eternity tradition – the theme of man in relation to God. So were the works of Thomas Wolfe – man's spiritual pilgrimage through life in search of a Father; and William Faulkner (also a Nobel prize winner), who analyzed the perversions of American bourgeois society, and of many others.

The real depression that began in 1929 produced in the 1930s a new wave of socially critical writers such as John Dos Passos, John Steinbeck, and James T. Farrell. Next to them the crisis also brought forth a vast body of self-styled *proletarian literature.* 'The economic crisis shattered the common illusion that American society was classless. Literary frustration, unemployment, poverty, hunger threw many writers into the camp of the proletariat. Once they were compelled to face the basic facts of class society, of necessity such writers faced the relation of poetry to class. It was impossible to share the experiences of the unemployed worker and continue to create the poetry of the secure bourgeois. However, like theory, poetry tends to lag behind reality. Suffering opens the poet's eyes but tradition ties his tongue. As a member of society he was forced to face the meaning of the class struggle; as a member of the ancient and honorable caste of scribes, he continued to be burdened with antiquated shibboleths about art and society, art and propaganda, art and class.'[67] Wrote Joseph Freeman (1935), himself a member of the Proletarian writers' circle,: 'In the past five years many writers have fought their way to a clearer conception of their role in the contemporary world. At first they split themselves into apparently irreconcilable halves. As *men,* they supported the working class in its struggle for a classless society; as *poets,* they retained the umbilical cord which bound them to bourgeois culture. The deepening of the economic crisis compelled many writers to abandon this dichotomy. The dualism paralyzed them both as men and as poets. Either the man had to follow the poet back to the camp of the bourgeoisie, or the poet had to follow the man forward into the camp of the proletariat.'[68] Those who chose the second camp were many at the time and included some of the best known authors who were after the war persecuted by both the Stalinists and the 'unamerican activities committee' of McCarthy (of which Nixon was also a member). Among the better known of the 'proletarian writers' in the 1930s were Erskine Caldwell, Albert Maltz and Richard Wright.

In conclusion, in the second half of the nineteenth century the bourgeoisie attained the position of power it had coveted, by the middle of the twentieth it had to acknowledge its inability to hold on to it. In the Charter of the United Nations the members stated among their objectives *'the promotion of a) higher standards of living, full employment, and conditions of economic and social progress and development; b) solution of international economic, social, health, and related problems, and international cultural and educational co-operation; and c) universal respect for, and observance of, human rights and fundamental freedoms for all*

---

67. Joseph Freeman, *Introduction to an anthology of proletarian literature in the United States,* New York, 1935.

68. *Proletarian Literature in the U.S.,* Granville Hicks etc. eds., N.Y., 1935, pp. 19–20.

without distinction as to race, sex, language, or religion.[69] These aims which had been agreed upon by Roosevelt and Churchill several years before the United Nations Charter received its formal recognition, in fact in one of the darkest periods of the war[70] reflected the changes that had been modifying the capitalist conception of the world for some time. In the place of 'the pursuit of happiness' or 'wealth', had come 'freedom from fear, and freedom from want'; in place of 'survival of the fittest' and the 'market forces', came the quest for 'fair labor standards and social security.'[71] Fascism, the remedy the bourgeoisie tried in dispair had conceded to employ against these changes, and by which it almost was destroyed itself,[72] was discredited and stopped, and the reformers on the left were gaining prestige. The communists gained well earned esteem for their part in defeating Fascist barbarism, and the socialists for their plans for a better and more just post-war world. In Britain Labor won the General Elections (July 1945) and set in motion an ambitious socialization program with the ultimate objective of making Britain a socialist state. Parliament repealed the Trade Dispute Act of 1927 which had hampered the Trade Unions' freedom of action; consolidated national insurance legislation, and introduced free national health services (1946); it nationalized the Bank of England, the coal industry, civil aviation (1946), transport (1948) gas

---

69.   *United Nations Charter*, Ch. IX, Article 55.

70.   *The Atlantic Charter*, 14th August 1941.

71.   *Ibid.*

72.   Thomas Mann wrote in 1938, 'It is heartbreaking to see the weakness of the older cultural group in face of this barbarism; its bewildered, confused retreat. Dazed and abashed, with an embarrassed smile, it abandons one position after another, seeming to concede that in very truth it no longer understands the world. It stoops to the foe's mental and moral level, adopts his idiotic terminology, adjusts itself to its pathetic categories, his stupid, spiteful and capricious propaganda – and does not even see what it is doing. Perhaps it is already lost.'

and electricity (1949) and iron and steel (1951).[73] In France the elections for the Constituent Assembly (Oct 1945), with women voting for the first time, also showed a strong shift to the left. The Communists obtained 152 seats, the Socialists 151, and the *Mouvement Républicain Populaire* only 138.[74] In Italy too the elections to the Constituent Assembly in 1946 showed a similar inclination. The Christian Democrats still topped the list of Assembly members (207) but the Socialists and Communists (115 and 104 respectively) together were a majority.[75] In Germany the first local elections in the western occupied zones (1946) returned the Christian Democrats in first and the Social Democrats in close second place. In the eastern zone, the Social Democrats united with the Communists in the Socialist Unity Party (S.E.D.) received the great majority of all votes. In 1949 the Federal Republic of Germany adopted a new *Basic Law* which was essentially not very different from the *Weimar Constitution*. In subsequent years East Germany came more and more under communist rule,[76] and the Christian Democrats continued on the whole to retain a small lead over the Socialists in West Germany. In Belgium the Catholic Christian Socialists received the largest number of votes in 1946 and 1949. In the Netherlands the Catholic People's Party, closely followed by Socialist Labor, won the 1946 elections. In 1948 the government lost some votes and in the new coalition Dr. Beel was replaced as Prime

---

73.   Iron and Steel, and road transport, were later denationalized again by the Conservatives in 1952.

74.   The elections to the Constituent Assembly in June 1946 gave the M.R.P. first place, the Communist second and the Socialists third. In the elections to the National Assembly in November 1946 the Communists polled 186 seats, the M.R.P. 166 and the Socialists 103. After 1947 the French left was weakened by the growing rift between the Communists and the other parties.

75.   In 1947 de Gasperi headed a cabinet of Christian Democrats, Communists and Left-Wing Socialists, but this government did not last very long. In the national elections in 1948 the Communists and Socialists together did not manage to gain 33% of the votes.

76.   More is said about this in the following chapter.

Minister by the Labor leader Drees. In Denmark Vilhelm Buhl, a Social Democrat, formed the first post-war Cabinet (1945). In three subsequent elections (1945, 1947, 1950) the Socialists emerged as the strongest party. In Norway, Eivar Gerhardsen, the leader of the Labor Party, formed the first post-war coalition government. Labor received a majority of the votes in the 1945 elections, and increased its majority in 1949. In Sweden Per A Hansson replaced the coalition government, which ruled the country before July 1945, by a Social Democratic cabinet. In 1948 the electorate gave again the greatest number of votes to the Social Democrats. Altogether then, industrialized western Europe had taken a step to the left. The old confrontation between labor and capital was temporarily pushed into the background while both left and center shared in Europe's reconstruction. The working class had won its moral hegemony and took the lead in the reshaping of post-war Europe. The few discordant sounds from the extreme left[77] seemed as yet no more than the rumble of the rising storm of the struggle for political hegemony between the U.S.A. and the U.S.S.R. The working class had become partner – no longer the servant, in the process of economic advancement.

---

77.   For example the wave of strikes in France in May and November 1946 and in November 1948.

9

The Rise of Egalitarian Society

*'Eine Gesellschaftsordnung geht nie unter,
bevor alle Produktivkräfte entwickelt sind, für
die sie weit genug ist, und neue höhere
Produktionsverhältnisse treten nie an die
Stelle, bevor die materiellen Existenz
bedingungen derselben im Schoss der alten
Gesellschaft ausgebrütet worden sind.'*
Karl Marx

The labor movement whatever form it assumed was essentially a
reaction to the social and economic evils that attended the rise and
development of Capitalism. Its *strength* lay in its opposition to
exploitation, alienation, insecurity and poverty; its *weakness* in its
inability to offer to most people an attractive alternative to the
prevailing order before industrialization reached a level of productive
efficiency capable of securing for everyone a decent living standard.
As long as Capitalism had not accomplished what Marx had called
its 'historical task,' of 'baking a cake' sufficiently big to satisfy most
if not all who felt entitled to share in it, labor's alternative to
Capitalism could only imply a fairer distribution of the 'cake' but
not plenty for all. It implied the reduction of poverty at the one end
of society at the cost of less affluence at the other end – not plenty

301

but justice. Until the middle of the present century this meant that on the whole[1] too many people would have had, or thought that they would have had, to reduce their living standards before the poor could be better provided for than they were. What seemed theoretically possible, i.e. the distribution of wealth in a way that everyone would be reasonably well provided, was practically and therefore politically, unattainable. Where and when it was attempted it met with the strongest resistance.[2] As explained in the earlier chapters, it was not that under Capitalism people with a Jewish-Christian upbringing were insensitive to the suffering of others, but their own fears of becoming destitute in a world in which the accumulation of wealth alone seemed to provide an adequate protection against privation led them into the 'Prisoner's Dilemma' of having to choose between an apparently fairly secure individual option and a promising but insecure collective option. In other words, fear led reasonable and charitable people to restrain their natural inclination to help others only to the extent that such help did not impair their own living standards. And as pointed out in the previous chapter, it was not before the middle of this century that the technological achievements of society reached the level of development that made possible the provision of bourgeois living standards for everyone in the industrially most advanced countries.

A truth that economists have discovered long ago is that men's *needs* though not their *desires* are limited. On the one hand economists acknowledged the fact that people can use only so much food as their stomachs can absorb;[3] can drive but one car at a time; and even when they dress differently for each meal can use a limited

---

1.   This excludes of course the spells of recessions and depressions when poverty and the prospects of destitution were particularly widespread.

2.   The Ukrainian peasants struggle against Lenin's economic policy is a good example for such resistance in a supposedly alternative regime. *Vide* Y.S. Brenner, *A Short History of Economic Progress,* pp. 217–28.

3.   The consumer may of course with rising income substitute caviar for bread and champagne for tea but his total volume of consumption will still remain limited.

number of suits and dresses. And on the other hand, they also observed that this fact need not and does not restrict men's desire to amass capital and accumulate wealth boundlessly. In fact this combination of limited needs and boundless desires has been used as a strong argument against the egalitarian clamors of the left. For in a growing economy – an economy with an improving productive capacity, much was seen to depend upon the rate of capital investment, and so, as *needs* are limited, any additions to the incomes of the rich are more likely to be saved and turned into economic-growth producing investments than similar additions to the poor whose demand for consumer goods is not yet satiated. Now, in spite of the fact that this particular justification of inequality in bourgeois society is one of those half-truths that are worse than lies[4] it is of course true that irrespective of political systems all economies that have not reached the level of efficiency at which they are capable of providing affluence for *all,* can only reach this level by devoting part of their output to the construction of more and better means of production, i.e. to the accumulation of real capital. In this at least the Capitalists' and the Socialists' roads to higher living standards are alike. Where they differ is in that the former system imposes the burden of the cost of growth upon the lower middle class and the workers, and allows market forces to determine the pace and direction of the process, and the latter system spreads the burden, or has hoped to spread the burden, more equitably over all members of society, and lets the pace and direction of the process be decided by its political leaders. Essentially however, it remains a fact that the better consumers' demand is satisfied immediately in a growing economy the less is saved for providing the capital for its better satisfaction in the future, and the greater the investment in the better satisfaction of future needs the smaller the share left over for current consumption. Hence the nineteenth century notion that everything is 'pregnant' with its opposite; that machinery gifted with

---

4.   Savings do not automatically become investment. They are necessary but not sufficient, for the expectation of profit must also be present in a capitalist system to encourage the owners of savings to invest them, and these expectations depend upon consumers' effective demand, i.e. on rising domestic incomes and/or on foreign (sometimes colonial) trade expansion.

the wonderful power of shortening and fructifying human labor causes starvation and overwork and new inventions stultify human life into a material force.[5] Yet since the middle of the present century there has been so great an advance in technology and in the accumulation of real capital in the economically most developed countries that industry has in fact become capable of producing all the material goods that society can use and more,[6] though, of course, this capability is not at all times and everywhere exploited.[7]

In fact when incomes rise above a certain level, consumers' demand tends to diminish at the upper margin because the desires for the material objects of comfort and well-being that bourgeois society values and can offer (except good accommodation assurance against unemployment, sickness and destitution in old age, and a fund for the children's education) have all their upper limits of demand.[8] It is after all impossible to enjoy more than *one* television set at a time though one may well install one but no more than one in each room of one's home. Unless this was true industry would not have found

---

5.   For this characterization of the capitalist mode of production *vide* Marx & Engles, *Selected Works*, F.L.P.H. Moscow, 1958, Vol. I, p. 359.

6.   One may think here of the surplus milk and wine 'lakes', and the large surplus butter and pork 'mountains', which accumulated in Europe in the 1970s, and led to the imposition of restrictions limiting the volume of production while millions of people were starving in Asia, Africa and South America.

7.   The restriction of the above statement to 'material goods' is necessary because some other objects of desire can never be fully satisfied. Fred Hirsch in his book *Social Limits to Growth* gives several convincing examples for this and shows why the riches enjoyed by a minority cannot be enjoyed by a majority because of what he calls the positional context of society. For example not all people can get a flat or house overlooking the sea because the sea-shore is not long enough.

8.   The observed tendency for the marginal propensity to consume to diminish with rising incomes is part of Keynes' explanation for the turning of a boom into recession in the business cycle. *Vide* Y.S. Brenner, *Introduction to Economics,* 'The interaction of the *Multiplier* and the *Acceleration Principle*', Part II, pp. 115–50.

it necessary to create *'false wants'*, or advertise new fashions every other week to convince people that what they already own must be replaced. To be sure, not even man's desire for leisure is unlimited. *The notion of the absence of such an upper limit is but a shadow of man's past poverty and the reflection of the capitalist's war of all against all in competition which forces upon him the choice: Accumulate or be destroyed.* But given that such an upper limit for material things exists, then it must also set an upper limit to what people can from time to time reasonably aspire to obtain.[9] Here then lies one of the essential differences between the pre and post World War II, situations in the rich countries before the middle of the present century, society was not, and since the middle of the century it is, or is at least rapidly becoming, technologically capable to meet most people's material needs and expectations with the customary investment of labor-time. In other words, technology has reached a level which allows simultaneously to sustain both the satisfaction of consumers' demand for the high living standards to which the middle class is accustomed, and the provision of the means of production necessary to perform this 'miracle'. A simple exercise should illustrate this point. One lists all the material goods owned by a well established upper middle class household and multiplies them by the total number of households in the society; and again, with the help of a Leontief type input-output matrix, one multiplies them by the production coefficients, i.e. by the volume of inputs which contribute to the final output at the given level of technology, and adds the households' food requirements in a similar manner, and sums it all up (allowing for imports and exports) in terms of labor-time. The result would then indicate how many people would have to work for how many hours per week to provide at the given level of technology the whole society with all the goods such a society may aspire to. Preliminary estimates for the Netherlands[10] suggest that even with an increasingly aging population there would remain labor

---

9. Leaving aside the urge to save which tends to wane in welfare systems that guarantee social security, and the declining prestige of the owners of capital in comparison to the managerial élite.

10. *Vide* Y.S. Brenner, 'Working paper scenarios for Planning and Beleid'.

to spare for the provision of the labor services which do not result in tangible goods which society of course also requires. It may therefore be concluded that while in the past the share of society's economic product which went into the production of means of production was relatively too large, and the productive efficiency of the available means of production too low, to satisfy simultaneously all the expectations of an increasing number of consumers and investors, this seems no longer to be true. As will be shown,[11] labor efficiency in the manufacturing industries and agriculture has increased dramatically. The recurrent and often prolonged crises of 'over-production' that plagued western society before World War II, had in fact not been crises of over-production but of under-consumption, not crises brought about by an objective productive over-capacity, but crises brought about by an ill-adjusted distribution of income that was, and still is, endemic in Capitalism. They were crises of under-consumption brought about by too few earners and/or too low earnings, i.e. by the absence of an automatic mechanism, like the price mechanism, to keep incomes and investments on a rising equilibrium trend. They were crises due to Capitalism's inability to maintain over time a rate of capital investment which is consistent with a steadily rising technological coefficient that matches a similarly steadily increasing effective consumers' demand in spite of a declining marginal propensity to consume at full employment.[12] In short, they were due to the only too well known phenomenon of the modern Business Cycle. Since the 1950s, however, things are different as the coincidence of inflation and unemployment seems to indicate.[13] It appears that the

---

11.   *Vide* pp. 307–8.

12.   Models exploring such steady growth were discussed by R.F. Harrod and E.D. Domar. For examples see *The Economic Journal,* Vol. XLIX, 1939; *Economica,* Vol. 14, 1946; *The American Economic Review,* Vol. XXXVII, 1947, and Harrod's *Towards Dynamic Economics.*

13.   Milton Friedman's criticism of the Keynesian notion about the Phillips Curve, that it is but a 'special' and not a 'general' case, may well be justified if pre-war capitalism is separated from post war capitalism as I suggested.

dual mechanism of competition (the competition between the enterprises on the one hand and the competition between capital and labour for the fruits of production on the other)[14] has in the industrially most advanced countries so forced the pace of productive-efficiency that the surplus production of agriculture and industry has turned from relative to absolute. In spite of the fact that state intervention (especially in the Welfare States) kept effective demand steady and even on a rising path in the 1970s, has the unemployment of labor and the idle productive capacity increased almost unabated. The butter mountain of the E.E.C. and the stocks of unsalable electronic gadgets should stand as monuments to this new true development. In other words, over-production and over-capacity which had in the past been relative – the product of temporary disequilibria between effective demand and supply, have increasingly become structural – an inherent characteristic of the system. The people in the rich countries have simply no use for all the goods industry can produce even though they may from time to time have sufficient earnings to acquire them. More goods are produced in the industrialized countries, in the time people are accustomed to or think fair to work, than they can use, but given the wages and other costs which go into the production of these goods, they are too costly to be purchased by the people who may well be able to use them in the economically less developed countries. And so, the survival of 'old style' capitalism becomes dependent upon the growth of purchasing power in the under-developed countries, – upon the new type of imperialism which in the 1960s Dr. Nkrumah named Neo-Colonialism.

Meanwhile, however, the rich countries were faced with a growing problem of structural unemployment,[15] and with the strains attending the transformation of their socio-economic systems into something that, but for the perseverance of the profit motive, increasingly come to resemble socialism. No longer meeting the old resistance from those sections of the working class and of the middle class which

14. *Vide* pp. 304–5.

15. I should be noted that this book was originally published in 1978.

had in the past opposed egalitarian notions for fear of having to share, i.e. of having to reduce their own living standards, in order to raise that of the others less fortunate than themselves, it had become increasingly easier to modify capitalism – in fact its modification has become politically almost unavoidable.

It is not difficult to show the staggering rise in productive efficiency due to technological and organizational improvements in the rich countries by comparing a few data. If one compares the efficiency of labor in more and less developed countries today, or in the same countries at, say, twenty-five-year intervals the changes in productivity are obvious. To satisfy all the requirements for food and materials of farm origin no more than 4 per cent of the American labor force is engaged in agriculture, but 58 per cent are still necessary in Asia.[16] In 1820 72 per cent of the American labor force was engaged in farming, but only 63 per cent in 1850, 36 per cent in 1900, 12 per cent in 1950, and 4 per cent in 1975.[17] Taking into account that in spite of this low labor input the U.S. is also a great food exporter it may safely be said that it takes no more than one man engaged in agriculture in America to produce all the food and agricultural materials required by 22 persons. A similar tendency towards lower labor requirements can also be observed in manufacturing. In spite of the increasing number of items on which people wish, and with rising incomes are able, to spend their money, and in spite of the growing accumulation of manufactured goods,[18] has the number of workers directly engaged in the manufacturing sector also steadily declined. The real product per man-hour in the United States has increased more than fourfold since the beginning of the century and the rise in western Europe and Japan was on the

---

16.   The percentage of the people engaged in agriculture in different parts of the world is: United States 4; Israel 7; Western Europe 12; Soviet Union 31; Latin America 40; Asia 58; Africa 73; Chad 91. *Source* Eli Ginzberg, *Scientific American,* Dec. 1976, p. 26.

17.   Eli Ginsberg, *op.cit.*

18.   In spite of the fact that unlike for food there is no real limiting 'stomach' to restrain the acquisition of manufactures.

whole no less impressive. It is of course true that the rise in the productivity of people directly employed in the production of agricultural and industrial goods was accompanied by a rise in the number of people engaged in providing the services that became necessary to hold the increasingly more specialized and intricate new economic system together. This increase is very obvious in spite of the fact that because all economic activities are fundamentally services it is difficult to make a clear distinction between directly and indirectly productive labor – between the services of a tractor driver and a bus driver, except by definition. If it is further taken into consideration that many sciences play a twofold role in modern industrial society – that they contribute to both the economic process and directly to the quality of life then the relative growth of the service sector in comparison with the producing sectors assumes an even greater significance.[19] In *France,* out of a total population of 38.451.000 in 1901, 5.812.000 were engaged in commerce, finance, transport, communications and other services, and 14.089.000 in agriculture, forestry, fishing and in the manufacturing, extractive and construction industries. In 1954, out of a population of 41.000.000,7.068.000 were engaged in commerce, finance, transport, etc., and only 12.198.000 in agriculture, forestry, fishing and manufacturing etc. And in 1962, out of a population of 46.500.000 there were already 8.160.000 engaged in commerce, finance, transport, etc., while the number of people engaged in agriculture, forestry, fishing, construction, and manufacturing etc. had diminished to only 11.333.000. In *West Germany,* out of a population of 50.787.000 in 1950, 8.032.000 were engaged in commerce, finance, transport, etc. and 15.046.000 in agriculture, forestry, fishing and manufacturing etc. One decade later, in 1961, out of a total population of 56.115.000,10.514.000 were engaged in commerce, finance, transport, communications and other services, and 16.209.000 in agriculture, forestry, fishing, mineral extraction,

---

19. It is for example difficult to separate for example a doctor's contribution to physical production for better health reduces the number of man-days lost at work owing to bad health, and his contribution to people's better quality of life from enjoying better health. The same may be said of teachers, and others rendering a service of this kind.

construction and manufacturing. In other words: while the total population in West Germany increased by a little less than 10.5 per cent, service employment increased by almost 31 per cent, but employment in agriculture and manufacturing etc. increased by no more than 7 per cent[20] i.e. relative to population the number of people employed in the production of food and manufactured goods diminished. In the *Netherlands* 1.936.000 man-years were spent on 'services' in 1958, and 2.480.000 in 1970. In the primary and secondary sectors of the economy (agriculture, fishing, production of semi-finished products and food, drink, tobacco products, textiles, shoes, chemical goods, oil refining, public utilities, etc.) taken together 2.126.000 man-years were employed in 1958, and 2.201.000 in 1970.[21] Even with the production-linked services and the services in the public utilities included in the 'directly productive' statistics the relative greater rise in employment in service occupations (544.000 as against 75.000) is obvious.

The ratio of the labor force to total population had been fairly stable in the past in countries with high immigration quotas like the United States in spite of longer life expectancy and longer schooling of the young. Since the middle of this century it began moving against labor – i.e. the share of the working population declined in the volume of the population as a whole. The ratio of labor (above the age of ten years) to total population in the United States was 33 to 100 in 1850; 35 to 100 in 1880; 38 to 100 in 1900; 40 to 100 in 1930; 43 to 100 in 1950. But in 1959 it fell back to 41 to 100. It is difficult to say how much of the early rise in the share of the labor force in total population must be attributed to the particular character of the age composition of immigrants, and how much to changing work habits – for example, to women taking up remunerated work, and to compensation for the steadily reduced length of the working-day, but the break in the trend is clear and

---

20.   Calculated from B.R. Mitchell, *European Historical Statistics*, London, 1975, pp. 20, 155-6.

21.   *Source*: C.B.S., *Statistisch Zakboek*, 1971, p. 70.

similar to that in other industrial countries where the pre 1950s rise in labor was not taking place.[22]

The share of the *government* in the employment of labor and of *not-for-profit* engagement as opposed to capitalist enterprises has also increased very greatly since the 1930s. Even in the U.S.A. the country fully committed to Free Enterprise 13.400.000 people out of a total labor force of 84.700.000, i.e. 31.9 per cent, were employed in *'not-for-profit'* organizations in 1973. Of these 13.400.000 were directly employed by the state and 7.100.000 by private firms working on government orders. 5.000.000 were directly engaged by 'non-profit making' organizations and 1.500.000 indirectly. The share of the combined output of the non-private sectors of the economy taken together amounted to 26.3 per cent i.e. to 338 billion dollars.[23]

In the Netherlands total employment (in man-years) was 3.773.000 in 1950, and 4.688.000 in 1974. Of this the state directly employed 392.000 in 1950 and 617.000 in 1974. So, while the overall labor force increased by 20 per cent, government employment increased by 58 per cent The share of government work in total employment rose from a little more than 10 per cent in 1950 to just above 13 per cent in 1974. Net investment (including stocks) increased in the Netherlands from Fl. 3.127 million in 1950, to Fl. 29.480 million in 1974. Of this the government share was Fl. 494 million in the former year and Fl. 5.680 million in the latter. It follows that the share of the Netherlands' government in the country's fixed investment increased from but 16 per cent in 1950 to almost 20 per cent in 1974.[24]

All this, – the growing share of the public sector in the Free Enterprise economies; the increasing impact of 'not-for-profit' organizations on employment; the rising level of social security and of living standards in general, and the many other modifications of

---

22. Hamberg, *op.cit.*, p. 144.

23. *Vide* E. Ginzberg, *Scientific American*, December 1976, p. 26, 'The Pluralistic Economy of the United States'.

24. Calculated from C.B.S., *75 Jaar Statistiek van Nederland*, 's-Gravenhage, 1975.

the classical capitalistic system which can no longer pass unnoticed in the economically advanced countries still do not toll the knell on capitalism altogether. They are but the early shoots of the new social system that germinates within the old. Whether or not this coming system will seem attractive judged by the standards of our generation remains still to be seen.[25] For as a rule our desires arise out of our most immediate wants in such a manner that what we most miss *here* and *now* affects our aspirations for the future strongest. Indeed, often it affects our aspirations so strongly that it overshadows everything else that we may also hope for tomorrow and the day thereafter. In the darkest era it was the hunger and the poverty that accompanied the progress of capitalism that made men raise the need for bread above all other wants, and so, in the first country in which Capitalism was abolished *output statistics* became the measure of man's value to society (Stakhanovism).

This may well be an improvement in comparison with the conception of man purely as a factor of production but it is less than mankind may expect. A man who has an elephant standing on his toes finds *this* the most pressing of all problems. He devotes all his thoughts and efforts to the removal of the beast and forgets for the moment all else that bothers him. Poverty was precisely such an 'elephant' and it was the removal of this ill that in those countries which today have become the technologically most advanced, occupied foremost people's thoughts. It was this aspects of capitalism – the poverty, hunger and alienation that accompanied it, that pushed into the shadow some of its more attractive aspects, such as the rule of law and the freedom of expression, at least in the minds of those who were deprived or observed the distress. So *economic growth*, i.e. the improving of the efficiency in the utilization of human and other resources, and only to a less extent *stability* and *equity*, came to the center of attention in macroeconomics. But *growth* was above all regarded as a technological problem assisted by the accumulation of wealth, while *stability* and *equity*, the two other great objectives of

---

25.   One cannot help wondering whether a lion in the Zoo where he is well fed and cared for is happier than a lion in the desert where he is often subjected to hunger and diseases.

society, were as long as this was possible left unattended, supposedly to be solved of their own accord by some mysterious economic mechanism.

This fact had an additional affect, namely that it provided science with a special status in society. As, unlike the pursuit of stability and equity, the pursuit of economic growth did not *per se* raise social contradictions this was the one area in which all classes could be united. For in effect the scientist or technician who advances man's dominion over nature may well serve simultaneously both private interests and the public good. In any case his achievements need not detract from one class of society in order to benefit the other as usually seems to be the case with the promotion of greater equity and in the short-run with stability.[26] For potentially all new discoveries, before society became conscious of the environmental hazards involved in their application, added to man's ability to overcome the reticence of nature, and to his ability to drive back the frontiers of ignorance, and thus improved the chances for a better life. Indeed, it is alone the use that society makes of its discoveries that determines their practical value for mankind. Hence, the scientist's ability to advance man's ascendancy over nature while he remains outside the antagonistic social class formations gave him, in fact to all those in the learned professions a special status in society which was far above their economic position. The masses romanticized his work and him into a selfless servant of society and truth, and the entrepreneurs recognized in him a useful tool to further their own interests. As a result of this confidence that was bestowed upon them the members of the professions began developing a kind of sub-culture of their own in the midst of the profit dominated society. They put the advancement of true knowledge before the pursuit of material advantages for themselves. Not that there ever was a lack of people in the professions who were keen on money, – like doctors specializing in the diseases of the rich, but these were not the men that determined the image of the

---

26. The distinction between short and long-run advantages has to be made for in the long-run stability would be better for all but in the short-run those who have to pay for it feel at a disadvantage. We shall return to this problem later.

learned in the eyes of the society at large. Many of the young people who studied the sciences or medicine before World War II did so because they wanted to help mankind. Even those who studied for more pecuniary reasons or to gain status or just because their family expected them to study, were seldom able to escape altogether the climate of this sub-culture with its special value system. In America where the bourgeoisie was firmly established earlier than in Europe, and its values less challenged by older ones, the intellectual elite never gained this type of social position and responsibility. Europeans were accustomed to social differentiations which did not rest upon a person's economic status – the hierarchical position of an aristocrat seldom reflected precisely his wealth, and had therefore little difficulty in accepting artists and scientists as 'a breed apart', as men of special status. This was not true of the Americans. In America the ascendancy of the bourgeoisie was more complete. There a scientist was long before W.W.II. valued by the amount of money his work was worth to industry – Einstein was valued by his contribution to the atom bomb and not by his new perception of time and space.[27] So, being better integrated in the system than his European colleague, the American intellectual had to earn recognition by his services to it in order to become part of the establishment. He was in fact the servant of *the establishment* whereas the European retained until the early 1980s some influence upon it. Motivated by the capitalistic spirit of competition, even among themselves, American scientists registered great achievements especially in those fields where science has a high degree of technological applicability, but they lost control over the direction of their work. They became concerned with 'does it work' and 'will it sell', rather than with 'is it true' and 'is it socially necessary'. They left the decision of what they ought to study in the hands of the industrialists because they expected their rewards and esteem from the industrial establishment; they worked for cash and for the appreciation of their fellow scientists, and not for the immaterial

---

27.   In America it is customary for Professors to negotiate their salaries with the Universities like merchants selling their goods.

benefits of knowing and the acclaim of the general public.[28] In contrast, the special status accorded to the intellectuals in Europe imposed upon them a particular code of conduct. The European intellectual was not supposed to be keen on money and was expected to take a leading part in the advancement of humanity – *noblesse oblige*. For this reason, until fairly recently, the European bourgeoisie was never really able to bend the intellectual elite fully to its will and alienate it from the masses. To avoid misunderstanding it must again be emphasized that it is not that American scientists did not drive back the frontiers of ignorance and did not contribute magnificently to man's ability to better satisfy his needs and wants, but that they left the decision about what these needs were and in economics how they should be satisfied to the whimsicality of the price mechanism over which they themselves had no control but which was if not wholly than still greatly influenced by the leading industrial establishment. Their achievements were progressive – they promoted man's mastery over nature, but from a social point of view they were not optimally so. The scientists' efforts were not directed where they would have been socially best employed but where they were expected to yield the highest profit for the directors of industry, only too often were therefore the negative social consequences of the results, for example on the environment, simply ignored as long as they did not involve a direct cost element for industry. Industrialists' 'love of gain' rather than society's objective needs were the direction towards which, first American and later also European, science gravitated. At first sight this may not seem of great relevance in the light of the truly great technological leap forward that society has made in the last hundred years, and in the light of the *potential* this achievement offered society to lead a better – more secure and comfortable life in the future; but this is not altogether true. While society was conquering nature it lost more of its ability to control itself. The mechanism which stimulated capitalist society to achieve its magnificent positive successes was competition. The incessant

---

28. The dominance of positive economics among American economists shows how far scientists can stray from the path of social relevance to serve the establishment.

drive of owners and controllers of industries towards innovation, to avoid being destroyed by their competitors, was in fact the hallmark of bourgeois society. But a society caught up in this relentless choice, advance or be destroyed, is no longer free to choose at all. It becomes the victim of its own utilitarian drives. It cannot really be concerned with questions regarding the long-term consequences of the solutions to its immediate problems. For example, whether or not the use of nuclear energy is safe, because *not* to use nuclear power, while others may well use it, would be directly self-destructive. In a world ruled by competition the fear of being outpaced by someone is a very real danger and not an imaginary one. If for example American industry should make use of nuclear power and German industry should not, and consequently American products become, at least for a time, cheaper than German products, it is of course a fact that not only German industrialists but German workers too will suffer the ill consequences. For the same reason any diminution of the forces that are capable of restraining the utilitarian spirit of capitalism, that can restrict the urge for unbridled competition in pursuit of profit, is likely to constitute a real danger for the human race. Like the sorcerer's apprentice in the fairy-tale capitalism has released forces it cannot control, and with one section of society after the other falling victim to the capitalist value system and shedding its own – the church, the aristocracy, the scientists, the chances of social considerations taking precedence over individual interests become more remote and eventually the latter become socially destructive. This then is the real danger involved in the scientists' loss of special social status. It is the end of an era in which people believed in what they had been taught was right and the coming of a time in which right is judged by success. The traditional system of morality which gave prime value to truth is replaced by one appealing to expediency.

There is perhaps no better example for the confusion of old and new values in modern society than the so called 'generation gap' exhibited in the late 1960s and early 1970s. On the one hand the young are encouraged by the literature selected for them and by the verbal admonitions of their teachers at school and by their religious instructors if they go to Church to put great store by patently non-utilitarian values – such as patriotism, human dignity, compassion, and the love of truth and beauty etc., and on the other hand, they are directed by the reality at home and by their parents admonitions to follow a narrow utilitarian path – to study or do what is useful for their personal advancement and behave in the way best suited to promote their immediate self-interest. The paradox of a student brandishing Marcuse's *One Dimensional Man* in the one hand and holding a banner reading 'We want it all, and we want it now' in the other, is perhaps the best illustration of the cultural confusion in modern society. The fact that American science did not fall earlier victim to the utilitarianism of its surroundings is probably also due to this dichotomy. Firstly the influx of foreign intellectuals which was particularly strong in the 'thirties when liberals and Jews fled Fascist continental Europe, and in the 'fifties and early 'sixties when England was no longer providing the necessary conditions for its intellectuals, injected some of the traditional values back into the American scientific establishment. Secondly, there was something in the American tradition itself that retarded the loss of traditional values. Though the teachings of the Church and the Calvinist traditions of the founding fathers of the United States were more 'honored' by transgression than by adherence they were still upheld before the young as the true values of American society. Without this would neither Lincoln nor Roosevelt have been able to rally the masses in support of their causes. So, utilitarianism and religion went together in the most developed parts of the United States unlike in Europe where they were in conflict. The particular character of American Calvinism combined the pursuit of worldly goods with Christian piety much better than its European counterpart. In fact what had in Europe developed as a mere legitimization for the pursuit of wealth – the test if one is chosen by the master of all destiny, became in America a source of inspiration in itself for the pursuit of wealth, almost a sacred duty of man to *make* his destiny. But the roots remained in an ethical system which was essentially a traditional – a Christian, system, and before these roots were wholly severed pure utilitarianism could not vanquish. There was no time in history in which the great majority of the American people, and for that matter people everywhere, felt sufficiently economically or physically secure to abandon all metaphysical appeals for succor. As Christianity was nearest at hand the appeal was mainly to christianity; and as christianity was upholding a pre-capitalist value system these values continued to play a role in American society restraining the hard headed utilitarianism. How long they will continue doing so remains an open question.

In fact it is altogether difficult to see how an individualistic and purely utilitarian community can maintain a modern system of production. It is hard to predict whether a secular ideology will continue to fulfill the task of preventing the slaughter of the goose which in the past has laid the golden egg. The failure of the Left to provide an alternative morality in an increasingly secular society was almost certainly a factor in its failure to modify the capitalist system in the way made possible by Keynes. The great industrial progress that advanced the modern living standards brought with it a high degree of complexity and specialization. Indeed so high a degree of specialization that without reliable co-ordination it must collapse. It follows that more than ever before everyone's welfare depends upon what everyone else is doing and how far everybody fulfills his task on time conscientiously and responsibly. Under early capitalism this responsibility was normally assured by the individual's fear of getting the sack, as a consequence of the fear of starvation, if he does not fulfil his task, and by a tacit acceptance of a social culture pattern which subjected people to a firm moral code of rules with socially sanctioned 'do and do-nots'. These were the rules by which entrepreneurs were free to destroy their opponents by competition but not by highway robbery. The rules were firmly anchored outside man's will they were the 'Laws of God', the Bible's 'thou shalt and thou shall not'. However, with the decline in the individual's immediate fear of starvation, – with the improved social security arrangements, and with the diminution of religious sanctions – with the spreading of materialistic individualistic utilitarianism, little is left to assure industrial discipline. But without discipline industrial society cannot survive. It follows that in the absence of the old compulsive forces new ones become necessary, and these can only rest either upon *consensus* or *force*. Indeed without the metaphysical sanctions of God's laws, and without the economic sanctions of the capitalist system, what else remains to elicit obedience but consensus or force? Under the circumstances the former would require *egalitarian democracy* and the latter *totalitarian despotism*. Where the laws of

God are replaced by the laws of men, and the rewards or punishments in the life to come lose their hold upon mankind, there the rewards and retribution 'upon this bank and shoal of time' must take their place. To be sure, it is by no means certain to what extent since the inception of industrial society, religion continued to influence man's conduct, and in what measure the 'here and now' became decisive, but it is impossible not to acknowledge the impact that it had on the cultural climate in which industrial society developed. In Professor Chadwick's opinion the laboring poor were in the eighteenth and nineteenth centuries too near subsistence to care much about religion. According to him they were simply indifferent. Yet Durkheim believed that there was something eternal in religion which will survive within industrial society; and Weber thought that when the new order has come to maturity it will lose the ethical tenets which, according to him, gave rise to it; And Marx, whose early views on this subject followed the rational criticism of religion of Bauer, Strauss and Feuerbach, later came to the conclusion that religion must be understood as an institution within the totality of social existence.[29] They all, each in his own way, acknowledge its great influence. Nor did metaphysical considerations disappear. Einstein, who believed that 'everything that the human race has done and thought is concerned with the satisfaction of deeply felt needs and the assuagement of pain', also thought that 'with primitive man it is above all fear that evokes religious notions – fear of hunger, wild beasts, sickness, death.' But not this alone: 'social impulses are another source.. . The desire for guidance, love, and support prompts men to form the social or moral conception of God.' In his view, this development from the religion of fear to the moral religion is admirably illustrated in the Old and New Testament. A higher development, he thought, was the coming of was the Spinozan *cosmic religious feeling.* 'The individual feels the futility of human desires and aims and the sublimity and marvelous order which reveal themselves both in nature and in the

---

29.   *Vide* Anthony Giddens' criticism of Owen Chadwick's book *The Secularization of the European Mind in the Nineteenth Century* in the T.L.S. 1976.

world of thought. Individual existence impresses him as a sort of prison and he wants to experience the universe as a single significant whole...' This is the 'love of God' which Spinoza championed, a religion with no dogma and no God conceived in man's image. It is communicated from one person to another by art and science, and it should lead to a world in which 'man's ethical behavior is based effectually on sympathy, education, and social ties and needs, for which no religious basis is necessary'. 'Man would indeed be in a poor way' Einstein concludes, 'if he had to be restrained by fear of punishment and hope of reward after death.'[30] But even he cannot find evidence for the spreading of his kind of ethical conception outside the intellectuals' sub-culture of his time, and has to admit 'that in this materialistic age of ours the serious scientific workers are the only profoundly religious people'

The realistic alternatives, if industrial society should survive, remain therefore, either the replacement of individualistic rationality by social rationality or the emergence of a new political system in which economic compulsion is replaced by legal coercion. Recent developments[31] are pointing in both directions. The increasing participation of labor in the management of industries, the proliferation of action-groups concerned with communal problems such as the use of nuclear energy and the environment in general, and the rising number of social services, seem to point to a growth in *social rationality.* Increasing state participation in industry, the proliferation of bureaucratic control over decision making processes, ranging from who may study [where, when, and what] to the most intimate spheres of individuals' lives – for example in some countries decisions about birth control, not to mention even the state direction of almost all aspects of existence in Socialist countries, seem all to indicate that society is moving in the second direction i.e. towards bureaucratic despotism. The third alternative, namely the continuation of total individualism is in fact no alternative at all. For

---

30.   Albert Einstein, *Berliner Tageblatt,* 11 November 1930, translated into English in *Ideas and Opinions,* New York, 1954.

31.   'Recent' at the time the first edition of this book was published, i.e. in 1978.

it implies self-destruction, atomic or otherwise, or chaos i.e. a return to self-sufficiency. As W.F. Ogburn[32] very correctly observed, 'periods of great social change are usually characterized by a decline in the authority of codes of morality and by greater dependence on experiment, expediency and rationality in conduct... by a deterioration in manners and by the frequent emergence of an uncontrolled egoism.' But whether in our period of accelerated change society is given the time to work out 'by a long process of trial and error what appears to be the most suitable adjustment of the individual to the culture and the best correlation between the parts of that culture,' remains to be seen. For such a harmonious transformation is not on the one hand, labor's inability to develop its own counterculture, i.e. its failure to embrace and make its own the idea of the *'dignity of labor'* that its intellectual leadership propagated in the early part of this century, and its almost total surrender to the *brute materialism* of the bourgeoisie; and, on the other hand, the bourgeoisie's progressive abandonment of its own code of business conduct, i.e. its failure to keep to its own rules of legality, and the ensuing decline of business confidence and freedom of competition, have extended over almost all strata of society that 'uncontrolled egoism' that in earlier periods of 'great social change' affected only certain sections of it while the rest were only marginally conscious of the developments. While the workers were exchanging the struggle against the *principle* of private ownership of the means of production for the more pragmatic efforts of gaining a greater share in the fruits of capitalist production, the capitalists have abandoned the principle of trust or confidence and legality upon which their part of the system rested in favor of a short-sighted egoism which is rapidly escalating from a legitimization of bribing foreign officials to wholesale corruption at home.

Yet industrial society rests upon every member's confidence that all other members make their contribution to the system on time in the expected manner. Now, for Classical Economics such confidence sprang from its mythical trust in *Natural Harmony,* in nature's inbuilt gravitation towards order. In its illusionary world of nigh

---

32.   William F. Ogburn, 'Social Change', in *E.S.S.,* Vol. III, p. 333.

Perfect Competition it relegated the task of coordinating the increasingly complex system to the 'invisible hand' of the Price Mechanism, assuming all the time the existence of a utilitarian urge that brings private and public good into one line. Because of its trust in Natural Harmony it simply ignored the contradictions that may arise between the pursuit of private and of public aims. It did not have a social but a strictly individualistic perception of the forces regulating human actions, – namely the pursuit of pleasure and the avoidance of pain. It took the social system and the people's patterns of behavior which were the product of this system with its class distinctions and social stratification for granted and made these patterns of behavior the foundations of its theory. And, to be sure, these patterns of behavior were in fact so well anchored in the European cultural legacy and so well established in bourgeois society that empirically testable economic laws could indeed be based upon them, though, of course, these laws are only of limited empirical validity.[33] But these patterns of behavior were no more than the reflection of a still desperately poor class-ridden social reality in which society was objectively yet unable to provide security and plenty for all. They were the product of fear – the reflection of a reality which left people no choice but to behave exactly as they did. The rich had to pursue greater riches to avoid destruction by competitors and the poor had to maintain industrial discipline to avoid dismissal and starvation. Take out fear and the whole structure crumbles, for why should the capitalist continue amassing wealth and why should the worker maintain the rigid labor discipline when both have no other urges to spur them on to action than the cold fear of poverty and starvation. Perhaps the love of gain? Yes; but only to the point of the satisfaction of *real* present and future wants, for without fear there can be little urge for an individual to go on accumulating wealth. If people still do – it only comes to show that old habits are slow to change.

The process of the transformation of a rural and economically backward society into an industrial and affluent one requires a

---

33.   For a discussion of the scientific status of economic laws see Y.S. Brenner, *Introduction to Economics,* Ankara, 1972, pp. 3–4.

mechanism to keep it in motion and to affect the distribution of the national income or product between the share devoted to current consumption and to the better satisfaction of future needs, i.e. to the production of more and more efficient means of production. Private ownership of capital and the availability of workers with nothing to sell but their labor combined in the shadow of the earlier mentioned economic fears in what is called the Free Enterprise economies and produced the great miracle of industrialization. Fear was also the cement that held together the inequitable partnership between capital and labor and determined for both the division of the national product between investment and consumption. As already explained, for the former it was the fear of lagging behind in the relentless competition of all against all and for the latter it was the fear of finding no work at all unless it accepts the work offered on the capitalists' own terms. The capitalist anxious to survive in business was therefore forced to reward labor as poorly as conditions allowed and labor, being deprived of alternative means of sustenance, was forced to work for much less than the full market value of its produce. To be sure, without labor's gradually growing ability to organize and thus to increase its share in the fruits of production foreign demand would never have sufficed to stimulate capitalism to its magnificent technological achievements,[34] but even so it was the low level of labor's remuneration for its work and capitalist competition that made the economic-growth-producing accumulation and concentration of capital possible. In other words, it was the working class which paid the bill; it was the working class which bore the cost of the industrial progress. It did so in the shadow of fear and with great misery and unnecessary deprivation. For on purely logical grounds there is no real reason why growth cannot follow an almost steady path; there is no reason why accumulation cannot proceed with less economic instability than the last century witnessed, and accompanied by a more steady rise in workers' living standards than it did. True enough such growth might have been somewhat slower than the one achieved by capitalism, but this would

---

34. *Vide* Y.S. Brenner, *A Short History of Economic Progress* for the growth of domestic demand.

not be a too high a price to pay in order to avoid the misery accelerated growth inflicted on its carrier. But such a solution would have required an impossible foresight, it would involve a social instead of individual rationality, and a mechanism as powerful as the fear it should have had to replace, which could not conquer the hearts and minds of men before the true causes of the old fear were really eliminated – i.e. before society was really technologically capable to satisfy its needs at a sufficiently high level to meet the wants of most if not all its members. What we have seen in Soviet Russia is that even with the 'foresight' – the knowledge of what man is technologically capable to achieve, and even with the social rationality promoted by its leaders, it was not possible to industrialize Soviet Russia without resort to fear.[35] The fear of the forced labor camps for those unwilling to work and to restrict their consumption to suit the high rate of accumulation determined by the country's bureaucratic leadership was as real as the economic fears of unemployment and starvation in the capitalistic system, though it was perhaps less effective in inspiring labor discipline and an efficient use of the accumulated resources. Whatever the social and political system happens to be, economic growth requires two things: that people wish to work and that current consumption is restricted to facilitate the accumulation of real capital for the better satisfaction of wants in the future. Therefore, irrespective of social and political systems a mechanism must in all cases be present which is capable of inspiring the wish to work and to restrict consumption. As it happened this mechanism was fear. When pre-industrial society in which all human activities were treated as falling within a single scheme, whose character is determined by God's chosen destiny of mankind – not by utility but by standards derived from the traditional values of the Church entered upon the path of industrialization partial adherence to some of the old values were kept as a precaution to assure man's spiritual well-being – a kind of an insurance lest there is an eternal justice a God in heaven after all. When, as the late R.H. Tawney claimed, man was transformed from a spiritual being, who, in order to survive, must devote a reasonable

---

35.   *Vide* Y.S. Brenner, *A Short History of Economic Progress,* pp. 217–28.

attention to economic interests, into someone who seems sometimes to have become an economic animal, who will be prudent, nevertheless, to take due precautions to assure his spiritual well-being, some of the old values were carried over into industrial society. They were proclaimed in church, passed on from parents to their children, and exalted in the books the children later read in school. To be sure, they gradually lost their Godly credentials and were taken simply as self-evident truths, and they could seldom stand up against the hard pressures of economic necessity – they could not prevent people from following the path prescribed for them by their economic fears, but they could and did maintain man's egoism within the bounds but for which society would have fallen into chaos. They were the anchor that held back the ship of industrial growth that floated on the current of individualistic utilitarianism from reaching the whirlpool of socially self-destructive egoism.[36] It is the combination of the diminishing influence of the fear of starvation, and the steady decline of the impelling force of these moral values, and the lingering economic expediency inherited from the era of high capitalism, that in the modern Welfare State constitutes the greatest danger for the future of society. It is this combination which puts in jeopardy the so dearly paid for technological achievements of mankind just at the point that they could liberate humanity from some of the worst ills that have plagued it for many centuries.

Let it therefore be stressed and repeated that it is perhaps the most disturbing feature of recent industrial society that its liberating diminution of economic fears – that the declining power of the capitalistic mechanism for the enforcement of industrial efficiency and work-discipline, is closely accompanied by an increasing acceptance of expediency as a justification for the abandonment of some of the traditionally held *absolute* values – absolute in the sense of being valid for all time. It is the tendency to substitute the question 'will it succeed' for 'is it true' and 'is it good for me' for 'is it good'.

---

36.   *Vide* p. 235–6.

This approach spread to all spheres of life without sparing science. The old science described nature with the purpose of explaining it and to take this explanation as a guide to human action. The objective of modern science is more limited and direct. It describes nature just to *imitate*, to reproduce, it. The order imposed upon nature is therefore entirely dictated by convenience, i.e. by the wish to predict. As in the previous era experience remains the basis of scientific laws. But experience can never yield absolute certainty. And when experience in human actions is emphasized then all it can show is that when everything else remained equal a given course of action taken several times in the past has yielded similar results, or that a given course of action has, like Mendel's experiment,[37] yielded a precisely definable result, i.e. a result that can be defined in a precise value indicating the probability of, or the odds for, its recurrence.[38] The more trials are made the greater becomes the degree of certainty. So *the belief in the absolute is replaced by probability* – the future is no longer determined as the old principle of 'cause and effect' had suggested, but is allowed a defined measure of uncertainty. Man's future has become neither teleologically nor strictly causally determined, – between the two it is allowed to move within a calculable area of uncertainty. The calculable limits of this freedom have been likened[39] to atoms in a

---

37.   *Vide* Rene Taton, *Science in the Nineteenth Century,* pp. 480–3.

38.   *Vide* von Neumann in *The Theory of Games* for the principle of uncertainty and the inseparability of observer and event.

39.   J. Bronowski, *op.cit.,* p. 124: 'Since the end of the last century there has been known one physical property which gives a direction to time. It is this. If you look at a stream of gas which has come out of a nozzle, you can tell which part of the gas is furthest from the nozzle, that is which has come out earlier, without seeing the nozzle. The part which flowed out earlier is by now more disorderly, and its molecules are drifting about more at random. They have lost the direction imposed by the flow through the nozzle. So the passage of time in the universe at large is marked by an increasing state of physical disorder or randomness this is the second law of thermodynamics. It is remarkable that this is itself a chance effect, yet only this gives time (and with it cause and effect) its direction.'

stream of gas under pressure. On the average they obey the pressure; but at any instant any individual atom may be moving across or against the stream. In other words, large events may, given a degree of uncertainty, be predicted but not small ones. But these, the 'small events', are precisely the ones which gain most attention in the study of modern science and society. This is of course hardly surprising, for the characteristic of the victorious bourgeois liberal democracy is that it maintains its rule by allowing individuals on the basis of competitive ability to rise and find their place *within* its social structure. It allows perfection within the system, and thus postpones or avoids a more rapid development of pressures capable of disequilibrating it. It can therefore use a science that is concerned with particulars, with the 'small events', which maintains that true knowledge is founded exclusively on sense experience, on individuals' here and now, but not a science with a global and historical perspective. It is this that has led to the emphasis of the local rather than the global character of the law of increase of entropy in thermodynamics and statical mechanics, and it is this aspect of Karl Popper's work that has so greatly appealed to the bourgeois mind. The 'large events' that might provide us with a clue to the future are relegated to the world of mystics and utopians. We are told that 'life imposes greater order from moment to moment while the physical universe is drifting into greater disorder' but we are not encouraged to study how this is affecting us. More than that, we are scared off the wish to look into the future – to search for an alternative to equilibrium. 'We are being told that if a star is sufficiently massive it eventually will undergo a runaway collapse that ends with the star's matter crushed completely out of existence. Not only that, but our entire universe may slowly stop expanding, go into a contracting phase, and finally disappear into a black hole, like an acrobatic elephant jumping into its anus.'[40] But this is precisely what may happen to society unless it takes precautions to meet the global challenges of the future, unless it reads the symptoms in the past and present and synthesizes them to meet the future. Organisms

---

40.   Martin Gardner, 'The Holes in the Black Holes', *The New York Review of Books*, September 29th. 1977, p. 22.

and species that could not foretell the future from the symptoms perished.

To use the words of the late Dr. Bronowski,[41] 'All living is action, and human living is thoughtful action. If this is plain enough as a statement about living, it still needs to be underlined about science: that science is a characteristic activity of human life. The characteristic of human action is that it is a choice at each step between what are conceived to be several alternative courses open to us. Man can visualize these alternatives and animals probably cannot; but in both, action means choice – and this, whether we suppose the choice to be free or circumscribed. In both, action is directed towards the future. Men are conscious of this direction and choose one action rather than another in the conscious hope that it will lead to one rather than another kind of future. I add that this statement describes what they do correctly, whether we think that their choice is free or determined'. So, the characteristic of living things, according to Dr. Bronowski is that 'their actions are directed towards the future... we see the shadow and close our eyes, we hear a noise and our glands squirt adrenalin into our blood, so that the pulses quicken, the muscles tense, and the nerves alert... our actions are directed towards some obscurely foreseen future.' And Dr. Bronowski adds surprised that 'oddly enough, this has had least attention in the past'. Well, it seems that he needed not be surprised. In the Middle Ages, when man had little chance to influence his fate, it was God's will, predestination, that obscured man's view. Later, with the rise of the bourgeoisie when man, at least some men, discovered a world and a society in motion, it was the mechanism of the clockwork of causes and effects – of before and after, that attracted all attention. And only now, when man has learned to synthesize, to mimic the work of nature, and abandoned God's willed destiny for his own, have his eyes also begun to discern what has always been there to see. Alone that his cognition is still individualistic – his rationality restricted by the fetters of capitalistic adaptation of means to ends, and not societal or holistic.

---

41.   J. Bronowski, op.cit., p. 109.

Heisenberg in his later years emphasized the role played by the intuition of those trying to interpret phenomena in the forming of new scientific concepts, i.e. in the scientists' philosophical background. He was convinced that the success of quantum theory in explaining the optical spectra of atoms or the structure of molecules in chemistry, indicates a return to the belief that a *unifying* principle exists behind the observed phenomena. If he is right then this should indicate that society may well be at the threshold of an era in which the social view will once again replace the individualistic. Altogether Heisenberg thought that although the philosophical background seldom influences the scientists answers it usually determines his questions. In his own words: 'The results of scientific work can be quite different if you either try to find out the plan according to which nature is constructed, or you just want to observe, to describe and to predict the phenomena. The final understanding can depend on this decision'.[42]

Man recognizes that the present is not like the future, but he also knows that it is not entirely unlike it. He understands that the present provides a set of signals which hold a meaning for the future, and he hopes that he can interpret these signals in an ongoing process of correction as more and more signals reach him with the passage of time. But it is an activity which must involve the whole society not a single observer or actor – it is a process of collective adaptation to the future. This is a process not guided by expediency but by truth – even if *truth* in this context is circumscribed by the definition that it is *what man can act upon with confidence.*

In this sense then, *the search for truth* may be taken as a constant *social value.* If all conscious action is forward looking and implies choice, and choice depends on the degree of confidence one has in the expected outcome of one's chosen course of action, then, confidence remains the closest thing to (unobtainable) certainty, and thus the search for truth for what one can act upon with confidence, must be a need which is independent of place and time. It becomes

---

42.   Quoted from a lecture given by W. Heisenberg in Dubrownik in 1975 on the Philosophical Background of Modern Physics.

an eternal social value, it becomes something 'good' in itself.[43] We must destinguish between two tendencies in our search for an understanding of the world. One stressing the unity of nature and the other its diversity; one emphasizes the abstract thought which goes beyond the notions obtained by the senses, and the other the results of reality as they present themselves to our senses. Marx illustrated this difference in the social sphere by contrasting the abstract with the concrete relations in the realm of capitalist production. On a concrete level the relationship between a capitalist-employer and his employee may be excellent, they may be friends and belong to the same sports-club, but on the abstract level, the one which Marx calls the objective level, the relationship remains one of exploiter and exploited however they may feel about it. The concrete relationship reflects a transient and individual situation, the abstract collective affinity. The one is akin to atoms in a stream of gas that move each in its own direction, or to persons pursuing their individual aims in the current of history; the other is more similar to the stream which determines the direction and the limits within which each atom can move, or the degree of freedom an individual is allowed within the current of time. In the nineteenth century a Democritian approach had the upper hand in the Natural Sciences. It coincided with a fragmented social reality – each individual finding his place according to his competitive ability. Gradually, however, more and more social needs came to light which were not met by individuals' pursuit of their immediate interests. Step by step society was becoming increasingly aware that the welfare of all and each of its members required the provision of some services which were not automatically met by the mechanism which was supposedly harmonizing private 'vices' with the 'public good'. One by one provisions were made to correct the system where individualistic self-interest failed to give an answer. These 'corrections' ranged from education and health to state intervention in the economic sphere to promote growth, stability and equity. But only when they became so

---

43.   My biologist friend Ad v.d. Linde suggests another such 'eternal' value, namely, *the urge to maintain the species*. The concept of truth as a value is raised by Karl R. Popper in *The Logic of Scientific Discovery*, London, 1959, pp. 275–6.

numerous, so overwhelming, that they were penetrating almost all spheres of man's existence did man begin to question the underlying truth of his conception, did he ask himself whether it is really valid or even useful to assume that an invisible hand leads individuals' pursuit of their own interests to the attainment of the greatest possible good for most people. Only when the risks of atomic nuclear annihilation, and the dangers from air and water pollution became so pressing that social action could no longer be postponed began an increasing number of people consciously to search for other forward looking *social* mechanisms to take the place of the no longer tenable Smithian belief in the harmony of individualistic self-centered gravitation. It is also at this time that a new Platonism began to gain ground in the natural sciences replacing the neo-Democritian view which had ruled there since the days of Newton.

10

The Great Era of Prosperity

'Our remedies oft in ourselves do lie,
which we ascribe to heaven:'
All's Well That Ends Well. Act I Sc. i 235

The future differs from the present but is not totally unlike it. Neither the social or economic model-builder nor the social or economic *indicative planner* can avoid being influenced by their contemporaneous background. The *model-builder* formulates the image of an aspired future as if it was already present. He tests its internal material consistency, and the practicability of its attainment given the available resources. The *indicative planner* studies trends and symptoms in the past and present and synthesizes them in the process of his plan elaboration. The former is no less affected by the fears and preferences in his socio-economic cultural environment than the latter is guided by them in the selection of the trends and symptoms he considers *relevant* from among the innumerable signals from the past and present that reach him. The one states his present aspirations in terms of a body of economic and social policies expressed, if possible, in quantified targets and defined tasks, with a time schedule for their accomplishment usually attached to them. The other presents a cluster of trends taken from the past and present and extended into the future in such a way that they reflect certain deviations which may either be expected, for example a decline in the marginal propensity to consume with rising incomes, or are the hoped for results of deliberate policy orientated 'outside' intervention. At first sight the model-builder may seem more 'revolutionary' or utopist in his conception than the indicative planner, – he appears to say how he would wish the future to be as distinct from the indicative planner who merely claims to show how either with or without 'outside' intervention the future is likely to be, but this impression is not altogether true. The real character of the expected changes depends upon the content of the model towards which the model-builder intends to steer society, and on the selection of the trends which are considered relevant and the measure of 'outside' intervention allowed by the indicative planner. Both evaluate the future in terms of their present likes and dislikes but their methods of depicting the desired future vary. The one does it by means of something like a set of static 'future photographs' taken at regular intervals of time from the last picture showing the desired future going backwards to the first showing the present state of affairs, which enable him to check and correct the course of events from time to time in the light of the pre-selected aims. The other does it by means of something like a cinecamera concentrating upon the movements of what from time to time appear to him to be the most relevant trends. It follows that from a methodological point of view the first method is therefore more rigid than the second, it is more strongly bound to the expectations of the society in the year of the plan's initiation, while the second allows more freedom for adjustments to newly arising aims as some of the old ones come closer to achievement with the passage of time. What both methods tend to neglect is taking account of the complex and unquantifiable effects that socioeconomic changes have upon behavior and human motivation. They tend to take 'human nature' as they know it from contemporaneous experience – as given, without asking whether or not these 'given' characteristics, say, the love of gain and fear of starvation, are not but the specific product of a situation which will no longer be the same once their expected future is approaching reality. They study the material balances admirably but they neglect the *mechanisms* by which the people transform aims into material reality.

What then are the economic and social tendencies in the economically most advanced countries upon which the eyes of the economic planners and model-builders have been focusing in recent years?

Firstly the changing employment patterns. The dramatic decline of employment in agriculture, the diminishing labor requirements in industry, and the rise in service occupations.

Share of Primary, Secondary, and Tertiary Sector in the National Product of the United States.[1]

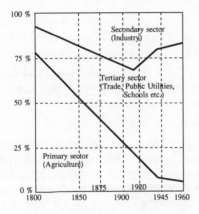

---

1.   *Source:* Jean Fourastié, *Die Grosse Hoffnung des zwanzigsten Jahrhunderts,* 2 Aufl. Köln 1969, quoted here from W. Dettling u.a., *Die Neue Soziale frage und die Zukunft der Demokratie,* München-Wien 2 Aufl. 1977, p. 66.

Share of the Labor Force Employed in the Primary, Secondary, and Tertiary sectors of the West German Economy.[2]

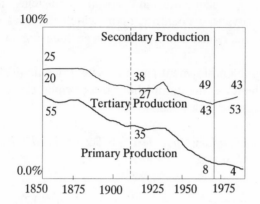

The share of employment in the Primary Sector declined throughout the whole period 1850 to 1975; the share of employment in the Secondary Sector increased on the whole until the Nineteen-sixties but then began falling (from 49% to 43%); and the share of the

---

2.   *Source:* Walther G. Hoffmann, 'Das Wachstum der deutschen Wirtschaft seit der Mitte des 19. Jahrhunderts', Berlin-Heidelber g-New York, 1965, and 'Quintessenzen aus Arbeitsmarkt- und Berufsforschung', Heft 1, hrsg. v, Institut für Arbeitsmarkt und Berufsforschung der Bundesanstalt für Arbeit, 1975. Quoted here from W. Dettling u.a., *op.cit.*, p. 66. *Vide* also OECD census for U.S., France, West Germany and U.K.

R.L. Heilbronner, *Business Civilization in Decline*, 1976, p. 65
Percentage Distribution of Employed Workers

Country	Year	Agriculture	Industry	Services
U.S.	1900	38	38	24
	1950	12	33	55
	1972	4	32	64
France	1950	35	45	20
	1970	17	39	44
W.Germany	1950	24	48	28
	1968	10	48	42
U.K.	1950	6	56	39
	1970	4	45	50

Services rose steadily from 20% in mid-nineteenth century, to 27% in early twentieth century, 43% in the 'sixties, and 53% and still rising in 1975.

In the United States rose the share of the services during the last three decades from 55% to 67% in terms of employment, and from 31% to 41 in terms of output.

Shift to services: The share of the goods-producing industries (agriculture, mining, manufacturing and construction) in total employment (left), and in output (right)[3]

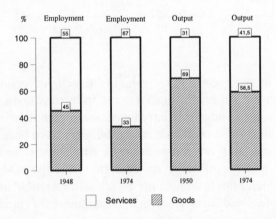

Secondly, the eyes of the planners and model-builders have been focusing on the rise of the public and non-profit making sectors of the economy. In 1929 the 'not-for-profit' sector of the American economy accounted for 15% of employment and 12.5% of output. Since then it increased slowly but steadily until the 1950's. In the 1950's it rose sharply, and it continued rising though at a much smaller rate than in the 1950's also throughout the 1960's. Early in the 1970's it declined a little, but began rising again since 1975.

---

3.   *Source*: Eli Ginzberg, 'The Pluralistic Economy of the U.S.' in *Scientific American*, December 1976, p. 28.

Growth of Government and other 'not-for-profit' sectors in the United States Economy.[4]

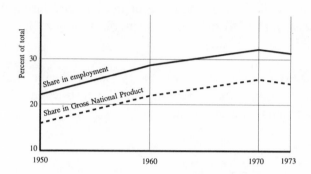

The trend in other economically highly developed countries was similar though the nationalization of some industries and sometimes denationalization of industries introduced some complications.

Thirdly, planners and economic model-builders have been studying the changing age and sex composition of employment seekers, and the changing patterns of work remuneration. On the whole young people spent increasingly more time at school or similar institutions and old people lived longer so that the number of producers of goods and services diminished in comparison with the number of their consumers. But at the same time there was also a fairly steady increase in the proportion of people included in the labor force in the total of the working-age population. Out of a total working-age population of 106.6 millions in the United States in 1950, 44.4 millions (41.5%) were not in the labor force. In 1976 out of 156 million working-age people, 62.2 million (39.8%) were not in the labor force. However, while the working-age population (16 years and over) increased by 47 percent, civilian employment increased by 48 percent, and unemployment from 3.3 million in 1950 to 7.3 million in 1976, i.e. by 122%. Most dramatic in this period was the

---

4.   *Source:* Eli Ginzberg, 'The Pluralistic Economy of the U.S.', *op.cit.*, p. 27.

influx of women into the labor force. In the 25 years separating the middle of the century from 1976, 20 million women entered the U.S. labor force (defined as people actively looking for work), and only 12.6 million men. In 1950 women made up just under 30% of the labor force, in 1976 41%. In summary then: the number of civilian jobs in the United States increased since 1950 by just under 50%. 'The rapid rate of job expansion unquestionably facilitated the increased participation of women in the labor force: one out of approximately three worked in 1950 and nearly one out of two worked in 1975. The rapid increase in jobs also helped to create opportunities for many, if not all, of the people in the larger pool of young entrants into the labor force, a pool that approximately doubled in the period after 1965. The number of job seekers who wanted (or settled for) less than full-time work increased three times as much as the number of those on a full-time schedule. Although adult women significantly increased their participation rates, mature men, beginning in their late forties, show striking declines.'[5] In Europe all these processes were less striking because of the great influx of mainly male workers from economically less developed regions. But here too the share of women in the labor force increased and was accompanied by a rise in the number of young people who remained longer at schools and by a decline of men over fifty years of age at work. The last was only partly the result of people's wish to stop working earlier in life, but more often due to the mounting difficulties men over 45 years of age found in getting new employment when for one reason or another they had to change jobs.

Studies of changing patterns of work remuneration have also yielded interesting results. One of these was the shift in the character and proportions of people employed in what may be termed 'good' and 'bad' jobs. The division is significant because, given the modern social security arrangements, many people tend to prefer to 'keep house, go to school, engage in illicit or illegal activities, or live off Social Security or some other form of income transfer,' rather than

---

5.   Eli Ginzberg, 'The Job Problem', *Scientific American*, November 1977, p. 47.

do unattractive work for little pay.[6] The characteristics which determine whether a job is good or bad are on the whole 'wages, fringe benefits, regularity (or intermittency) of employment, working conditions, job security and opportunities for promotion. Although certain jobs must be performed under poor working conditions, such as those on an automobile assembly line or in a foundry, they may pay above-average wages. More often than not, however, favorable elements go together. Accordingly we can differentiate between good jobs and poor jobs, with earnings as the most reliable indicator.'[7] Now, while in the last 25 years (this was written in 1978) the number of all jobs increased, the number of those with above average wages increased less sharply than the number of those with less than average pay. Significantly the high pay sector includes mining, construction and manufacturing, and also transport, utilities and wholesale trade, and the low pay sector services and retail trade where the low pay is often the result of a combination of wages and part-time work. In the United States 'between 1950 and 1976 about two and a half times as many new jobs (18.2 million v. 7.1 million) were added in industries that provide below-average weekly earnings as were added in industries that provide above-average earnings. More than three out of every five new jobs created in the past 26 years (to 1978) have been in retail trade or services, where many jobs are part-time and wages are traditionally low.'[8] The wage differences are very significant: they ranged in the United States from weekly earnings (1976) in retail trade $.114 and the services $.146 to between $.258 and $.284 in construction and mining. Altogether it seems that two labor markets developed in the last decades in the economically most advanced countries: One for 'good' jobs, taken up mainly by the male nationals of these countries (and the whites in the U.S.A.) and another for 'bad' jobs taken up to an increasing extent by women and foreign workers *Gastarbeiter* (and

---

6.   Eli Ginzberg, *ibid.*

7.   *Ibid.*, p. 47.

8.   *Ibid.*, p. 47.

blacks in the U.S.A.). *[The reader should bear in mind that all this was written before the end of the 1970s, i.e. before automatization eliminated a lot of routine jobs and created considerable unemployment in a great variety of sectors and caused important social changes. This points was discussed in the new introduction to this book, and in several others more recent books of mine.].*[9]

Another significant development which took place in the last 25 years was the relatively rapid expansion of government employment. In the U.S.A., at all levels, it accounted for more new jobs than any other industrial group except the services.[10] Twenty-five years ago (to 1978) earnings in government service had on the whole been average but tended to move into the 'good' jobs bracket in the course of time.

Now, Ginzberg[11] asks: How if most of the jobs that were added in the last quarter century were on the whole poor, how does one explain the near-absence of criticism and discontent among Americans who obtained those jobs? His answer is that most of the new jobholders were 'secondary' workers whose earnings supplemented the income of the family's principal bread-winner. For Europe it may be added that many of the 'bad' jobs also went to foreign workers who were both afraid to complain and found their 'bad wages' still well above those they were able to earn in their countries of origin. As for the future Ginzberg projects that the number of young people reaching working age will decline sharply because of the lower birth rates in recent years; that the number of women in the work-force will continue to grow; and that the increasing number of women, because of their heightened attachment

---

9.   *Vide* for the recent changes in the economy and society: *Capitalism, Competition and Economic Crisis*, Wheatsheaf Books & Kapitan Szabo Publishers, Washington, D.C., 1984; *The Rise and Fall of Capitalism*, Edward Elgar Publishing Limited, Aldershot and Vermont, 1991, and in Y.S. Brenner and N. Golomb-Brenner, *A Theory of Full Employment*, Kluwer Academic Publishers, Boston/Dordrecht/London, 1996.

10.   Eli Ginzberg, *ibid.,* p. 48.

11.   *Ibid.,* p. 49.

to the labor force, (greater share of divorced, separated and single women in total female population), will be seeking good jobs and a career, not just jobs.

Fourthly, I myself and other students of socio-economic trends have been analyzing the characteristic intensities of demand for labor in the various sectors of the economy and particularly the difference between labor requirements in the directly producing sectors and in the expanding service sectors of the economy. The main difficulty here is that the output of services is less easy to quantify than the output of agriculture and manufacture, and that many services are provided in a way that does not lend their 'output' to the normal measurement of cost accounting in a capitalist systrm. For example the ratio of pupils to teachers in state schools is determined by an administrative decision and not by the market forces of supply and demand. And indeed, some parents prefer, where this is allowed, to send their children at great cost to private schools. This alone shows that at least for part of the public certain services are offered well below their 'equilibrium' or 'natural' price, and there are many such services, (normally provided by public authorities,) for which people are ready to pay extra such as, for example, private health care. Moreover, because many of the services are provided by the public authorities out of taxes or similar 'anonymous' revenues the direct pecuniary link between consumer and supplier is distorted. Hence, neither the conduct of the person who provides the service nor that of the receiver is directly influenced by the regulating effect of the price mechanism. It is of little immediate consequence for the physician examining a patient whether the same has contributed much or little to his salary, – whether he has or has not made a large contribution to the health insurance scheme out of which the physician is paid. In theory this should of course have a progressive democratizing effect on the service but in reality it has often the opposite result. In a society brought up to judge individuals' status in terms of money, and in which the providers of certain services are chronically understaffed, it is hardly surprising that the quality of public services has a tendency to be low in terms of the time and effort its providers are willing and able to devote to their 'customers'. The fact that the receiver of a service has almost no means of directly influencing the provider's status and income, creates, to say the least, an unaccustomed situation in an otherwise cost-benefit-accounting culture. In addition, the fact that the person who pays for public services does not directly recognize the *value* he obtains for his money, or may even suspect that he receives too little value or no value at all, and that he is paying for services given to others, is often, even unconsciously, so abhorrent to people grown up in a capitalist environment, that only with the greatest reluctance they make their contributions to the authorities responsible for the services. In consequence, the authorities are continuously pressed to provide these services at low cost – at the expense of quality. This is the reason why teachers have to teach classes with 40 or 30 pupils instead of 20, or 15, or even less, which would be to the advantage of pupils and teachers alike. The difficulty of measuring the output of services, of welfare as distinct from wealth, thus leads to its measurement by the cost of its inputs; and in the shadow of the conception borrowed from the sphere of goods' production, increased efficiency is erroneously linked to cost reductions. So, because people are not used to pay out money without expecting a directly related return, and are not accustomed to social as distinct from individual cost-benefit accounting, and have not learned to value additions to collective welfare as they do with individual wealth, it is difficult indeed for the authorities in charge of the collective welfare services to raise the funds that they require. It is difficult to make people understand that there is a difference between the introduction of some new production technique which enables a worker to produce more units of output in a given time and the addition of some extra pupils to a class. The shift of employment away from the goods producing occupations towards more services is indeed posing a severe psychological problem for a society which in the course of the last centuries became accustomed to measure efficiency in terms of quantities of goods. And the psychological problem is even more confounded by the fact that this shift to services greatly involves the public sector in the midst of a still essentially individualist and competitive society.

There is something touchingly Physiocratic in people's attitude towards the services. The Physiocrats were unwilling to accept that any other type of labor than farming is productive. In their view people engaged in manufacturing merely convert one thing into another – they take wool and make cloth and in the process the wool is consumed, whereas the farmer who tends the sheep and sees to it that they multiply does actually *add* to the nation's physical stock of wealth. Since then, people have learned to regard work – the work invested in the transformation of wool to cloth, as a source of wealth. Having been for centuries desperately short of goods they accepted this view only where *this* production increased, and hold on to this view even now, when more goods than can be used in the rich countries are produced (mountains of butter and hills of gadgets). People find it difficult to accept that all work is productive including services. In fact all labor is a service, whether it is turning screws in a factory, turning switches in a television studio, driving a crane on a construction site or driving a taxi in a city – it all adds to the Gross National Product. As long as mankind was not yet technologically capable of providing for itself sufficient of the physical goods to satisfy its most fundamental wants it was only natural to consider farming and manufacturing the prime sources of welfare – for wealth and welfare seemed on the whole to go together. But now that in the industrially most advanced countries this is no longer the case – that wealth alone can no longer be regarded as the prime factor in man's welfare; that the production of wealth often implies a direct threat to welfare, through pollution for example, there remains little valid cause for the mental relegation of the services to second place in the list of the factors contributing to the richness (or welfare) of societies. It is therefore the mental legacy of an earlier materially much poorer age, and its competitive individualistic utilitarian social culture pattern, which are the cause of modern society's unwillingness to expand and remunerate services to meet its new needs in a measure commensurate with its materially productive capacity.[12]

---

12. This does not imply a desirability of expanding *all* services. It is quite reasonable to do with less but more efficient bureaucrats It is quite probable that, say, a better paid official would be encouraged to do the work of three poorly paid. The problem in this case remains the cultural (or psychological) willingness to carry responsibilities which are assessed differently from those in the market economy.

Now, one of the late causes of unemployment seems to be the sharp rise in the technological capacity to produce goods. Not unlike Thomas More, who claimed in the sixteenth century that sheep were devouring men, many people now put the blame on machines for the recent increase in the unemployment of labor. They claim that the present crisis is not one of too little money but of too many goods. There can be little doubt that labor-requirements in the goods producing sectors of the economy are falling-off.[13] But this is not the main issue, which can be best understood by comparing the changes during the transition from a basically agrarian into an industrial society. Then too the transfer of labor from one sector of the economy to another was accompanied by painful social dislocations and mental adjustments. The interdependence of the developments in the two sectors, agriculture and industry, was very complex for without some of the technological innovations made in industry agriculture could not have sufficiently advanced to make possible the transfer of labor to industry, and without innovation in agriculture industry could not have obtained the food and raw-materials that were necessary to sustain the growing number of industrial workers who were no longer able to provide their own. Moreover, the changes in outlook that accompanied the transformation of an economically self-sufficient and socially feudal or family-centered rural society into one which is orientated towards cash crop production and individualist urban existence are hardly much greater than the changes that must accompany the transformation of a primarily goods and wealth focused society into one in which the service sector is central and welfare-consciousness ought to replace individualism in *production*.[14]

Altogether then, the sharp rise in the efficiency of goods-production, which gives rise to the current fears of increasing structural unemployment, may well signify society's capacity to provide all its material requirements with less and less labor and

---

13. *Vide* p. 334–7.

14. *Vide* in the new introduction to this book for a more extensive explanation of this point.

therefore its increasing capability to provide more services without at the same time reducing the satisfaction of the customary material wants.[15]

For many years economists have accepted as a fact that man's requirements for food are limited – that people's stomachs set an upper limit to consumption. What they did not regard finite was man's other wants. In an economy which was still incapable to produce enough industrial goods to satisfy all its members' needs a confusion between an unlimited capacity to accumulate wealth and the propensity to obtain more and more industrial goods is well understandable. But with the technological efficiency approaching a point where, like in farming before, industry is producing with ever lesser labor more and more output which cannot find domestic markets, not merely due to a lack of disposable incomes but because people already possess the goods industry offers for sale, this confusion must be sorted out. If one was to make a list of all the manufactures a person can possess, and multiply them by the number of households or individuals who may wish to possess them in an industrial society, one must soon discover the limits of the potential demand for industrial products and the limits of their replacements' market. Given then the technological production coefficient, the capital-output ratio, it may, in spite of the inability to foresee all new inventions, not be too difficult to see how much labor is required to satisfy the demand for industrial products at its potential upper limit. It follows that each new advancement in laborsaving technological efficiency reduces the number of working places in

---

15.   This is of course something very different from *zero growth*. Firstly the expansion of services contribute to the growth of the G.N.P. in the same manner as industrial production, and even the most environment conscious can have no good reason for holding back the expansion of services. Secondly, until all members of industrial society will be able to satisfy their wants for goods at a level equal to that of the economically better situated there seems little chance for industrial production to stagnate permanently. Thirdly, there is no reason to believe that scientific and technological progress can be stopped (even the Church did not manage to do this in the Renaissance) or indeed ought to be. It may of course be directed towards safer and less environmentally harmful avenues. (This note was written in 1978 and the subject is reconsidered in the new introduction to this book).

productive industry – just as it happened before in modern agriculture, and lowers the *real* cost of goods in terms of services.[16] The desperate efforts of the industrial nations to prevent the loss of working places in the industrial sector by creating additional demand for its produce in the poorer countries with the help of foreign aid may well delay but cannot stop the process. In fact the manner in which foreign aid is currently being expended even by well intentioned governments and international organizations, tends to diminish the welfare of the majority of people in the rich countries in favor of only temporary advantages for a minority in the poor countries – to increase the wealth and welfare of a small minority of people in the poor countries at the cost of the majority. In the long-run it neither solves the rich nor the poor countries' real problems.[17]

As less and less people become necessary to satisfy our material needs, more and more people become free to supply us with services; only that services are on the whole far less suited than goods for the direct 'cash and carry' relationship to which we are accustomed. Their worth is less measurable than that of goods and their advantages are more often collectively enjoyed than individually, and some of them, for example the work of the housewife, have customarily been regarded as free of charge. These essentially psychological factors add significantly to the prevention of the labor released from industry being more smoothly absorbed in the services.

Now, all that was said earlier in connection with the low perspective of much further industrial expansion must not be understood to imply that all people's desires are bounded, nor should it be taken to imply that artificial needs, the so called 'false wants', do not exert an influence, or that new inventions cannot put new life into

---

16.   *Real* is here in italics to distinguish it from *nominal*.

17.   Further on this subject *vide* Y.S. Brenner and M.J. Weggelaar, 'The Rich, the Poor and the Ugly' in *Intermediair* 4, maart 1977 (Amsterdam). See also the discussion of the transfer of production to the less developed countries and the indifference of the new élite to the fate of the poor, in the new introduction to this book.

consumers' desires to obtain more goods. But all these 'false' or 'genuine' wants have to be seen in their right perspective. In this context desires are always concrete, – not vague aspirations for something unknown. In the familiar social context they are either for objects, status, affection or other things that give pleasure. The closer people approach the point at which they can obtain the material objects of desire they tend to wish for more and more immaterial things and for 'positional' advantages. They compete for social power or prestige and for the things that by their very nature cannot be had by everyone or cannot be produced for the 'masses'. In this sense then man's desires are really unlimited, but this has little bearing on the expansibility or inexpansibility of industrial demand at any particular time.

Fred Hirsch in his book on the *Social Limits to Growth* (Harvard 1977) well illustrates how the real advantages of wealth have become 'positional' advantages. The positional advantages, or the 'positional goods' as Hirsch calls them, are the advantages which arise mainly out of the circumstance that they can only be owned by a minority and wane when the majority can also obtain them. An example is the urge to raise one's income which continues unabated. 'If one's own income remains unchanged while the income of other people rises, one's command over the positional sector will fall. The income that earlier supported a downtown apartment, a country home, the acquisition of elite educational qualifications, or simply an active life protected from crowds, is no longer sufficient... It makes a difference if others earn more than you, even if you are interested exclusively in your own consumption possibilities... The flaw in the affluent society lies not in the false values of affluence but in its false promise.'[18] But then, even if on the whole man's desires are insatiable his desires for industrial goods are *not,* and the shift in the balance of employment away from industry and towards the services is likely to continue. The creation of false wants for industrial products can only have a marginal influence on this process. Precisely the same reasons that make 'positional goods' desirable are of course the reasons that give to 'new' goods their temporary

---

18.   F. Hirsch, *Social Limits of Growth*, Harvard U.P., 1977.

attraction. The same forces that reduce labor requirements in industry as a whole apply also here. As the 'false wants' do not actually *add* new wants but merely substitute new products to satisfy old wants differently, false wants only reduce the life-span of old goods. For example, instead of using a black and white television set for the full 'natural' length of its life, say, for five years, it is replaced by a color set after three years. This constitutes a 40% increase in consumers' demand, which, together with the necessary labor for retooling in the factory, may therefore provide 50% more working places in the industrial sector. Taking into account the rate at which labor efficiency has been improving in this sector throughout the last decades, this means no more than a delay of two decades in the industrial redundancy.

Demand for labor with and without 'false wants' in a hypothetical industry without real growth perspectives.

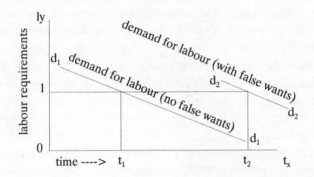

The demand curves d_1 and d_2 are downward sloping from left to right because of the assumed technological labor-saving improvements. After the year t_1 increasingly more labor becomes redundant in this industry, but the creation of 'new' wants which raises labor requirements to curve d_2 postpones this redundancy beyond the year t_2.

The same rule applies also to improvements in the society's distribution of income. As long as there are people in the society whose demand for industrial goods is not yet satisfied at the saturation level the demand for labor described by curve d_1 may tend to shift upward, like in the case of 'false wants' – these people become potential consumers. For each significant improvement in the distribution of income in favor of the classes of people who until this time were unable to satisfy their demand for industrial goods a new curve describing the demand for labor must be drawn up to the right and above the curve d_1. This is also true for the expansion of exports. Trade among rich countries has its obvious limits, and trade with economically backward countries is initially restricted by the paucity of their *effective demand* – by their poverty, and later, when they develop, by the output of their own industries; for, after all, what else is development than the growth of productive capacity? So, again, 'false wants', exports, and Foreign Aid, can delay unemployment in the goods producing industries, but they cannot prevent it altogether.

With services things are different. There is still ample room for service expansion, above all, as Daniel Bell has shown, in research, health and education.[19] *The expansibility of services has to do with their specific character: The direct contact between their 'producers' and 'consumers', the impossibility of storing their 'produce', their unsuitability for transportation and transference, their lack of homogeneity, their high income elasticity of demand, and their inaptness to be rationalized and mechanized.* Taking the direct contact between 'producers' and 'consumers' – the *'Kundenpräsenz'* or the *'Uno actu'* principle, as some German authors call it, it is easy to see how the demand for services can be, and actually is, expanding in 'post-industrial' societies as they become richer. Doctors and patients, teachers and pupils, waiters and diners, cannot be separated in the performance of their respective services. This gives the services a special time-dimension which influences their quality. This time – dimension describes a positive relationship – the longer the time allowed for the performance of the service the better on the whole becomes its quality. The longer a doctor can spend (within reason) with his patient, and the longer a teacher can spend with each individual pupil, the better becomes the service he renders.

---

19.   Daniel Bell, *The Coming of Post Industrial Society*, New York, 1973.

Presently many doctors, especially in the employ of National Health Services, can devote on average no more, and often less, than seven minutes to each patient. This time-pressure, which is the result of too many help-seekers wanting the services of too few doctors, is partly due to the restrictive practices in the medical profession and to the long study period required to become a doctor. But the main cause, which also makes the restrictive practices possible or at least easier rather than necessary, is the state's inability, mainly for financial reasons, to provide more study places and money allowances for medical students. If all prospective students of medicine would be supplied with allowances and study places the doctor/patient ratio would change significantly, and doctors would be able to examine their patients more thoroughly. Health care – welfare, would improve. The same applies to the education services. If governments were in a position to employ more teachers and pay them adequately, the size of school classes could be reduced and teachers would be better able to concern themselves with individual students. Educational standards and the welfare of pupils would be improved. It is no secret that even now many parents who can afford it send their children to costly private schools not only because of snobbery and the wish to give them certain social and educational advantages but also because they think that they will receive there more personal attention from the teachers and 'feel happier'. Moreover, rich people tend, in spite of higher prices, to frequent shops and restaurants where they are served by better trained, politer, staff, which is allowed more time to serve customers, and to avoid establishments were attendants are poorly trained and overworked. It may therefore be said that the expansion of services depends on the height of people's incomes and the character of service remuneration. If the remuneration of services was subject to the same market-mechanisms as the supply of goods there would be little to hinder their expansion as the incomes of all members of society rise; but as many of the most important services are traditionally paid for by public author- ities react more slowly to the laws of demand and supply. In a world of *perfect competition* the solution would have been automatic, but as by definition *perfect competition* is un-obtainable the progress towards the solution can only advance in pace with the transformation of society's direct short-sighted individualist logic into indirect long-term social rationality.[20]

People were for thousands of years gathering fruit and hunting animals for their sustenance. When they became too numerous to do so comfortably they gradually learned the more reliable and efficient way to provide for themselves by farming. They learned that by the indirect effort of sowing and planting the land and rearing certain animals they can gain more food than by the direct efforts. To more primitive man this must have seemed irrational – why put something that can be consumed into the ground and feed animals rather than eat them? Later again people discovered that by devoting more time and effort to the production of tools and instruments which themselves also have no use i.e. cannot be eaten or yield any other kind of direct pleasure, they can in the long-run gain more of the things they desire than by devoting all their time to the direct pursuit of the things they want. Eventually, people even came to understand that by a division of labor, – by a collective effort of many individuals of whom each is engaged in work which even indirectly has no separate meaning whatsoever (like making a machine-part without ever seeing the complete machine let alone the final object of demand) they may actually increase the volume of goods they wish to enjoy thousandfold. Now, having learned all this, it seems not beyond reason to believe that people will also gradually come to recognize that their individual wants for things other than tangible goods, i.e. for services, can often be better satisfied by indirect and collective efforts through greater financial contributions to *public* authorities, than by the traditional, direct way to which they are accustomed. That such a wondrous conversion may well be happening can be concluded from the manner in which public revenues are spent in recent years and how since the days of Keynes

---

20. For the hypothetical character of the concept of *perfect competition* and its lack of realism or its unattainability *vide* Y.S. Brenner, *Introduction to Economics*, p. 146, and see also in the new introduction to this book a comment on the unfortunate current reaction to this tendency.

they have become a major instrument for regulating entire economic systems.[21]

Fifthly, economists concerned with social tendencies in the more developed countries point out the price-inflation and the re-emergence of widespread unemployment of labor which attend all the earlier mentioned processes in recent years. In seven industrial countries taken together the rate of change of consumer prices compounded annually from calendar year 1955 to 1960; 1960 to 1965; 1965 to 1970; and 1970 to 1975 was as follows:

1956–1960 2.8
1961–1965 3.7
1966–1970 4.1
1971–1975 9.3 [22]

The seven countries concerned were France, Germany, Italy, Japan, Sweden, The United Kingdom, and the United States. In the Netherlands the price index for household consumption (base 1938/9 = 100) rose from 218 in 1955 to 319 in 1960; 389 in 1965; 499 in 1970; to well above 700 in 1975. The purchasing power of the Guilder fell in comparison to 1899 as follows:

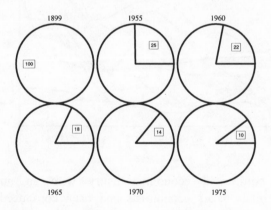

---

21. *Vide* Y.S. Brenner, *Introduction to Economics,* pp. 115–58.

22. *Source:* Milton Friedman. Nobel Lecture: 'Inflation and Unemployment.' Quoted here from *Journal of Political Economy,* 1977, Vol. 85, No. 3, p. 461.

In Britain where on the whole unemployment rates were the highest among the industrial nations in Europe, 281.000 registered unemployed in 1966 and 1.332.000 unemployed in 1976. Average weekly earnings rose from £.20.78 to £.65.10 in the same period; and retail prices rose from 168.8 points to 436.8 in comparison with the index base 100 in 1951. In other words, prices rose two-and-a-half-fold, and wages more than threefold in spite of the mounting unemployment. This relationship between prices, wages, and unemployment is more or less true for all industrial countries.

Unemployment in the 'sixties increased from below 3 per cent of the labor force in most industrial countries, (with the exception of the U.S.A. and Canada where it was below 5 per cent) to well above 4 per cent in the 'seventies in all countries (with the exception of Japan and Sweden where it remained about 2 per cent).

Comparison of unemployment rates in nine industrial countries[23]

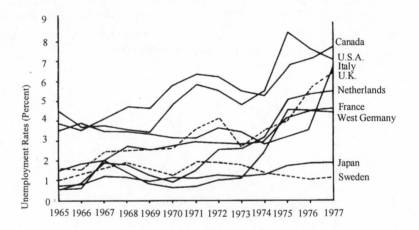

Now, this confronted economic theory with an unexpected problem. For many years economists had been convinced that an

---

23.   *Source:* Eli Ginzberg, *op.cit.*, 1977, p. 46. Note must be taken that the data are not strictly comparable because countries count their unemployment data in different ways.

inverse relationship between annual price changes and the employment rate can be taken for granted. That in what is called the 'full employment economies' unemployment declines when wages and prices tend to rise and that unemployment rises when wage and price increases tend to diminish. Professor A.W. Phillips showed by empirical evidence that this was really what happened in the 1950s and 1960s.[24] It also seemed logical to assume that when employers vie with each other for the services of workers, i.e. when business prospers, wages will tend to rise, and when little work is available the unemployed will be content to work for what wages they are offered and the employed will recognize that they are not in a good bargaining position for higher pay. However, looking at recent evidence,(in 1978) for example at the earlier cited statistics, this view can no longer be uncritically accepted. A number of explanations come to mind for this apparent anomaly of simultaneously rising prices, wages, and unemployment rates. 1) In prolonged periods of inflation workers may take anticipated price developments into account in wage-negotiations and insist on wage increases which employers will for the very same reasons not powerfully resist. 2) The influx of more women, part-time employees, and young people who tend to shift more frequently between jobs than mature male workers. 3) The reduced pressure to seek work immediately and accept almost any work when unemployed because of the very much improved unemployment provisions. 4) The increasing specialization which adds to the rigidity of the labor market by reducing occupational mobility (though in fact unemployment tends to be lowest among the highly skilled). 5) The pension and social security legislation which make employees over the age of 45 years increasingly more expensive for employers than young workers and therefore less employable. 6) The expansion of government expenditure. As government expenditure is not strictly determined by

---

24.   In *Economica* (1958) Professor Phillips set out the empirical evidence for the significant relationship between the percentage change of money wages and the level of employment, and draws the conclusion that a low rate of inflation may not be consistent with low unemployment. From his data it appeared as if a 3% unemployment rate is consistent with 0% inflation, and a 1.5% unemployment rate with 8% inflation.

purely economic considerations and by normal cost-benefit accounting maximization criteria, it may well tend to introduce disequilibria into the Free Market System by raising demand for goods and services in excess of the value produced by its employment of labor. 7) The mounting power of labor-unions to claim wage improvements for their members which are then passed on as higher prices to consumers in all sectors of the economy. This in turn, affects the discrepancy between earnings of well organized labor, mainly in the goods producing sector, and of less powerfully organized labor in occupations in which wage increases cannot readily be passed on to consumers, which are mainly in the service sector. In other words the rising incomes of people in 'good jobs' compensates for the loss of purchasing power of people who are unemployed but who receive transfer payments – social or unemployment assistance which is not much below 'bad jobs' wage rates.[25] 8) The unexpected coincidence of high wages and unemployment of labor may be the existence of large multinational enterprises which, because of their enormous financial reserves, enjoy a great measure of independence from governments' monetary and fiscal means of control, and which can often monopolize key sectors of the economy as long as demand is maintained on a satisfactory level by export subsidies (Foreign Aid etc.) and transfer payments to pensioners and unemployed. 9) Sudden increases in the price of imported raw-materials, as were experienced in the 'Oil Crisis', may also contribute to inflation without reducing unemployment. Finally high taxes on profits and the possibility of earning without taking entrepreneurial risks – profits of eight or nine per cent interest from 'paper investments', may also maintain profits without creating employment opportunities. [Today, in 1997, one may of course also add the rapid progress of automatization which is not always attended by a reduction of prices equal to the reduced expenditure on labour][26]

---

25. For definition of *good* and *bad* jobs *vide* p. 339.

26. I have discussed this point at length in Y.S. Brenner and N. Brenner-Golomb, *A Theory of Full Employment*, Kluwer Academic Publishers, Boston/ Dordrecht/London, 1996.

Now, any combination of these explanations may well answer the question how it is possible for inflation and unemployment to move for a number of years in the same direction. But the question which has to be answered is whether this phenomenon reflects a true change in the socio-economic reality, or is no more than the result of coincidental concatenations of several independent events; – whether the old theoretical premises of economics are still valid or ought to be abandoned. Milton Friedman is apparently of the opinion that this situation cannot last. 'It will either degenerate into hyperinflation and radical change, or institutions will adjust to a situation of chronic inflation, or governments will adopt policies that will produce a low rate of inflation and less government intervention into the fixing of prices.'[27] The 'villains' in his piece are Keynes, who, in his view, confused a special case, which happened to have lasted for several decades, with the true character of economic relations, and those who, misled by Keynes' confusion, prescribe more rather than less state intervention to regulate employment and prices and must now seek their answer for the causes of stagflation in the coincidental concatenation of events 'outside' the economic system. Professor Friedman's conclusion that the combination of unemployment and inflation cannot last is of course correct; but his inability to free himself from the nineteenth century myth of natural harmony etc., and to see the socio-political impossibility (and un-desirability) of a return to nineteenth century 'Free Enterprise', is a sad reflection on how far 'positive economic science' is removed from reality. Everyone of the great streams of economic thought reflected a different economic and social reality. Classical economics was concerned with wealth and reflected mankind's inveterate subjugation to forces which were still far beyond its control. Adam Smith wrote an inquiry into the true nature and causes of wealth of nations, – an inquiry into the *wealth*, not the *welfare*, of *nations*, not of *individuals*. Malthus, Ricardo and Mill did not put the blame for the deplorable plight of the poor upon the inadequacy of human arrangements, but upon the laws ordained by God or nature. Neoclassical economics was concerned with *utility* and its

---

27.   Milton Friedman, *op.cit.*, p. 470.

maximization, and reflected the technological progress that enabled late nineteenth and early twentieth century society to produce much more than its predecessors but not yet enough to meet everyone's expectations. It reflected a society beset by *scarcity,* by scarcity that made its members vie one with another for their share of that which could be divided by scarcity which became poignant once man began to recognize that it can be overcome. In fact no new realization has abandoned old conceptions nor did neoclassicism abandon the belief in nature's harmony, – in an invisible regulating hand. Those in power felt better served by economists who held on to theories of dynamic equilibrium than by new analyses of reality. For dynamic equilibrium precisely reflected the chance of everybody to find his place within the social system on the basis of competitive ability, – it reflected the fact that some people's wants could, and others could not, be well satisfied at the current level of technology, and it provided a mechanism by which the former were separated from the latter. Keynesian economics reflected another reality. Keynes recognized mankind's newly gained and growing technological capability to satisfy its basic wants, and understood the forces that democracy has unleashed. Neoclassical economics was the product of the era of individualism, – of a belief in personal advancement on the basis of competitive ability which affected one class – a minority. Its orientation was micro-economic, suitable for solving the maximization problems of the firm. It was ill equipped to meet the challenges of collective problems of the State, of mass unemployment. Conventional *classical economic thought* was theoretically in a much better position to tackle such problems, but not practically. In both classical and neoclassical economics profits play a central role, and therefore, the *controllers* of investable funds. With the exception of State intervention profit is regarded as the major independent 'variable' in the economic system. Most people's expenditure is determined by their incomes and by force of habit, they alone can determine if and when they wish to spend, i.e. to invest. The factor that influences their decisions is profit. When profit rises they invest and when it falls below their expectations they do not. In the first case they set in motion a cumulative 'multiplier' process generating ever more employment and incomes as it spreads throughout the system, and in the second case unemployment persists, production stagnates and incomes fall. So profit is the heart of the matter.

But what is profit? It is the difference between the cost of a good or service and the revenue obtained from its sale. It follows that profit can be realized in either one of two ways: when demand is brisk and prices rise above costs, or when demand is slack and costs are lowered. It follows that when unemployment is high, and hence demand is slack, the way out is to reduce costs. If lower interest rates do not do the 'trick' then all that can be done is to allow unemployment of labor to increase till wages fall to their 'natural level' i.e. to the point where the difference between costs and revenues can satisfy investors. By that time the old stocks of goods will also be depleted and the sequence of employment, incomes, demand, and more investment will be on its cumulative upward trend again. All this wass very sound at the beginning of the nineteenth century, but is irrelevant to day. For people who have come to realize, or are increasingly coming to realize, that all their misery is not the work of God or the result of nature's retentiveness but the result of mismanagement of human institutions, for they can see that food and other things are being destroyed while they have none, will not sit idly starving until in its good time things will improve.

The dawning upon people of the recognition that not God's imperfect world, but mankind's imperfect social arrangements were the cause of their deprivation, led many of them to seek for new solutions. Instead of leaving their fate to be determined by the mysterious equilibrating forces appealed to by liberal democratic capitalism, many people sought for the guiding hand of man. Some found this guidance in the personality of leaders, and others in the application of scientific socialism. The former became fascists the latter revolutionary socialists or communists. It is in the light of these developments, and against the background of the rising power of the working class to brush away the old system at the ballot-box,[28] that the success of Keynesian economics must be seen. It represented the only possible compromise between liberal

---

28. As said before the socialists' political influence went far beyond their strength in numbers.

capitalism and its alternatives. It introduced just enough state direction into the 'self-adjusting' system to satisfy the wish for conscious human intervention without causing the whole system to falter. Essentially Keynes' ideas were not so far removed from conventional economic thought. He too believed that profit was the key to the problem. But unlike other economists he was convinced that the lock to which this key fitted could be unlocked from both sides of the door, i.e. that effective demand – money in the pockets of workers, can no less 'accelerate' investment than low labor costs and interest rates. Conventional economists allocated to the 'captains of industry' the position of an almost independent variable in the system, and made them into the 'lords' of the economy, who ought best be humored by low labor-costs and interest-rates to 'save' the nation. Keynes deprived them of this independent position and tore them off their pedestal. Given the technological production coefficient – the ratio of the real capital required to produce a desired volume of output, Keynes maintained, that industrialists tend to adjust their capital equipment to changes in the demand for their final products. When demand exceeds the volume of goods which can be produced with the existing capital, industrialists will invest and when it does not they will refrain from investing. Further increases in the supply of money will then be added to idle balances, and wage cuts or not; the economy would 'stick' at this point with chronic unemployment. Hence the masters of industry need not be humored by the working-people, for the 'equilibrating mechanism' of the system is not the rate of interest but the level of employment. The practical policy which flowed from this perception of the economic system was that deliberate human intervention was not only desirable but necessary to maintain the economic mechanism's mechanism working. Rather than allowing unemployment to persist until wages reach their 'natural' (low) level, and interest rates follow their 'natural' tendencies, the government should directly invest in construction, public utilities etc. in order to create employment and demand, and banks should be made to influence the interest rates in the desired manner because without this the system will not return to its former equilibrium position but change.

Whether Keynes's general theory of employment was correct or relied too much on special cases, such as wage rigidity, insensitivity of investment to the rate of interest, etc., it has been presented as an intermediate position between the traditional economic *laissez faire* with the hegemony of the bourgeoisie which went together with it and the new tendencies towards centrally directed economic systems with one or the other type of dictatorships that accompanied them. It presented a sufficiently wide and realistic alternative to permit both the survival of the capitalist economic and social system and uphold the newly gained self-consciousness of mankind and the dignity of labor. In short, it reflected the new economic, social and political reality. That these ideas upset conventional economists and politicians of the establishment is hardly surprising. They deprived them of two of their most cherished beliefs: The low-wages ideology and the universal remedial powers of low interest rates. More than that, as already pointed out, they undermined the very foundations of establishment morality – of all that was held right and proper. What Keynes proposed was to put money into workers' pockets by allowing governments to initiate public works, i.e. to provide employment with tax-payers' money from the Treasury during a time of depression when revenues were low. He wanted to prevent wages from falling to their 'natural' level, and worse, he expected the Exchequer to pay for this purpose not only out of current surpluses and reserves but also from future incomes. In other words, he wanted to increase spending out of 'borrowed' money, a sheer aberration of all that was held prime virtue in bourgeois society such as thrift and good husbandry. No wonder therefore, that Keynes's ideas appeared to many both sinful and foolish. Sinful, because implicitly they approved of spendthrifts and debunked the reasonable, parsimonious and provident. Foolish, because instead of reducing the forces which distort the natural order of things, they tended to strengthen them. Rather than recommending the elimination of labor's resistance to wage reductions, Keynes wished to impose upon governments the duty of sustaining full employment. Rather than restricting the role of the State in economic matters to that of the guardian of the price-mechanism against distortions, he proposed the extension of continuous and massive government interference in the economy, and all this not for compassionate reasons, for providing incomes for the poor, (reasons which would not have been too alien for bourgeois society to accept), but for what he claimed sound economic reasons, also in the interest of the rich.

With elections approaching in the United States both major parties contesting for the presidency were of course pressed to provide programmes which could at least give the impression that they could give an answer to some of the most immediate problems of the majority of voters. Even for the purpose of vote-catching alone it was therefore necessary in the 1930's to approach the problem of unemployment not from a detached theoretical long-term aspect but from a practical, committed and immediate point of view. It would hardly have been good electioneering to say to the majority of the American people, who were at that time experiencing all the evils attending unemployment, wage-cuts, and falling living standards, that they should vote for a President who intends to let wages fall even further and unemployment increase until sometime, who knows when, an inherent regulative mechanism of the economic system would restore prosperity. In other words, it was never the absolute certainty that Keynes's theory was correct, and that the evidence that seemed to support it presented more than a special case (as Professor Friedman claims), but the cultural framework, the changes in the social and political reality, which was its source of strength. The democratization of political life simply shifted the center of gravity in economic thought from its preoccupation with optimalization problems and micro-economics, to the solution of human problems such as mass unemployment and to macroeconomics. Slowly, under the pressure of democratic institutions, and of the masses growing consciousness of their political power, economics was becoming a social science in the service of the majority of the people. From a discipline concerned with wealth, which often gave the impression that people were on this earth to serve the economy rather than the economy to serve the people, it became a tool for regulating the economic system in the service of people's welfare. It is therefore hardly relevant whether Professor Friedman is right or not, and he may very well be right, when he claims that less state intervention can prevent stagflation, for a return to *laissez faire* has become politically untenable and socially undesirable. The curtailment of labor-unions' power, the reduction of social security arrangements, and the diminution of state intervention to maintain employment at a high level, just do not fit the *Zeitgeist*[29] which reflects and influences social reality.

For centuries man's fate had been dominated by nature. Gradually he learned to understand some of its regularities and turn this knowledge to his own advantage. As described earlier in the example of steel production. eventually he also learned to synthesize – to reproduce nature in precisely the way he wanted. In other words, first man chanced upon certain materials he needed. Then, he learned how to extract them from the ores in which they were embedded. And finally he found ways to produce them synthetically in a quality that often served his purposes even better than their natural precursors. Something like this also happened in man's relation to the economic system. Keynes's ideas fitted well the second stage of such a development. For Keynes accepted the system as it was but interfered with its working to serve the social purpose. The next stage may be that man will structure the economic system to suit his needs, – the satisfaction of real wants, not profits, will become its moving force, and planning will take the place of the profit-loss accounting incentives. Whether from our ethical point of view this development will be *good* – will augment people's freedom of choice, or *bad* – will reduce humanity to a new state of slavery, remains to be seen, but the alternative can not be *laissez faire* or a reversal to pre-industrial conditions.

What brought planning and state control into disrepute, and also highlighted many of their negative effects, was the way they were employed by the communists in Russia. The fact that state planning in Russia must be seen against the background of an economically backward society with a long tradition of despotism, and not against the background of an economically advanced society with a

---

29. I avoid the term *paradigm* for recent writers, following Kuhn, have used the term in a manner that gives the erroneous impression that it is more than only descriptive. In fact, however, it provides no more than a moment's 'photograph' which can be compared with an earlier 'photograph' but tells little about the processes which transformed one into the other. In other words, the term is descriptive and has recently been too often passed off as if it were dynamically explanatory. The proces of transformation by which one paradigm is turned into another has remained a mystery.

democratic liberal tradition, is too often lost out of sight. So is the fact that planning in Russia was a device for the acceleration of economic growth, while in the industrialized western countries it would become,and in some countries already is, an instrument for the maintenance of economic stability and equity. Contrary to Marx's expectations the first successful communist revolution took place in a quasi-feudal and economically retarded country without an industry. In addition to this, the revolution was followed by an armed intervention staged by some capitalist countries. This left behind a legacy which was to influence events in Russia for many years to come.[30] To raise living standards and to be able to repel another attack from the capitalist world made the Soviet government to regard rapid industrialization its first and foremost priority. Now, there is ample evidence from the industrialization of the capitalist countries for the high price in human terms that industrialization costs in the initial stages. It requires an enormous concentration of capital, the transfer of labor from the countryside to cities, and the termination of traditional institutions. In the west it led, at least temporarily, to sinking living standards, greater insecurity of livelihood, and recurring periods of mass unemployment. With the exception of unemployment, these ills, – the natural by-products of transition, were also unavoidable in the Soviet Union. In the west industrialization had progressed gradually, in Russia 'in a race against time', and this acceleration left its mark on the emergent sociopolitical structure. In the western countries the hardships which accompanied industrialization gave rise to labor's opposition – to the evolution of the trade union movement and socialist parties. The same causes of discontent that had given birth to labor's opposition in the west were also present in the Soviet Union. And this is the main reason for the heavy-handed suppression of all real or apparent opposition in Russia. The fear that such opposition may lead to more of the national product to be spent on current consumption, and therefore to a diminution of the rate at which the Soviet Union can

---

30.   Although some historians doubt the real extent of this threat, and ascribe its exaggeration to the Bolshevik's strategy for maintaining power, this is irrelevant.

industrialize, was a major factor in the establishment of that particularly unattractive system, associated with the name of Stalin, which gave such a bad name to planning.[31]

Most important for the understanding of the horrors that accompanied central planning in Russia was that it was historically 'premature'. In the west the growth of industry and of an industrial working class progressed gradually and preceded the development of labor's class consciousness. In the Soviet Union the process was reversed. Industrialization had still to be achieved by a working class which was already becoming class conscious and had just emerged victoriously from a revolution: a working class which now, after the old regime had been toppled, was expecting to reap the fruits of its victory. Returning from the battlefields each and every worker must have had his small private hopes and dreams about the future to be fulfilled now that things were going to be different in Russia. Yet what was the reality? The country's economy was in a state of utter chaos. The government was neither able to follow the traditional line of financing the country's industrial progress out of the sale of agricultural surplus to the capitalist countries. To finance the development of industry from export earnings would have made its growth dependent upon the 'good will' of the hostile camp of capitalists who could engage in fixing prices or refuse to sell to Russia the most necessary goods for the aspired industrialization. The required policy was that as much as possible of the national product should be diverted to the production of capital goods, but this implied that as little as possible was spared for the direct satisfaction of consumers' wants. To slow down the rate of industrialization and

---

31. A point to remember is that the great European socialist movement had been unable to prevent World War I. Only the Bolsheviks and a small number of socialists in the west really opposed the war efforts. The majority of the social democratic movements supported the war once it had begun. In Russia Lenin made great efforts to secure an alliance with other workers' parties but was unsuccessful. Consequently the Russian Revolution did not acquire some of the best humanist traditions of the western and of the non-Bolshevik Russian labor movements. Worse than that, even the old Bolshevik leadership, before Stalin became the undisputed tyrant, developed a suspicion towards all other working-class movements, and this again helped Stalin to suppress all independent, even left-wing, thought in Russia.

permit a gradual and staged transfer of labor and resources from agriculture to the industrial sector was, or seemed to be, out of the question, because, the government felt that unless it was able to industrialize the country very rapidly, it would soon have to succumb to internal or external pressures. For these reasons the government could do little else but tell the workers to wait and in the meantime tighten their belts even further, and then stress and overstress the pace of industrialization in the hope that through the accelerated rate of capital production it would soon reduce the cost of consumer goods and raise the real income of the population. Now such a policy would be difficult to implement at the best of times even in a well educated society, let alone in a time when armed and not well educated men were returning from a war and after a victorious revolution which had raised their hopes and expectations for a prosperous future. So the innocent and just demands of the revolutionary workers, which in the west played such an important role in the advancement of industrialization, underwent a metamorphosis in the Soviet Union and became a damaging factor in the process of development. Particularly the richer peasants, who had been relatively well off in pre-revolutionary Russia, were unwilling to reduce their living standards after the years of war and deprivation. In the hands of Stalin this lack of enthusiasm to take part in the building of the future at the expense of the present was transformed into treason. To accelerate the rate of industrial growth Stalin tried to extract from the agricultural sector as much as possible. When ideology failed he used force. As events were to show this was not a well conceived idea: farmers hid as much as possible their productive capacity and turned against the new regime. The tremendous planning apparatus had to be supplemented by another to suppress possible outbreaks of discontent and to spy after hidden resources. Together with the bad traditions inherited from the pre-Revolutionary bureaucracy, this soon gave rise to the development of officialdom into a class by itself; a class which was content to carry out orders and instructions from above, without worrying about the nature of those orders and their content in exchange for personal privileges. At the same time this class was also suppressing all criticism of those instructions from below, killing as it were all germs of independent reasoning. In time, Stalin alone remained capable of thought and decision making. The party, supposedly the ideological vanguard, merged with the whole body of State bureaucracy, to become merely an apparatus for carrying out instructions. All criticism became tantamount to attacks on the party and its leadership. The natural by-product of this state of affairs was the well-known 'cult of the personality'. As independent thought was taken to be heresy, only those with no imagination could serve their party well, i.e. a rule of mediocrity emerged.

There was more at stake. Socialism set out to replace Christian charity by the rule of rights and responsibilities, by the idea that every human being is *entitled* to a share of material and spiritual well-being and that every member of society is individually responsible to all fellow men – 'for each according to his needs and from each according to his ability'. Yet again, what peculiar twist did these ideas receive under the Stalinist tutelage! While Soviet education was successful in discrediting Christianity as a hypocritical manifestation of pity, it did not succeed in raising responsibility and human dignity to the required moral plateau to take their place. Both justice and responsibility were denuded of their moral values and transformed into a system of technology. The rights of the individual were reduced to barely the right to work and eat. The idea of social responsibility was transformed into a mere scheme of figures of output and production. Even where this stimulated economic growth they certainly did not produce a new type of socialist morality. Thus, ill equipped to withstand the perversion of socialist morality and dominated by the mediocrity of officialdom Russian literature and philosophy were also brought to stagnation. After having flourished by the end of the nineteenth century and in the early days following the revolution, Russian and socialist literature and political thought were reduced to mere propaganda. In an ill-fated attempt to use it as an educational instrument, literature became primarily concerned with the description of society as it should be according to the imposed ideology rather than as it is. The heroes became all-round ideal stereotypes and the villains all-round vicious enemies of the people and the party. No room was left for development of character and circumstantial influences. Literature became therefore increasingly estranged from life, and in the main (there were exceptions) hardly worthy to be called literature at all. In this form it could hardly play a valid role in the education of people towards socialism. Not dissimilar was the fate of communist philosophy. All that remained of it in Stalin's time were scholastic exercises, quoting and explaining Marx without taking any notice of the changing reality since his days. History, too, was made to share the fate of literature and philosophy. Regardless of the fact that all Marxist and socialist analyses were supposed to be founded on detached historical studies, the party wilfully distorted historical facts to serve imaginary objectives. By all this it not only brought the development of socialism to stagnation but did harm to progressive thought far beyond the boundaries of the Soviet Union. As Russia was the first socialist country both friends and foes judged the merits and demerits of socialism, state intervention, and economic planning by the image the Soviet Union presented to them. The fact that what had happened in Russia may well be regarded as a special and not the general case is but too often forgotten.[32]

In fact Soviet Russia was neither socialist nor was its economy scientifically planned. Marx had foreseen the socialist revolution in a highly industrialized society. As a result, the theoretical problems of Marxist communism were mainly concerned with the distribution and not with the creation of wealth. The development of industrial society was regarded as the 'historical task' of the capitalist stage. The source of Marxism was the outrage people felt with the injustices of capitalist society. Marxism was therefore essentially the offspring of a humanist liberal morality – an ethical movement (in spite of its claim to be scientific) which saw the main cause of the deplorable state of much of mankind in an alienating economic system and the institutional arrangements which were inseparably linked with it. The termination of the capitalist production relations were thus never, or not necessarily, an aim in itself but a means for the abolition of the various types of alienation and social injustice which were the direct consequences of those relations. The public control over the means of production therefore was also not necessarily the final aim of socialism but the necessary means by

---

32.   The discussion here of Russia is a shortened version of pp. 218–23 in Y.S. Brenner, *A Short History of Economic Progress.*

which the ethical objectives were to be realized. So, in Russia Lenin not only stood 'Marx on his head' by instituting a Communist Government (a superstructure) before Capitalism had fulfilled its historical task of creating an industrial basis (an infrastructure) for it, but in doing so he had laid the foundations for a system in which the aims were confused with the means. What had begun as socialist construction became in time State Capitalism. That the control over the means of production was not directly inheritable in the Soviet Union as it is in the Capitalist States makes little difference to the workers in Russia who were no less alienated from the processes of production and from the privileged class of government and party officials that control them than the workers in the capitalist countries. For all practical purposes there is indeed little difference for the person whether he cannot enter a shop to acquire the things he wants because he has not got the money or because he does not hold the necessary card identifying him as a member of the privileged class of bureaucrats for whom the special shops were opened. From this point of view Soviet Socialism was in fact nothing but a new kind of capitalism in which the fear of the labor-camp took the place of the fear of starvation as the whip which ensured labor's discipline and acquiescence throughout the process of capital accumulation and concentration which is necessary for industrialization.

What was true for Russian 'socialism' was also true for Russian planning. 'Accounting and control – that is the main thing required for arranging the smooth working, the correct functioning of the first phase of communist society', wrote Lenin in *The State and Revolution*. Economics was turned into a procedural administrative matter centrally controlled like a single big firm with little regard for the limitations of centralized management and work motivation. In 1926 P. Popov published an attempt to quantify the volume and structure of the output which flew into the national economy of the Soviet Union from individual branches and its distribution among the separate branches and classes of society. His work was not taken seriously and Strumulin's view prevailed that 'the accuracy upon which strict science insists is by no means necessary for practical purposes.' In 1928 Soviet planning took the form of a series of five-year plans devised to overtake the United States in *per capita* production. In 1936 Stalin proclaimed that Socialism had been

achieved in the Soviet Union, and with the adoption of the new
constitution he laid down the rule that economic growth could
henceforth only result from policy directives and their executions.
Organic growth was no longer relevant, being part of the capitalist
structure. In the future output targets were no longer to be regarded
as based upon technological predictions but as government
instructions to be carried out. This led to *maximum* rather than
optimum planning. Ignoring costs, as the 'affair of small
shopkeepers' mentality', Stalin regulated the economy regardless of
any cost-benefit accounting for individual enterprises or sectors. The
losses were hidden in the lump sums of centralized averages and
ignored, because general social utility cannot be measured by the
cost-benefit accounts of individual firms or sectors. Not before 1957
did anyone dare to challenge this view publicly in the Soviet Union.
Though theoretically it appears common sense to sacrifice investments in one sector to achieve higher overall gains, in practice, this
can only be done on the basis of careful examination, and in a well
integrated, highly organized, system where plans are strictly adhered
to. But this was not the case in Stalin's Russia. Plans were not only
frequently changed, but there appears to have been an endless
sequence of revisions to eliminate disproportions, which led to the
introduction of ever higher priorities, until by the end plans lost all
consistency. From supreme law, setting intransgressible principles for
the allocation of factors of production and the distribution of the
national income, plans became no more than approximations
susceptible to changes at any moment if the non-written plan
required it. They became no more than a list of macro-economic
choices. But central planning without detailed profit and loss
accounting for each subsector of the economy becomes impossible
without constant modification, and modifications distort the overall
plan unless they are very carefully adjusted in its light. Moreover,
the absence of cost-accounting for specific investments invited
excessive overhead costs, 'empire building', nepotism, inefficiency
and maladministration. This we were told by no lesser authorities on
the Soviet Union than Mr. N. Khrushchev *(Pravda* November 14th
1958) and Mr. L.I. Brezhnev *(Pravda* March 26, 1965). Only in the
1960s did mathematical economics which had been struck off the list
of subjects taught in Russia when Stalin called it 'playing with funny

figures', return to the Universities under the name of Planometrics. Russian planning can therefore hardly be taken as evidence either for or against the desirability of planning in a highly industrialized country with a western democratic tradition but should be a warning to over enthusiastic planners.

The fact that Nazi barbarism struck roots in Germany which was one of the relatively most liberal and advanced countries in the 1930s (though it must be admitted without a long democratic tradition), and that many of the manifestations of bureaucratic insensitivity and mediocrity which accompanied state control and planning in the Soviet Union are also discernible in the western welfare systems, and that a 'fourth estate' of civil servants and managers has been developing in North America and western Europe which displays many of the worst characteristics of its Russian counterparts (especially the tendency to cover up their incompetence and illegal activities by laws which criminalize those able to bring them to public attention), should not be left out of sight when the tendencies towards, and the desirability of, more state interference and planning are being considered in the west. The foregoing excursion into the history of the Soviet Union, to show that it was neither socialist nor its economy really planned, was therefore necessary not only to eliminate the widespread apprehension that a planned or socialist economy must per force lead to a Russian situation, but also to stress the objective risks which became visible in Russia, which are not linked to any particular stage of social and economic development or political system of government but threaten all planned societies unless steps to avoid them are taken in good time.

Sixthly, economic planners and model-builders have been worried by the diminishing profit incentives of investors in many sectors of the capitalist economies. There seems to be a tendency, which is by no means unequivocally confirmed, that capitalists are becoming less keen to invest capital in new labor intensive enterprises, i.e. in enterprises in which there is a considerable use of labor in relation to the amount of capital equipment per unit of output. Sometimes this tendency is given as the main cause of 'stagflation'. The argument then is that investors find it more profitable to buy government bonds than to take entrepreneurial risks because due to

Labor-Unions, labor costs have risen in excess of what can be compensated by higher prices and greater production efficiency. This argument of falling profit rates is often reinforced by allusion to the rising prices of imported raw-materials – oil prices for example. In fact average wages rose more sharply than prices in recent decades. For example in the Netherlands nominal average incomes from work, and the cost of living index, rose between 1955 and 1975 as follows:

Income from work and the index of prices[33] in the Netherlands (Index 1955 = 100)

Year	National income from work	Cost of living index
1955	100	100
1960	127.3	114
1965	193.9	138.1
1970	298.1	170.8*
1975	516.8	264.2*[34]

Yet, the *real* rise in wages was also accompanied by a sharp rise in productivity which greatly compensated employers. Again, in the Netherlands, real wages and productivity rose as follows:

---

33.   *Source: Centraal Economisch Plan* (C.P.B.), 's-Gravenhage, 1974 & 1976.

34.   The figures marked * were calculated by a different method of computation than those of earlier years.
The comparison is however not fully representative for in the industrial sector where most of the 'good' jobs are located real labor costs rose from 1953/63 to 1963/73 by 1.3%, and in the service sector where most of the 'bad' jobs are located by only 1.2%.

Real wages and productivity in the Netherlands[35] (Index 1955 = 100)

Year	Real Income from work in Industry	Index of productivity (all)	(industry)
1955	100	100	100
1960	111.9	117	130.6
1965	142	143	162
1970	178	186	227*
1975	201	221	274*

This suggests that profits should have increased. But this is by no means certain because labor costs for the employer are not the same as laborers' take-home incomes. The difference lies above all in the amounts of money employers have to contribute for each employee to pension, health and other social security funds. In the Netherlands the relationship between workers' take-home pay and employers costs per worker developed as follows:

Cost of labor to employer and workers' incomes[36] (Index 1955=100)

Year	Nominal income from work	Labor costs payable by employer
1955	100	100
1960	127.3	139.1
1965	193.9	219.7
1970	298.1	370.8
1975	516.8	716.3

---

35. *Source: Centraal Economisch Plan, op.cit.*, pp. 202–3. Again data marked by * were calculated by a different definition of industry.

36. *Source: Centraal Economisch Plan, op.cit.*, 1974 and 1976.

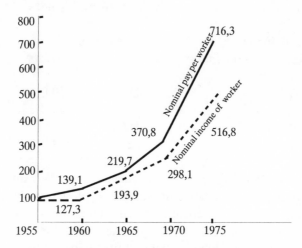

The profit of a firm, then depends on whether it can or cannot reduce its labor force by raising technological efficiency. If it can, then profits will remain satisfactory and may even rise in spite of the higher labor-costs to employers; if it cannot, profits will diminish. In the latter case a trend seems to develop in the welfare states for the managers of such industries to ask for government assistance. The governments are then forced to make a choice between, on the one hand, becoming full or temporary partners in what may well turn out to be insolvent enterprises, or, on the other hand, finding new employment for the workers of the failing businesses, or finding money for unemployment pay. In the short-run it is usually cheaper to support weak enterprises than to support unemployed workers out of social security funds, and miss the taxes and other contributions which the state collects from the same workers when they remain employed; but in the long-run such support is of course untenable, and threatens the nation's competitive efficiency. As a matter of fact it appears that even among the industries which are not directly affected by low-cost labor competition from the third world, as the textile industry is, there is a growing number in which profits tend to fall below investors' habitual expectations of profit. Rising taxes, mounting expenditures to keep the environment safe, and growing costs for certain imported raw-materials, for example oil, may therefore well have contributed in a number of industries to lower profits, less investment incentives, and unemployment. However, what is true for some industries need not be true for others, and in fact a trend seems to emerge which separates the technologically most advanced enterprises from the rest. The former will continue growing and improving technology; the future of the latter is less certain. But the expansion of the former is hardly likely to increase the volume of employment sufficiently to compensate for the loss of posts in the remaining industries. With this in mind, it seems not unreasonable to assume, that next to the expansion of services, the share of the state in the second type of industries will increase in the wake of the growing need to find employment for workers, who without government participation may become unemployed due to the diminished incentives for investment.[37]

Seventhly, economic planners and model builders have become increasingly conscious of the limitations that monster enterprises and especially multinational ones impose upon the decision making power of the state. The enormous resources which such organizations have at their disposal and the ease with which they can shift their resources and operations from one country to another makes them almost uncontrollable by national governments and almost insensitive to their customary instruments of fiscal and monetary direction. For example, in the Netherlands, five monster organizations together with the state mines (D.S.M) control so large a share of the food (UNILEVER), electronics (PHILIPS), oil (SHELL), chemical (AKZO) and metallurgical (ESTEL) industries, and so great a share of the labor force – 18% of all workers employed work directly for the above mentioned five enterprises and many more indirectly) that it is inconceivable that any government can make any decision that would infringe upon their vital interests.[38] The threat alone that they may transfer part of their operations to another country is sufficient

---

37. As can be seen in the new introduction to this book, what was only *likely* in 1978 has been amply confirmed since then only that the commitment of government to generate full employment was abandoned and unemployment soared.

38. *Vide Selective groei,* Economische structuurnota. Tweede Kamer zitting 1975–76, 13955, No. 1–3, pp. 240–1, and 258.

to make any government think twice before it makes such a decision. For no democratic government could survive the economic chaos that 'hard actions' from the side of these enterprises would bring down upon the country. At the same time it is of course also true that no multinational or other monster organization would resort to such 'hard actions' easily, unless its most vital interests are threatened. They too cannot wish to put democratically elected governments in impossible positions vis-à-vis the electorate, for they too have a vested interest in political stability. They too fear the unpredictable. It follows that a kind of tacit agreement exists between the most powerful economic organizations and the states in which they are based. This tacit agreement reflects the truce between the great national and international capital and the various governments in power which clearly defines the democratic freedom of the peoples concerned. This is no 'sinister plot' but the obvious result of a socio-economic reality.

From all these points follows that social and economic planners and model-builders in the Welfare States are by no means free, if they wish to remain realistic, to plan what may theoretically be regarded the most rational solutions to problems, but they must plan politically tenable ones. They must compromise. This recognition of necessity has given rise to a deep rift in the progressive movements in the Welfare States.[39] The revolutionary and utopist left was quick to point out the lack of logical consistency in reformist planning, and the reformist left was equally quick to point out the lack of realism in revolutionary schemes. It is of course not inconceivable that a revolution will brush aside all the political impediments to planning, and turn planning into an administrative optimization problem, like that of an army or of a single firm. But in practice such a sudden conversion cannot change the fact that plans turn out in reality just as good or as bad as they are implemented, i.e. that the advantages of plans depend on the people who transform them into practice. In an army, or in a business firm, the realization of a plan depends

---

39.   The term *progressive* is used here in the earlier defined sense of the augmentation of free choice and the diminution of divisions between people of different sex, color, race or background.

upon a system of rewards and penalties; the soldier or worker who does not do his job properly is penalized, and the soldier or worker who does, expects to be rewarded. Now, given the fact that society, even in the richest countries, has only very recently emerged from the era of fear, it is still everywhere firmly in the grip of this individualistically determined utilitarian mentality. A sudden transformation to a rationally planned economic system would therefore, at least for a time, require the introduction of a similar rewarding or punitive mechanism. With no economic mechanism to assure compliance, the task would become administrative – the job of supervisors. In other words, it would become the task of a bureaucracy which before long would develop class characteristics as indeed it has done not only in Russia but also in East Germany and Czechoslovakia which were both economically relatively economically advanced countries of which the last mentioned also had a democratic heritage. The point is that there is a highly intricate relationship between economic and social factors which cannot be arbitrarily separated. A sudden change in the economic structure, imposed upon a civilization, without its members having gained the social consciousness that suits the altered economic structure, as it indeed happened after the war in eastern Europe, can hardly guarantee progressive changes in social relations. It had on the contrary the opposite effect. It transferred power from the hands of a weak class, which was prepared to make concessions to socially progressive forces, into the hands of a vigorous new class of technocrats with self-seeking utilitarian tendencies, and thus have delayed rather than advanced the humanization of mankind's socio-economic relations. To hide behind primitive Marxism and say that the new economic relations will produce new social relations tells nothing about whether these relations will be progressive or retrograde – whether they will raise mankind to higher spheres of freedom or reduce it to a new type of slavery. But also to recognize that the capitalist system is illogical from a societal point of view, and that planning is superior to spontaneity, is simply not enough – the alternatives must be made explicit together with the motivational mechanisms that will replace the capitalist profit motive. In fact the fascination that a planned social system has, vis-à-vis the ill-functioning and inequitable capitalist system motivated by the pursuit of profit, can sometimes so estrange the revolutionaries from reality that they no longer distinguish between their objective friends and foes. For example, it totally escaped the view of the revolutionary student movement of 1968 that they were courting the wrong section of society when they were pleading for the help of the industrial working class. They never recognized the division between the people who hold 'good' and hold 'bad' jobs. They were unaware that skilled workers in industry were much better paid, had much better social arrangements and security, than other workers; that in fact the skilled workers, particularly in the largest firms and in the multinationals, had a direct interest in the continuation of the capitalist order – that they had far more to lose than their chains. The mutinous students never accepted the fact that their natural allies were teachers and intellectuals. They never saw that the really worst exploited in modern capitalist society were women and the minorities – negroes and foreign workers. They never even recognized that the little sympathy they really gained from the industrial working class was not for the abolition of the system, but against progressive taxation and bureaucratic interference, – a 'march through the institutions' not against capitalism but for its adjustment. They brandished Marcuse's book, and waved it about, but they did not read it. The failure of the student movement was therefore no coincidence, it was the logical consequence of its lack of touch with reality. And yet, it really was a progressive movement though not for the reasons that students put forward. The stir it caused and the sympathy it commanded in wide circles of the population had less to do with the egalitarian slogans of the young people in the streets than with the widespread feeling that democracy is threatened by the ruling establishment, – that the system and institutions that gave workers the power to resist exploitation, and gave all people a sense of freedom, were being undermined and vacated of their content. The explosion of 1968 attracted most sympathizers outside the universities not because it promised a new fair world but because it opposed the new way in which capitalism had learned to protect its vital interests against democracy.

In the postwar era, after the failure of Fascism, capitalist establishments acknowledged the inevitability of having to operate within the democratic system and its institutions. Therefore, rather than resist them it quickly learned to subvert them to its purposes. Almost unnoticed were the democratic institutions and their bureaucracy absorbed into the establishment; what had been the stronghold of liberty, the means by which society had protected itself against the excesses of capitalism, and the source of labor's strength for the promotion of social and economic equity, had step by step become an instrument for people's subjugation. Exploiting the East West confrontation to withdraw ever wider spheres of public interest from the public view, all, of course, in the 'national interest', the new alliance between big capital and state bureaucracy deprived society of the most essential factor in democracy namely access to information. McCarthyism in the United States, and the wider and wider interpretation given to the Official Secrets Act in the United Kingdom may serve as good examples, the former for the atmosphere, and the latter for the actual mechanism by which this was achieved. The press was left free but its access to real politically relevant information was restricted by prohibiting those who have access to it to reveal it under the pain of heavy penalties. That such an arrangement was not anathema to politicians and civil servants is obvious. It enabled them to hide their mistakes and inefficiency. That it was not unwelcome to monster enterprises and multinationals is equally understandable. It frees them from the need to deal with governments in the full glare light of public scrutiny. C.I.A. (a United States government organ) and I.T.T. (a multinational business organization) were willing partners in efforts to topple Dr. Allende (the elected President of an independent state) but both were much too shy when they succeeded, to claim their 'credit' publicly.

To be sure, illegal acts have also been committed by the 'servants' of the State before, – the first labor government of Ramsay MacDonald was crushed half a century ago with the help of the infamous Moscow Letter which had been forged by MI5, and played into the hands of the British press to mislead public opinion with the assistance of the Foreign Office and the Secret Service (MI5). What is new is the mechanism by which the perpetrators of such deeds are nowadays officially protected. Indeed there seems to be no law in any country which by pain of prosecution prohibits the Head of State, Cabinet Ministers, or high ranking state officials, to lie to Parliament or the public in matters of state. Even senior civil servants who misinform their Ministers seem immune to prosecution. Daniel Ellsberg, in 1974, could not defend in Court his publication of the Pentagon Papers by the obvious fact that he was telling the truth and that this was in the public interest to do so because the elected representatives of the American people had betrayed the trust of the people by misinforming them about Viet-Nam. He had to hide behind the legal technicality that the truths he had revealed had already been revealed by others before him and were therefore not a breach of secrecy. It seems that before the coming of democracy there was no need to enact laws prohibiting the holders of political power to lie to the public, and with the coming of democracy it must have been inconceivable that they may do so. After all there was always the free press to explore into the darkest corners of political manipulations. But as Bernard D. Nossiter,[40] the London correspondent of *The Washington Post,* wrote: 'It would be absurd, of course, to claim that Britain is a police state or that it is ruled even fitfully by an invisible government. Even Merlyn Rees is miscast as an enemy of civil liberties: as the minister in charge of Northern Ireland, he simply demonstrated an unhealthy reliance on his civil servants, and this could again account for his order against Agee and Hosenball. It is clear, however, that there are certain matters that are ventilated here at a journalist's peril. This is not because the British spy agencies are malevolent; they are bureaucracies, much like others. Any agency unrestrained by law will inevitably use its imagination rather than due process to deal with annoying little threats to an otherwise untroubled life.' But this, that any agency unrestrained by law will inevitably use its imagination... to deal with annoying little threats to its otherwise untroubled life,

---

40.   *Vide New York Review of Books*, April 14th 1977, p. 32. For example, no one thought it possible that Section Two of the British Official Secrets Act of 1911, could be used to gag the press, i.e. threaten with a two year prison term any civil servant who provides, and a reporter who receives, an unpublished government plan to cut certain normal rail services. But such ridiculous things actually happen in Britain.

is precisely the issue.[41] Newsmen, like members of other trades, have families, and on the whole wish to live normal lives, and though there are probably more brave and public-spirited women and men in this profession than in most other, newsmen too cannot spend all their lives defending themselves against defamation and worse.[42] Deprived under the rules of official secrecy of access to the evidence against them, and therefore unable to refute it, newsmen become less and less keen on obtaining and publishing that kind of information that will engender the wrath of the bureaucracy. Eventually political reporting becomes little more than the reformulation of official hand-outs. No knock on the door in the middle of the night, no censor in the editorial room, but the discrete hint of the bureaucrats in one country to their equivalents in another or to a complaisant newspaper, and the 'offensive' reporter's freedom to travel, and his personal reputation, is gone. There are of course great differences between countries in this respect. In the smaller countries with a long egalitarian and humanist tradition and with a strong heritage of bourgeois legality (such as The Netherlands), the bureaucracy is far less able and inclined to use such methods. In countries without such traditions, and in which officialdom had always regarded itself above the people, this type of abuse is more common. It is indeed surprising that under these conditions some relevant political information does now and then become public after all. In some cases simply because there were just too many people directly involved to prevent a 'leak'. For example, there were too many Viet-Nam veterans, who told friends and members of their families what they knew to be the truth, to keep the public misinformed forever. In other cases the truth leaked out because of personal differences between high office-holders who tried to discredit each other by

---

41. For the fascinating story how such agencies deal with the 'annoying' little threats, and ruin people's lives, *vide* Nossiter's account 'Outcasts of the Island.' *New York Review of Books*, April 14th, 1977.

42. Nossiter writes that three weeks after publishing an 'offending' article, 'two of the less restrained writers' of the London *Times* denounced him for endangering British journalists abroad. One wonders who told them?

giving information about their opponents to the gentlemen of the press whom they expected to support them. On other occasions things reached the public by coincidence: the innocent remark by a technician who remembers that a certain statement can or cannot be verified by a tape recorded on a device he was instructed to place somewhere. But most important of all were those instances where the persons who normally enjoy the privileges which flow from keeping the public uninformed fell out one with the other. For those interested in the maintenance of secrecy are of course not a homogeneous lot. The interests of the bureaucrats are not in all matters identical with those of the great economic bosses, and the businessmen lobbies also often represent opposing interest groups. Even a President who in a certain moment overestimates his power and makes a deal with the 'Milk Lobby' against the wish of Senators or bureaucrats who are at the same time dealing with the agriculture lobby, may suddenly, as it happened, find that information, which had been carefully withheld from the public by common consent, makes headline news. The press, then, is not only 'fed' the damaging information, but is protected by one part of the establishment against the other, while each side is trying to rally public opinion behind it by discrediting its opponents. All at once the demand is heard for the protection of State Officials who disclose illegal activities of the government, and for making State Officials answerable in law for covering up such activities, say, for not reporting the illegal spying after citizens. (Herman Badillo for New York in House of Representatives).[43] All at once it is suggested to make it illegal and punishable by law for members of the F.B.I. to engage in political espionage in the United States and to harass people for their political opinions, something which from the presentation of the newly suggested law must have been common practice. (Daniel Inonye Commission).[44] All at once the new F.B.I. chief only admits that for *forty* years many Americans were illegally malevolently defamed because Mr. Edgar Hoover did not approve of

---

43.   *Vide de Volkskrant*, Agency report 22.4.1977.

44.   *Vide New York Times* report reprinted in *de Volkskrant* 22.4.1977.

their political views.[45] All at once the public is told that the C.I.A. misinformed even the President of the United States to further its own policies[46] that it deliberately spread false news about China;[47] that it experimented with the drug L.S.D. on unsuspecting citizens;[48] and that it paid some 400 journalists to misinform whosoever it thought ought to be misled.[49] All these were not disclosures of unfortunate departures from what on the whole remained a democratic system, but the reflection of a fundamentally undemocratic oligarchical paternalistic state of mind in the circles that rule the United States. They simply do not think that they owe any information to the electorate. They tell the people just as much as they deem necessary for maintaining public support for what *they* think is best, or, in the cases when they fall out with each other, what they think will influence the public to support one group against the other. Nixon said this quite openly in his interview with David Frost on television. He claimed that the President had the right to order illegal actions if he considered it in the national interest.[50] But then, why only the President? Why not any official in his sphere of authority if he acts in the national interest? That this was the view of the people who ordered the various operations of the Watergate team became quite clear in the course of the investigations. By now Nixon and his group have been replaced, and business returns to be as usual, – the children in New York schools find in their textbooks that Richard M. Nixon never knew of the Watergate affair before the scandal became public, and was 'very

45.   Reported by Reuter and UPI, 10th May 1976.

46.   Reported by *de Volkskrant* 18.1.1977 from Reuter and AFP. Ted Sorensen's report.

47.   *Washington Post*, PDA, Reuter, UPI, vt. 19.1.1976.

48.   *New York Times*, vt. 21.9.1977.

49.   *New York Times*, vt 13.9.1977.

50.   Reuter Vr. 21.5.1977.

angry' when he heard of it. (Elizabeth Holzman about New York school books).[51]

In Germany, which in the immediate post war period had adopted a very democratic constitution, the democratization process has taken on a somewhat different form. Article 20 of the constitution, *Grundgesetz,* has given every German the right to resist illegal actions by the executive. But there too only officials are likely to have access to information about such breaches of the law, and these are bound by rules of silence. When the rules do not suffice, the people who are likely to uphold the rule of law at their personal peril are excluded from the civil service in advance by *Berufsverbote.* Where *Berufsverbote* cannot be applied a smear campaign is unleashed to silence the critics and their criticism and scare others – Böll, Gollwitzer, etc. Everyone in Germany is free to read whatever he wishes, only the publishers, distributors and sellers of undesirable writings are threatened by the 'anti-terror' paragraphs of the law.[52] The CDU chief, Helmut Kohl, wants even to go a step further. He wants a law like the one in East Germany which makes the 'defamation of the State', *Staatsverleumdung,* an offence punishable by law. As only officials, who will not or are not allowed to provide damaging information, can substantiate whether or not a certain statement was true or defamatory, and as the same bureaucracy that may be accused of malpractices will define what is and what is not defamatory, one may well wonder if Mr. Kohl was really listening to what he was saying.

Peter Noll, the Professor of Law at the University of Zürich in Switzerland, gives some very good examples how democratic freedoms are being restricted.[53] It is sufficient to object to some specific financial item, say, in the military budget, to be publicly marked a Communist, though one may really be a life-long Liberal or Conservative. From this point on, the administration needs no

---

51.   Reported in *Der Spiegel* 30.5.1977.

52.   For a discussion of this subject see 'Der Ramponierte Rechtsstaat' in *Der Spiegel,* 5th December 1977, p. 33.

53.   *Vide* Professor Noll's article in *Die Weltwoche,* 24 November 1976.

longer provide reasonable arguments about the item of actual complaint, because the critic is busy defending himself against the false accusation. When Böll speaks out against the prostitution of the German Constitution and against official excesses he is branded terrorist-sympathizer; the discussion shifts from the question whether or not he is right, to the question whether or not he is in favor of the stupid criminal activities of a small group of young people whose political sense is as large as a bird's. The evidence for the waning of bourgeois-liberties in Germany is too massive and well publicized to be repeated here in detail,[54] but its most essential feature must be stated, for it seems that even those politicians and capitalists who short-sightedly support it because it gives them some opportunistic advantages, have not yet become aware of the real danger it holds also for them. *Berufsverbote* deprive the civil service of critical minds and make only people prepared to carry out orders from above, without questioning their content, capable of serving the state. In the end only the man at the top remains free to take decisions, and once this happens the truce between capital and bureaucracy is gone. For their interests are no longer identical. Capital becomes the servant instead of the master of the political power and political power holders in this case are no longer intent on anything but the continuation of their position. If this implies the 'nationalization' of capital they will not hesitate to nationalize, for the bureaucracy will feel no less entitled to run industry than all other spheres of life. In fact, German capitalism should be better aware of this danger than any other capitalism; in any case it should be more scared of it than of the democratic left. A bureaucracy which develops into something like a class, and remains unrestricted by law and uncontrolled by a

---

54.   For examples see *Der Spiegel* 15.11.1976, pp. 39, 41; 10.3.1977, 14.3.1977; 21.3.1977, pp. 7, 22; 16.5.1977, pp. 228–9; 12.9.1977, pp. 136–8; 3.10.1977, p. 29; 14.11.1977, p. 131; 5.12.1977, pp. 32–4; and reports in *de Volkskrant*, 4.5.1977; and 17.12.1977, p. 23.

free press with good access to information, will no better honor the rights and privileges of the bourgeoisie than of the working class.[55]

Taken together then, the rise of democratic government, which seemed to have vanquished with the fall of Fascism, and which gave to the workers in the industrial countries of the West a real share in the ever rising fruits of production, has also brought with it a new social formation – a 'class' of managers. This 'class' had two origins. Firstly, public administrators charged with the task to correct the ill-effects of the capitalist system – to avoid the unemployment of labor and the inequitable distribution of wealth, and to support the weaker sections of the population by the distribution of pensions, unemployment pay etc., gradually developed class characteristics of their own that alienated them from their social base. Rising in constant confrontation with conventional capitalist interests, this 'class' was ready to satisfy the economic demands of the working class but not share power and position with it. It was prepared, indeed willing, to tax the capitalists and transfer the revenue to other sections of society but not willing to regard itself on equal footing with the beneficiaries of the services it rendered. It was ready to weaken capitalism but not to put the working class, or indeed anyone else but itself, in its place. As happened, it was more successful in the task of taxing the small capitalists and the self-employed than with the large and multinational organizations. The second origin of the new 'class' was industry. Industrial management was changing. The small employers, running their businesses more or less independently with their own and borrowed capital, were becoming rarer under the heavy hand of the fiscus and competition from the large producers, and their place was taken by large, often multinational, enterprises run by professional managers who, like their equal numbers in government, were also operating with other people's money and developing a separate life-style on expense accounts. Before long the two managerial groups became indistinguishable from each other. Managers of monster industries

---

55. This is exactly what Rosa Luxemburg was afraid would happen, and did indeed happen, in Stalin's Russia, and which is in progress also in the western world.

became top government officials and top officials directors of industries.[56] Married by the bonds of the expense account, and distinguished from the rest of the nation by the life-style the account enables them to maintain, they soon discovered that the stifling of criticism was a common interest. The workers in the monster firms were kept happy by high incomes relative to those employed in other firms made possible by the rapidly advancing technology and the often monopolistic position of such firms. The rest of the population was silenced by social security payments, lack of opportunity to voice their complaints, and, when neither worked, by the long arm of the forces of 'law and order'.

It was this idyllic situation into which the student opposition to the Viet-Nam war exploded in the United States. For years people were led to believe that all goes well in South-East Asia. That the enemy was all but exhausted. That America is defending western civilization against the onslaught of barbarity. Criticism and disbelief were put aside as Communist propaganda. But every day more Americans were killed, the war lasted on and on, and more and more young men returned to the United States and told the truth. And all at once everyone knew that not only the government but all the media were lying. The students in the streets had broken the conspiracy against the American people. They became a threat to the system. A real danger. Above all it demonstrated that the system was vulnerable – that the people were still capable of shaking the establishment. It gave hope to the malcontents and showed their potential strength should they unite and find the necessary leadership. And malcontents were many: The blacks and other minority groups who were frustrated by the host of unkept election promises. Small shopkeepers and self employed who were hard pressed by competition from the politically influential large enterprises and by rates and taxes. Teachers and other members of the less well-remunerated intelligentsia who were appalled by the cultural waste-land into which the 'experts' in public relations who dominated government were turning the United States. And young

---

56.   John Conally, Richard Helms, William Rogers became investment advisers for Iranian and Arab oil dollars see *de Volkskrant*, 17.1.1978.

America, the 'Dr. Spock generation', the generation of young people who were not yet thoroughly infested with the crude materialistic utilitarianism of their elders and who had been spared their elders' recollections of an era when economic fears had been real and very horrifying. But the American student movement never recognized its allies and never introduced them to full partnership; it lacked leadership and historical perspective. It therefore remained a protest movement, an explosion of resentment against a world without firm values ruled by short-sighted expediency – against insensitive bureaucrats, uncouth officials and policemen; a revolt against a society led by an elite that was incapable to distinguish between good and evil, truth and untruth. In summary, the student movement was a spontaneous outburst – a desperate though unconscious attempt to save the traditional values of the Jewish-Christian heritage. Like all spontaneous protest movements without a leadership with a clear political conception, like all movements that gather support on the basis of what they are *opposed* to, and not on the basis of a practicable alternative programme they favor, the student movement attracted many persons from the fringes of society. People who gave vent to their frustrations by shouting obscenities and by wanton, senseless, destruction of property. They alienated the liberal middle class, and gave the guardians of the establishment the opportunity to retaliate with atrocious violence. Paradoxically, however, it was this 'retaliation', which was seen by millions of Americans on television, that saved the movement much of the sympathy the mad fringe had lost for it. People who watched on their T.V.'s the legalized brutality in front of the Chicago Convention hall could not but begin to wonder about the type of people that was leading American society. All the establishment's efforts to minimize the damage done to its public image by stressing the demonstrators' provocative behavior – and provocation there was – had only limited effect. As Thomas Paine once said, there is no word to *'unsee'* in the English language. Chicago was the curtain-raiser to the drama which unraveled before the eyes of the American people in the Watergate and subsequent

Senate Hearings and found its echo in Carter's successful bid for the Presidency under the banner of moral revival – of 'human rights'.[57]

In Europe the student movement was also fed essentially by frustrations and was ethical in character, but in many other respects it differed from the American, and from one country to another in Europe itself. Having no ideological conception of its own, and no programmatic perception for the future,[58] it reached back for the slogans of traditional Marxism. Unaccustomed to historical analysis, its leaders never bothered to examine these slogans' contemporary relevance. Dogmatically, without bothering to analyze their contemporary social reality, they forced upon the movement pre-war class perceptions. It totally escaped their view that the industrial working classes of western Europe did not live in the 1960s on the verge of starvation and in constant fear of unemployment and destitution. The student leaders did not notice that especially the industrial working-men in the larger firms felt that they had never had it so good, that the system allowed them to obtain all the things they wanted – vacations with pay, private automobiles, television, economic security, things that until a few years before no worker ever dreamed of getting, and they felt an illusionary confidence that this security will last for ever. But it was to this section of the working population that they appealed with Marxist slogans from the late 19th and early 20th century. At the same time they ignored the middle class which felt both economically and politically alienated by the system. What *united* the working with the middle-class was resentment towards bureaucratic arrogance. Economic interests, at least short-run economic interests, *divided* them, for a great part of the industrial working class knew that it was a minor partner of the establishment, but it felt that it stood more to lose from shaking it than from its preservation. *Labor Unions* and *Parliamentary representation* had proven themselves successful instruments for the

---

57.   For what happened to some of the student leaders of the 1960s in later years see *Der Spiegel*, 16 January 1978, pp. 104–16.

58.   How indeed could the students have a historical perception having been educated in a strong positivist or neo-positivist anti-historical tradition?

advancement of the economic objectives of organized industrial labor, why abandon them? Why throw the system into confusion, the outcome of which cannot be predicted, and risk concrete achievements because of the theoretical proposition that exploitation – the gathering of 'surplus value' by employers, still continues? After all, revolutions are very serious matters; they take place when people feel that they can no longer stand a situation, or that all legitimate avenues to right some wrong have been explored and found of no avail They do not occur for the promotion of theoretical propositions even when these may be perfectly correct. To be sure, there cannot be a progressive revolution without a theoretical conception of an alternative social order as an aim, but such a theory alone does not suffice to make a revolution. As Marx himself might have said: the industrial working-class of western Europe had far more to lose than 'its chains'.

While the Marxist slogans of the student movement did not serve to engage the active support of the industrial working class it frightened a great section of the intelligentsia and the middle class. The intelligentsia and the middle class wanted human dignity – that dignity it felt deprived of by the new establishment. These were also objectives of the students. But the vulgar Marxism they mistakenly assumed to carry favor with the working class scared them. Worse than that, this primitive Marxism and the students' life-style also alienated many of the really poor – the deeply religious foreign workers, and the small self-employed. Ill-educated in the social sciences, the students mistook their initial success, and the early manifestations of sympathy by wide sections of the working-class, as indications of agreement with their slogans while in fact they were symptoms of exasperation with the establishment. Intuitively most workers felt that the establishment of managers of monster national and multinational enterprises and of state and party organs was depriving their public institutions of their democratic content – that from instruments of social and economic reform the democratic institutions were being turned into tools for the confirmation of the new oligarchy in power. Most European workers knew that the democratic institutions had helped them to a good share of the fruits of economic growth, but they also felt that in the process they had little by little restricted people's individual freedoms. At the time they hardly imagined that this could in the long-run threaten also their continued economic progress, but they saw that it deprived them of their human dignity whenever they came face to face with the bureaucracy.

Not that bureaucrats are different from other people, but precisely because they are like all others, they tend to develop an *esprit de corps* which leads them eventually to confuse loyalty to the institutions they see with loyalty to the objectives for which the institutions have been called to life. They find that their own rank and position depends upon the smooth functioning of their office within the organization and not upon the attainment of the objectives the organization as a whole is supposed to meet. But as the public criticizes exactly the last aspect of their functioning, they feel that they are treated unfairly and their alienation from the public is the result. The lower and intermediate levels of officialdom who come into immediate contact with the public and who therefore are the direct targets of its anger about unpopular, nonsensical, or plainly anti-social measures, upon which bureaucrats of these ranks have themselves little influence, and which they can only challenge in peril of their chances of promotion, can therefore hardly avoid to seek to justify themselves by finding excuses for the measures they have to carry out. Spending most of their time in offices with other officials struggling with similar problems an atmosphere develops which in time leads them to believe in their excuses, – if 'everyone' thinks so then it must be true, and they become genuinely convinced that the policies they implement are really justified and in the public interest. Their attitude towards the public hardens, critics become trouble-makers and subversives. Without wanting it they arrogate for themselves the place of the nation, and before long they really believe that what *they* think or do is in the national interest, they feel that they *are* the nation, and the rest of the people can only be trusted as long as they conform with their ideas. Like the capitalist industrialists of old, who genuinely thought that they are also public benefactors because they provide work and sustenance for the poor, so does the bureaucracy, where it is not under strict democratic scrutiny, adopt self-congratulating attitudes which in time become increasingly derisive towards the people. This then is the body behind which *managerial capitalism* hides. And what is true of the state bureaucracy is often also true for the officials of Trade Unions and of political parties. As with only few exceptions all political leaders, Cabinet Ministers etc., who had come to power since the war arrived there by way of the civil service or the party machine it is hardly surprising that most of them share the bureaucracy's attitudes. Those who do not are still dependent on their top officials' information for the formulation of policies. There are indeed very few political leaders in Europe whose parties have adequate research units with access to facts which could provide them with alternatives to the analyses of the permanent top civil servants.

There is a fundamental similarity between Western and Eastern bureaucracies is spite of their *real* differences. In the East the bureaucracy was in fact a distinct *class*, – it had common economic interests; it had economic privileges, its own shops with goods unobtainable for other people etc., and though these privileges vary with rank (as there are also richer and less rich capitalists in the capitalist class) which had a strong combining factor. In the west the bureaucracy has no such economically unifying interests. Most of its members are economically no better situated than other members of the working class, and often they are even worse off. Only the bureaucratic top is really separated from the working class and belongs to another 'class' – to the 'managerial class'. It is separated through the enjoyment of economic privileges, such as high salaries and expense accounts, that are not available to the rest of the working population nor to the bureaucracy's lower rank and file. Not unlike the Russian establishment it holds these advantages due to its control, not ownership, of the means of production and coercion. This joins the state's managerial top with its equals in the management of private enterprises. Consequently, the bureaucratic top in the west, as distinct from the eastern bureaucracy, must be regarded as part of an establishment which includes the leaders of the private enterprises. But the latter, due to their day in day out practice – their need to make profits for their business's share-holders, belong also into the sphere of the old establishment of capitalism. Nevertheless, in spite of the obvious differences between real capitalists and managerial controllers of capital, and in spite of occasional conflicts between bureaucratic and private interests, capitalists and managers of both types are on the whole united by similar interests and attitudes. Together they form an oligarchy whose power could only be restricted by public supervision. But public supervision depends upon the public's access to all the necessary information which could be obtained only by the complete freedom of the media to disseminate such information. And this is precisely what this new class manages to prevent. For indeed, reformist ministers come and go, but top civil servants are 'permanent', and they provide the information, and its analyses, upon which ministers must base their policies; – by which they must judge whether their reforms are financially or otherwise bearable. Even their morning paper does not give the ministers more information than what the civil service decides to give or 'leak' to the press, and this is also what their supporters read and take as valid information in support of, or against their policies. It must therefore be concluded that it is not the growth of the state sector of the economy – not state intention, which threatens western democracy and its achievements, but the lack of democratic supervision. And this was what the public sensed and the reason why the working class, the intelligentsia, and the middle class sympathized with the student movement in its early stages. The public supported the students' revolt against authority and not their revolutionary dreams. The people wanted the establishment of what used to be called the bourgeois liberties – the freedoms that had served them well in their ascent to greater economic affluence and that were progressively eroded by the new elite. They wanted free access to information, freedom of expression, participation in the decision-making processes that affected their life at all levels where such decisions were taken from the shop-floor to international politics. They wanted to be able to make up their own minds whether or not wage-claims threaten the viability of their working-places – 'open books', or whether or not nuclear power is necessary or dangerous. In short they wanted the continuation of the progressive movement that had swept over western Europe at the end of the war and whose liberal institutions were since the fifties step by step vacated of their progressive content. They did not wish to abolish the 'bourgeois' institutions but to make them again into the powerful instruments for social and economic advancement. They wanted human dignity – not the dogmatic verbalism and the long attained economic objectives that the student movement was offering.

No one thought that profit is the best motivational mechanism for social action, or the best allocator of resources, but no one wanted either the bureaucratic *dirigism* that seemed to be the eventual perspective of the students' aims. And so, the student-movement was abandoned by the masses not because it was too progressive but because people felt that the students were speaking in terms of a capitalist society that was no more. People were already struggling with the problems of a post-capitalist society in most western countries. They were aware that they had toppled the old style capitalism which the students made their verbal target, but they were not yet able to meet the onslaught of the new power combination, and they had not found the new forms of social organization that could meet the new challenges and eventually take the place of profit incentives.

There were also great differences between the nature of the state bureaucracy, and the structure of capitalism, and the students-movements, and popular reactions to the movements, in the different parts of western Europe. In Britain, where the working class had learned from sad experience that the state bureaucracy cannot be trusted; and where the workers have become accustomed to have confidence in no one but their own directly elected leaders in the pit or on the shopfloor; and where the division between the working class and the intelligentsia is fraught with deep suspicions, the student movement went almost unnoticed outside the intellectual circles in the cities and remained in fact confined to the universities. In France with her traditionally class conscious and politically experienced working class, and her tradition of political skepticism in all classes, the student movement had initially a considerable following in the cities but this was lost partly due to its earlier mentioned self-isolation and partly due to the negative attitude of the French Communist Party. In Germany, where working class traditions had been eradicated by the Nazi era, and where democratic traditions had had little time to develop, and where the *Untertan* mentality of the middle class and bureaucratic arrogance had strong historical roots, and above all, where the industrial working class was extremely successful in attaining economic objectives even under the authoritarian regime, the student movement was almost totally isolated. Made more radical than in other countries by the particularly ferocious reaction of the authorities and by the tolerance with which the bourgeoisie accepted this reaction – in contrast to other countries with better founded liberal traditions, the German student movement displayed itself also less tolerance than those of other countries, which further isolated it from its objective allies. Against the background of an essentially authoritarian society the vicious circle in which student violence was answered by legalized violence and more student violence by even more incommensurate state violence, part of the movement was eventually driven into the politically irrational underworld of senseless individual terrorism. In the smaller countries with a longer tradition of bourgeois liberty, for example in the Netherlands, where the bureaucracy never lost touch with the masses to the extent it did in the larger countries where at least initially, it took a leading part in the economic and democratic reconstruction of the country, and where the Nazi occupation had trust home the lesson of what happens when the legal safeguards of the rights of individuals are abrogated, the student movement met less opposition and was itself less virulent than in the larger countries. To be sure, the same forces that isolated the students from the working class in other countries were also effective there, but the atmosphere was different. Moreover, both the students and the government were on the whole ready to air their differences in a democratic manner. Neither the students nor the police really abandoned or deviated far from the legally accepted norms of a liberal society.

On the whole the practical achievements of the student revolt were very limited in Europe. It produced no more than some university reforms. But its general impact on society was tremendous. It showed that common people could still shake the system, could force the people at the top to take notice. It broke the spell of public resignation under which Europe's social and political life had lain dormant since the 1950s. The spell that had held in its grip a generation experienced in the deprivations of the pre-war economic crises, of war, of ideological and political disillusion; a generation that had spent its energies in the reconstruction of post-war Europe, and in the class struggles of the early 1950s; a generation which at the end of all this discovered affluence, that it could get all the things that it had wanted for so long once it submitted unconditionally to the new God of crude materialism. In short, the student revolt fell like a blessed rain upon the moral desert of a society obsessed by the spirit of acquisition to the exclusion of all else. A society that without really noticing had turned acquisition into a social value dwarfing all other values in its shadow. Religion, compassion, the dignity of man and labor, all these lost their status in the big orgy in honor of the great God Mammon. Entropy, increasing chaos, became the scientists image of the universe. Nothing remained definite and stable, values like *good* came to mean *useful* and *true expedient*. As long as the new elite could assure the progress of individuals' material advancement its moral status remained irrelevant. If individual's rights were trodden on, who cared? Too bad for those afflicted as long as the others could go on building their new private home, purchase their motor-car, and fill their rooms with the latest electrical gadgets. Into this atmosphere burst the student movement. A new generation which had never experienced the deprivations of their elders rediscovered some of the old values of society. They found their elders lacking. *There* was the generation gap. And this then was the progressive element in the revolt: it awakened the old moral values from their sleep and put them like a mirror in front of their society to see its new-won face. It gave new hope to those members of the older generation which had given up the struggle because they had lost it, and it opened new perspectives for the young. As it turned out Marx was enlisted in the 'sixties not in the service of the proletarian revolution but in the service of traditional morality. Neither the violence nor the obscene language employed by some fringe members of the student movement made any difference to the fact that it ushered in a new period for Capitalism.

11

Towards the Future

Earlier in this analysis it was said that Capitalism had been changing since the war and that these changes affected both its infrastructure, forms of organization, and superstructure. Its infrastructural character including its forms of organization[1] were altered firstly by the dramatic rise in production efficiency and the changing employment patterns that accompanied it;[2] namely, the decline of employment in agriculture and industry and the rise in service occupations. *Secondly,* by the increasing share of the public and non-profit-making sector in the economy,[3] i.e. by the rise of the share of the non-capitalistically owned sectors of the economy in the gross national product and employment. *Thirdly,* by the changing age and sex composition of

---

1. The terms *infra- and superstructure* are used here in a vague form to separate the material and organizational factors from the socio-psychological.

2. *Vide* pp. 334–7.

3. *Vide* pp. 337.

employment seekers, and the changing patterns of work remuneration: young people joining the labor force later in life than before and more women seeking full and part-time employment,[4] and by the sharper division between 'good', namely well remunerated, and 'bad' poorly remunerated jobs. *Fourthly,* by the growing discrepancy between the increase in per head output in the goods producing sector and the comparatively stable or rising demand for labor in the service sector, and the consequences of this development on government expenditure as the former sector is largely private and the latter mainly state-owned. *Fifthly,* by the continued rise in prices and wages, which in the 1970s also went together with high unemployment.[5] *Sixthly,* by the changing patterns of ownership and control of the means of production; by high taxes and consequently reduced investment incentives and rising costs; and by rising real incomes and greater social and economic security for most workers.[6] And *seventhly,* the capitalist infrastructure and mode of organization was altered by the rising political and economic power of multinational and other monster enterprises, managed by a 'class' of professional directors with long-term globe-embracing interests and plans, which are either in control of or independent of financial institutions;[7] and by the powerful position of State enterprises and organizations and their managers. But above all, the most important change in capitalism is the *objective* technological capacity of industrial societies to produce sufficient goods to meet all needs and more.

Altogether then, alienation, the private ownership of the means of production, the profit motive, etc., – in short, *capitalism,* is still with us, but it has changed. Ownership has increasingly become separated from control, the State and other non-profit-making organizations have captured part of the capitalist terrain, workers' living standards

---

4.   *Vide* pp. 337–47.

5.   *Vide* pp. 347–50.

6.   *Vide* pp. 350–4.

7.   *Vide* pp. 354–72.

have improved, and workers have gained greater social security, and occasionally also some degree of influence on managerial decisions. Upon this modified basis of Capitalism arose a new superstructure, – an *amended social stratification, a revised type of institutions,* and a *modified mentality.*

The *amended social stratification* is reflected in the rise of the managerial 'classes'. The *revised institutions* are reflected in the development of the negotiating machinery between labor and employers, in the regulating functions of the state in economic matters, and in the host of social security legislation and the setting up of the organs for its implementation. And the *modified mentality* is reflected in the decline of conventional business ethics among employers, and among laborers the end of fear and decline of pride in their work. As more and more firms engaged in different stages of production of the same commodity,[8] or in the same stage of production of the same commodity,[9] amalgamate – as the *vertical* and *horizontal* integration of business increases in order to achieve greater economic power and higher profits, business becomes less and less manageable by a single person or a single managerial board. And so, as the amalgamations become syndicates, trusts, and holding companies, management is delegated along hierarchical patterns to 'sub-managers', heads of branches, departments, sections etc.[10] Eventually, the organizations become so powerful that their top managers, the men who replace the old-style capitalist owner-manager, find that their decisions are far less influenced by market forces than market forces by their decisions. They discover that their share in consumers' expenditure is so large that subject only to the limitations imposed upon demand by the magnitude of

---

8. For example, the 'American Steel Trust consists of firms engaged in transport, coal an iron mining, steel production and rolling' (Alan Gilpin, *Dictionary of Economics*, 'Vertical Integration').

9. For example, the 'Bradford Dyers Association' which is a combination of all firms engaged in dyeing.' (Alan Gilpin, *op.cit.*, 'Horizontal Integration').

10. *Vide* Alfred D. Chandler, Jr., *The Visible Hand: The Managerial Revolution in American Business*, Harvard University Press, 1977.

the year to year changes in the country's Gross National Product their decisions have a greater impact on markets and prices than markets and prices on their decisions. Let this be illustrated by an hypothetical example from a conglomerate in which, say, the production of motorcycles takes an important part. The managers of the motorcycle business examine the size and age composition of their market, and then, on the basis of population statistics calculate how many more people will enter their customers' age group in the years to come. Further they study, again on the basis of national accounts, the income trends of this age group, and its habitual division of expenditure, and so they ascertain the maximum amount of money that can be expected to be spent on motorcycles in the following years. Finally they also study their 'target group's' demand-elasticity to price variations and susceptibility to advertising. And then, on the basis of all this information, they formulate their production plans. But often this is not all. The general management of the whole conglomerate, of which the motorcycle business is only one section, may also examine whether it is not more profitable to transfer part or even all the customers of its motorcycle business to its motor-car business. If it finds this desirable it can do so simply by raising its motorcycle prices to a height that will tempt a good part of its potential customers to buy cars instead of cycles, i.e. will tempt customers to behave in precisely the manner the conglomerate wishes them to behave. Because due to the high costs involved in the establishment, or rapid expansion, of motorcycle industries, and due to the length of time required for it and the risks involved in the invasion of markets which may have to be shared with the old established powerful firm, it is on the whole unlikely that a diminution of motorcycles output by the original firm will immediately give rise to strong new entrants to fill the gap. In other words, the shifting of custom from one product to another is possible when a conglomerate has a virtually monopolistic market position. At the same time, if the conglomerate operates in several countries simultaneously, and is not prevented doing so by law, it will of course continue to sell motorcycles abroad at the old price if the foreign market is too poor to shift to cars. In short, the managements of such organizations do not react to consumers' choices 'as they are communicated to them via the functioning of the *Price Mechanism*[11] but determine consumers' choices via their manipulation of prices. Very correctly unemployment in the motorcycle industry is blamed on high prices and less correctly the public is left to believe that the high prices reflect growing costs of production, and the latter are put at the doorstep of the Labor Unions and the State. As the saying goes; Two birds with one stone; the conglomerate's profits are maximized, and the workers are blamed for the price-inflation. Finally, both unemployment and high 'costs' are used as arguments to influence public opinion and the government to prevent competition from abroad.

When it is born in mind that, for example in The Netherlands, five big conglomerates directly employ 18 per cent of all the working population, and indirectly many more; and that, but for foreign competition, these five virtually control the whole field of electronics, metallurgy, food processing, chemicals and oil, it becomes clear that these conglomerates become states within the states, and their top managers plan just like the top planning officials in government service. Similarly in Germany, some 2000 businesses employ about 50 per cent of the total labor force, as against 200.000 businesses which employ the rest, and in the United States some 2000 corporations control about 80 per cent of all resources used in manufacturing,[12] so that even the most confirmed Free Enterprise economists cannot deny the price-fixing powers of the large conglomerates.[13] There is only one difference between the planning of the conglomerates and that of top officials in government service, the former plan for the maximization of profits and the government planners, where they exist, are supposed to plan for stability, equity

---

11. Wisdom of textbooks in economics for students written by people who continue believing in the myth that even under 'imperfect competition' the consumer is still King.

12. All data refer to the situation in the mid–1970s.

13. *Vide* also John Kenneth Galbraith, *The New Industrial State*, Ch. VII and the hearings before the Subcommittee on Antitrust and Monopoly practices upon which Galbraith's evidence is based. (Signet ed. 1967, p. 86).

and growth. But, not unlike the government officials at the top, the new type of managers in the private sector develop 'class' character-istics which distinguish them from both the rest of the people 'below' them and from the old style Capitalist-owner class of entrepreneurs. They are united with the top bureaucracy not only by their position but also by their life style and training. David Noble, for example, discovered that the chief executives of the five largest corporations in the U.S.A., General Motors, Singer, General Electric, DuPont, and Goodyear had all been classmates at M.I.T.[14] What Eton and Harrow had been for the managers of one Empire, the Ivy League, and the engineering department and business school of M.I.T. have become for the managers of another. Only that for those privileged to take part in the games on the 'playing fields' of Eton fair play was on equal footing with winning, while on the playing fields of the new elite only victory counts. The old-style owner-manager capitalists took pride in his and his childrens' humanistic education, – they sent their sons and daughters to universities and not to schools of technology, which they regarded necessary but inferior. They belonged to a civilization in which status was connected with control over people but was not entirely based on it. Unlike them, the new members of the managerial 'class' have only one criterion for achievement, namely the position a man holds in the organizational hierarchy. To be sure, like the capitalist of old the new manager in industry, government and in international organizations, is also caught up in the relentless race of all against all, only that the race for property – for ownership of capital, has become a race for position – for rank in the organization. The rules of the race have not changed; halt and you are soon overtaken by others, and being overtaken you fall back and might reach the bottom of the hierarchy. But, without the fetters of things 'done and not done' of the western heritage, the race has become much nastier. Is it not more than half a century ago that a soccer player who made a foul would admit it freely and even be applauded for admitting it by the supporters of his team? With what contempt would he meet

---

14. *Vide* David F. Noble, *America by Design. Science, Technology, and the Rise of Corporate Capitalism*, Knopf, 1977.

today if he were to do the same! Walk through the top floor of any international organization today and you can sense the unsavory atmosphere. The point is that the 'race' has become free from the *unwritten* rules that traditional education had imposed on old-style Capitalism, now only the *positive law* counts. All is right that the law does not forbid.

Moreover, unlike the old-style capitalists the new managers operate with other people's money, not with their own. Consequently they are also prepared to take much greater financial risks to promote their personal advancement than old-style capitalists would have dared to take, and they are also far less restrained in making personal expenses on the business's account. What matters to them is not whether their expenses are really necessary but whether or not they can be correctly booked. What matters is not whether or not they had to go round half the world to meet a business associate whom they might reach by phone but if they have sufficient receipts to satisfy the accountants that they actually spent the money they claim to have spent on the trip. In short, the new elite gave to the old term honesty a new meaning. From a nebulous term made meaningful mainly introspectively by a specific culture pattern they turned it into a precise term which takes its meaning from the wording of positive laws – they separated honesty from its traditional ethical context and turned it into honest calculations. Without going into the wider question whether or not Capitalism was as such always unethical in terms of non-Capitalist moral standards, it is of course true that old-style capitalists were often also corrupt even within the meaning they themselves gave to the concept honesty; but they were aware of it. When they transgressed *against* the unwritten rules of their society they did their utmost to hide it from their peers, and when they were found out it usually meant their ruin. For the need to play by both the written and the unwritten rules was essential to the capitalist system, because without *confidence* the whole system could not exist. 'My word is my bond' was the slogan of the Stock-Exchange; 'the Bank of England Promises...' was the statement printed on the British currency which made it acceptable as a medium of exchange. In short *confidence*, as any first year student of economics knows, is the very essence of capitalist economic relations. It is this confidence which the new managerial class is threatening to undermine. What it offers instead seems to be the rule of laws. but what it really leads to is loss of values and the risk of a reversal of society to medieval social and economic relations. The ability of the new managerial class to plan on a world-wide scale shows mankind's ability to be master of its future, but its tendency to divorce itself from the premises of the ethical heritage of western civilization indicates the great dangers it may hold for humanity if its freedom of action is not restricted by powerful and *really* democratic institutions. It may lead to a planned world as Huxley so vividly described.

A good example to illustrate the mechanism by which traditional ethical conceptions lose their hold upon society can be given from the sphere of bribery. Not that traditional capitalism did not indulge in this practice, but no self respecting capitalist would ever publicly admit having given or having received a bribe. This is no longer so. To quote the words of the ex-Gulf chief, Dorsey:[15] Ethics, morals, customs, values, principles... are all nonsense – *'Es gibt keine absolute universale Ethik. Moral, Gebräuche, Werte und Prinzipien sind überall Verschieden. Wir müssen uns anpassen, alles andere ist Unsinn'*. (There is no absolute ethics. Morals, habits, values and principles are different everywhere. We must adjust to them, all the rest is nonsense). Dorsey is not alone. When the United States agency Business International questioned the managers of fifty-five multinationals about their experiences with bribery it was told that with the exception of the People's Republic of China the practice of bribery is universal. In some countries like Kuwait, Saudi-Arabia, Indonesia and in Latin America it is indispensable, but it is also common in western Europe and in the Socialist countries, (the Russians like to have their bribes made over to bank accounts in Switzerland). In several countries, so the inquiry showed, established firms exist specializing in the sale of forged bills and receipts, to assist the multinationals and other large companies in this practice.[16] In the Netherlands, Mr. Harm van Riel, Chairman of the V.V.D.

---

15.   *Der Spiegel* 9/1976.

16.   *Der Spiegel*, 'Korruption gehört zum Geschäft', 27.12.1976.

fraction in the Upper House, also thinks that under certain circumstances bribery is quite respectable. 'No business manager, no high state official, can avoid doing wrong in the service of his interests... no outsider should arrogate to pass judgement.'[17] Bribes are deductible from taxes in Germany, in Japan, in France and in Italy, practically in all the industrial countries. Unlike the French, however, German enterprises have to show proof for their 'NA's' – they must convince the tax authorities that they have honestly spent the money they want to deduct for bribery and corruption.[18] *Ordnung muss sein.* When a study group on this subject was organized by the United Nations Social and Economic Council (ECOSOC), and the American delegation suggested that all payments to persons involved in the arrangement of contracts should be public to avoid corrupt practices, it met with the strongest opposition. The West Germans claimed that too many 'sensitive' things would come to light, and the Swiss claimed that it was unacceptable because under Swiss criminal law it was an offence to inquire into private business transactions, especially if foreigners were involved.[19] That in business sharp practices are not uncommon, says Roderick Maltman Hills, the Chairman of the American Stock Exchange Commission, is well known but what has been discovered lately must really shock the American public. 'We must ask ourselves if American business can continue enjoying the liberties it does'. A. A. Sommer, another top man in the Stock Exchange Commission, fears that if the public becomes convinced that the corporations cannot be trusted abroad it will say: 'If they bribe foreigners they are probably doing the same in the United States'.[20]

Corruption, like the life-style of management, is common to business and government. This, and the magnitude of the problem

---

17.   Report on VVD Congress in Rotterdam. *de Volkskrant*, 15.3.1976. The V.V.D. is a Dutch right of center liberal party then in government coalition.

18.   *Der Spiegel*, 'Und alle wollen sie ein Bakschisch', 3.5.1976, pp. 38–55.

19.   Associated Press report in *de Volkskrant*, 9.7.1977.

20.   *Vide de Volkskrant*, 20.2.1976. Report from Washington.

can be illustrated by a number of outstanding examples mentioned in 1975/6 in the *New York Times,* the *Christian Science Monitor,* and in the *Wall Street Journal.*[21] According to these reports, *Exxon* contributed $1.25 million to the funds of Canadian political parties, and between $46 million and $49 million to the funds of Italian political parties. *Gulf Oil* gave $4.8 million to the ruling party in South-Korea, $0.46 million to the President of Bolivia, and some $0.05 million to Arabs in the Lebanon. *Mobil Oil* supported Italian political parties with $2 million. *Phillips Petroleum* gave 50.7 million to foreign officials and advisers. *Northrop* $30 million to foreign advisers and $1.8 million to Swiss agents. *Lockheed* $7.1 million to Yoshio Kodama, $3.2 million to Marubeni Corp, and $2.8 million to officials, all in Japan. Beside this Lockheed also paid $0.2 million to Colombian air force officers, $7.9 million to influential foreigners, $1.1 million to Dutch personalities, $0.11 million to Mexican officials. *McDonnell Douglas* bribed government officials and air company directors with $2.5 million. *Grumman* bribed some contact man with the Iranian government $6 million. *Rockwell International* paid $0.57 to foreign government officials. *General Motors* $0.25 to political groups in South Korea, $0.23 Ministry of Defence South Korea, and $0.1 Canadian political parties, all million dollars of course. *G.D. Searles* paid $1.3 million to foreign government officials; *Schering-Plough* – $0.2 million to people in various countries, and *United Brands* – $0.75 million to Italian government officials and $1.25 million to government officials in Honduras.

Money for bribing state officials did however also go in the opposite direction, namely from governments to business. The most publicized case of this kind (in the late 1970s) was the Tongsun Park affair. The South Korean business-man who was promised immunity from jurisdiction if he agreed to give evidence against the allegedly corrupt members of the United States Congress.[22]

---

21.   *Vide Der Spiegel,* 23.2.1976.

22.   *Vide de Volkskrant,* 19.11.76 and NYT report from Washington in *de Volkskrant,* 12.1.1978, UPI report from Seoul.

Nor did corruption remain restricted to what may be termed 'the public interest'. Other cases of corruption which attracted public attention in the 1970s were: Ex-President *Nixon* receiving some two million dollars worth of presents from foreign heads of states, in spite of the 1966 law prohibiting U.S. Presidents to accept gifts valued more than \$50.[23] *British Defence Ministry officials* receiving hundreds of thousands of pounds in bribes for 'arranging' the purchase of certain radar systems.[24] And *Swedish politicians, top-civil-servants, and labor union officials* who received for their families and themselves free flights with the Scandinavian air line *S.A.S.*[25] The evidence for the spreading of corruption is in fact so massive that it is simply impossible to believe that it is only the greater publicity, not the greater incidence, that makes it appear so overbearing. A cursory inspection of the newspapers during the last months provides the following crop: *Lockheed* is mentioned as having bribed people in *the Netherlands*,[26] in *Japan*,[27] in *Germany*,[28] (where all parties, however, deny having received the bribes), in *Italy*,[29] in the *United Kingdom*,[30] in *Turkey*,[31] (where the military

---

23.   Reports of *Reuter*, UPI, 24.8.1977 and AP, Washington, 8.9.1977.

24.   *Reuter*, UPI and DPA reports reprinted in *de Volkskrant*, 15.4.1976. All following reports are taken from the *de Volkskrant* (a Dutch liberal daily morning paper) unless otherwise stated.

25.   Stockholm, DPA. 13.1.1978.

26.   16.1.1976, 7.2.1976, 11.2.1976, 13.2.1976, 14.2.1976, 21.2.1976, 1.7.77.

27.   6.2.1976, 11.2.1976, 14.2.1976, 17.2.1976, 18.2.1976, 30.7.1976, 7.1.77, 14.4.1977, 3.6.1977

28.   12.2.1976, 23.6.1977 and *Der Spiegel*, 15 March 1976 and 20 Sept. 1976.

29.   3.3.1977, 11.3.1977, and *Der Spiegel*, 10 January 1977.

30.   30.8.1976.

31.   10.2.1977.

prosecutor accepted the plea of not guilty of all the suspected Air Force officers), in *Spain*,[32] in *South Africa,* and in Nigeria.[33] But Lockheed is no exception. The other organizations mentioned in the course of the same period in connection with corrupt business practices were: *British Leyland,*[34] which admitted that its practices were 'perhaps unethical but not illegal' (for bribing foreigners is quite acceptable in British law.)[35] *Shell,*[36]   *Firestone Goodyear,*[37] *Coca Cola* and *Pepsi Cola,*[38] *General Motors, Chrysler,*[39] *Boeing,*[40] *Werkspoor NL.,*[41] *General Telephone and Electric Corporation,* and *Uniroyal,*[42]   *Gilette,*[43]   *Mercandia,*[44]   *Nederland   International Transport,*[45] *Dessault.*[46] In addition there were also the 'normal' cases

---

32.   8.11.1976.

33.   12.2.1976.

34.   20.5.1977, 23.5.1977, *Der Spiegel,* 23.5.1977.

35.   25.5.1977.

36.   12.4.1976, 14.4.1976, 17.2.1977.

37.   9.6.1976, 24.12.1977, and *Der Spiegel,* 1.8.1977.

38.   14.12.1976, 12.8.1977.

39.   2.4.1977, 15.6.1977.

40.   30.12.1976, 14.1.1977, 12.9.1977, 13.9.1977.

41.   15.3.1976, 16.3.1976, 17.3.1976, 19.3.1976.

42.   29.1.1977.

43.   22.9.1976.

44.   24.3.1976.

45.   30.7.1977.

of corruption, i.e. the cases which do not necessarily show a *qualitative* change in morals. These were, during the same period, the allegations brought against twelve Scotland Yard detectives in England, and against the Warmoesstraat policemen in the Netherlands,[47] against Bishop Simonis,[48] the British Conservative M. P. John Cordle,[49] the United States' Presidential Adviser Mr. Bert Lance,[50] and many others whose cases did not merit reporting in the international press.

What then is the reason for the great excitement about this qualitative change in corruption? The answer lies in the changing character of Capitalism, and in the threat these malpractices pose for its survival. One reason for the spreading of corruption since the war is the increasing business contact with countries where the giving and receiving of 'gifts' is part of an accepted way of life. Another, that much of the business with such countries goes via state officials who do not deal with their own but with public funds, and that much of the business in such countries is done with *'unearned'* funds, i.e. with Foreign Aid and long-term loans. While the first reason creates the necessary climate,the second, provides the stratum of society which has the opportunity to benefit from such practices without much financial and personal risk, because it is provided with funds which can be appropriated without causing an immediate *visible* loss to the people who are cheated. The donors in the rich countries – the American or European tax-payers, have no direct interest in the manner in which the funds are utilized abroad because they do not expect a calculable return on their payments, and the assumed beneficiaries in the poor countries have little directly noticeable loss from the malpractices for they cannot feel deprived of something

---

46. 8.11.1975, 11.2.1976, 12.12.1976, *Der Spiegel*, 25.10.1976.

47. 1.3.1976.

48. 11.1.1977, 13.1.1977, 1.12.1977.

49. 23.7.1977.

50. 7.9.1977, 12.9.1977, 14.9.1977, 15.9.1977, 16.9.1977, 23.9.1977.

they never had. As it is 'unearned' money that is stolen, and not individuals' earnings, the sensation of loss is not sufficiently concrete to elicit real resistance. Now, had it but been the fear that malpractices 'learned' abroad might occasionally be also attempted at home, where conditions are less favorable for their spreading than in the poorer countries, Capitalism would in all probability have been able to live with them. After all, corrupt practices had tempted businessmen abroad, particularly in the colonies, for centuries without posing a real threat to the system as a whole. What is different now is that conditions in the *developed* countries have changed. At least with regard to doing business with other persons' money the conditions for spreading corruption have become very similar in developed and underdeveloped countries.

It is worth repeating here some of the causes for this change. In earlier times it was not only the social climate which did not favor massive bribery and corruption in the industrial countries. There were also powerful material forces at work which restricted malpractices of this kind. These forces have gradually eroded under the influence of the changes which accompanied the rise of managerial and regulated capitalism. In the past the people who bought in bulk were owner-capitalists, i.e. people who were directly interested in gaining the best possible bargain, and the money they spent was their own earned money. Now, the rise of the large corporations in which the owners have only indirect control over expenditures and of the non-profit-making sectors, over whose expenditure the public has only a 'book-keeping' but no real supervision, has created in the economically developed countries a category of people who control other people's money and have the same opportunities for corruption as their equals in the poorer parts of the world. In addition to this, the great secrecy in which the expenditure is shrouded for public goods, such as military equipment, space technology and research, energy, etc., provides almost optimal conditions for financial irregularities. The funds used for these purposes are 'unearned', from the point of view of those who disburse them, and their utilization cannot be subjected to the price-mechanistic tests of strict cost-benefit analyses. Only the input can be measured, not the output. Add to this Official Secret Acts and the opportunities for theft, maladministration, and inefficiency are obvious. Few firms 'experienced' in bribing officials in the third world will be able to resist for long the temptation to bribe officials at home who are in a similarly favorable position to accept and give favors. It is for this reason, i.e. because of the erosion of the inbuilt protecting mechanism of manager-owners self-interest-dominated-capitalism, that part of the establishment feels threatened by the spreading of corruption. It is the recognition of this threat that has recently given rise to some hasty efforts to introduce legislation to contain the spreading of corrupt business practices. Yet, as the proposed legislation can only attack the symptoms of the disease not the disease itself, for this would require thoroughgoing changes in the established political order with far reaching effects upon the social and economic power structure, little is likely to result from it.

The real opposition to the declining business standards comes from another direction. Firstly, from the direction of traditional Capitalism, i.e. from the great number of still surviving small enterprises. Less able than the large multinational corporations to disguise illicit operations abroad, and to exert political pressure on the state, and also financially less capable to 'buy' government officials in charge of the allocation of subsidies and similar advantages at home, the old style capitalist firms' economic viability is directly threatened by the new system, and therefore they simply cannot avoid resisting it. Yet, being also hard pressed by their workers to pay higher wages, and by the state to make greater and greater contributions to its social security schemes, which the large multinationals find much easier to bear, their resistance is weak. For it is not received by the public as opposition to the transformation of payments to the state into subsidies for their competitors, i.e. to the monster enterprises with 'good relations' with the government, but as opposition to the provision of greater social security for the workers. Secondly, the opposition to the new style capitalism came in the 1960s and early 1970s, from the ranks of the young workers who gradually seemed to realize that in spite of the considerable economic progress neither exploitation nor alienation has ceased.[51] They notice that the differences in incomes have not narrowed. In fact, for example, in West Germany, 5% of the salary- and wage-earners still receive 7.2 times more in *net* incomes than the 20% of earners at the bottom of the wage pyramid; and the pension of a public servant, who contributes little to the pension fund, is about twice that of a qualified factory worker who worked the same length of time and contributed normally to the fund.[52] They found out that more than half of the working people receive from the state, in all forms of assistance, almost precisely the sum of money that is taken from their monthly wages, but some privileged groups, public officials and farmers, get more. Finally the young workers have learned that capitalism is still a hard reality by the recent wave of unemployment. But their resistance to the system is also weak. It is blunted by the relatively good pay when they are working and by the social security arrangements when they are not, and by the absence of an undogmatically committed political leadership. Thirdly, the opposition to the new capitalism comes from the intelligentsia which was brought up upon the traditional values of western civilization and which has recognized that the abandonment of these values and the submission to the materialistic utilitarianism of the bureaucratically directed welfare state must lead towards a system of 'valueless' totalitarianism or chaos. Exponents of this group are people so varied in their formal political and ethical conceptions as Böll, Sartre, and Gollwitzer, but who are united in their common belief in the dignity of man. It is this group that either recognized or sensed that the effective means to restrict the power of the new elite is in the utilization of the bourgeois institutions themselves. The people belonging to this group understood that under present conditions the

---

51. As explained in the *new introduction* to this book, this observation of the reaction of young people to the changes in the system is no longer true. In the later 1970s and certainly in the course of the 1980s and 1990s young people have become accustomed to the new ways and very few can still be counted among those who oppose it.

52. *Source:* for Germany, Christof Helberger and Georg Haubeck, for America, Irwin Gillespie. *Vide* also *Der Spiegel*, 20 January 1978, pp. 32–44.

only practical way to stop society from reverting to chaos or medieval despotism is to uphold the power of the democratic institutions and bourgeois legality. Their opposition has therefore taken on the form of a struggle to subject the people's political representation to public criticism and to force the various executive organs of the state to abide by legal rules. Their strength lies in their appeal to the widely accepted and recognized norms of behavior, which the new elite does not yet dare to challenge openly. Their weakness lies in the absence of mass support of a class which is already conscious of the direction into which the new elite is leading it. The ferociousness with which the media that serve the new elite attack the representatives of this group indicates how acutely it feels threatened by them. For they are the people who might unite the forces of traditional capitalism with the disillusioned young working class and the idealistic youth from the middle class in a bid to stop the managerial bureaucracy from attaining its aspired position of unrestricted social and economic hegemony.

What then is this direction into which the new elite is leading industrial society? The answer is quite simple: some kind of despotic feudalism. The feudal ranking of people within each organization, with increasingly more privileges (expense-accounts, official cars, etc.,) attached to each rank as it comes closer to the top management positions, is already a well established practice in government service and in the larger business organizations. And as the share of these organizations in total employment increases, more and more people are sucked into this hierarchical system. In fact, close to half of all the working people in the industrial countries have already been sucked into it,'[53] and with the spreading of services,[54] (in which the state has again a major share), this tendency is bound to continue. Now, as most services do not lend themselves to easy cost-benefit evaluations, and when state controlled,[55] are insensitive to the normal functioning of the *Price Mechanism,* a state of affairs which also

---

53. *Vide* pp. 334, 405.

54. *Vide* p. 334–6.

55. *Vide* p. 410.

applies to many of the functions in the multinational business conglomerates, the test for employees' efficiency becomes less dependent on the effectiveness of the service they render than on the hitchless operation of their office. Consequently, promotion becomes less and less a function of individual performance and more and more dependent on obedience or on the personal relationship between inferiors and superiors in the organization. The personal 'nexus', – who one knows and whom one serves, becomes the overriding element in one's advancement. In this way a new vertical relationship is forged by which the whole hierarchy within one organization or office is held together. The lower layers protect the ones above them, for their position depends upon their status, and the higher layers protect the ones below, for any mistakes the latter may be responsible for will eventually be put at their doorstep. As each member of the hierarchy has personally nothing to gain, but much to lose, by way of chances for promotion, by challenging either the quality of the service rendered by the organization or its efficiency in rendering it; and as all members of the organization will be adversely affected if either is criticized from outside, i.e. from the general public, it usually develops a self-sustaining ethos, – a belief that what it does is right. More than that, it accepts that what is is necessary. For example, the people making up the organization accept as right that manual workers and clerks are entitled to good wages and salaries (where good means good in comparison with other employees of the same categories in other enterprises), by virtue of their *position* in the organization – not by virtue of their contribution to, say, production; because this is the way it is. For the same reason the accept that particularly qualified personnel receives higher incomes, but again by virtue of their position not the quality of their expertize; and that administrative staff at managerial level gets next to greater income, again by virtue of position, additional advantages such as tax-free expense-accounts, interest-free company loans, the use of company-vehicles etc., which together often add up to much more than their salaries.

At the same time the hierarchical system is also made strong by influences from outside. For example workers' children, as distinct from the children of professionals and administrators, have not found their way into higher education, in spite of many genuine efforts by various progressive governments to change this situation. Those who did usually preferred purely technical studies. Consequently with few exceptions, they are excluded from the managerial strata. They remain qualified workers and this adds a hereditary element to the new hierarchical stratification. The son or daughter of a manager receives an education that suits a member of the managerial or top government service class, the son of a professional family or of a middle level administrator receives a similar level of education, but as on the whole he lacks the connections that can place him at the top of the scale, he becomes a teacher or a lower member of the hierarchy; and workers' sons or daughters receive their elders' status. A similar process also separates the receivers of state assistance. Workers can obtain far less advantages from tax deductions and government subsidies than members of the better remunerated strata of society. For illustration, in the Netherlands workers with low incomes and most in need of mortgages for buying a house, which are greatly tax deductible, find it more difficult than people with higher incomes to obtain a mortgage. Altogether then, the mounting share of the state in the economy, and the decline of manager-owner capitalism, and its replacement by the new type of monster enterprises, and the great increase in affluence and social security without greater social justice, that accompanies these changes, threatens to usher in a new type of socio-economic feudalism.

At first sight the rise of socio-economic feudalism might not seem as frightening as it really is, for it appears to be founded upon so high a level of technology that even without social justice it can provide all people with a living standard and economic security never attained before by any known society. Alas this is illusory. To date society has only experienced two mechanisms by which people were encouraged to work and produce the goods they require. The one was *fear*, and the other *the prospect of great gain*. The pyramids in Egypt and the Colosseum in Rome, and, more recently, the great canal in the Soviet Union, were all built by slave-labor, i.e. by the power of fear. The same is true, though less directly, for most of the achievements of capitalist construction, where the fear of starvation took the place of the fear of the slaver's whip.

Yet, together with the fear inspiring 'non-alternatives' of working or starving, Capitalism, as distinct from earlier forms of social and economic organization, contained also a powerful dynamic element. The so called 'love of gain' provided a realistic prospect for a greater number of people than ever before to advance socially and economically if they were suitably placed and naturally inclined to grasp the opportunity on the basis of competitive ability. It transformed the direct control over people into indirect control via the ownership of not only land but all means of production. But the ownership of means of production also implied accumulation, and the need to accumulate implied the choice between going on doing so or fall victim to competitors and be eliminated in the race for power and status. So, legitimized avarice, – the love of gain, on the one hand, and the fear of starvation, on the other, gave Capitalism its progressive dynamism and its labor-discipline. To be sure, 'the motives of capitalistic entrepreneurs are by no means restricted to acquisitive drives: among them we find a motley array – the desire for power, the craving for acclaim, the impulsion to serve the common good, the urge to action. But as all these motives work Out in the capitalistic enterprise they become, by virtue of an inner necessity, subordinate to profit making.'[56] They simply cannot be attained without economic success. Moreover, 'in addition to an aim distinct from the purposes of its owners the capitalist enterprise has a separate intelligence: it is the locus of economic rationality which is quite independent of the personality of the owner or the staff. At first rational business methods, objectively adapted to make the business profitable, are developed only in the course of time as a crystallization of experience, but in the period of full capitalism we observe the characteristic activity of artificial and self-conscious creation of economic rationality. Rational business methods are steadily and systematically developed and improved by persons who devote all or part of their time to this pursuit, which may itself be directed toward profit making. Thousands of people... become engaged in a perpetual quest for perfecting economic rationality.'[57] Eventually, the system becomes so complex, its degree of

---

56.   W. Sombart, 'Capitalism', *E.S.S.*, Bk. III.

57.   *Ibid.*

specialization so high, that no part of it can continue functioning in separation from all others. Individuals become dependent on millions of other people completely unknown to them, and millions become dependent on a few individuals who are quite beyond their control. If for one reason or another capitalists desist from investing; if Arabian Sheiks stop the flow of oil, if train drivers refuse to drive their engines; if electricians will not man the power plants; in fact if any strategically placed group of people refuses to do its job, the entire economic life of a city or a country is threatened with dislocation. In short, the system cannot function properly to ensure the high productivity that makes possible the developed nations' affluence unless all it's component parts click in place with each turning of the clockwork. Each part must fall into place at precisely the right time − if not, the whole system falls into disarray and can no longer maintain the customary living standard. But precisely this, the harmonious functioning of the system, was assured by the two great motive forces of capitalist society − the love of gain and the fear of starvation; take out either, and the wheels will turn erratically, take out both, and unless you have something else to put in their places, the whole clockwork will grind to a halt. Affluence will be no more.

This then is the essential factor that economic planners and model builders have ignored. They have neglected to consider the complex and unquantifiable effects that socio-economic changes have upon human behavior and motivation, and herein lies their failure.[58] For the rise of the great business conglomerates and progressive taxation have deprived Capitalism of much of its vitalizing competitive element and of its customary opportunities for gain, while at the same time better social security arrangements have also deprived it of its old stand by − fear, for the assurance of the necessary labor discipline. People capable of accumulating wealth and competing with the large established firms have become fewer and fewer, and people exerting their power diligently at work for fear of dismissal and unemployment have also become rarer in high industrial societies. The *bourgeois virtues* of industry, thrift, stability and

---

58.   *Vide* p. 333-5.

efficiency, which symbolized the aspirations of classical capitalism's entrepreneurial class have all but disappeared with the rise of 'jet-set' management. So have to a great extent the dignity of labor, the pride in work, and the fear-inspired diligence of workers.

As long as *fear* and *greed* could be regarded as firmly-set in 'human nature', indicative planners and economic model-builders could also feel quite confident that given the use of the normal Keynesian and post-Keynesian instruments of economic control things would on the whole turn out the way they expect them to turn out. However, when these firmly-set 'foundations of human nature' are shaking, as in the richest countries indeed they are since the 'sixties, confidence in the state's ability to control, regulate, or guide the economic system along desired lines, must wane. When the structure of the economy becomes so specialized that it introduces hitherto unknown occupational rigidities into the mobility of labor, and when the greater security-of-income removes much of the urgency to take whatever employment offered and wherever it is offered as soon as possible, it is hardly surprising that expectations based upon economic laws which arose out of empirical observations in another period, when these changes had not yet materialized, can no longer be relied upon. If contrary to Professor A.W. Phillips observations in the past, that when unemployment rises wages and prices tend to fall, unemployment, wages, and prices rise together; and if as Professor M. Friedman suggests this 'anomaly' is not the result of a temporary coincidence of special circumstances; and if it is not only the Phillips Curve which no longer describes the economic relationships correctly, then confidence in the predictions which are based on economic laws which are the product of no longer reliable observations must diminish.

Economic Laws are founded upon assumptions about human behavior, for example that 'people seek to maximize their utility and act rationally towards that end...' It is tacitly assumed that one knows what is *rational* as indeed as far as one's own cultural environment is concerned one does. It is therefore taken for granted that given the choice between a larger and a smaller sum of money people will act rationally when they take the larger sum as indeed they do in our society. But there is no guarantee that this 'law' holds in every society. For example, it may not have been correct in

Medieval Europe when people's concern was much more with religion, with their fate in the world hereafter, and when taking the larger sum might have been regarded as the deadly sin of avarice. Medieval man would have acted rationally taking the smaller rather than the larger sum because his objectives were different. And even today a Buddhist monk or a New York hippie are as rational within their framework as a good capitalist within his own. No wonder then that economic laws which were based upon a rationality that suited a society dominated by fear and in which power and status depended on the ownership of means of production, no longer hold good in a society in which fear is diminishing and power and status tend more and more to depend on control than on ownership. To be sure, the old system is still very much alive but there are cracks appearing in its shell and the cracks are widening. The ownership of capital still confers enormous advantages but they are steadily reduced by the power of the state and labor unions. The owners of capital still invest but their spirit of enterprise is declining. They seek security rather than high profits, they often invest in safe government loans rather than in new productive enterprises. They think of state subsidies rather than of greater work efficiency. The same is true of the working-men; people are still afraid of unemployment but not as much as they used to be. They absent themselves from work longer than before because of sickness, they make longer tea-breaks, they work less diligently and responsibly, they allow more time to pass between leaving one post and finding another, they sometimes misuse the social security arrangements and evade taxation by working 'black'. So while capitalists gradually cease to fulfil their expected function, i.e. do not invest in pursuit of maximum profit, and the state is ill-equipped to take their place effectively, and workers can be less and less relied upon to work diligently and responsibly in the expected manner, the whole system begins to operate on a lower key. In spite of continued technological innovation efficiency declines and eventually no longer assures the high standards of living people have come to expect from it.

Taken in isolation, the fact that the post in Italy was burned on a certain occasion because it had become too much to be delivered, or that a postman in Bourg-sur-Gironde in France,[59] or in Amsterdam in the Netherlands,[60] found it too tiresome to distribute the mail to whom it was addressed, does not amount to much. Certainly this must have happened before. But, seen in its present context of the highly specialized and integrated economic system such events take on a much greater significance. For when the system of communication breaks down the whole modern economic structure can no longer function adequately. As already pointed out, what is true of the postman is of course equally true for almost all workers in sensitive industrial positions. The failure of one worker to oil a certain component of a machine on time can bring production in an entire factory to a standstill. Thousands of automobile workers, for example at Fiat in Turin, can be left without work for hours if not days. Not only the concerted and deliberate effort of a group of people but even the lack of diligence of a single worker is enough to dislocate the system and reduce its overall efficiency. The truth of the matter is simply this: Without an adequate motivating mechanism to assure that all the necessary tasks to keep the complex industrial system going, the system cannot function. At least not at the level of efficiency that is expected from it. The demise in the 1960s of capitalists' 'expectation of plenty' due to the high level of taxation, and of labourers' 'fear of starvation' due to the improved social security arrangements, threatened to deprive post-industrial capitalism of such a motivating mechanism. If one adds to this the social climate of materialistic utilitarianism that has grown with and was part of the capitalist system, and which has dwarfed in its shadow almost all other social values, the future viability of industrial society must appear even more questionable. Classical capitalism had always made a clear distinction between legitimate and illegitimate practices in people's efforts to enrich themselves. Thieves, swindlers, embezzlers, hold-up men, forgers, extortionists, and the rest of that ilk, were always, as a matter of course, excluded from the list of practitioners of 'free enterprise'. This is still so. But

---

59.   *Vide* AFP report in *de Volkskrant*, 6.12.1977.

60.   *Vide* ANP report in *Het Parool*, 13.9.1977.

the mode in which all these practices are performed has undergone a change which has taken out their social disapprobation; in their new guise they tend to become less and less prosecutable and more and more socially acceptable. Few people bother nowadays to prosecute the clerk who appropriates to himself the employer's stationary, postage stamps and use of the telephone. In fact the clerk himself has ceased to regard his actions for what they really are. Nor does anyone take to court the garage owner who produces a bill for four hours labor-time for a job which but for his mechanic's mistakes would have required only one hour. The garage-owner himself would never regard it theft to charge the four hours because this was the actual time his mechanic worked until the car was again ready for use. Officially prescribed prices are here of little consequence. Again, it ought to be stressed that the point is not the existence of corruption. Corrupt practices are not new; they were employed by individuals in all periods, but their legitimization to near institutionalization is new and threatening the efficiency of the industrial system, let alone its moral fabric. Finally the system is threatened by a host of other tendencies in post-industrial society. For example, as people can obtain an income from unemployment benefits, and as other people can often ill-afford the quasi-monopolistic prices of the firms that provide such services as home repairs, the so-called unemployed and the people in need of workers to do these repairs conspire against the state. The former to obtain some extra money and the latter to avoid the cost of middle-men and social security contributions and other impositions. As a result the number of contributors to the schemes that provide the nation's welfare diminishes and the number of claimants increases. Another example is the diminishing efficiency in the utilization of natural resources. Due to high labor costs people are less and less inclined to repair faulty equipment and prefer to replace it by new. Altogether therefore, it must be obvious that unless society develops new motivating mechanisms to replace the old fading ones the affluent welfare state will not survive.

Which then are the alternatives that present themselves for the future of industrial society? One is decline and fall. A second, is a command economy. A system of imposed production targets enforced by the prospects of rewards and threats of penalties administered by a state bureaucracy. A third possibility is democratic participation – a system in which each member of society not only feels that he has, but in which he actually has, an equal share in the fruits of production.[61] The first alternative needs no further explanation. The second is the one towards which society seems to be drifting. It implies more economic and social planning and less economic insecurity; more state intervention and less freedom for the individual; the replacement of property-founded hierarchies by hierarchies of positional status; the replacement of the fear of unemployment and poverty by the fear of administratively determined penalties for the non-fulfillment of production targets, and the substitution of profit incentives by bureaucratically fixed rewards (and it makes no difference whether the bureaucracy is of the government or of an even more powerful multinational business enterprise); and the transformation of our strongly introspective ethics into a formalistic system of morality. The greater intervention of the state will in all probability rationalize the utilization of resources but this will be at the expense of restricting people's freedom of choice. For public administrators will decide what ought to be produced, in what quantities, and by which methods of production. Dire poverty will disappear together with price variations, the economic mechanism by which consumers have in the past communicated to producers their preferences. The administrators will become the final arbiters of 'the public good', and by the earlier described 'class' crystallization process in the bureaucracy,[62] the public good will turn out to be precisely what will cause them least bother and what is in their own best interest. By virtue of their claim to superior information about desires and practicable possibilities, they will arrogate the right to decide what people ought and ought not to be supplied with. They will decide what people have to learn and which jobs they have to take by virtue of what they will claim to be necessity. Deprived of the means to resist these tendencies

---

61.   This is in fact Rawls' point that the share need not be literally equal, provided any inequality is justified by some morally accepted reason.

62.   *Vide* pp. 410–5 on the rise of industrial feudalism.

effectively, and their opposition blunted by economic security, the people will gradually become accustomed to this Aldous Huxley's new world, and acquiescent in their roles. As bonuses and penalties become the only means by which the ruling bureaucracy is able to reward and punish those who do and who do not fulfil their assigned tasks, i.e. who do or do not contribute to the smooth functioning of the system, the ethical values *good* and *bad* will become *obedience* and *disobedience,* and *the public good* will become *expediency,* the fulfillment of the plan. The *best* man will be the one who contributes most to the volume of production and obeys his betters. This process is already well advanced in our society. Not much imagination is necessary to see how it will go on. It is sufficient to think about the *real* necessity to prevent terrorists from taking control of some nuclear materials to see how some freedoms of the people should an can be restricted with their own consent, but also, how these restrictions can then be abused, for example, by the exclusion of all nonconformists from studying the natural sciences at the universities. After all, the step from a *Berufsverbot* to a *Studierverbot* is but a small one.

The third alternative, the alternative of democratic participation, implies greater social and economic equity and an enormous educational effort. It implies *real* freedom for the media of mass communication, and workers' participation in *all* decision making organs in their working-places, and unrestricted insight into all documents with but few exceptions such as medical reports. Only when all people have an equal share in the wealth of the nation so that the welfare of each person depends and is seen to depend upon the effort of everyone else can a social mechanism be expected to develop that is capable of taking the place of the traditional ones of coercion and economic fear. After all, such a mechanism already functions within most families in which husbands and wives share incomes and expenses. Optimistically a social tendency to stop the drift towards the new bureaucratic despotism and towards a more equitable and liberal society can be detected in a number of recent developments, as in the 'wild-growth' of movements outside the establishment's 'democratic' system. The first among these are the extra-parliamentary 'action-groups', the movements which organize mass opposition to such things as nuclear reactors in their regions, the pollution of air and water, the destruction of historical monuments and the natural environment and others. Sometimes the establishment reacts to them by police brutality, other times by efforts to absorb them into the system in a subverted form. Both methods have till now met with limited success. The second, are workers' attempts to gain a greater say in the running of the enterprises in which they work. This too presents a direct challenge to the hierarchical system upon which the new administrative oligarchy rests. As a rule the establishment tries first to 'buy' this opposition by the offer of better wages. But when it is either unable to do so or unsuccessful in the attempt it resorts to the old subterfuge of 'divide and rule'. It bestows privileges on the workers' chosen representatives to alienate them from their following. It allows them certain economic achievements, to draw the attention away from their lack of success in other respects. It attempts to absorb the demands for greater workers' participation in the system and thus deprive them of their progressive character. Again, the attempts have so far met with partial success. The third opposition comes from some, mainly young, members of the church, the intelligentsia, and the students, who are, perhaps unconsciously, united in their adherence to *conventional morality.* This is perhaps the most dangerous opposition the new establishment has to deal with for conventional morality is as deeply rooted in the teachings of Christianity as in the writings of Karl Marx and both still command widespread respect. In fact conventional morality is still implicit in most of the values taught at school in spite of many efforts in the last decades to transform the schools from educational institutions into places where children are encouraged to learn 'practical' things that will allow them to find their places in industrial society, i.e. to learn the things that best suit the purely economic needs of the system. Here too the new establishment uses a mixture of force and stratagems to meet the threat. On the one hand it labels all those who stand up for conventional morality Communists or terrorist-sympathizers, and on the other, it tries to dress all its despotic deeds and institutions in a mock-garment of morality. It restricts the freedom of the individual in the name of liberty and it imposes the autocratic rule of the administrator in the place of the capitalist in the name of greater social equality. It speaks about the need for an ethical revival and means a campaign against long hair and a woman's freedom to live the way she wishes. It's top functionaries fill their mouths with speeches about human rights and then allow themselves to frame or malign the ones who practice them. In short, the new establishment tries to avoid an open confrontation with the forces of conventional morality by retaining its shell but depriving it of its content. Like the Cat in Lewis Carroll's *Alice's Adventures in Wonderland,* that 'vanished quite slowly, beginning with the end of the tail, and ending with the grin, which remained some time after the rest of it had gone', the new establishment makes liberal society disappear. 'Well! I've often seen a cat without a grin, thought Alice, but a grin without a cat'. It's the most curious thing I ever saw in all my life'. Unfortunately then, this third alternative is not very feasible ecause just when part of humanity attained a technology that is capable of ending all economic fears that have plagued it for so long, a new threat to its freedom emerges-'from that spring whence comfort seem'd to come, discomfort swells'.

The special in modern man is that he has learned to use *indirect* methods to achieve his objectives; that he has learned to devote time and effort to make things which have no direct use but which help him to obtain other things which have such use more efficiently and in greater abundance. Man has learned to create machines that satisfy none of his immediate wants for food and drink apparel and shelter and aesthetic pleasure, but which have it in their power to reward him in the end with much greater affluence than he could ever have obtained had he applied himself directly to the satisfaction of his wants. This subjugation of passions to reason, which taught him not to eat the cow he chances upon but to feed it so that it will reward him in the fill of time with milk and calves and more cows, that rendered him mountains of butter and meat and rivers of milk and wine and manufactures galore, has alas been confined to his economic activities alone. In other spheres mankind remained pitifully short sighted. Whether this short-sightedness is but the reflection of the lingering fears from an era in which mankind was yet unable to produce enough to satisfy all wants for comfortable living; when man did really need to vie with one another for a share in the means of sustenance, or whether it has deeper roots, is hard to say, but if it is fear alone then there is hope. For with the growing recognition of mankind's ability to satisfy these economic needs its confidence will grow and it will learn to restrain its individualistic immediate urges in favor of collective indirect efforts to gain welfare and security. It will replace competition by co-operation and the struggle for power by common sense. It will come to see that individuals' desires can also be best satisfied by working for the common good. It will substitute social for individualistic rationality. But none of this will happen by itself, only the struggle against the masters of the new industrial feudalism and their pervert values can give mankind a chance to find new ways.

'If Winter comes, can Spring be far behind?'

Index

427